C0-AUT-099

WALL STREET

A PICTORIAL HISTORY

WALL STREET

A PICTORIAL HISTORY

BY

LEONARD
LOUIS
LEVINSON

ZIFF-DAVIS
PUBLISHING
COMPANY
NEW YORK

This book is dedicated to the memory of my father
NAIMON LEVINSON
who saw more than seventy years of this story . . . as a child and youth living through panics, depressions and hard times . . . as a soldier, a business man, a speculator in stocks which were mostly disappointing, and finally as an investor in American industry, like another million men, for whom Wall Street was a second, and most fascinating, occupation.

Library of Congress Catalog Card Number 61-14234

PRINTED IN THE UNITED STATES OF AMERICA

Foreword

HAVING DEVOTED the past five years to reading, writing, selecting pictures, and thinking about Wall Street and those realities in which Wall Street deals — the practical, financial side of life in the United States — I could not help but arrive at a number of conclusions. At this time I would like to bring one of these to the attention of the reader: Whether we realize it or not, believe it or not, or enjoy it or not, *today* is the best of all times, for never have so many people had so much health and money and leisure to savor life as they have right now. Mind you, I am not claiming that these people are enjoying all of these advantages—just that they are here for most of us to enjoy.

Anyone with a hard-headed memory of the past fifty years and a clear comprehension of what happened before that time must come to the inescapable conclusion that those people who sigh after the good old days, the quaint old customs, the dear old times, are the most impractical of dreamers, blessed with rosy, fuzzy hindsight, or a truly distorted comprehension of what happened.

Today we have every material and physical advantage over the past: more security, protection, and years to our lives. Even the hydrogen bomb has forced us into an impasse — a cold peace — because everyone realizes that after a nuclear war there would be little to distinguish the victor from the vanquished.

So today should be for happiness, and it is, for those who have the sense and balance to realize their blessings, the physical and material advantages we have over the people of the past. Yet there are too many people who cannot hold happiness in the hand, but who can only find it by looking backward to some previous scene, from which the memory of pain and hardship has been wiped away by time. "Happiness," a wise man once said, "is the ability to strike a balance between what we are and what we have."

But please do not think that the author is a male Pollyanna or that this book is a record filled only with sweetness and light. There is as much effort needed ahead to achieve a better state of living as there has already been. And this book reports the very imperfect progress we have made—a journey filled with horror, amusement, sensation, chicanery, devotion, mass anarchy, and unified unselfishness.

Much of this story is told in the scenes of celebration and disaster that have taken place in Wall Street, which, for a century now, has meant much more than just the narrow, stubby thoroughfare, pocked, patched, and speckled with manhole covers, that runs from Trinity Church to the East River. Today it means all of Manhattan Island below City Hall Park, and the thousands of branches of establishments with world headquarters located here.

You will be amused by the alarms and dire warnings set up to block every progressive move and needed reform that has been accomplished. So beneficial and innocent an innovation as government insurance of bank deposits, now proudly advertised by almost every financial institution, was the subject of savage attack and prophecies of doom by the banking associations of the nation before it was enacted.

You may reach another conclusion to which the author has come as a result of his study of recent history: that in addition to the statue of Washington, the man who made the United States possible, there should be another monument on Wall Street, one to honor the man who saved the Street, rescued the capitalistic system, and conserved our form of government—the man of our darkest hour, Franklin D. Roosevelt.

A further conclusion drawn from the years of absorption in the story of this street is that, if every trace of civilization were to be wiped away and the whole process of geographic evolution were to begin over again, New York, lower Manhattan, and Wall Street would inevitably evolve once more as they have this time.

This is a book which has been most difficult to confine to its present large number of pages, words, and illustrations because Wall Street offers so many faces and facts to a biographer, so many fascinating figures both statistical and human, so many angles, curves, circles, pyramids, and spirals, that a whole literature could be devoted to its story and an entire museum of pictures to its portrait.

It has also been a book most difficult to stop working on and send to the printer because every day something new and wonderful or strange happens on Wall Street. Recently, there was released a Harvard study of New York's financial district for the next twenty-five years which corroborated the general tenor of the predictions which appear in the last chapter. Also, the fledgling National Stock Exchange was preparing to open for business.

And the President of the New York Stock Exchange, in commenting on the expulsion of a member accused of embezzling securities of clients, stated for the first time that "the exchange feels that its moral responsibilities to these investors are not ended with the act of expulsion."

Shades of Richard Whitney and his "private club run for the benefit of its members"!

LEONARD LOUIS LEVINSON

Table of Contents

I

The Street

THIS BOOK is a history in pictures and words of a small V of land at the tip of Manhattan Island and of the men who shaped its growth during the past 350 years. If, as Shakespeare wrote in *Macbeth*, life is a "tale told by an idiot," the story of Wall Street should make no sense or have any significant pattern. There should be no plot, no heroes or villains. But an almost perfect plot exists, and there are heroes and villains galore. Indeed, the same actor very often plays hero and villain simultaneously, depending entirely on the eye of the beholder.

In some ways the plot of the Wall Street story resembles that of the medieval morality play *Everyman*. In each case there was the sweep to heady, dizzying heights, the swift plunge to despair, then reformation and regeneration until, purged, both Everyman and Wall Street could look to a better life ahead.

Sometimes it is easy to tell the heroes from the villains, and sometimes not. George Washington was our first great hero, and his splendid physical image has been used ever since as the yardstick in choosing our leaders. Surely Jim Fisk and Aaron Burr were villains. But Fisk was the comic hero of the New Yorkers of his time, and there are ardent Burrites to this day who will hold you spellbound with a recital of his virtues and Alexander Hamilton's defects.

The historical jury is still out on Peter Stuyvesant; the verdict on Captain William Kidd keeps changing; friends and foes put halo or horns on Jacob Leisler and Thomas Paine. Many people who admire the sterling qualities of John Pierpont Morgan, regarded by some as the greatest public villain of his generation, have only hatred for Franklin Delano Roosevelt, the greatest popular hero of the era that followed.

If we look back at Wall Street and see it year by year during the three centuries of its existence, we encounter a cast of characters more colorful than all the stages of the world can provide. The scenes of celebrations and alarms, glorious moments and nightmare panics, have been more dramatic than those any playwright has dared to create. No other street in America has had so varied or exciting a history. No other street is so well-known. No other

Where the Wall Once Stood (BERENICE ABBOTT)

Bush Terminal Building (BERENICE ABBOTT)—*on the site where John Howard Payne (who wrote "Home, Sweet Home") was born.*

street so strongly affects the lives of people everywhere.

For nowhere else on earth is so much of the business of buying and selling, borrowing and lending money, transacted. Because the United States has grown to commercial greatness as the result of a series of business adventures—from the first voyages of the explorers to the latest attempt to explore space—more of the history of this hemisphere has been shaped in the district of Wall Street than any other place, including the District of Columbia.

From the very beginning the southern tip of Manhattan was a place of excitement and challenge. It began one night in November, 1613, when Adriaen Block's ship the *Tiger* burned offshore, leaving him stranded on this wild island at the edge of an unknown, savage continent three thousand miles across the Atlantic from The Netherlands.

Forty years later, Wall Street, now the world's most influential center of finance, marked the northern border of the little village and trading post that sprang up after Block's departure. Father Isaac Jogues, who was to become a saint, and Captain William Kidd, who was to be hanged, walked the lanes of the tiny settlement. Adventurers, pioneers, settlers, immigrants poured through this funnel of lower Manhattan. Pirates and privateers found the authorities and inhabitants tolerant, hospitable, and easy to do business with. The town's reputation for wickedness began early and, in 1735, Dr. Andrew Hamilton of Philadelphia wrote about the Battery: "To walk after dark upon this platform was a good way for a stranger to fit himself with a courtesan."

The moralist points out that Wall Street emerges from a graveyard and winds up in a river. However, the purist will tell you that the churchyard of Trinity has not received a corpse since 1831 and the East River is no river at all but a salt-water estuary between New York Bay and Long Island Sound.

Until the year 1800, Manhattan was a town that terminated below the present City Hall. Today this southern tip of the island, scarcely a mile long and 120 acres in area, is what is meant and thought of by the words "Wall Street." Here, in spite of every effort to decentralize, to move the money market away, to spread out into more comfortable quarters, "Wall Street" remains.

The reason for this is that Wall Street is a "walk-around" market, where people must work close together, for the actual physical movement is the trading back and forth of little slips of paper. In addition to the traders, there are a hundred thousand people who create the slips, shuffle them around the district by hand and on foot, send them out to the ends of the earth, and destroy them after they have served their purpose.

The slips of paper represent cash and promises to pay cash, labor, transportation of goods and people, many different services, protection of property, and tiny slivers of huge industries.

And Wall Street is a leading market place for slips of paper which represent heads of cattle, tons of coffee, bales of cotton, silos of corn, bars of copper, tankers of oil, bushels of oats, drums of lard, and pigs of lead. It is also a market where you can buy such materials, ranging from the ordinary to the exotic, as: #2 A grade raw silk at $4.25 a pound, crack Tossa raw jute at 14 cents, ducks for 31 cents a pound and Army duck cloth at 80, old radiators at $400 a ton and platinum at $82—$85 an ounce. Butt-branded steer hides are 12½ cents a pound and whole steers sell for double that price per pound. Next year's Santos coffee, at 36½ cents a pound, is ten times the price of the sugar to sweeten it. If you need Glauber's salt, you can get all you want at $34 a ton, or boric acid at $128 a barrel, and you have your choice of cocoa by the pound at 27½ cents, antimony at 31, potatoes at 4, hogs at 15, soy beans for 4¼, and No. 1 standard rib smoked sheets of rubber at 41¼ cents. Sperm whale oil will run you 14 cents a pint.

In the bargain stores of Wall Street, where the discount houses had their origin during the Depression of the thirties, you can buy quill pens with ball points for a quarter, affectionate orangutans for three thousand dollars, Civil War surplus muskets for $7.50, and hot charcoal-broiled pretzels from a vendor named Baruch for eight cents each.

Wall Street can be all markets to all men and no two people seem to have the same picture of the place in their mind's eye. Viewed from afar, from a ship or plane at sunset or sunrise, it is a dream city, an incredible mass of white castles sparkling in the pink light. Seen from the bottom of one of its canyons during the rush hour of a dreary day, it can be a terrifying ant hill, built to enslave the souls as

Liberty and the City (LEONARD STERN)

Jeweled Tip of Manhattan (ANDREAS FEININGER)

well as the bodies of the human insects who scurry about.

Somewhere between these two vistas one can find his own Wall Street. It may be like "a gladness . . . with such a sparkle in her air and in her people," as John Masefield said—long before he was poet laureate of England—when he was seventeen and janitor in a Manhattan saloon. Or it may be like Dr. Oliver Wendell Holmes' 1835 description: "The tip of the tongue that laps up the cream of the commerce of a continent." To Lloyd Morris it was "a gilded, gleaming cesspool," to Christopher Morley, "the terrible, magnificent jungle" where "men cannot even worship God without quarrelling about it." F. Hopkinson Smith, contrasting Trinity Church and the surrounding skyscrapers, wrote: "The Old Church, undismayed, fearless, guarding its dead—still lifts its slender finger pointing up to God."

There are countless people to whom Wall Street means only the New York Stock Exchange. They are only vaguely aware of the other exchanges (American, Commodity, Cocoa, Coffee and Sugar, Cotton, Mercantile, and Produce) or the tremendously active over-the-counter share-trading or the concentration of banking business in the area. These people, and shoals of students, crowd into the visitors' gallery of the big brokerage barn at the rate of a thousand a day. It has been a sightseer's high point

for almost a century. Even before 1900, Karl Baedeker in his United States *Handbook for Travellers* advised: "Strangers, who are admitted to a gallery overlooking the hall, should not omit a visit to this strange scene of business, tumult, and excitement, a wilder scene probably than that presented in any European exchange."

To that always-perceptive reporter, Anne O'Hare McCormick, the Stock Exchange was "a unique and fascinating village which has the distinction of being a very small kingdom, a very great power. It contains the greatest of all markets, though it never sees the things it buys and sells. Nobody lives there, yet it is the most populous spot in one of the most congested centers in the world. It is more international than Geneva and more insular and homogeneous than Emporia, Kansas."

As for the architecture of the district as a whole, seen close up it may be "a delirium of inanimate anarchy bordering on terrorism," but viewed from a mile away on the bay, from the air, from Brooklyn Heights, Governor's Island, Stevens Institute of Technology in Hoboken, or the Empire State building, it becomes the crown of Allan Nevins' "imperial city of the Western World." The island city is framed in a magnificent silver sheet of water. These rivers, bays, straits, and the Sound, all pouring into the Atlantic, created the geographical destiny that has made New York what it is today — and made Wall Street inevitable.

This destiny has not been achieved lightly. Many have fought against it. The leading enemy general, Karl Marx, defined capitalism as "the inhuman offspring of greed and irresponsibility, committed by its master, Wall Street, to a long life of monopoly." *The Great Soviet Encyclopedia* (1955) described Wall Street as "a street in the southern part of Manhattan [that] is a synonym for monopolistic capitalism in the United States." Today the Soviet definition of 1955 is as out-of-date as that set forth by Marx eighty-eight years before. Each year the ownership of American industry sees its base broadened. More people find the money to purchase securities. More subscribe to mutual funds. More pension funds, controlled outright or in part by labor, are created and growing, and Marx must start whirling in his London grave every time another labor-union pension fund leaps over the hundred-million-dollar mark.

Criticism of Wall Street is not confined to its functions and purposes. Even the spectacular skyline comes in for its share of disapproval. The European architect Le Corbusier complained that the skyscrapers are too small and too numerous, but, like almost every critic, turned poetic when he tried to describe the place after dark: "New York at night is like a limitless cluster of jewels. . . . No one can imagine it who has not seen it. It is a titanic mineral display . . . shot through with an infinite number of lights . . . a violent silhouette like a fever chart beside a sick bed. A diamond, incalculable diamonds." H. J. Dutiel, a Frenchman whose opinions of America will never win him an honorary citizenship, wrote: "Nowhere in the world is it possible to have such a spectacle of the play of light across a city plunged in night . . . a firework which has been immobilized at the exact second it burst." Henry James, who compared the row of skyscrapers to a giant haircomb "turned upward and . . . deprived of half its teeth," felt differently about the place after nightfall and likened "the flash of innumerable windows" to "the flare . . . of the lamps of some permanent celebration." And F. Hopkinson Smith admitted: "No, ours is not a beautiful city—not by day. But see it by night! . . . Then Manhattan rises in compelling glory, the most brilliant, the most beautiful and the most inspiring of all the cities of the earth."

An unusual and amusing form of entertainment would be to walk around the Wall Street area substituting the old buildings and historical events for today's skyscrapers and activities. The north side of the Street itself becomes the wooden wall which was erected in March, 1653, and formed the town limits of New Amsterdam. Apparently, it was not much of a wall, for parts of it fell down or were eventually stolen for firewood. Intended by Governor Peter Stuyvesant to protect the town from the English, who were making warlike gestures from their settlements on the eastern end of Long Island and in Connecticut, the wall was totally ignored when the English did come ten years later. The enemy simply sailed up to the Battery with a strong naval force and demanded the surrender of the town.

Stroll down to Bowling Green at the foot of Broadway. No building has ever stood here. The iron fence around it is the same one that was put up in 1770. Only the royal crowns which topped the pickets are missing, knocked off during the celebration of the signing of the Declaration of Independence on the glorious night of July 9, 1776. A gilded lead statue of King George III was also knocked off its pedestal that night and the lead was melted down and returned to His Majesty's loyal troops, one bullet at a time.

Across the street is the block-square Custom House, with the magnificent Reginald Marsh murals which hardly anyone sees. The building, designed by Cass Gilbert, is as different from his Woolworth tower as the Woolworth tower is from the Gilbert-designed George Washington Bridge. The Custom House occupies almost the exact space on which the original fort of New Amsterdam was situated. All the land to the south and west has been filled in, as was everything west of Trinity Church and east of Pearl Street, so called because of the oyster shells that once littered the beach and were used as its first paving.

Look at Number 1 Broadway which advanced from hovel to home to mansion, British headquarters, hotel, tavern, office building, and shipping center. Broadway is the other great thoroughfare of the Wall Street district and it has kept pace with its neighbor in all its changes. Its two churches, Trinity and St. Paul's (actually a chapel of Trinity), offer quiet oases of green grass and eroded headstones in the shadows of the giant buildings. It is a street of solemn business towers and frantic shops, of old-fashioned massive building blocks, newly erected

Beginning of Broadway, 1938 (BERENICE ABBOTT)

Manhattan from 7,200 Feet (WILLIAM SAMENKO, JR.)

The Glass-Eyed Jungle (CHARLES ROTKIN)

sleek office spires, and jam-'em-in luncheonettes. It has heaped applause, cheers, and salutes on Washington, Lafayette, Washington Irving, Lincoln, General Grant, Charles Dickens (who immortalized Broadway's scavenging pigs), Jenny Lind, and Admiral Dewey, and three future kings of England. Ticker tape and shredded telephone books were added to the welcomes of Teddy Roosevelt, General Pershing, Lindbergh and sundry other fliers, a dozen kings and queens, and a score of athletic heroes.

But return to the corner of Broadway and Wall, across from Trinity Churchyard, where the bones of Robert Fulton, Alexander Hamilton, and a thousand others are at rest, and start walking eastward. You soon come to the brief, ancient alley called New Street. At this corner the Irving Trust Company building occupies the site where Washington Irving shared an office with his brother and wrote America's first satirical classic, *Diedrich Knickerbocker's History of New York.*

Across the street and east stood the First Presbyterian Church and, next door, John Simmons' highly respectable tavern. From the tavern door, looking south, you could see Broad Street (originally an inlet of the East River, later the "Graft" or canal), the scene of a terrible explosion in 1845 and, until 1920, the battleground of the outdoor Curb Market. Another and more terrible explosion shook Broad Street and Wall in 1920, killing thirty people, injuring three hundred, and remaining an unsolved mystery ever since. After the First Presbyterian Church was dismantled and transferred in sections to Jersey City and Simmons' Tavern was torn down, a half dozen progressively higher structures occupied the site until the Bankers Trust Company building sank its formidable foundations.

Only three buildings, however, have ever stood across the street on Wall. The first was the City Hall, started in 1700 and transformed into Federal Hall in 1789, then in the early 1800's a row of private homes, later converted to use as the United States Custom House, and, in 1845, the Greek temple known as the Sub-Treasury building until 1939 when the name was officially changed by order of the

Trinity Church, 1904 (EDWARD STEICHEN)

Secretary of the Interior to Federal Hall. On this spot, when Wall Street was the site of our first capitol, Washington was sworn in as President (he took the oath almost exactly where his statue stands today). Here the Bill of Rights was adopted, the Supreme Court created, and thirteen ill-matched colonies were welded into the United States of America.

Cater-corner to Federal Hall stands one of the three buildings which house the New York Stock Exchange, the other two stretching down Broad to Exchange Place. This site has, retrocessively, held the turn-of-the-century Wilks building, a cable office, a bookstore, and private houses. Across the street, at the fourth corner, is the squat fortress known as the House of Morgan, where a larger counting house, the Drexel, Morgan and Company building, stood before. Prior to that there was a rabbit-warren of a structure on the plot, full of stockjobbers, with a coal merchant in the basement, a watchmaker occupying quarters upstairs, and a sidewalk oyster bar in front. When the City Hall stood opposite, the Morgan corner was occupied by the pillory, stocks, cage, and whipping post of the town.

Continuing eastward, as Paul Revere did on May 17, 1774, when he brought dispatches from the Boston Committee of Correspondence to the Merchants Coffee House at Water and Wall, we pass the site of the graceful Merchants Exchange, which was burned in 1835, and its monolithic successor of 1842, now occupied by the First National City Bank. Along this route we would have seen the buttonwood, or sycamore, tree with the brokers of an earlier day bickering under its leaves, the Tontine Coffee House, into which the first brokers moved, and Murray's Wharf, where Washington landed on the way to his inauguration. One afternoon in 1692, Captain William Kidd walked along this street, immensely pleased at having sold the lot at 56 Wall Street for thirty-five dollars, making a neat five-dollar profit on the deal. No matter how many people crowd into Wall Street today, they are outnumbered by all the ghosts.

Although 56 Wall will never again sell for thirty-five dollars, the Street is still the Land of Opportunity. An honest young man with the ability to

Smoke, Steam, and Sun (BERENICE ABBOTT)

make the right friends can build up a list of brokerage customers yielding an annual income of fifty thousand dollars within five years. A dishonest one can sit in a "boiler-room" and unload phony stocks at so swift a clip that he rakes in five thousand dollars a week in commissions, which are unreported and hence untaxed. Wall Street is still the place where a man can run a nest egg into a goose egg, but today no one in any exchange or brokerage office stacks the cards against him.

The Street has never been so clean, so honest, so ethical. In a number of ways the exchanges and the brokers have better business morals than some of the companies and industries whose securities they trade back and forth. And there is constant vigilance by exchange officials and the Securities and Exchange Commission to keep it that way.

Terror has gone out of the market place, but for several hundred years the Street was either headed for disaster or recovering from one. The miracle is that it survived. It has survived because at its most cataclysmic depths there were men tough enough and brave enough and acquisitive enough to fight, to rebuild, to win. Wall Street has been burned out, blown up, wiped out, panicked, threatened, investigated, regulated, cursed, rigged, held up, and looted —but it has come back every time.

Wall Street is a cat with ninety-nine lives.

2

In the Beginning

WALL STREET has been here for more than three hundred years, which is a long time by our standards. But the tough old granite that sometimes lies less than a foot below its pavement has been there since the earth cooled to a hard crust some 2,500,000,000 years ago — a time-span almost impossible for the human mind to comprehend.

Yet for thousands of millions of years before man evolved, the forces of nature were at work shaping the physical structure of what was to become the world's greatest trading place. Not long ago, geologically speaking, the Hudson River was a wild torrent with great falls that roared through a canyon forty miles long, seven miles wide, and two miles deep. Manhattan was 150 miles inland and 3,500 feet above sea level. Then, about twenty thousand years ago, the most recent glacier melted and the Atlantic rose to its present shoreline.

The last great glacier did an excellent job of dredging the harbor of New York, carving Manhattan roughly in the shape of a giant airplane carrier made of rock as it reached what is now Staten Island and began to recede. In many other ways, nature has been good to the island of Manhattan. The rivers and estuaries which converge around it, the rich hinterland which needs an outlet for its products, the midway location on the Atlantic seaboard — these are only a few of the geographical factors responsible for the pre-eminence of New York City and its treasure vault, Wall Street.

In past ages the climate of the entire area has ranged from sultry tropical heat to frigid arctic cold. Several times it has lain beneath a mile-thick coat of ice; periodically it has been inundated by rising ocean or covered densely with lush, exotic vegetation. During the Triassic Period, giant reptiles prowled the land of eastern North America and fossil remains of some of these creatures have been found close to the shores of Manhattan. Between a million years ago and 25,000 B.C., enormous ground sloths, huge bison, musk oxen, and lumbering mastodons trampled paths across what later became Wall Street and Broadway.

Not long after the last glacier receded, early man came to North America. A Mongol from Central Asia with slanted black eyes and a wild mop of black

Digging foundations for the skyscrapers in lower Manhattan, builders often find bedrock lying just beneath the surface. The tough, two-billion-year-old granite is so hard it can only be split by drilling holes so close together that the rock walls resemble corduroy cloth.

Before the arrival of the Dutch, the Algonquins lived an easy communal life on Manhattan Island, which provided an abundance of game, wild fowl, and fish. Indian dwellings were sometimes bark-covered long houses, resembling the Quonset huts of World War II. One found by the Dutch was 180 feet long.

The natives also lived in huts made by planting a circle of saplings, binding their tops to form a roof, and covering the frames with birch bark. In winter women usually wore a deerskin cape for protection against the cold.

hair, he was a nomadic hunter in search of food and hides who had crossed a land bridge that extended between Siberia and Alaska. Eventually these people multiplied, spreading to all parts of the continent, and anthropologists have uncovered evidence of their settlements in various regions of the United States.

The Indians who descended from these early people frequently lived in caves and rock shelters in and around Manhattan, but neither these natural homes, nor the circular or long communal huts which they built of bark, were year-round dwellings. Manhattan was apparently a summer camping ground, a stopping-off place for tribal groups roaming up and down the coast.

The first Indians who settled permanently on Manhattan Island arrived about a thousand years ago. They were Algonquins, driven from upper New York by the more savage Mohawks. They lived a pleasant, ideal life on the shores of the Hudson, the men hunting and fishing while the women cultivated the "Three Sisters"—corn, beans, and squash—as well as millet, sweet potatoes, melons, and tobacco. At that time Manhattan was covered with rolling hills, thick forests, and swamps. Wild grapes, strawberries, apple and oak trees grew in undisciplined profusion. The air was full of birds, the land abounded with game, the water swarmed with fish.

Then the white man came. Because of the wild grapes, some scholars think that Manhattan was the Vineland of Leif Ericson, who probably discovered America at the beginning of the eleventh century. Others lean to the belief that the initial visitor may have been a Welsh prince named Madoc, or an Irish missionary, or the Venetian navigator Niccolò Zeno, who is said to have reached the New World a hundred years before Columbus.

Whether Columbus was the first or the fifth or the fifteenth explorer to cross the Atlantic, he certainly had the best timing. Spain had driven the last of the Moors out of the country and could now turn to new business; people were ready to believe that the world was round; and the invention of the printing press made it possible to spread the news quickly and fairly accurately.

The total cost of discovering America did not exceed one hundred thousand dollars—some say no more than twenty-five thousand. As soon as it was discovered, the continent became the target of every sailor-of-fortune able to gain a royal ear. Several of these adventurers, sailing up or down the North American coast, swept right past New York. It is not known if any of them actually stumbled into the world's greatest harbor. For despite the claims made for John Cabot and his son Sebastian, for the Portu-

Christopher Columbus, whom the Spanish call Cristóbal Colón—and claim as a native Spaniard—believed to his dying day that he had found Zipango (Japan) or its outlying islands. For the next 150 years, explorers continued to seek the Far East in the West.

In April, 1524, Giovanni da Verrazano entered the BELLISSIMO LAGO, *as he described New York Bay, but a sudden storm forced him back to sea. Some writers say he was a humanitarian and humanist; others claim he was a cunning, greedy pirate.*

guese brothers, Gasper and Miguel Cortereal, and for Amerigo Vespucci, the first recorded visit came thirty-two years after Columbus' initial voyage, when, early in 1524, Giovanni da Verrazano sailed his *Dolphin* into a "very pleasant situation among some steep hills, through which a very large river . . . forced its way to the sea. Up this river we found it formed a most beautiful lake. . . . All of a sudden, a violent contrary wind . . . forced us to return to our ship, greatly regretting to leave this region, which seemed so commodious and delightful, and which we supposed must also contain great riches, as the hills showed many indications of minerals."

This was from the captain's report to his patron, Francis I of France, but by the time Verrazano returned to Dieppe, Francis was in no position to develop Angoulême, as the discoverer named New York. Francis, who was defeated at Pavia on February 24, 1525, was spending a year as a prisoner of Emperor Charles V in Spain.

In 1609 Henry Hudson explored the river named for him, seeking a short cut to China, but was halted by shallow water near Albany. About a year later, he was set adrift by a mutinous crew and perished in the icy waters of Hudson Bay.

Adriaen Block, lawyer, sea captain, trader, and cartographer, was also the first European house- and shipbuilder on Manhattan. He explored and mapped the East coast almost to Boston and claimed the entire area for the Dutch.

It was almost eighty-five years later that Henry Hudson made the next visit from Europe to New York. Verrazano had been a Florentine in the service of France; Columbus was a Genoese sailing for Spain, and Hudson, an Englishman, worked for the Dutch. This is not at all surprising, for these projects were business ventures rather than nationalistic enterprises. At first the sole purpose of these voyages was to search for a new route to the rich spice and pepper country of the Orient. No pepper was found, but the explorers discovered coffee, chocolate, sugar, corn, bananas, potatoes, and tobacco. These profitably salable items, some previously unknown in Europe, kept bringing them back to America. They also made another valuable discovery—the land seemed to contain a limitless store of gold and silver.

For the next hundred years, the Spanish neglected almost everything else in the Americas in their hunger for the precious metals. During that time, their vessels brought back to Spain at least one hun-

According to Icelandic sagas, America was discovered by Leif Ericson, son of Eric the Red, and thirty-seven venturesome companions who, around 1000 A.D., sailed and rowed their way from Greenland to the mainland of North America, where they spent one winter at a still-unidentified site which they called Vineland.

On his first voyage, Columbus, in the one-hundred-ton SANTA MARIA, *was accompanied by the forty-ton* NINA *and fifty-ton* PINTA. *Most of his crew of eighty-eight had been released from Spanish prisons. On his second voyage in 1493 he led an expedition of seventeen ships and 1,500 experienced seamen.*

dred million dollars' worth of gold and silver. (Today the banana crop alone for a single year is worth more than this.) When a ship of another nation was outfitted and financed for a journey to the New World, one of the inducements to investors was the possibility that it might capture a Spanish gold galleon, for the captains of that day sailed under letters of marque, which were simply licenses to steal.

Authorized robbery on the high seas did not die out until after the War of 1812. Known as privateering, it was distinguished from piracy, considered a nasty word, because the privateer operated against some country at war with the nation that had issued his permit to pillage. Indeed, he was generally regarded with respect as a businessman because he was supposed to divide his loot with the country or individual who had signed his *carte blanche*. Between the privateering and the smuggling industries, business was a great deal more exciting, zestful — and profitable—then than now. The island of Manhattan with its numerous quiet coves and ready access to the sea was perfectly designed for smuggling, and Wall Street, in its early days, was a center for the disposal of loot at very reasonable rates.

The elder J. P. Morgan, all of whose yachts were painted black and named the *Corsair*, once confided to Henry Collins Brown that he was a remote descendant of that other Welshman, the buccaneer Sir Henry Morgan. "The only difference between us," Brown reported, "is that he operated at sea and I work on land."

Verrazano had been a corsair preying on Spanish bullion ships for Francis I before his visit to New York. He is reported to have returned to that trade afterward and died, presumably in 1527, either at the hands of Spaniards who resented his way of doing business or those of West Indian natives who, some historians say, roasted and devoured him. But before his demise he had left records of his Atlantic coastal survey and his brother, Gerolamo, a chart-maker, had put New York on the map as Angoulême, the name of Francis' domain in the Bordeaux country. The bay was named Santa Margarita, in honor of the King's sister, Margaret of Navarre, author of the *Heptameron*.

The waters around New York led the discoverers to theorize that a vast sea existed a few miles inland and that beyond this sea lay China. This theory found its way onto maps and one of them guided Hudson to the neighborhood. Hudson's orders from the Dutch East India Company were to find a Northwest Passage to Asia, but, halted by icebergs and the extreme cold of the polar seas, he turned southward to seek Verrazano's inland sea. He entered the Lower Bay of New York on September 3, 1609. The sweet breeze of the land blended with the salt air of the sea and he found the country "as pleasant with grass and flowers as any we had ever seen." He sailed up Verrazano's "very large river" almost to Albany and then sent a boat ahead which returned with the disappointing news that this was not the short cut to the Orient which he had hoped to find. On October 3, he sailed out of the river that now bears his name and returned to Europe.

His glowing description of the country and the rich cargo of furs he obtained from the Indians did not impress the aristocratic members of the Dutch East India Company, but there were independent traders who saw the potential wealth of the land.

John Cabot (Giovanni Caboto in Venetian) received a patent from England's Henry VII to seek a Cathay passage by sailing west and north. However, he found only a forbidding northern American coast and returned to Europe, his mission unfulfilled. The later British claims to America were based on this voyage.

As a result, a number of trips were made by venturesome Dutch sailors who traded cheap novelty goods and baubles to the Indians for the fine pelts which were in great demand in Europe. Captain Adriaen Block was one of the first of these traders, and he, like the other sea merchants, found the island of Manhattan an ideal port.

On a night in November, 1613, his ship, the *Tiger*, was anchored off the southern tip when it caught fire. Block and his crew barely managed to escape to

This map by Gastaldi, 1550, shows the influence of Verrazano's reports. Angoulême (New York) is the peninsula at lower left (above vessel); Flora (Long Island) is shown on the mainland. Verrazano was delighted with Port du Refuge (Newport).

When fire destroyed Adriaen Block's TIGER, *at anchor near what is now Greenwich and Dey streets, he spent the winter of 1613–14 on Manhattan. Here he built the Sixteen-ton* ONRUST *("Restless"), took her up the East River through Hell Gate, into Long Island Sound, where he discovered the island he named "Adriaenbloxeyland."*

A section of Block's Figurative Map of East coast. Original, presented at The Hague, October 11, 1614, led to the granting of a three-year charter to the United Netherlands Company. Manhattan appears as an island for the first time; the map also is the first to place the "Manhattes" tribe on the island.

shore. All the other trading vessels had already returned across the Atlantic, and Block and his men were faced with spending a bleak and desolate winter in a savage land. They scooped out crude shelters, in the vicinity of what is now 39–41 Broadway, and occupied their time building a new ship. By spring they had floated the *Onrust* (or *Restless*, in English), a yacht of sixteen tons burden. Now Block began to explore the neighboring waters. Passing through Hell Gate (he called it Hellegat), he entered Long Island Sound and discovered the Housatonic and Connecticut rivers. The latter he named the Fresh River, in contrast to the Hudson, which was salt water as far as he explored it. Sailing around Long Island, he discovered the isle at the east entrance to the Sound which bears his name, as well as Roode (red) Island, since corrupted into Rhode Island.

For the next dozen years Dutch explorers, sailors, and traders lived on Manhattan at irregular intervals. The Dutch West India Company was chartered in 1621 and given the exclusive right to trade wherever Dutch authority extended in the New World. The company's first vessel, the *Nieuw Netherland*, brought thirty families of settlers to Fort Orange, near Albany, on its initial voyage, and, in 1625, two ships with settlers and cattle were disembarked on Manhattan. The following year the little *Sea-Mew* arrived with the Director-General of the colony, Peter Minuit (or Pierre Minuet), a Belgian Walloon (or French Huguenot), depending on the historian consulted. He either arrived, or bought the island, on May 4, or 6, 1626.

The purchase of Manhattan Island for trinkets valued at twenty-four dollars is the most familiar

This popular conception of the most famous real-estate deal in history is probably misleading, since no contemporary description or picture of the purchase of Manhattan Island exists. The entire story is based on one brief mention in a letter.

fact in the history of New York, but exactly where the transaction took place and from whom the island was bought are unknown. The price and size of the purchase were recorded by Pieter Jansen Schaghen, Deputy from Amsterdam to the States-General, Holland's parliament, in a document dated November 5, 1626: ". . . they have bought the island Manhattes from the wild men for the value of 60 guilders . . . [it] is 11,000 *morgens* in area." As a result, the Dutch West India Company's "stock soon stood at a high premium."

If the Indians had taken the twenty-four dollars in cash instead of trinkets and invested it immediately at 6 per cent interest, compounded quarterly, today they would have had more than the sixteen billion dollars assessed value of Manhattan Island and the buildings thereon, such being the wonder of compound interest. Some historians claim that Minuit paid off the wrong tribe and had to negotiate over again with several others. In any event, Minuit should be nominated as the patron saint of real-estate men, for they have ever since used his purchase as the prime example of a profitable property deal. A *morgen* is two acres, which means the island was sold for one-tenth of a cent an acre.

Of all New York's colonial governors, Dutch or English, Minuit seems to have been the best. He was an honest, fair, and energetic man who had a winning way with both the Indians and the settlers. About the latter it is recorded that "most of them could neither read nor write. They were a wild, uncouth and most of the time a drunken crowd. They lived in small log huts, thatched with straw. They wore rough clothes, and in winter were dressed in skins. They subsisted on a little corn, game and fish. They were afraid of neither man, God, nor the devil.

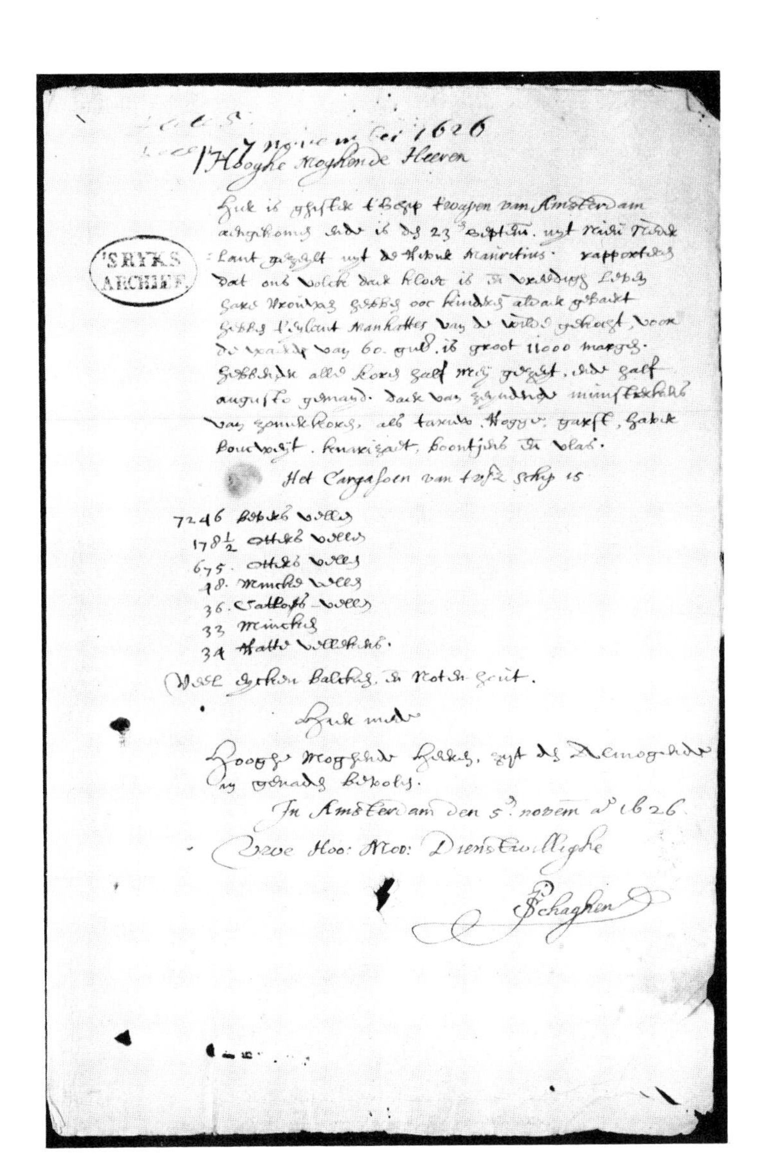

Recepi 7 novemb 1626

Hooghe Moghende Heeren

Hier is gisteren 't schip 't Wapen van Amsterdam aengecomen ende is den 23 septemb. uyt Nieu Nederlant gezeylt uyt de Riviere Mauritius. rapporteren dat ons volck daer kloeck is en vredich leven. haere vrouwen hebben oock kinderen aldaer gebaert, hebben 't eylant Manhattes van de wilde gekocht, voor de waerde van 60 guld. is groot 11000 morgen. hebben alle koren half mey gezayt, ende half augusto gemaeyt. daer van zenden monsterkens van zomerkoren, als tarwe, rogge, garst, haver, boeckweyt, kanarisaet, boontjens en vlas.

Het Cargasoen van 't voorsz schip is

7246 bevers vellen
178½ otters vellen
675 otters vellen
48 mincke vellen
36 catlossen vellen
33 mincken
34 ratte vellekens.

Veel eycken balcken en noten hout.

Hiermede

Hooge Moghende Heeren, zyt den Almogende in genade bevolen.

In Amsterdam den 5e novem. aº 1626.

Uwe Hoo: Moo: Dienstwillighe

P. Schaghen

In Pieter Schaghen's letter from Amsterdam to the States-General, dated November 5, 1626, he reports the arrival of the ARMS OF AMSTERDAM from New Netherland, tells of the purchase of Manhattan, the birth of the first girl, Sarah Rapaelje, and lists the vessel's cargo of furs.

Earliest view of New Amsterdam, 1626-28. This sketch, which appeared in a Dutch book published in 1651, shows the island in reverse as viewed from the East River. The stepped-gable building below the fort held the Counting House and stood at what is now Whitehall and Pearl streets.

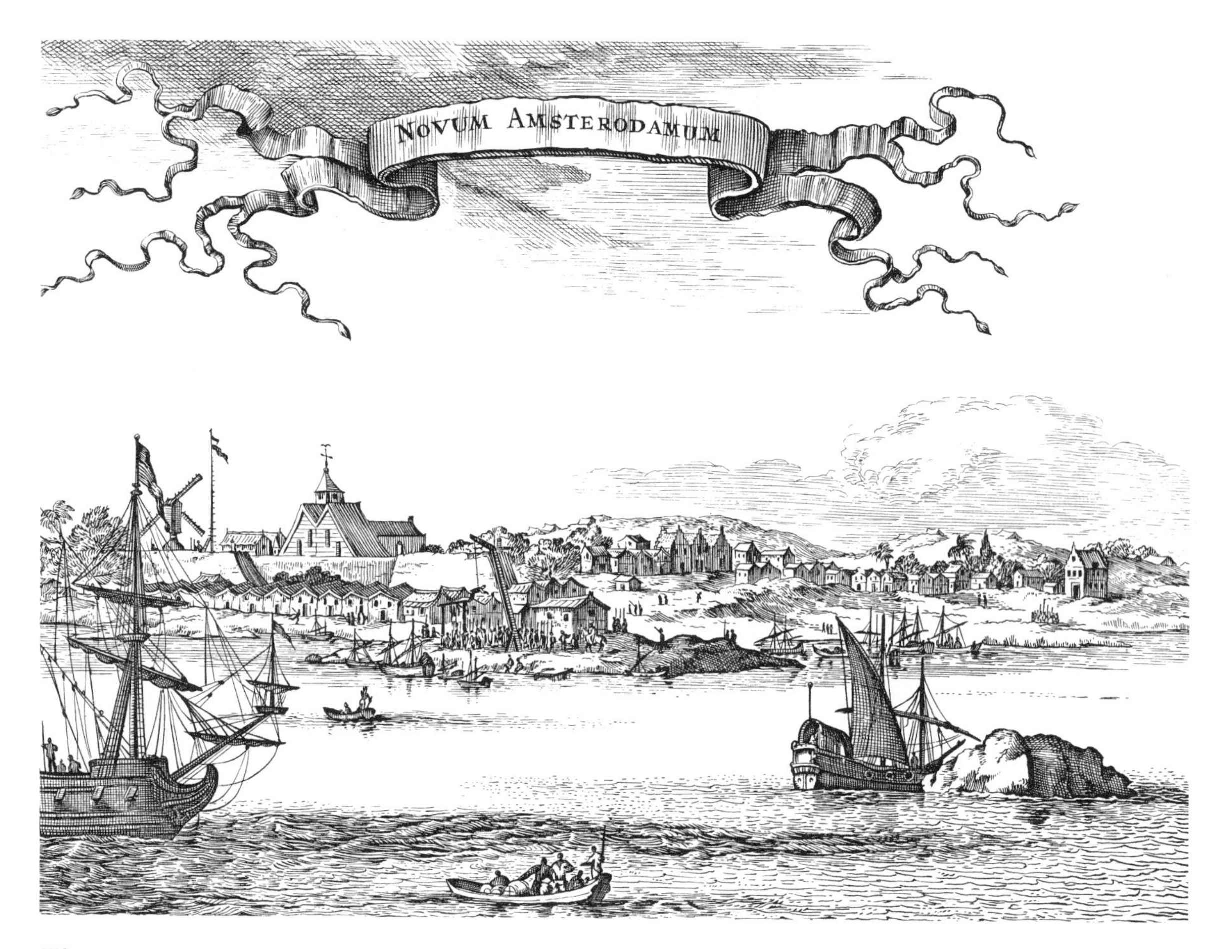

The second known view of New Amsterdam, 1642–43. This drawing is a puzzle to historians because it shows a belfry on the church but no city tavern, which was supposedly completed before the belfry was added. In the center, near the shore, is a gallows with a crowd looking on at a man suspended from his waist, a typical punishment in New Amsterdam.

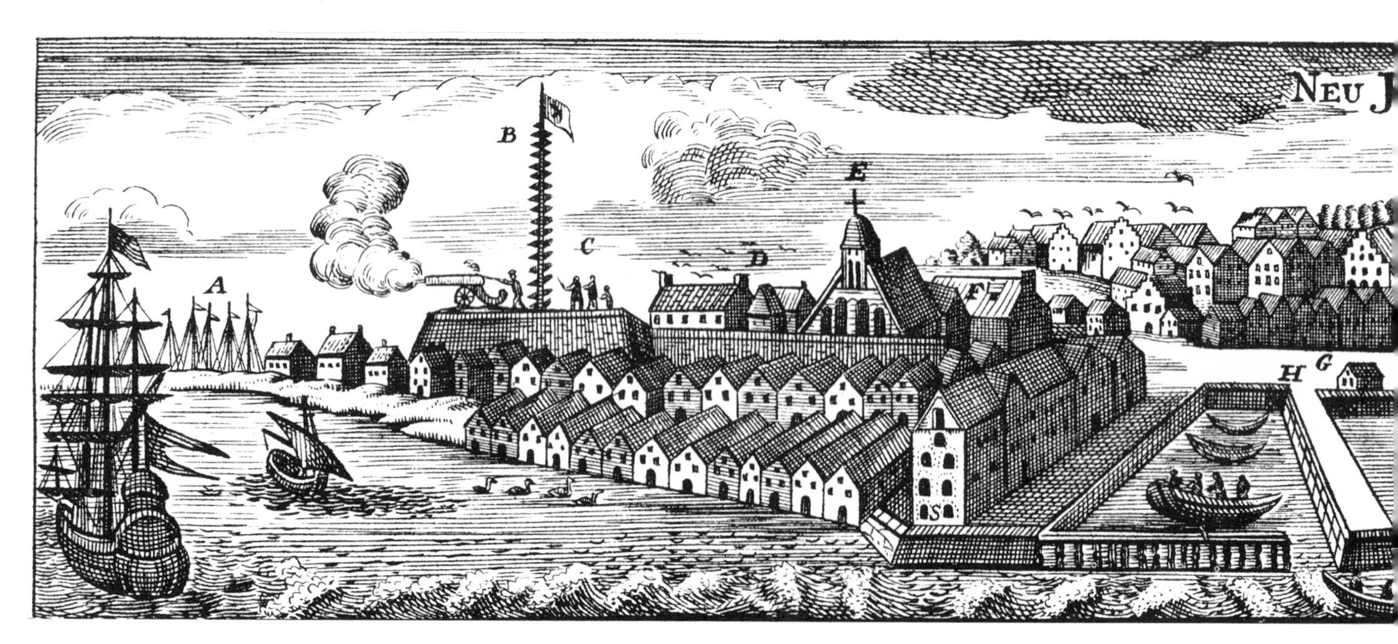

New York, or New Orange, recaptured by the Dutch from the English in August, 1673, and surrendered in November, 1674. (A) *Albany sloops anchored in the Hudson.* (B) *Flagstaff.* (C) *Fort William Hendrick.* (D) *Jail in the Fort.* (E) *Church of St. Nicholas.* (F) *Governor's House in the Fort, occupied by Anthony Colve.* (G) *Public storehouses.* (H) *Scales or weighhouse.* (I) *The Great Ditch, or "Graft," now Broad Street.* (K) *Stadt Huys or City Hall (belfry and gallows not shown).* (L) TO RIGHT AND ABOVE K: *Lutheran Church, southwest corner Broadway and*

They were laying deep the foundation of the Empire State."

Almost from the first, there were Negro slaves in New Amsterdam, brought from the Dutch West India Company's islands in the Caribbean to work on the first stone building, the company warehouse. New York was not only America's first frontier town, but also a company town, which means a town in continual ferment against the vested interests and authority. Minuit was fair and progressive in his administration, but was recalled after six years because he had authorized the building of a large vessel of eight hundred tons which exceeded its budget. He was replaced by Wouter Van Twiller, described by one historian as a gluttonous, hypocritical drunk and by the colony's dominie, Everardus Bogardus, as "a child of the devil and a consummate villain."

Bogardus married the widow Annetja Jans, whose *bouwerie*, or farm, known as the Queen's Farm toward the end of the century, became the nucleus of Trinity Church's extensive real-estate holdings. When the Jans family relinquished the property, one son failed to sign the papers, and this was, for two hundred years, the basis for a flood of hopeless suits by persons of the remotest relationship to him. These suits were mainly inspired by lawyers who advertised for heirs and obtained a series of fees from each of thousands of hopefuls. It took a Supreme Court ruling, after World War I, to bar any further litigation in the Annetja Jans case.

Wouter Van Twiller was followed in 1638 by Willem Kieft, a military man who ran the town and province for nine years. He was considered an improvement over his predecessor until he tried to tax the Indians. This resulted in a two-year Indian war and much justified dissatisfaction with the Governor, so that he was consequently replaced by Peter Stuyvesant on May 11, 1647.

According to Washington Irving's *Diedrich Knickerbocker's History of New York* (1809), Stuyvesant was a tough, sturdy, valiant, weather-beaten, mettlesome, obstinate, leather-sided, lion-hearted, generous-spirited old governor. Irving bestowed on Stuyvesant a better reputation than he deserves. While he must have had an overpowering personality, his treatment of religious dissenters, especially Lutherans, Baptists, and Quakers, ranged from shabby to downright cruel. He made no bones about being a dictator and warned that if anyone dared appeal to the home government, "I will make him a foot shorter and send the pieces to Holland and let him appeal that way."

Stuyvesant himself was a leg shorter than the average citizen, his right one having been amputated after

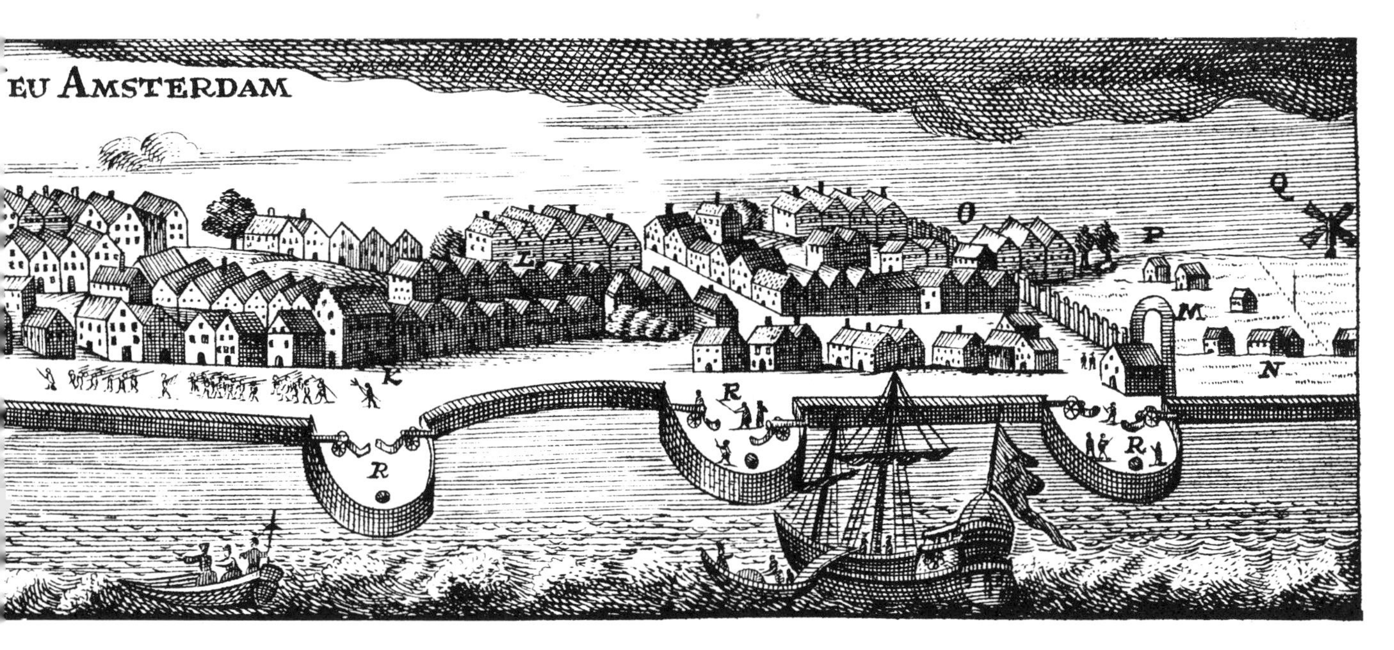

Rector. (M) Water Gate of city wall at East River. (N) The Smith's Valley or Fly, Pearl Street from Wall to Franklin Square. (O) Land Gate of city wall at North River. (P) The way to the Fresh Water Pond, now Broadway. (Q) Probably Peter Jansen Mesier's windmill on Broadway between Liberty and Cortlandt. (R) Redoubts or half-moons (LEFT TO RIGHT), *Stadt Huys Battery, Burgher Battery, and Wall Street Battery. (S)* AT SHORE BETWEEN E AND F: *House of Peter Stuyvesant, who died the previous year. (T) East River, between Manhattan and Yorkshire (Long Island).*

Bird's-eye view of New Amsterdam, 1660, when every house had its garden or orchard. At right is the wall from which the street takes its name. The Broad Street canal runs from the East River almost to Exchange Place. The Fort stands where the Custom House is today. Only Bowling Green remains the same.

he was wounded in an attack on the Portuguese island of Saint Martin while he was Governor-General at Curaçao. His wooden leg, still being sought by collectors of antique curiosities, was decorated with bands and nails of silver. When he stumped onto shore for the first time, he found New Amsterdam a rather miserable little town. He proceeded to clean it up, halting the sale of firewater to the Indians, repairing the fort at the tip of the island, and establishing Manhattan's first night watch. In 1653, fearful that another dictator, Oliver Cromwell, would order Englishmen from Connecticut and the eastern end of Long Island to capture New Amsterdam, Stuyvesant decreed that a wooden wall be erected across the island, just beyond the town's northern limits.

Unlike the walls of European cities, the Manhattan stockade was similar to the palisades the Indians built around their villages in time of war. It was 2,340 feet long and extended from Pearl Street, on the shore of the East River, to the rear of the present Trinity Churchyard, where the bank fell sharply to the Hudson. Soon the Dutch, great experts at reclaiming land from water, started expanding the island. From Pearl Street the East River was pushed back to Water, then Front, and finally South Street. To the west the shore became Trinity Place, then the Hudson, too, was pushed back, first to Washington and then to West Street.

The wall which the Governor ordered was constructed of wooden logs, sharpened to pointed ends at the top and planted in the ground. It cost $1,300 and the contractor was Tomas Bacxter, who later turned to piracy. When Stuyvesant presented

When Oliver Cromwell made warlike noises and the British cast covetous eyes on New Amsterdam, Peter Stuyvesant ordered his "children" to build a wall along the city limits. It stood for fifty years.

Looking east on Broad Street before 1676, when the canal was filled in. The view fails to show Brooklyn Heights across the East River. The bridge is at Bridge Street.

Peter Stuyvesant

Sir Edmund Andros

Colonel Thomas Dongan

Earl of Bellomont

Lord Cornbury

William Burnet

Colonel William Cosby

General Robert Monckton

Earl of Dunmore

Bacxter's bill to the town council, the members refused to pay it, saying that the Dutch West India Company should defend its property at its own expense. They held their ground until Stuyvesant agreed to turn over the excise tax on liquor to the city treasury, instead of keeping it for the company. When Cromwell signed a peace treaty with the Dutch in December of the same year, the thrifty citizens began stripping away the palisades for use as firewood and the wall gradually fell into disrepair. But every time a war alarm was sounded, the fence was once more repaired and some additional breastwork was added.

In March, 1664, Charles II of England blithely gave all the land between the Connecticut and Delaware rivers to his younger brother, the Duke of York and Albany. On August 29, four frigates with ninety-two guns and 450 men sailed into New Amsterdam harbor, completely ignoring the wall at the other end of town, and demanded the surrender of the city. Stuyvesant was all for resisting, but recognizing the superiority of the enemy's forces and faced by the reluctance of his people to put up a fight, he surrendered the island to Colonel Richard Nicolls, who came ashore, took command of the town, and promptly renamed it New York. Samuel Pepys, Secretary of the Admiralty, wrote in his celebrated diary on September 29: "We have been doing them [the Dutch] mischief for a great while in several parts of the world, without public knowledge or reason."

Nicolls and his successor, Sir Francis Lovelace, were capable, popular administrators, but during the next hundred years New York suffered from a succession of rumpots, crackpots, rogues, and ruthless rulers. But first there was a brief return to Dutch rule, less than two years (1673–1674), when two Dutch admirals, Evertzen and Binckes, captured the port and appointed Anthony Colve as Governor. However, when the Dutch signed the Treaty of Westminster with England, the island reverted to English rule, and Sir Edmund Andros (1674–1680) took over. Sir Edmund was a tyrant who was finally recalled only to bob up again eight years later as Governor of all the crown colonies from Massachusetts to New York. Colonel Thomas Dongan (1683–1688) gave the city a charter and stole a sixty-four-foot-wide strip from Wall Street. Through dummies, he acquired that much of the one-hundred-foot-wide parade ground in front of the wall, generously leaving thirty-six feet for the city street. He added his sixty-four feet to a strip eighty feet wide on the other side of the wall which he bought through another dummy and thus had a subdivision 144 feet wide and one thousand feet long.

Jacob Leisler, a militia captain, set up the first popular native government in 1689 during religious dissensions that were then plaguing the colony. After two years, he surrendered his powers, was tried for treason, and executed by Colonel Henry Sloughter, who ruled drunkenly for four months in 1691, then died. Sloughter was succeeded by another colonel, Benjamin Fletcher (1692–1698), a great crony of pirates such as Captain Thomas Tew, whom the Governor "was trying to reform." Fletcher was accused of official larceny, tried for conniving with the pirates, and was ousted, but he took with him the proceeds of a thriving under-the-counter business in land grants.

His successor, Richard Coote, Earl of Bellomont, was hampered by his prior association with Captain William Kidd. Although he captured Kidd and sent him off to Execution Dock in London, his rule, from April, 1698, to March, 1701, was hardly notable. He died of the gout and was succeeded by Edward Hyde, Lord Cornbury (1702–1708), the most eccentric of all the governors. Appointed by his cousin, Queen Anne, who had just ascended the throne, Cornbury felt that, since he resembled her physically, he should endeavor to be the living embodiment of the Queen in order to represent her in the New World. He would therefore put on his wife's clothes, parade forth from his residence in the Fort, and proceed up Broadway until the aroused citizenry chased him home. The people considered him either drunk or mad, and sympathized with his wife and seven children. After six years of this odd behavior, he was removed and sent home to England, where he was jailed for debt until his father died and he inherited the title of third Earl of Clarendon.

Lord John Lovelace, Baron Hurley, arrived in December, 1708, after a rough ocean voyage and only survived for five months. Lord Robert Hunter (1710–1720) provided a distinct change of pace. He was a good governor; his only offense, it seems, was that he wrote a play. Governor William Burnet (1720–1728) was a young widower of thirty-two who fought continually with the Assembly which became so irritated with him that it appealed to the crown for

Stadt Huys or City Hall, at head of Coenties Slip, was first built as the city tavern in 1642 and became the Municipal building in 1653. When it began to fall down, in the 1690's, Colonel Abraham De Peyster donated land at Wall and Broad for a new one.

Residence of Captain William Kidd on Pearl Street near Water Gate at the east end of Wall. When Trinity Church was being built, 1696–98, Kidd supplied the block and tackle used for hoisting the wall stones into place.

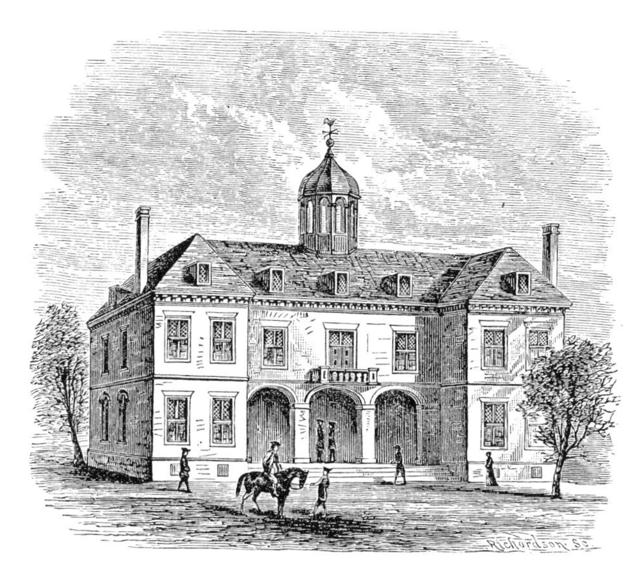

The second City Hall was completed in 1700. The first floor left contained a prison with a dungeon beneath it and a fire engine in the rear; the second floor held courtrooms and the third was a debtors' jail.

his removal; this was accomplished by elevating him to the governorship of Massachusetts. Next came John Montgomery who died of the smallpox, but not before giving the city a charter which divided it into seven wards, one of which was named in his honor and known, therefore, as Montgomery Ward. Colonel William Cosby, who died of tuberculosis after a four-year rule (1732-1736), is chiefly remembered as the persecutor of John Peter Zenger. Sir George Clinton (1743–1753) and Sir Charles Hardy (1755–1757) were both admirals whose ineptness as administrators makes it obvious that they should have stayed at sea, and Sir Danvers Osborne was a widower afflicted with melancholia. His brother-in-law, the Earl of Halifax, thought that it might cheer him up to be Governor of New York, but Sir Danvers was so discouraged after his first official banquet that he went into the garden and hanged himself five days after he arrived. General Robert Monckton (1761–1765) was a working general and an absentee governor. Then came Sir Henry Moore, Earl of Dunmore, who wept when he was transferred to Virginia, where he is still remembered for an attempt to kidnap Martha Washington and burn Mount Vernon during the Revolution. The last royal Governor of New York was Sir William Tryon, who tried to have George Washington assassinated and viciously persecuted helpless civilians in raids on Connecticut after the outbreak of hostilities. Why the beautiful park at the northern end of Manhattan Island was named for him is one of the major mysteries of New York.

From the beginning of English rule, the city grew rapidly. Rough thatched houses gave way to stone and brick homes, those of the Dutch adorned with gabled roofs and corbiesteps. In 1688, three years after Governor Dongan acquired his Wall Street property, he began selling off parcels. One lot, at what is now 56 Wall Street, was acquired by William Cox, who is said to have built the first house on the north side of the street. In 1689 Cox "took too much water in" and died. His widow remarried, but on May 15, 1691, her new husband followed Cox to the grave. The next day Sarah Cox married a respected and able ship captain, William Kidd, who sailed a New York-London packet boat for many years.

Kidd was in London in 1695 when King William, whose Navy was busy fighting the French, gave orders that a stock company be formed to wipe out piracy. Many titled and notable personages subscribed, including the Earl of Bellomont and Robert Livingston of New York, who recommended that Kidd be drafted to command the *Adventure Galley* and sail to Madagascar, headquarters of the Red Sea trade, as that branch of piratical endeavor was known. According to a recently unearthed version of the Kidd saga, he was unable to capture any corsairs but, since his commission ordered him to proceed against the French, he gathered in two ships of the Grand Mogul, who, the newly found documents assert, was an ally of the French. However, since England and France had signed a peace treaty before Kidd's action, which infuriated the French and strained the new peace, William appeased his former enemy by making Kidd the sacrificial goat. Not that the captain was hanged for piracy. The charge was much more prosaic—bashing in the skull of a mutinous gunner with a bucket.

Kidd and his wife had lived around the corner from Wall Street on Pearl, two blocks north of the Stadt Huys, or State House, which actually was the City Hall. It had been built in 1642 as the city tavern and became the center of more formal civic activities in 1653, while the Fort was the headquarters for provincial business. In Kidd's time the Stadt Huys had become so ramshackle that the magistrates feared for their heads and rented rooms in private houses to hold court. At the same time, the remnants of the wall were fast being turned into fire-

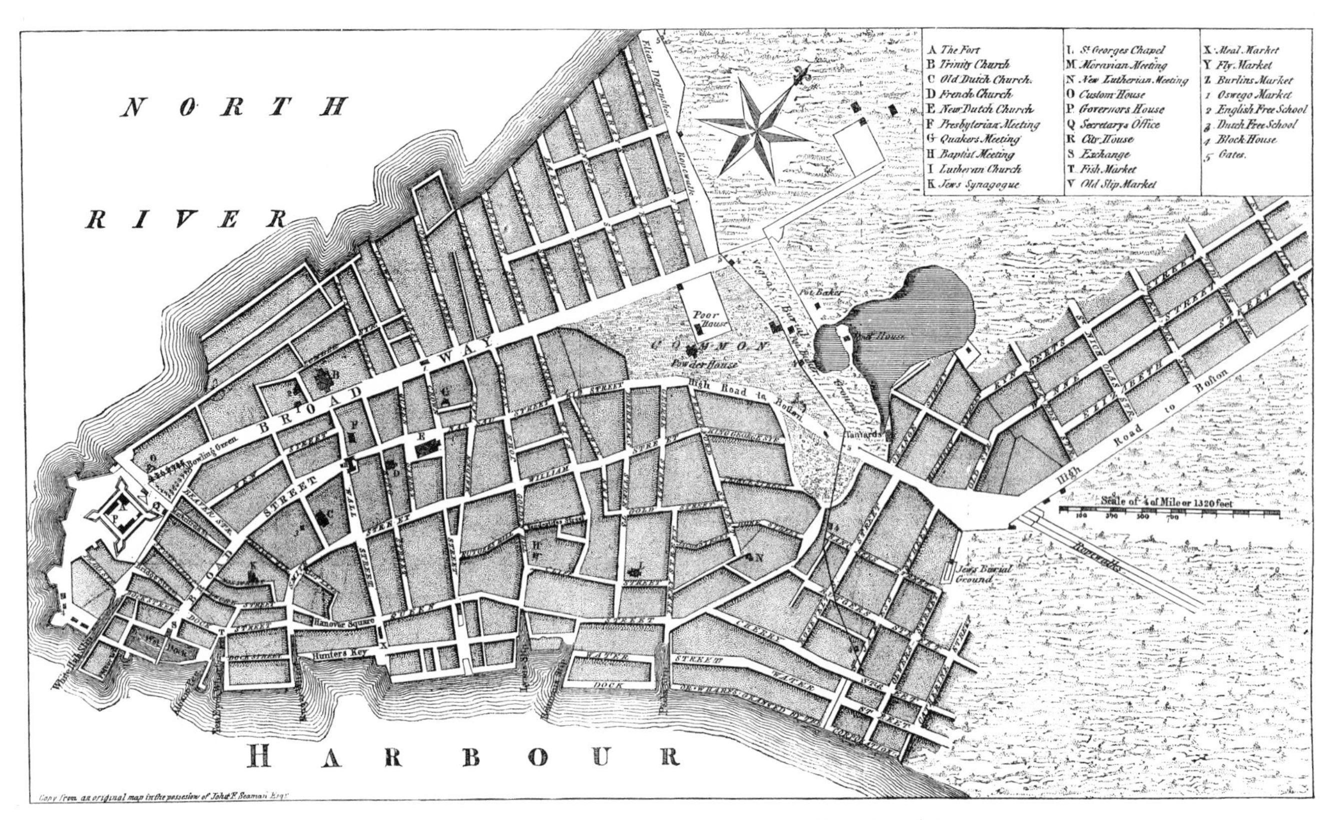

By 1763 New York had expanded not only north along the Bowery (High Road to Boston), but west, as the Hudson shore was filled in, and east, with the addition of Water Street and Dock, now Front Street. The Common is now City Hall Park.

wood. Colonel Abraham De Peyster, who had bought many of the Dongan lots on Wall Street, gave the town the site for a new City Hall on that thoroughfare, at the top of Broad Street. Alongside the north end of the new site was a cartway, now Nassau Street, then known as "the street that runs by the pie woman's, leading to The Fields."

The remnants of the wall came down and the new City Hall went up, utilizing the stones from the wall's bastions for the foundation. In 1703 the cage, the pillory, the whipping post, and the stocks were moved up from the Stadt Huys and placed across the street, where the House of Morgan stands today at 23 Wall Street.

The City Hall was the scene of a prosecution in the summer of 1735 that stirred all of the English colonies in America—the trial of John Peter Zenger, a printer who had founded the *New York Weekly Journal* late in 1733. This paper soon became the most popular sheet in the province, for it was filled with entertaining squibs, low satire, lampoons, and ballads, many of them aimed at officials of the royal government. There were also well-written, barbed criticisms of the dismal way affairs were being run in the colony. Zenger was encouraged and supported by the party opposed to Governor Cosby, led by two leading lawyers, James Alexander and William Smith. Cosby became increasingly indignant. "Sometimes heavy, half-witted men get a knack of rhyming," he fumed, "but it is time to break them of it when they grow abusive, insolent and mischievous with it." He ordered copies of the offending papers to be burned by the public whipper, or hangman, near the pillory. He also ordered the Mayor and the other city magistrates to witness the burning.

The city fathers protested, ignored the Governor's order, and even forbade their hangman to carry out the burning, which was done later by a Negro slave of the sheriff. Zenger was then arrested and, because he could not meet the high bail that was set, jailed in a cell on the first floor of City Hall. In his issue of November 25, 1734, the editor apologized for missing publication of the previous week's *Journal*, "as the governor had put him in jail," but added "that he now has the liberty of speaking through a hole in the door to his assistants, and shall supply his customers as heretofore."

Since a grand jury refused to indict Zenger, the

Attorney-General filed an information "for false, scandalous, malicious, and seditious libels." Smith and Alexander began their defense of the printer by attacking the legality of the judges' commissions. The judges ruled this contempt of court and struck the two lawyers off the roll of attorneys who could practice before them. As a result, Andrew Hamilton, the eloquent Philadelphia lawyer, was engaged for the defense and the trial brought all other business in New York to a halt. Hamilton's defense was that truth was no libel and he had little difficulty convincing the jury that what Zenger had published was the truth. Following lengthy arguments, during which the truths and/or the libels were given much wider circulation, the jury acquitted Zenger. The principle of freedom of the press was established and the first seeds of defiance against the divine right of the English kings were planted in the American colonies.

Government by remote control was a source of great dissatisfaction on both sides of the Atlantic. The crown looked upon the colonies as a potentially rich source of revenue, a cow requiring attention only at milking time. The colonies wanted to keep every drop of their own milk and, wherever possible, did so. The people were stubborn and growing in number. From 1735 until the outbreak of war forty years later, the citizens increased their opposition and the representatives of the King, once overbearing, arrogant autocrats, were shorn of their power and reduced to the level of figureheads.

New York continued to expand northward without plan or design. The path the girls took on their way to launder the family wash became Maiden Lane and houses were built on either side. The tanning pits, originally along the Broad Street canal, which was filled in after the arrival of the English, were relocated in the region called The Swamp, where the leather industry still flourishes. Little attention was paid to the west side of the island, since ice formed in the Hudson in winter and the East River shore provided all the year-round anchorage needed.

As New York grew, Wall Street became the center of fashion and quality, the Park Avenue of the time.

Andrew Hamilton, celebrated Philadelphia lawyer, pleaded the case of John Peter Zenger, accused of libel, before judges and jury in the City Hall courtroom, 1735.

The First Trinity Church was consecrated in 1698 and enlarged in 1737. Standing at the head of Wall Street on Broadway, it held title to lands stretching to Christopher Street in Greenwich Village.

The foot of Wall Street had been the site of a gun emplacement, then a slaughterhouse, a ferry house (shown above), and a slave market.

With Trinity Church, built in 1697, at its head, the First Presbyterian Church in the first block, and City Hall at Broad Street, the thoroughfare became the favored address for aristocrats, professional men, and merchants who erected mansions and elegant residences, some towering as high as three stories. Often these houses were built with a Dutch *stoep*, leading to a high first floor, a carryover from the houses of Holland, where the sea frequently flooded the streets.

At the river end of Wall Street, where there had been a blockhouse in Dutch days, the Slave Market stood until 1762. Here, Negroes were not only bought and sold, but rented out. Many citizens who purchased slaves as an investment sent their chattels to Wall Street each morning to hire themselves out for the day and return at nightfall with their day's rental in hand. Also in the middle of the street, at the foot of Broad, was the Merchants Exchange where traders and storekeepers met to discuss business, credit risks, concerted action against the crown, and attend the auctions of ship cargoes. Another meeting place was the Merchants Coffee House on the southeast corner of Wall and Water which provided refreshment as well as shelter for the businessmen of the day.

Life in early New York was almost always turbulent. There were fearful epidemics which took a toll of hundreds; religious controversies, which, in spite of the city's reputation for tolerance, kept various minorities in a state of constant misery; and a spate of incendiary fires in 1741, rumored to have been set by slaves as a signal to revolt. At the time a fifth of Manhattan's ten thousand souls were slaves, and the town was soon caught up in panic and hysteria, pell-mell flight from the city, hasty hangings, and the rule of lynch law, all with no actual evidence of any organized plot. Nothing so wild and chaotic was to grip the city again until 120 years later during the Draft Riots of the Civil War.

Trouble with the Indians to the west and the French to the north brought soldiers to New York, as well as more persistent attempts by His Majesty's governors and His Majesty's ministers in London to wring new taxes from the reluctant, defiant New Yorkers. Then, in 1761, old George II died and his grandson, George III, ascended the throne. Now the crown was under new management, a management that set to work briskly, and with great firmness, to make its American branch show a profit.

3

The First Revolution

THE AMERICAN REVOLUTION against the British, like the Southern revolution against the North in 1861 and the New Deal revolution against Wall Street in the 1930's, was a revolt originally caused by economic factors. The threat of annoying taxes and trade restrictions fired the blood of our forefathers. Although New York was the third city of the colonies, neither Philadelphia nor Boston was more vigorous in opposing England. During the century of English rule in New York, the mother country had imposed a long list of onerous restrictions on the colonies for the benefit of the King's treasury and for the merchants, shipowners, and manufacturers of the homeland.

Each time the King's purse became light, or business was poor, or a new ministry rose to power, or the government had spent millions of pounds on the periodic wars of the eighteenth century, new regulations were adopted or vigorous attempts were made to enforce the laws already on the books. Every such move was met with savage opposition by the colonists and their leaders in the Provincial Assemblies. New York City, with its large Dutch population, good businessmen but poor monarchists, was especially vociferous in its protests.

After the coronation of George III, the government revived the idea of raising money by taxing legal documents. The plan, first advanced sixty years before, was passed into law as the Stamp Act in 1765. Witlessly, the sponsors added a stamp tax on newspapers. Even today, the meekest of newspapers will fight furiously against laws which threaten its circulation. This was certainly the case two hundred years ago when the struggling weeklies of the period stood out as leaders in the battle against the hated stamps. Since Wall Street was even then the center of economic agitation, the call went out to the other colonies from a meeting of businessmen at the Merchants Coffee House for a Stamp Act Congress, which was held in the City Hall, with nine of the provinces participating, during the month of October, 1765. While this first American Congress was in session, the hated stamps arrived from London. This was the signal for a day and evening of uninhibited rioting, which ended only after the stamps had been surrendered to the city authorities by the royal Lieutenant-Governor.

In February, 1766, Benjamin Franklin, agent for several of the provinces, appeared before the House of Commons, "sitting as a Committee Of The Whole" on a bill to repeal the Stamp Act. Like Thomas Paine, whom he sent to America with letters of introduction, Franklin was a brilliant propagandist. He also made a superb witness before the House of Commons, which he used as a sounding board to reach all England.

Since many members were sympathetic to the colonists, he probably benefited from a number of leading questions. Here is part of his examination:

Q. *What is your name and place of abode?*

A. *Franklin of Philadelphia.*

Q. *What was the temper of America towards Great-Britain before the year 1763?*

A. *The best in the world. They submitted willingly to the government of the crown . . . the people . . . cost you nothing in forts, citadels, garrisons or armies, to keep them in subjection. They are governed by this country at the expence of a little pen, ink and paper. They are led by a thread. They had not only a respect, but an affection for Great-Britain, for its laws, its customs and manners, and even a fondness for its fashions, that greatly increased the commerce.*

Q. *And what is their temper now?*

A. *Oh, very much altered.*

Q. *What do you think is the reason that the people of America increase faster than in England?*

A. *Because they marry younger, and more generally.*

Q. *Why so?*

A. *Because any young couple that are industrious, may easily obtain land of their own, on which they can raise a family.*

Q. *Are not the lower rank of people more at their ease in America than in England?*

A. *They may be so, if they are sober and diligent, as they are better paid for their labour.*

Q. *What is your opinion of a future tax, imposed on the same principle with that of the Stamp-Act; how would the Americans receive it?*

A. *Just as they do this. They would not pay it.*

Q. *What will be the opinion of the Americans on these resolutions [that Parliament has a right to tax the people of America]?*

A. *They will think them unconstitutional and unjust.*

Q. *But who is to be the judge of that, Britain or the colony?*

A. *Those that feel can best judge.*

Q. *Will it not take a long time to establish that manufacture [of cloth] among them; and must they not in the meanwhile suffer greatly?*

A. *I think not. They have made a surprising progress already. And I am of the opinion, that before their old clothes are worn out, they will have new ones of their own making.*

Q. *Can they possibly find wool enough in North-America?*

A. *They have taken steps to increase the wool. They entered into general combinations to eat no more lamb, and very few lambs were killed last year. This course persisted in, will soon make a prodigious difference in the quantity of wool. And the establishing of great manufactories... is not necessary... the people will spin, and work for themselves, in their own houses.*

One of the most brilliant triumphs in the life of Benjamin Franklin was his examination in the House of Commons as chief American witness for the repeal of the Stamp Tax. His testimony, reported in American papers, "made the name of Franklin dear to every patriotic heart."

New Yorkers expressed their sentiments regarding the Stamp Act by rioting, hanging and burning an effigy of the royal Lieutenant-Governor, Cadwallader Colden, as well as his carriages, right under the Fort's guns. Companion effigy to Colden's is that of the Devil.

Q. Can nothing less than a military force carry the Stamp-Act into execution?

A. *I do not see how a military force can be applied to that purpose. . . . Suppose a military force is sent into America; they will find nobody in arms; what are they then to do? They cannot force a man to take stamps who chooses to do without them. They will not find a rebellion; they may indeed make one.*

Q. If the act is not repealed, what do you think will be the consequences?

A. *A total loss of the respect and affection the people of America bear to this country, and of all the commerce that depends on that respect and affection.*

Q. How can the commerce be affected?

A. *You will find that if the act is not repealed, they will take very little of your manufactures in a short time.*

Q. Supposing the Stamp-Act continued, and enforced, do you imagine the ill-humor will induce the Americans to give as much for worse manufactures of their own, and use them, preferably to better of ours?

A. *Yes, I think so. People will pay as freely to gratify one passion as another, their resentment as their pride.*

Q. Would they [farmers] suffer the produce of their lands to rot?

A. *No; but they would not raise as much. They would manufacture more, and plough less.*

Q. But in places where they [the stamps] could be protected, would not the people use them rather than remain . . . unable to obtain any right or recover, by law, any debt?

A. *It is hard to say. . . . I can only judge . . . by what I feel within myself. I have a great many debts due me in America, and I would rather they should remain unrecoverable by any law, than submit to the Stamp-Act.*

Q. Is there a power on earth that can force them [the Americans] to erase [their resolutions against being taxed without their consent]?

A. *No power, how great soever, can force men to change their opinions.*

Q. What used to be the pride of the Americans?

A. *To indulge in the fashions and manufactures of Great-Britain.*

Q. What is now their pride?

A. *To wear their old clothes over again, till they can make new ones.*

Franklin's testimony proved most effective, for on March 18, 1766, the Stamp Act was repealed. Two

From the Merchants Coffee House, at southeast corner of Wall and Water streets, the New York Committee of Correspondence dispatched a historic letter which resulted in the convention of the first Congress of "United Colonies of North America" which met in Philadelphia.

months later the news reached New York and a "sudden Joy was immediately diffused thro' all Ranks of People in the whole city." To celebrate, the first Liberty Pole was erected in The Fields, now City Hall Park. The British soldiers quartered nearby cut it down on the night of August 10 or 11. A new pole was raised the next day, amid the cracking of skulls and bayoneting of flanks—the first blood shed for liberty in the colonies. The second Liberty Pole was destroyed by British sympathizers six weeks later. Battles over succeeding flagpoles of freedom continued as long as the redcoats were quartered in New York before the Revolution. The most serious fight occurred at Golden Hill, near William and John streets, on January 19, 1770. A sailor was killed and four sons of Liberty were wounded. Although this skirmish took place six weeks before the Boston Massacre, it was never accorded the same degree of historical attention. New Yorkers claimed that they had always led the opposition to England. Indeed, the first Non-Importation Agreement was signed by the merchants of Manhattan in 1765 and the other colonial ports followed.

On May 23, 1774, from that hotbed of defiance, the Merchants Coffee House, the New York Committee of Correspondence sent out a letter rallying the colonies to join together. This urgent call to arms led to the convention of the first Congress of United Colonies of North America, which was held in Philadelphia on September 5.

Defiance became more open among the patriots of New York during the next two years and the British authorities did little to combat it. The arms stored at City Hall were seized by the Sons of Liberty, the organization which took its name from Isaac Barré's description of the rebels in a speech delivered in the House of Commons. Another strong defender of the colonial position in Parliament was John Wilkes. Together the two Englishmen were honored for their sympathetic stand in this time of trial by having a city in Pennsylvania named after them.

Only about a third of the people in the colonies were in favor of the rebel cause. Another third were staunch loyalists. The remainder were indifferent to the conflict. Yet in the agonizing struggle that followed, the green, outnumbered, ill-provisioned, badly fed, and seldom-paid revolutionists defeated some of the finest British and Hessian troops, splendidly equipped and armed, along with the loyalist regiments and their Indian allies. The greatest asset the rebels possessed was a leader who was forced to learn his military tactics as he went along, a Commander-in-Chief who would let lesser men overrule him, Congress nag him, and jealous officers seek his job behind his back.

George Washington wanted the responsibility of

View of New York from the northwest, before 1773. On bluff at left is Trinity Church; other spires, to right, are Lutheran, Middle Dutch, Wall Street Presbyterian, French (next is the City Hall cupola and flag), and South Dutch churches.

Rallying points for rebels were Liberty Poles erected on commons of colonial towns. The New York pole was repeatedly cut down by British soldiers and loyalists, leading to the Battle of Golden Hill, where the first blood of the Revolution was shed.

When news reached New York that the Declaration of Independence had been signed, the document was read to Washington's troops and from the balcony of City Hall. Jubilant citizens ripped the King's coat of arms from the courtroom and burned the symbol of royal rule "amid thrilling cheers."

On the evening of July 9, 1776, soldiers and civilians gathered at Bowling Green and pulled down the statue of King George III. The scene is seldom depicted authentically, and most outrageous fake is this French view of a Parisian New York, horseless statue, turbaned "Indian" rioters—and no Bowling Green.

leading America's troops because he felt, without false modesty, that he was the best man for the command. He appeared at the sessions of Congress, where he represented Virginia, in his state militia uniform and quietly let it be known that Colonel Washington was available. After he was selected, he came through New York on his way to embattled Boston on June 25, 1775—the same day the royal Governor, Sir William Tryon, arrived from England.

Washington's leadership at Boston was successful. After the British sailed away, Franklin wrote: "Britain, at the expense of three million [pounds] has killed one hundred and fifty Yankees in this campaign, which is twenty thousand pounds a head . . . and at Bunker Hill she gained a mile of ground, half of which she lost again. . . . During the same time six thousand children have been born in America. From these data . . . [you] will easily calculate the time and expense necessary to kill us all, and conquer our whole territory."

Despite this optimistic estimate, Washington realized that the next British move—the attempt to capture New York—could end differently. Although he was filled with doubts that the city could be defended, he hastened there, arriving on April 13, 1776. General Charles Lee had done his best to fortify the exposed town, but Washington knew, from the experiences of Peter Stuyvesant and the British, who had briefly lost New York to the Dutch admirals, Evertzen and Binckes, in 1763, that only a superior fleet could protect the city. But not to defend New York at the start of the Revolution was unthinkable and the city was soon a bustling camp.

The final break with England came on July 9, when copies of the Declaration of Independence arrived from Philadelphia and were read to the citizens in front of City Hall and to Washington's Army at The Fields. This was the signal for the burning of the King's coat of arms, ripped from the wall of the courtroom and set afire in the street, the ringing of church bells, and a general celebration in which defiance of Britain was the theme. In the evening the people assembled at the Bowling Green, where six years before an equestrian statue of George III had been erected in gratitude for the repeal of the Stamp Act. Now the gilt and lead statue was pulled down. Although British sympathizers were able to rescue the head, the rest of George and his horse, about four thousand pounds of lead, was sent off to a Connecticut bullet-maker. It was estimated that 42,088 bullets melted down from His Majesty's statue were shot back at His Majesty's troops.

Two weeks before, there was, according to one horrified account, "a most hellish plott . . . a most Infernal plott . . . a plott most damnable" to assassinate Washington. Financed and instigated by Tryon, the Tory Governor, and David Matthews, the Tory Mayor, the plot had as its key figure Thomas Hickey, an Irish soldier who had deserted several years before from the British Army. When the Revolution broke out, he joined the Continentals. Because of his previous military experience and his manly bearing, he was appointed a member of Washington's Life Guards, the elite troop attached to the General's headquarters. The exact method by which Washington was to be slain is not known, but the version most frequently accepted is that poison was to be mixed with his green peas at dinner. If this failed, he was to be stabbed, or captured and turned over to the British to be hanged.

Hickey is said to have relied on his friendship with Peggy Fraunces, daughter of the West Indian who operated the inn that bore his name, to assist him in his plan. Peggy was Washington's housekeeper and her warning resulted in the capture of Hickey and a half dozen barroom characters who were to aid him in burning the city, hatching a mutiny among the troops, providing arms to the Tories in the city, and signaling the British fleet to launch a naval attack on Manhattan from both rivers—all of which was to take place once Washington was disposed of. Too many people were involved and too many steps were to be taken in the hope that the Revolution might be crushed in one night. As Rupert Hughes wrote in his biography of George Washington: "Simplicity is the very essence of an artistic assassination." And the Hickey Plot collapsed through sheer mass of details. The Irishman was the only one known to be hanged, the execution taking place—after a court-martial and a civilian investigation by John Jay, Gouverneur Morris, and Philip Livingston—before a crowd of twenty thousand in a field near the Bowery on June 23, 1776.

Sir William Howe and his forces were already anchored off Sandy Hook. On the day Hickey was hanged, the British General was joined by his brother, Admiral Sir Richard "Dirty Dick" Howe, with the entire British fleet and additional troops from Hali-

Following the American defeat at the Battle of Long Island on August 27, 1776, Washington, by an elaborate deception that completely fooled the British, executed a classic retreat across the East River, evacuating nine thousand troops without losing a man or gun.

fax. This was an expedition larger than the Spanish Armada and surely more than enough to crush the local amateurs at war. But the behavior of Sir William, and, for that matter, his successors, contributed as much as any other factor toward ultimate American success. Time after time the British failed to follow up victories in battle when the patriots were still reeling. Howe's lack of decisive action in pushing the war was attributed both to laziness and a reluctance to wage war on fellow Englishmen. The British leader was a stickler for the formal conduct of war and allowed the Americans to slip out of his grasp while he fought according to the "gentlemanly" rules of the time. They, however, were fighting for their very lives—and a new country.

For the British there was a "war season," which ended before the cold weather set in. One did not fight in winter. Washington was to take advantage of this during the dark days toward the end of 1776. His forces not only sneaked up on Trenton in the snow, but were unsporting enough to attack the day after Christmas, when the Hessian mercenaries were presumably suffering from monumental hangovers.

That victory at Trenton, in which some nine hundred prisoners were captured, helped to compensate for the poor showing the American Army had made in New York three months before. The British had landed on Staten Island, then moved their troops to Brooklyn and Long Island. Washington sent his forces across the East River to meet them. The green American troops were without discipline or organization. They scrounged for food, looted hen roosts, and burned barns belonging to friends and foes alike. Military activity was confined to unauthorized skirmishes with the enemy. In the belief that the Americans numbered at least forty thousand, Howe took his time to build up his forces. Had he known that there were only seven thousand Americans facing him on August 26, he might have exercised less caution with greater success, since he outnumbered the rebels three to one. Washington added to his troops during the night, but the next morning a force of redcoats marched to the Jamaica Pass, where there was a vast gap in the American line, swung around behind it, and soon the colonials were under fire from front and rear. When the bloody day was over, the British had pushed the rebels into a small area between the Gowanus Canal and the Brooklyn Navy Yard. However, the Americans had fought bravely. "Had they been military experts," wrote Martha J. Lamb in her *History of the City of New York*, "they would doubtless have surrendered without contesting the ground inch by inch."

The British generals under Howe wanted to renew the attack at once, but he said: "Enough has been done for one day." His troops dined and spread their tents less than a mile from the trapped Americans, who dug trenches and huddled in the storm of pelting rain which followed their defeat. Behind them was a swift river, a half-mile broad. Howe had a great fleet at his command which, once the wind changed, could cut off all communication between Washington's beleaguered forces and Manhattan. He could afford to be deliberate, certain that the next blow he struck would mark the death-knell of the American Army and the collapse of American resistance.

It continued to rain the next day and Howe did not stir. Washington conferred with his staff and decided that a retreat in the night was their only chance for salvation. To divert the British, and keep his own troops from learning his plan, Washington had his men line up in parade formation, informing them that they were about to be relieved by fresh battalions from New Jersey. Meanwhile, with the greatest secrecy, small craft of every description were recruited on the Manhattan side and placed under

After the British successfully landed on Manhattan, driving the raw American militia before them, they stopped near what is now Grand Central, while General Howe and his staff were entertained at Murray Hill by Mrs. Robert Murray. Meanwhile, American troops in lower Manhattan slipped past them along the West Side.

Desperate for information about enemy plans, Washington sent Captain Nathan Hale, disguised as a schoolteacher, through the British lines, via Long Island, to New York. Here Hale wandered freely among British troops (as shown in this old print), gathering military information, which he set down in notes written in Latin and secreted beneath the innersoles of his shoes.

the command of Colonel John Glover and his regiment of pea-jacketed Marblehead fishermen. The rain fell all day. As soon as it was dark the regiments piled into the craft brought across the river to evacuate them and glided silently toward what became known as Fulton Ferry on the Manhattan shore.

The retreat from Long Island was brought off with almost miraculous success. An army of nine thousand men, with all its gear, camped within earshot of the enemy, vanished across the water without losing even a member of the rear guard.

The miracle of the retreat was quickly forgotten in the gravity of the situation on Manhattan. Many of the soldiers, enrolled for short terms, now returned to their farms to harvest the crops. The rest were battle-weary and dispirited. If Howe had sent his men up the Hudson, landed, and moved southward, he would surely have pushed the rebel force into New York Bay. But with the British fleet anchored just off Governor's Island, he fortified every point on Long Island facing the eastern shore with earthworks and cannon. Then a line of English men-of-war ascended the East River and anchored off Turtle Bay, where the United Nations building now stands.

"Whereas a Bombardment and Attack upon the City of New-York, by our cruel, and inveterate Enemy, may be hourly expected," Washington urged the women and children, the ailing, aged, and infirm, to leave the city. The more prudent gathered their belongings and departed, while Washington waited for Howe's next move. It came on the morning of September 15. First there was the most terrifying bombardment ever loosed in the New World. From the Long Island shore and the ships in the East River a deadly barrage of shot fell upon the nervous Connecticut militia entrenched along the shore. Then came barge after barge filled with spick-and-span troops. "It looked like a clover field in full bloom," said an observer. The redcoats landed under scattered fire and formed ranks for a bayonet charge. The rebels hastily scrambled from their trenches and fled west in terror. At what is now Third Avenue near Forty-second Street they were met by General Washington, General S. H. Parsons, and a few officers who vainly tried to halt the pell-mell retreat.

According to legend, the American Army was

After he was captured and sentenced to be hanged, Hale, flanked by a guard of redcoats, was marched to his execution wearing a coarse white tunic and cap trimmed in black. A rough pine coffin was carried beside him. At the rear of the procession are William Cunningham, the notoriously cruel British Provost-Marshal, and Richmond, the hangman, bearing a ladder and rope.

saved that day by Mrs. Mary Murray, who detained Howe and his staff at her home on nearby Murray Hill by serving them an elaborate luncheon. True, the British slowed down, or halted, close to the streets where General Israel Putnam and his troops were making their escape from lower Manhattan, in some cases sneaking across lots and through back alleys, guided by a young local officer, Major Aaron Burr, with Captain Alexander Hamilton and his artillery as rear guard. But Mrs. Murray or not, it was the custom of the British Army to halt on the offensive, survey the situation, eat, and ponder the next move. Washington and his troops headed north and were able to retreat in fairly good order to the area in the vicinity of the present campus of Columbia University. That night he made his headquarters in the Jumel Mansion.

From here (or possibly from the Apthorp Mansion where he had spent the preceding night) he dispatched a handsome young Connecticut captain, Nathan Hale, on a mission to penetrate the British lines and bring back desperately needed information on Howe's intentions. In the disguise of his former occupation, a schoolteacher, Hale walked fifty miles to Norwalk, sailed across the Sound to Huntington, Long Island, and finally reached New York, where he made a thorough survey of the entire British military force in the city. With sketches and other valuable information concealed under the innersoles of his shoes, he returned to the spot where he had landed for a rendezvous with the sloop that had brought him. Instead, he was surprised by a barge filled with British marines who captured him, found the drawings and the information (written in Latin), and sent him to Howe's headquarters at Mount Pleasant, the Beekman Mansion at Fifty-first Street and First Avenue.

Hale was brought to British headquarters the morning after the great fire which left nearly one-third of New York in ashes. Almost five hundred houses were burned and the conflagration was thought by the British to be the work of rebel agents. Hale's arrival could not have been more ill-timed, and, since he at once confessed his identity and mission to Howe, he was ordered to be executed as a spy at daybreak the next morning. Where he was imprisoned and where

Shaded area of map depicts the havoc wrought by the great fire of September 21, 1776, which destroyed one-third of the city. Howe believed that rebel spies had deliberately set the blaze. The ruins were still smoldering that evening when he sentenced Hale to be hanged.

The fire, which broke out in a tavern on Whitehall Street, crept up Broad, then leaped across Broadway and destroyed everything west to St. Paul's and King's (now Columbia) College. This view of the ruins of Trinity Church was sketched by a British officer during the Revolution.

he was executed are much-disputed locations, but he was the prisoner of the detested William Cunningham, Provost-Marshal of the British Army, who tore the letters Hale wrote to his family into shreds "so that the rebels should never know they had a man who could die with such firmness." Wearing a coarse white jacket trimmed in black, with a cap also trimmed in black on his head, Hale was marched to the tree that was to be his scaffold, followed by Cunningham and other officers as formal witnesses and Richmond, the Provost's mulatto hangman. In the early morning light of September 22, he mounted the ladder, felt the hangman's knot touch the large hair mole on his neck, and must have recalled that in his youth the other boys had said this was a sign he would one day be hanged.

Then he made his dying speech: "I only regret that I have but one life to lose for my country."

"Swing the rebel off!" Cunningham shouted, and Richmond twisted the ladder, dropping Hale about five feet and leaving him to choke to death.

One of the officers present at the Beekman Mansion when Nathan Hale was brought before Howe was Major John André, who was destined to suffer Hale's fate. The following year André moved with British headquarters to Philadelphia, where he met Margaret Shippen who later married General Benedict Arnold. When the disgruntled Arnold offered his services to the British, it was Major André, back in New York with the new commander, Sir Henry Clinton, who conducted the negotiations. A great opportunity opened up when Arnold, through the influence of Washington, was given the command of the impregnable fort at West Point, which was the key to control of the Hudson and the entire region surrounding it. Arnold was now ready to betray his country, in return for ten thousand pounds sterling and a brigadier-generalship in the British Army. From Clinton's headquarters in the Kennedy House at Number 1 Broadway, André, now Adjutant-General of the English forces in America, departed aboard the sloop-of-war *Vulture* for a rendezvous with Arnold near West Point.

The two men met on the west bank of the Hudson at midnight, September 21, 1780. They talked until daybreak, then went to the house of Joshua Smith, who thought they were negotiating under a flag of truce. Here, near Haverstraw, Arnold furnished every proof of his willingness to commit treason. He handed André maps and lists, in his own hand, showing where he would assign the West Point garrison so that it would be least effective, plans of the fortifications, location of cannon and stores, and every detail needed for a successful assault on the fort. When they were ready to depart, Smith refused to row André to the *Vulture*, because it had moved its anchorage downstream to avoid the fire of American sharpshooters on the river banks. Arnold persuaded the Major, against André's better judgment, to change his British uniform for civilian clothing, hide the papers in his boots, and return to New York by horse. He provided the Englishman with a pass made out to "John Anderson." Smith accompanied André, and on the road to White Plains they were stopped and searched, but Arnold's pass saw them through.

The next morning they continued to Pine's Bridge, across the Croton, where they parted. Smith returned to Arnold's residence and reported. André was near Tarrytown when he was stopped by three American militiamen. One of them, John Paulding, had escaped from the New York Sugar House prison three days before, wearing the uniform of a Hessian Jäger. Seeing this, André made a fatal mistake. He identified himself. So did the American irregulars. Then André tried to use the "John Anderson" pass, but the suspicious rebels insisted upon searching him. When they found the Arnold documents, they brought him to the nearest military post. Lieutenant-Colonel Jameson, who was in charge, could not imagine that Arnold was disloyal, and proceeded to send the prisoner straight to Arnold! "He had a passport signed in your name," he wrote, "and a parcel of papers, taken from under his stockings, which I think of a very dangerous tendency." The papers, he informed Arnold, were being forwarded to General Washington, who was then returning from a conference with Rochambeau and his generals at Hartford. When Major Benjamin Tallmadge, a classmate of Nathan Hale's at Yale and the next in command, returned to the post, he was informed of André's capture. He was immediately suspicious of Arnold and persuaded Jameson to send after the prisoner and his guards. André was overtaken and returned to the post, but Jameson insisted that the letter to Arnold be sent on.

Arnold and his family occupied the Robinson House across the Hudson from West Point. The morning after André's capture, he and his aides-de-

Benedict Arnold, once an apothecary in Norwich, Connecticut, was an intrepid leader during early part of the war, but was in constant financial trouble. "He plunged into the Revolution as he would have dashed into a jungle for game, with an eye for the rewards," wrote one historian.

camp were waiting for Washington and his staff to arrive and have breakfast with them. Several of the officers turned up and told him that Washington had gone down to the shore to examine the redoubts there. When they sat down to eat, Arnold was interrupted by the letter from Jameson informing him that André was a prisoner. Arnold, concealing his agitation, excused himself, saying that his presence was required at once across the river but that he would return soon. He went up to Mrs. Arnold's room and told her what had happened. Then he rode to the dock, climbed into his barge, and directed the six oarsmen to row swiftly across. When they reached midstream, he altered their course, stating that he must board the *Vulture* under a flag of truce. Once aboard, he introduced himself to the captain, urged him to get under way immediately, and had the crew of his barge made prisoners of war.

Washington reached the Robinson House a few minutes after Arnold's hasty departure. Informed that his host had gone to West Point, the Commander-in-Chief had a hurried breakfast and, instead of waiting, went across to meet Arnold. Alexander Hamilton, one of Washington's aides, remained

Head Quarters Robinsons
House Sepr. 22d. 1780

Permit Mr. John Anderson to pass the
Guards to the White Plains, or below
if He Chuses. He being on Public
Business by my Direction

B. Arnold M Genl

After the meeting between Arnold and Major John André, rebel shore fire drove the VULTURE *downstream, making it impossible for André to return to New York by ship. General Arnold persuaded him to change into civilian clothes and proceed on horseback, providing him with this pass, made out to "Mr. John Anderson."*

On October 1, 1780, one day before he was executed, André made this pen-and-ink sketch of himself. The original is now in the possession of Yale University.

A contemporary engraving entitled: "The Unfortunate DEATH *of* MAJOR ANDRE *(Adjutant-General to the English Army) . . . who was found within the American Lines in the character of a Spy."*

behind, but the others, including Lafayette, accompanied the General. Crossing the river, he was surprised that there was no salute from the fort, and when they reached the west shore, Colonel John Lamb, in command, was confused to see the party. General Arnold, he told them, had not been there in two days. Washington was puzzled, but remained several hours, inspecting the fortifications. At noon he returned to the eastern shore and was met by Hamilton, who was in a grave and agitated state. The documents from Colonel Jameson had caught up with Washington's party at last.

The evidence shocked Washington, who had always considered his companion-in-arms a loyal friend. Although Arnold's betrayal made him wonder for days whether he could trust any officer on his staff, he wasted no time in ordering the defenses of West Point reinforced and alerting the entire Army north of New York. Then André was interrogated at West Point. Two days later he was taken to Tappan, where he was tried, convicted as a spy, and sentenced to be hanged. The British command tried strenuously to save his life. Washington would have exchanged him, if he were given Arnold in return. This Clinton refused to do and André went to the gallows on October 2. News of the Arnold-André affair made the war in America even more unpopular in England than it had been, for there were possibly more pro-American Britons at the time than there were rebels in the colonies.

A year later, after the defeat of Cornwallis at Yorktown on October 19, 1781, most of the people in England were eager to bring the war to an end, with the exception of the stubborn George III. Not until September 3, 1783, did the various peace commissioners appointed by Great Britain agree upon terms for a treaty that would end hostilities. On that date David Hartley signed for England, while John Adams, Benjamin Franklin, and John Jay affixed their signatures for the now-recognized United States of America.

It was almost three months before word of final victory reached America and suitable celebration ceremonies could be arranged. The British troops were happy to leave New York. However, the native loyalists who accompanied them, either because they feared reprisals from their neighbors or were determined to live somewhere under the benevolent despotism of a king, were hardly elated, since they were compelled to leave their property behind.

The end of the war and the beginning of the Republic were marked by the ceremonies of November 25, 1783, when the redcoats left and the Americans entered New York City. Known as Evacuation Day, it was celebrated as a holiday for almost a century, but thereafter suffered from neglect, possibly because it conflicted with the more general celebration of Thanksgiving Day. On the day the British Army quit the city and sailed out of the country, fifty thousand people were present to witness the departure, including many deserters from the British and Hessian ranks. Almost simultaneously, Washington, at the head of his battered but victorious troops, entered the city, marching down the Bowery.

Benjamin West never finished his painting of the American ministers who signed the peace treaty with Great Britain in Paris on September 3, 1783. They are (LEFT TO RIGHT) *John Jay, John Adams, and Benjamin Franklin. Standing behind Franklin is his grandson, Temple Franklin, and seated at the right is Henry Laurens.*

Headed by Washington and Governor Clinton, the American troops returned to battered, war-torn New York on November 25, 1783. For almost one hundred years the event was celebrated here as Evacuation Day.

The scene was one of joyous emotion as General Washington and Governor George Clinton,. "preceded by a Party of Horse and followed by the Temporary Government Officials of the Southern Parts of the State and more Gentlemen both on Horseback and on Foot, passed down Pearl Street and up the Broadway, reviewing the line of Troops and a-lighting at Cape's Tavern." The committee appointed to conduct the ceremony announced they "hope to see their Fellow-Citizens conduct themselves with Decency and Decorum on this joyful Occasion."

As a final act of derision and defiance, the British had nailed their flag to the top of the mast at the Fort, then removed the cleats used for climbing, and greased the pole, confident that the Stars and Stripes would not be raised until they were out of sight. Several unsuccessful attempts were made to climb the pole, until bystanders ran to Goelet's hardware store in Hanover Square and brought back tools and

The last act of British defiance was to nail the Union Jack to the staff in the Fort, remove cleats, and grease the pole. John Van Arsdale proved to be the hero of the day by raising the American emblem before the British sailed out of sight.

nails so that new cleats could be made and driven into the pole. Then young John Van Arsdale slowly made his way to the top and tore loose the British standard. The American flag was raised and a thirteen-gun salute was fired. For many years afterward, a member of the Van Arsdale family repeated the traditional climb up the flagpole at every Evacuation Day celebration.

During the war Wall Street had been the scene of much military activity. The British turned the City Hall into a guardhouse, the Presbyterian Church in the block to the west was used as a hospital, and the fine houses abandoned by their American owners were confiscated and used as quarters for such Hessian generals as Knyphausen and Riedesel; Robertson, the military Governor; and even Benedict Arnold, who lived in the Verplanck Mansion, next to City Hall, for a short time after he turned traitor.

However, Arnold moved to Number 3 Broadway, and from there Washington tried to have him kidnapped and returned to American custody. The Commander-in-Chief was not seeking vengeance, but was more concerned with learning if other officers were about to follow Arnold's example. For this purpose, Major Henry Lee of Virginia detached Sergeant-Major John Champe, who dashed out of camp and "deserted" to the cause which Arnold had just joined. Once in New York he enlisted in the "American Legion" which Arnold was recruiting and then made arrangements with rebel sympathizers to abduct Arnold from the garden of his house, where he walked nightly. They planned to overcome and gag the traitor, carry him down the adjoining alley and onto a boat, which would take them to Hoboken. If challenged, they intended to explain that they were carrying a drunken soldier to the guardhouse. On the day preceding the night of the kidnapping, with everything in readiness, Arnold and his legion moved. Poor Champe, instead of crossing the Hudson that night with his prize prisoner, found himself on board a British transport bound for Virginia, his home state, to fight his friends under the command of the traitor. Eventually he deserted and returned to his old regiment, but was absolved and discharged from service, because if the British captured him, he would most certainly have been hanged.

On the evening of the first Evacuation Day, Washington was guest of honor at a great dinner at Fraunces' Tavern given by Governor Clinton. Foremost among the thirteen toasts which were proposed were "May the Remembrance of THIS DAY be a Lesson to Princes" and "May America be an asylum to the Persecuted of the Earth." It was a season of relaxing and rejoicing. Another dinner, for three hundred, was held at Cape's on November 28 and 120 gathered on December 2 to honor the French Ambassador at a dinner, which was followed by a dazzling fireworks display. On Thursday, December 4, Washington took leave of his officers in the Long Room at Fraunces'—an occasion filled with the deepest emotion. Benjamin Tallmadge, by then a colonel, wrote in his diary:

At 12 o'clock the officers repaired to Fraunces' Tavern, in Pearl Street, where General Washington

The tattered but triumphant Continentals marched up Wall Street to the cheers of exuberant crowds. This old woodcut of the scene makes the error of showing Trinity Church intact, although it was burned down in 1776 and was not rebuilt until 1790.

Washington bidding farewell to Henry Knox and other officers at Fraunces' Tavern on December 4, 1783. The occasion is especially memorable because brave, strong men embraced, kissed, and wept as they parted.

had appointed to meet them, and to take his final leave of them. We had assembled but a few moments, when His Excellency entered the room. His emotion, too strong to be concealed, seemed to be reciprocated by every officer present. After partaking of a slight refreshment, in almost breathless silence, the General filled his glass with wine, and turning to the officers he said: "With a heart full of love and gratitude, I now take leave of you. I most devoutly wish that your latter days may be as prosperous and happy as your former ones have been glorious and honorable."

After the officers had taken a glass of wine, Gen. Washington said: "I cannot come to each of you, but shall feel obliged if each of you will come and take me by the hand."

General Knox, being nearest to him, turned to the Commander-in-Chief, who, suffused in tears, was incapable of utterance but grasped his hand; then they embraced each other in silence. In the same affectionate manner, every officer in the room marched up to, kissed and parted with his General-in-Chief.

Such a scene of sorrow and weeping I had never before witnessed and I hope may never be called upon to witness again. It was indeed too affecting to be of long continuance—for tears of deep sensibility filled every eye—and the heart seemed so full that it was ready to burst from its wonted abode. Not a word was uttered to break the solemn silence that prevailed, or to interrupt the tenderness of the interesting scene. The simple thought that we were then about to part from the man who had conducted us through a long and bloody war, and under whose conduct the glory and independence of our country has been achieved, and that we should see his face no more in this world, seemed to me utterly insupportable.

But the time of separation had come, and waving his hand to his grieving children around him, he left the room and passing through a corps of light infantry, who were paraded to receive him, he walked silently on to Whitehall, where a barge was in waiting. We all followed in mournful silence to the wharf, where a prodigious crowd had assembled to witness the departure of the man who, under God, had been the great agent in establishing the glory and independence of these United States.

As soon as he was seated, the barge put off into the river, and when out in the stream, our great and beloved General waived his hat, and bid us a silent adieu.

No other country was so fortunate in its choice of Father as the United States. He, in turn, was supported by the most brilliant array of talented men, or able men who rose to a splendid challenge.

This portrait of Washington standing on Broadway, with Bowling Green and a view of the British fleet sailing away in the background, was painted by John Trumbull during 1789–90 by commission of the City of New York. The President put on his old Continental uniform to pose. The portrait now hangs in City Hall.

Robert R. Livingston

Philip Livingston

William Livingston

John Adams

Robert Morris

Gouverneur Morris

Lewis Morris

Henry Knox

Thomas Paine

Nathanael Greene

John P. G. Muhlenberg

William Alexander

Thomas Jefferson

Benjamin Franklin

James Clinton

George Clinton

Israel Putnam

Marquis de Lafayette

Together they made possible the birth of a nation. If there had been a group of comparable men in the French Revolution, or in Cromwell's day, France and England would have fashioned enduring republics out of chaos. Washington and his aides, the Founding Fathers, both military and civilian hammered out through trial and error a way of government which still remains far from perfect, but, like the human body with all its ills and faults, is above all a miracle and the finest political organism the world has yet known.

The Revolution and its victory can well be termed "a happy conjunction of men of talents and genius on a scale perhaps unexampled in the history of the world." There were Samuel Adams the Boston radical and John Adams the cultured, snobbish conservative. (It was John who commented on New York: "With all the opulence and splendor of this city, there is little good breeding to be found. We have been treated with assiduous respect; but I have not seen one real gentleman, one well-bred man, since I came to town. At their entertainments there is no conversation that is agreeable. There is no modesty, no attention to one another. They talk very loud, very fast and altogether.") Also from Boston came Henry Knox, the young, beefy bookseller who taught himself everything about artillery and served so well that he became Secretary of War. Then there were the rich John Hancock and the zealous John Otis as well as the colonial Cellini, Paul Revere. From Washington's home state came Thomas Jefferson, the skillful negotiator in Europe and democratic pioneer, and the pastor, John Peter Gabriel Muhlenberg, who ended a sermon to his congregation at Woodstock late in 1775 with: "There is a time for all things; a time to preach, and a time to pray, but those times have passed away." Then in a voice that echoed like a trumpet-blast through the church: "There is a time to fight and that time has come." And laying aside his clerical gown he stood before his flock in the full regimental dress of a Virginia colonel. Ordering the drums to be beaten for recruits at the church door, he marched forth followed by nearly three hundred of his male audience.

There were such generals as Nathanael Greene, the anchor-smith, and Israel Putnam, the tavern-keeper; Thaddeus Kosciusko, the Polish refugee, and Baron von Steuben, the Prussian drillmaster who whipped an untrained, awkward army into shape;

and, regrettably, there were generals who tried to supplant Washington, such as the ex-redcoat Charles Lee, who was eventually dismissed from service, and Horatio Gates, a great politician but a poor military tactician and commander.

New York contributed Livingstons and Morrises and Clintons. William Livingston, the "razor blade" with thin face and sharp nose and wit, was the great wartime Governor of New Jersey (succeeding William Franklin, the Tory bastard son of Benjamin). His round-faced brothers, Philip, who signed the Declaration of Independence, and Robert, first Secretary of Foreign Affairs and first Chancellor of New York, were the leaders among a dozen Livingstons who served with distinction during the Revolution. Lewis Morris and his half-brother, Gouverneur, were no relations of Robert Morris, the Philadelphia financier whose devotion to the American cause spurred him to perform prodigies of financing under the most difficult emergency conditions. Gouverneur was a brilliant one-legged aristocrat, while his older half-brother signed the Declaration, represented the state in the creation of the Constitution, and had three stalwart sons in the Army. There were two other Morris brothers, Staats Long, who was a general in the British Army for many years but did not participate in the Revolution, and Richard, who became the first Chief Justice of the New York Supreme Court in 1779.

The Clintons, who furnished New York and the nation with outstanding leaders, had no family ties to Sir Henry Clinton, the British general and son of Admiral George Clinton, the early colonial Governor, who became the second Commander-in-Chief of the King's forces during the war. James Clinton, the father of De Witt, was in command of the Highlands of New York and a Continental general, like his brother George, who was also the first Governor of the state.

General William Alexander, Lord Stirling, had a title which was recognized in Edinburgh but not in London. A fervid American patriot, he lost his estates and died before peace was signed. Another aristocrat who served the cause of freedom with dash and distinction was Marie Joseph Paul Yves Roch Gilbert du Motier, Marquis de Lafayette, who came to America at the age of nineteen, fought bravely, endured the winter of Valley Forge, and returned to France to plead the cause of American liberty at the court of Louis XVI. As a result, French military aid helped the revolutionists stem the British tide and Lafayette sailed back to America to serve with honor until the victory at Yorktown.

There were a score of other men of ability among the Founding Fathers: Roger Sherman; Francis Hopkinson; Dr. Benjamin Rush; Robert Treat Paine; Elbridge Gerry; Oliver Wolcott; Patrick Henry; the future presidents, James Madison and James Monroe; General Benjamin Lincoln; John Jay; Albert Gallatin, the Swiss-born Secretary of the Treasury; Rufus King; Judge John Marshall; Silas Deane; Philip Schuyler; Philip Van Cortlandt; Arthur St. Clair; Richard Montgomery; and Henry Laurens.

Then there was Thomas Paine who wrote phrases that were bugle calls to freedom and whose eloquent pamphlets were full of ideas which all men could understand and adopt as their own. In the winter of 1776, at the lowest ebb of American fortunes, he sat beside a campfire, blue-nosed, bleary-eyed, ragged, and sniffling, and, on a drumhead, wrote of the crisis: "These are the times that try men's souls. The summer soldier and the sunshine patriot will, in this crisis, shrink from the service of their country; but he that stands it now, deserves the love and thanks of man and woman. Tyranny, like hell, is not easily conquered; yet we have this consolation with us, that the harder the conflict, the more glorious the triumph."

Next to Washington the greatest man of the day was old Benjamin Franklin, the embodiment of the Yankee spirit. Curious, inventive, ambitious, a rock of integrity, he epitomized the rags-to-riches story. Indeed, he was the "Man of the Eighteenth Century" and his life enriched the colonies, the struggling young Republic, and the world. No one had so many diverse interests and notions and no one was so successful in making his ideas work. Franklin's influence on the vital documents of the new nation was only exceeded by his diplomatic services in Europe before and during the Revolution. And with it all he was as famous for his down-to-earth common sense and his cogent wit. But perhaps the war's neatest witticism was William Livingston's regret that General Clinton had been recalled, "because as fertile as England is in the production of blockheads, I think they cannot send us a greater blunderbuss, unless . . . it should please his Majesty himself to do us the honor of a visit."

4

The Federal Period

WHEN THE smartly clad, well-fed, sharply drilled, but beaten British marched out of New York and the tattered, exhausted Americans marched in, the victors found a town devastated by seven years of enemy occupation, the great fire of 1776, and another in 1778. Decay, neglect, and British depredations had cast a blight upon the city. Once the victory celebration had run its course, Manhattan had the appearance of a ghost town, with empty, gutted buildings, weed-choked lots, and droves of prowling pigs. Almost half of the twenty-five thousand people who had lived in New York when the war began were gone, and those who remained were demoralized victims of malnutrition and harsh enemy treatment. Well-to-do patriots had scattered before the English took over and Tories of means had moved out before the departure of the redcoats, seeking refuge in Canada, the West Indies, and Europe. Shipping was almost nonexistent and what little other business still went on was severely hampered by the lack of money, for the currency which the Continental Congress had printed by the bale was now altogether worthless.

The states were far from united, each legislature clinging to every conceivable right, leaving the central government in the position of a large debating society with hardly any power or authority. In fact, the New York Legislature repealed an act which granted the revenues of its port to the United States and established a custom house and duty system of its own.

"An Act for the speedy sale of the confiscated and forfeited estates" of royalist adherents redistributed a great deal of New York real estate. The property of James De Lancey, for instance, with over a mile of East River frontage, was split into lots and sold for $234,198.75. The De Lancey family was the leading loyalist clan, but, as Martha Lamb wrote: "Their attachment to the crown was peculiar from the fact that the race was a mixture of Dutch and French blood without any English alloy." For twenty-five years before the war, the De Lanceys and the Livingstons had opposed each other in an extremely bitter feud. In power now, the Livingstons divided the control of the river counties with the Van Rensselaers and Schuylers. Many of the lead-

The north side of Wall Street from Nassau to Broadway in 1784 shows Simmons' Tavern, Presbyterian Church next door, ruins of Trinity Church. The scavenging pigs helped to remove garbage.

ing families had intermarried, with the result that the war saw many curious mixtures of conflicting interests. Two Van Cortlandt cousins fought on opposite sides; rebel General Philip Schuyler was first cousin to royal General Oliver De Lancey; the De Peysters, chiefly loyalists, had intermarried with the Van Cortlandts, one of whom was the mother of John Jay.

Jay, along with Governor Clinton, Mayor Duane, and Baron von Steuben were leaders in the attempt to quell the ridiculous Doctors' Riot of April 13, 1788. This fatal comedy of errors began at the City Hospital, which had been completed just as the Revolution began and was used throughout the war as a barracks for troops. When the hospital was reopened, two rooms were assigned to Dr. Richard Bailey for anatomical lectures. A rumor began to float about town that his medical students were raiding the better cemeteries for cadavers. On the eventful day some venturesome boys climbed a ladder, peered through a window, and were greeted by a young surgeon with the wave of an arm—not his own. The boys fled, spread the news, a mob gathered, and soon the town was in one of its fits of popular fury. The swarm of outraged citizens stormed into the hospital, smashed the equipment in the dissecting rooms, and then poured into the streets hunting

To push state legislators into adopting the Constitution, New York staged a mammoth procession, featuring the Federal ship HAMILTON, *a miniature frigate named for the popular Federalist. Here it is saluted by members of Congress on the Fort.*

Once the Constitution was adopted, Washington, proposed for the Presidency by Hamilton, was elected unanimously in January, 1789. Notified at Mount Vernon on April 14, he set off for New York on the 16th and was greeted along the entire route with ceremonial arches, parades, and banquets.

for doctors. At the height of the riot they passed the residence of the British Consul-General, Sir John Temple, on Wall Street, and, mistaking the Sir John on the nameplate for "surgeon," attacked the house furiously, and were barely restrained by some of the more educated among them from leveling the building to the ground. The wild riot subsided during the night, but boiled over again the next day when the mob was joined by sailors from ships in the harbor. Now the enraged rioters threatened to break into the jail, drag out the doctors, who had taken refuge there, and hang them.

Jay, driving to the scene, was injured by a stone thrown through the glass of his carriage. The riot had become so violent that the Mayor was about to order the militia to fire on the mob. While kindly Baron von Steuben pleaded with him not to give the command, a brickbat flew through the air and struck the Baron in the forehead, knocking him to the ground. "Fire!" roared the Baron, "Fire!" The soldiers did, with the result that five rioters were killed, more were wounded, and the mob was dispersed. Von Steuben was carried to the home of William Duer, but, since no physician dared show his head in public, the Baron's wounds were bound up by his hostess, the daughter of the late Lord Stirling.

Congress, which had met in Trenton, moved to New York, the new capital of the nation, on December 23, 1784, but the Federal government was without power—even to prevent one state from declaring war against another. Then a convention to draft a new set of administrative laws met in Philadelphia in May, 1787, with George Washington presiding. After four months, the delegates adopted the present Constitution and submitted it to the states for ratification. Approval did not come easily. Patrick Henry said: "It has an awful squinting; it squints toward monarchy. Your president might easily become king." In Massachusetts, Fisher Ames argued the other way: "The State government is a beautiful structure, but it is situated on the naked beach. What security has it against foreign enemies?" In New York, Alexander Hamilton, aided by Jay and James Madison, wrote the brilliant series of eighty-five essays entitled *The Federalist* as a reply to the objections that had been raised against the Constitution.

Since nine states, the required majority, had already adopted the Constitution, New York either had to join the Union or secede. A State Convention was called at Poughkeepsie on June 17, 1788. While the arguments and scrimmages went on, news was received that Virginia had ratified on July 3. A three-hour speech of spellbinding eloquence by Hamilton pushed the measure through by a margin of three votes on July 26.

The New York decision may have been influenced by the mammoth parade held in Manhattan three days before ratification. In addition to the elaborate miniature Federal ship *Hamilton*, there were trumpeters, artillery, foresters with axes, farmers with oxen, and a new threshing machine manipulated by Baron Polnitz processing grain as it went, gardeners in green aprons, bakers drawing "The Federal Loaf" on a float, brewers with hogsheads, coopers making kegs, cordwainers at work, Indians, hatters, peruke-makers, whitesmiths and blacksmiths, ivory-turners, printers at work turning out copies of a commemora-

On April 20, Washington received a tremendous ovation at Gray's Bridge over the Schuylkill River leading into Philadelphia. The bridge was decorated with a magnificent bower of greenery and flowers arranged by the artist, Charles Peale. When Washington passed under the last arch, the artist's daughter, Angelica, "hidden among the evergreens and by means of certain machinery, lowered on the hero's brow a wreath of laurel."

The following day, at Trenton, Washington once again crossed the Delaware cheered by crowds lining the shores.

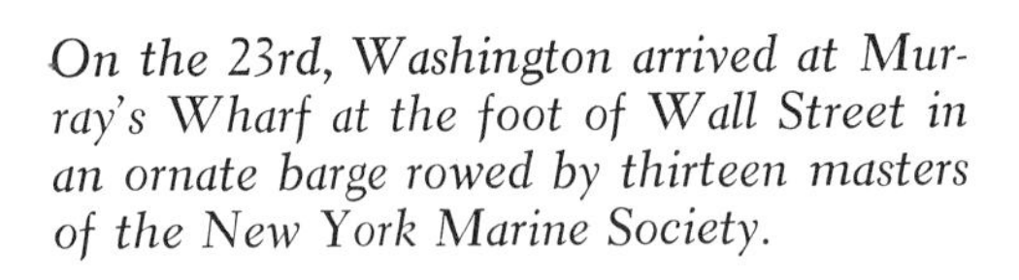

On the 23rd, Washington arrived at Murray's Wharf at the foot of Wall Street in an ornate barge rowed by thirteen masters of the New York Marine Society.

For his inauguration, President Washington rode to Federal Hall (the renovated City Hall) in his imported canary-colored state coach. Drawn by six white horses, it was shaped like a half pumpkin, ornamented with cupids and garlands of flowers, and emblazoned with the family coat of arms.

Only contemporary view of Washington taking the oath of office omits the mass of people who came from all thirteen new states to witness the "most glorious day in history."

The President was so overcome with emotion and moved by the crowd's reception that he had to rest several minutes in a chair before being sworn in by Chancellor Robert R. Livingston on April 30. John Adams is at the right.

Each Friday night, from eight until ten, Martha Washington held a formal reception or levee which was attended at one time or another by every prominent figure of the period. In addition to Mrs. Washington and the President, this painting by Daniel P. Huntington depicts sixty-two of the country's most eminent people.

The upper floor of the former Royal Exchange at the foot of Broad Street, near Water, was used as the first courtroom of the United States Supreme Court.

tive poem, "a horse-doctor bearing a standard with a curious device," chocolate-makers carrying a banner showing one man with thirteen heads each facing in different directions on one side and ten men supporting one presidential head on the other. Also, marching as a group, was the entire membership of the Philological Society, including Noah Webster. A great banquet with tables spread for six thousand people beneath a rustic pavilion temple, designed by Major Pierre Charles L'Enfant, who had directed all the details of the parade, concluded the exuberant day.

The French engineer was also placed in charge of remodeling the eighty-year-old City Hall into Federal Hall, a reconstruction job that kept exceeding its budget until the final cost was sixty-five thousand dollars, part of which was raised by running a lottery. But the reconstruction converted the drab old Municipal building into a magnificent capitol, regarded by proud New Yorkers as the largest and most elegant building on the continent. Native marble, carved woods, decorated draperies, and fine

On May 17, 1792, a group of Public Stock (government bond) brokers met under a buttonwood tree near what is now 60 Wall Street and signed an agreement to deal only with each other, thus forming the parent organization of the present New York Stock Exchange.

ironwork made it a showplace to all except the Anti-Federalists, one of whom called it ". . . the *Old New Building*, nicknamed *Federal Hall* and by others who are ill-natured called *Fool's Trap*. . . . I believe that it is expected that this medley of a house will induce us to forget that wrong is not right and that two and two are just equal to four."

Congress met here for the first time on March 4, 1789, and occupied the building for two sessions. After the Federal government moved to Philadelphia, it reverted to its old function and title. In May, 1800, a new City Hall was proposed; the cornerstone of the present building was laid on May 26, 1803, and it was completed in 1812. The Wall Street City Hall was sold at auction for $450 and the four lots on which it stood for $34,999.98.

For ten years Philadelphia was the nation's capital. The shift of location to the new Federal City on the Potomac came about as the result of a deal made between Hamilton and Thomas Jefferson. The latter led the faction which sought to relocate the seat of government in the South. Hamilton wanted the national government to assume the debts contracted during the war by the states, estimated at twenty-five million dollars. Those states with few or no war debts, such as Virginia, fought the plan so stubbornly that a split in the Union seemed inevitable. The two men happened to meet outside Washington's house at 39 Broadway and strolled up and down for a half hour, arm in arm. The result was that the deadlock over Hamilton's Assumption Bill was broken by two "yes" votes from Virginia, and Hamilton and Robert Morris persuaded the North that the capital should be located at what was to become Washington, D.C.

Of all the world's major countries, the United States is the only one where the principal city is not also the capital. As a result there has never been the close relationship between finance and government that exists abroad. Whether we have prospered be-

Wall Street became Bank Row in 1792 when the New York branch of the first Bank of the United States opened at Number 52, third from corner. The Bank of New York was built at the William Street corner in 1798. In 1812 the City Bank took over Number 52, where it remained for ninety-two years before moving across the street as the First National City Bank.

cause of or in spite of this is a question which no amount of debate can answer. But the fact remains that the deal to establish the nation's capital in Washington gave Wall Street its start as the financial capital of the country.

The Assumption Bill brought to eighty million dollars the amount of bonds, then called stock, issued by Congress. These securities were traded by the merchants and auctioneers of New York, frequently for out-of-town customers. Some of the traders began to specialize in this business alone and these men became the first stockbrokers. In early March, 1792, a Stock Exchange Office opened at 22 Wall. It was operated by five firms of auctioneers. On the 21st of that month, at a meeting in Corre's Hotel, at 63 Wall, the other dealers in United States stocks resolved that, beginning a month from that day, none of them would attend the Public Auction, nor would they buy or sell for a rate less than ¼ per cent commission. They also agreed to give preference to each other in their negotiations. This agreement was signed by twenty-one individuals and three firms under a sycamore, or buttonwood, tree which stood either between 58 and 60 or 68 and 70 Wall Street. Here the brokers did business until the following year when the Tontine Coffee House, at the corner of Water Street, two blocks east, was completed and became their headquarters. In addition to five government issues, the brokers dealt in shares of the first private commercial bank in the United States—the Bank of North America, established in Philadelphia in 1781—and bales of cotton and bags of pimento. They also took wagers on everything from elections to executions during the French Revolution.

Later, they dealt in the shares of the Bank of New York, which began business at the former Walton House on Pearl Street in 1784 before moving to its present site at 48 Wall Street in 1798. One year later,

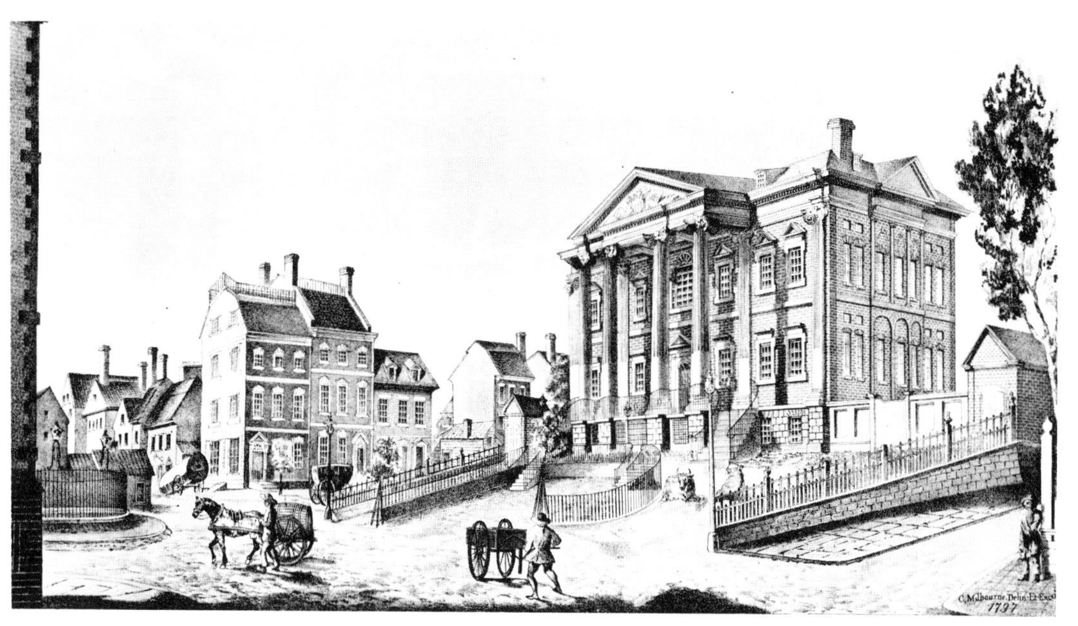

The Government House, on the site of the old Fort at Bowling Green, was built as the Presidential Mansion but was not finished when Washington and the government moved to Philadelphia in 1790. It became the official residence of Governors George Clinton and John Jay, then the Custom House, was razed in 1815.

Wall Street at Water in 1794 with the new Tontine Coffee House at the left. That year the Stock Exchange moved here from under the buttonwood tree, two blocks west. Ships' cargoes were scattered along the length of Wall Street, to be sold by haggle or auction to city merchants and out-of-town buyers.

the monopoly of the first New York bank, organized principally by Alexander Hamilton, was broken by Aaron Burr, acting as attorney for the Manhattan Company, ostensibly created to furnish the city with water, but permitted in the charter granted by the Legislature to use any surplus capital "in the purchase of public or other stocks, or in any other moneyed transactions or operations not inconsistent with the laws and constitution of the State of New York." While the company built a reservoir, ran wooden mains through the streets, and supplied some water until 1842, it quickly went into the banking business as the Bank of the Manhattan Company, which merged in 1955 with the Chase National Bank.

Just as Hamilton, who had become Secretary of the Treasury, and Burr, who was first a United States Senator and later Vice-President under Jefferson, opposed each other in bank organization and in the courts, the two political parties they represented became more and more antagonistic. Hamilton was the leading Federalist, while Burr headed the Republicans in New York and exerted enormous influence on the Tammany Society. The leadership of George Washington had previously unified the nation, but even before his second term as President expired, the country became embroiled in the relentless political warfare which has continued to this day. The battle was particularly hard fought in New York State, where foreign events increased the frictions between the two parties. When France declared war on England in 1793, the Federalists espoused the cause of our old enemy, while the Republicans were hotly pro-French although the excesses of the French Revolution made our former ally unpopular with many people.

In 1796 John Fitch ran the first successful steamboat with screw propeller on Collect Pond, where civic buildings now stand. However, unable to raise capital to finance his invention, he abandoned the boat there and, hounded by endless frustrations, committed suicide.

In the summer of 1795, John Jay, the first Chief Justice of the Supreme Court and newly elected Federalist Governor of New York, returned from England with a new treaty that revised some of the terms of the peace treaty of 1783. The provisions, which in effect bound the United States to strict neutrality in any war between Great Britain and other nations, were vehemently denounced by the Republicans. When Hamilton tried to speak in defense of the Jay Treaty from the stoop of an old Dutch house at Wall and Broad, he was pulled down and dragged through the streets. Another historian describes him as addressing a mob from the balcony of Federal Hall only to be answered by a shower of stones. "These are hard arguments to encounter," said Hamilton, smiling.

From the end of the Revolution to the end of the century, the population of New York City increased to fifty-five thousand, although several thousand perished in the yellow-fever epidemic of 1798, which threw the town into another of its recurring panics. From August to November the business streets were deserted; even the churches were shut down, and everyone who could moved out of the stricken town to the more salubrious climate of the country, principally in and around Greenwich Village to the north, which was to remain the refuge from epidemics for the next thirty or forty years.

At the end of the following year, on December 14, 1799, George Washington died, and New York went into mourning, along with the rest of the country, Actually, his death was lamented throughout the civilized world; sixty ships of the British fleet at Tor Bay lowered their flags to half-mast and Napoleon Bonaparte ordered the French Army to hang crepe from all standards and flags for ten days. The illustrious image which Washington left as a legacy is so exalted and powerful that, for the next 150 years, the American people have constantly sought to match it with another father, another victorious general.

5

A New Century

THE BEGINNING of the nineteenth century marked the dawn of a new, less colorful, bourgeois era. The French Revolution had put an end to silk stockings, knee breeches, powdered wigs, and the absolute privilege of kings. A trend toward clarity and simplicity in style had eliminated the "long" ſ in printing, although it would be fifty years before all the people who used it in their script died off. The dollar sign came into use, and many mechanical innovations that were to change the course of history were introduced.

But the situation of the fledgling nation, struggling to survive as an independent Republic, remained rather grim. The United States, caught in the crossfire between two powerful warring states, suffered severe economic blows as well as humiliating indignities. Great Britain, either forgetting that it had lost a war to its former subjects, or else smarting under the memory, adopted a naval recruiting policy which asserted that any seaman who spoke English was to be considered an Englishman. Instead of waiting for volunteer recruits, officers of the British Navy intercepted American merchantmen on the high seas and dragged off reluctant enlistees. The English also placed an embargo on any of our vessels suspected of trading with France. That nation, beginning its sweep across Europe under the command of Napoleon, captured and confiscated hundreds of American ships simply because they had touched at English ports.

On the other hand, in April, 1803, the United States acquired the greatest real-estate bargain since the purchase of Manhattan Island when Napoleon ceded to America the entire Province of New Orleans for a sum of fifteen million dollars. The area included the present states of Louisiana, Arkansas, Missouri, Iowa, Minnesota, Nebraska, Kansas, and Oklahoma. Napoleon may have thought he was getting the better of the bargain, for it had cost him nothing to recover the vast territory from Spain only three years before. But the purchase of the Louisiana territory was a triumph for Chancellor Robert R. Livingston, aided by James Monroe, who arrived in Paris a few days before negotiations were concluded.

As the country grew in size, New York City also expanded. Docks sprouted into the Hudson, nine of

Dey Street, corner Greenwich, was a busy residential neighborhood in 1810 when Baroness Hyde de Neuville drew this watercolor. The pump, corner, and second house disappeared when Greenwich was widened.

The Manhattan Company, organized by Aaron Burr, was originally chartered to supply water. It built this reservoir on Chambers Street and laid some wooden mains through the city, but soon went into banking by means of a trick clause in its charter.

them, in comparison to forty-eight in the East River. Built for President Washington, who never occupied it, the splendid Government House served for a time as the Governor's Mansion, and then was turned into the Custom House when the state capital was moved to Albany. As the richer families left Wall Street to live farther uptown near the new City Hall, their houses and mansions were taken over by banks and such firms as the New York Marine Insurance Company, the Mutual Fire Insurance Company, and the Washington Fire Insurance Company. Three stages now left from Baker's Tavern, at Wall and New Streets, on a round-trip service to Greenwich Village, Harlem, and Manhattanville.

At an opposite corner of New and Wall, Washington Irving was soon to begin writing in his brother's law office. Alexander Hamilton had sold his property down the street, the L-shaped lot next to the present Morgan building, extending around to Broad Street, and was living and practicing law on Broadway, where the Standard Oil Company building now stands. Aaron Burr was Vice-President and made his home at Richmond Hill, a fine estate above Canal Street, near the Hudson. The differences between the two men, courtroom and political antagonists since the end of the Revolution, were mounting now. Despite these differences, there were many striking similarities. Born only a year apart (Hamilton was the older), they were both brilliant men, slight in build, handsome, almost of a size, war heroes—and each had a winning way with the ladies. By profession both were then, and would be termed today, Wall Street lawyers.

But the similarities ended there. Burr, descended from an old American family, was the son and grandson of Princeton presidents, Aaron Burr, Sr., and Reverend Jonathan Edwards. As the guiding light of Tammany, he was the first real political "boss" in the United States. He was also a leader of the Republican party—the people's party of the day—which was later to change its name to Republican-Democratic and then simply Democratic party. Alexander Hamilton, born out of wedlock, a West Indian immigrant and a self-made aristocrat with little faith in democratic processes, was the spokesman and leading theoretician of the aristocratic Federalist party. If, Burr wanted to be Napoleon, then certainly Hamilton, for his part, would have liked to have been Prime Minister.

It is easy to see how Wall Street — and even the whole United States—soon became too small to hold both of these men. As each climbed the tree of government, the one about to grasp a higher branch would find the other above him, waiting to slash at his knuckles. Hamilton kept Burr from becoming President when the vote in the Electoral College after the election of 1800 ended in a tie between the two Republicans, Jefferson and Burr. The final decision was made in the House of Representatives where Hamilton used his influence to have crucial votes

The delicate, graceful second Trinity Church lasted only a half century. Heavy snows in the winter of 1839 buckled the roof and supporting columns so severely that repair attempts proved fruitless. The building was therefore demolished and replaced by the present third edifice, which was consecrated in 1846.

thrown to Jefferson whom he hated as a politician but respected as a man. In turn, Burr checkmated Hamilton and his aristocratic Schuyler in-laws time after time. Nevertheless on the surface, the two antagonists were always extremely formal and polite in their dealings. When they faced each other in court, Hamilton would often sum up his side of a case with two hours of brilliant logical oration. Then Burr, in opposition, would pick out the few vulnerable points in Hamilton's argument and demolish them, speaking in a reasonable, almost casual manner and making no other comment on the case. Burr would frequently win.

By 1804 there had been a dozen years of checkmating and triumph, frustration and revenge. Burr was not renominated that year as Vice-President, his place on the Republican ticket going to Governor George Clinton of New York. He therefore broke with the Jefferson Republicans and ran for Clinton's office as an independent. When he lost, he attributed his defeat to Hamilton's powerful influence. During the campaign, Dr. Charles D. Cooper had written and published letters urging Burr's defeat, letters which contained such lines as "Gen. Hamilton looked upon Mr. Burr to be a dangerous man and one who ought not be trusted with the reins of government. . . . I could detail to you a still more despicable opinion which General Hamilton has expressed of Mr. Burr." That Hamilton was right, in light of what happened later, cannot be denied. That Burr's history would have been different had Hamilton kept his opinions to himself is a distinct possibility. But Hamilton's honesty would not permit him to remain silent. And Burr's pride would not allow him to swallow insults from his enemy.

Alexander Hamilton opposed Aaron Burr at almost every step of their parallel careers, until the Vice-President forced him into a fatal duel.

Burr demanded a retraction from Hamilton and refused to be satisfied with the replies he received. He either forced a senseless duel upon Hamilton, as the Hamiltonians claim, or he justifiably insisted on avenging the long list of outrages to which he had been subjected, according to the Burrite version. Burr had had some experience in dueling, on one occasion exchanging shots, which missed, with John B. Church, Hamilton's brother-in-law. On the other hand, Hamilton's aversion to dueling undoubtedly stemmed from the fact that his son, Philip, had been involved three years earlier in a misunderstanding with George L. Eacker, a young lawyer and Burr adherent, which terminated in a duel and the death of the younger Hamilton. Now Burr made it impossible for Hamilton to avoid his challenge and, late in June, 1804, the time was set for the morning of July 11.

During the two intervening weeks, Burr and Hamilton met at the Fourth of July banquet of the Society of the Cincinnati and at the New York Marine Society, as well as at several patriotic rallies, and observers later recalled the deference and courtesy they displayed toward each other. This was not unusual, because until then they had always been outwardly courteous in their relations and even occasionally dined together at Richmond Hill or The Grange, Hamilton's country home which he had built in upper Manhattan in 1802.

The morning of July 11 was warm and bright as the two parties arrived in boats at the Weehawk, New Jersey, dueling ground just across the Hudson from the city. The place was chosen as a field of honor because it was almost inaccessible, being situated on a shelf half way up the side of the Palisades, with a steep path leading from the water. Lots were drawn and Hamilton won the choice of position.

The most famous duel in United States history took place on a wooded ledge above the New Jersey shore. It not only brought death to Hamilton (LEFT), *but also*

He chose to face the river and New York. He also won the right to give "the word," which meant he would call out: "Fire!" When the time came, and the opponents stood just twelve paces apart, he gave the word and then did what he had instructed his son to do three years before. He held his fire. Burr did not. His pistol roared in the still air, and Hamilton fell to the ground. Burr, his face shielded from view by an umbrella spread by his second, briskly descended to the waterside and was rowed back to Richmond Hill.

Even before Dr. David Hosack reached him, Hamilton knew that his wound was fatal, for the bullet had torn through his chest, lodging in his spine. Transported back to Manhattan, he was taken to the home of a friend, and his wife and children were summoned to his side. He died at two o'clock the following afternoon.

Fearing that he was about to disappear into political oblivion, Aaron Burr felt that Hamilton was responsible and demanded apologies the latter could not give.

ended the career of Burr who "avenged honor" only to live under a cloud of ill repute for the rest of his life until he died at the age of eighty in 1846.

The swift and universal reaction of people of every shade of political opinion to the news of the duel and Hamilton's death came as a complete surprise to Burr. He had been so cool and unconcerned following his return home that a young cousin who had breakfast with him had no intimation of the event until he went to Wall Street later that morning and found business suspended while everyone waited for the hourly bulletins on Hamilton's condition.

Even the liberals who had bitterly opposed him mourned Hamilton's tragic death, which served to immortalize him as a martyr. While it is futile to speculate as to what might have happened had Burr missed his mark, it is possible that Hamilton had already reached the apogee of his career. In light of the Republican triumphs of the next several decades, his political influence might have waned, but, considering his character, it is doubtful that he would have suffered the harsh fate that dogged the career of his slayer until the very last day of Burr's life.

Although Aaron Burr did not realize it at the time, he ceased to be a political leader from the moment news of the duel was known. He treated the affair lightly in his conversation and correspondence, but he was the only one who did. A coroner's jury in New York found him guilty of murder and he fled, hidden by friends along the way, to Washington, where he was still Vice-President of the United States. A grand jury in New Jersey, site of the duel, indicted him, but he continued unmolested in his office and presided over the Senate until his term expired on March 2, 1805.

Meanwhile, Richmond Hill was sold by Burr's creditors for twenty-five thousand dollars, which was seven thousand dollars short of meeting his debts. Since he was liable to imprisonment for debt if he returned to New York, Burr set out on an expedition to the Western territories, where he either became innocently involved in a scheme to establish an independent nation or was the initiator of the idea. As a result, he was arrested in 1807 and tried for treason. The charge was "not proven," and he departed for Europe, where he lived for four years. He then returned to New York, renewed the practice of

Handsome, graceful, talented, Robert Fulton was an artist, civil engineer, and favorite of society as well as the inventor of the first durable, successful steamboat. He is buried within a few feet of Alexander Hamilton on the south side of Trinity Churchyard.

"The CLERMONT *on the Hudson," a French print with French river scenery substituted for that of the Hudson. After its auspicious debut in 1807, when it was simply known as the "Steam Boat," the ship was lengthened, registered as the* NORTH RIVER STEAMBOAT OF CLERMONT, *usually called the* NORTH RIVER *until 1810 when it was designated the* CLERMONT. *It was withdrawn from service by 1814.*

It took nine years and $500,000, exclusive of furniture, to build the present City Hall. Contemporary description stated: "The first story, including the portico, is of the Ionic, the second of the Corinthian, the attic of the Fancy, and the Cupola of the Composite orders."

law, becoming a local landmark until his death in 1836.

The purchaser of Richmond Hill was Manhattan's richest man, the fur-trader and real-estate collector, John Jacob Astor, the first real giant of Wall Street. Astor created techniques in exploitation and financing that are still used with much success in finance and in the opening of new territories everywhere. When the Louisiana Purchase was completed, Astor, who had graduated from furrier (and pioneer piano

Duncan Phyfe, leading American craftsman, opened his shops and warehouse on Fulton Street in 1795. The first to win recognition for United States furniture, he was paid as much as $250 for a table.

Booths line City Hall Park, citizens fire pistols and guns, and members of the Tammany Society (the famous Tammany Hall is at left) dress up as Indians for annual Fourth of July celebration in 1812.

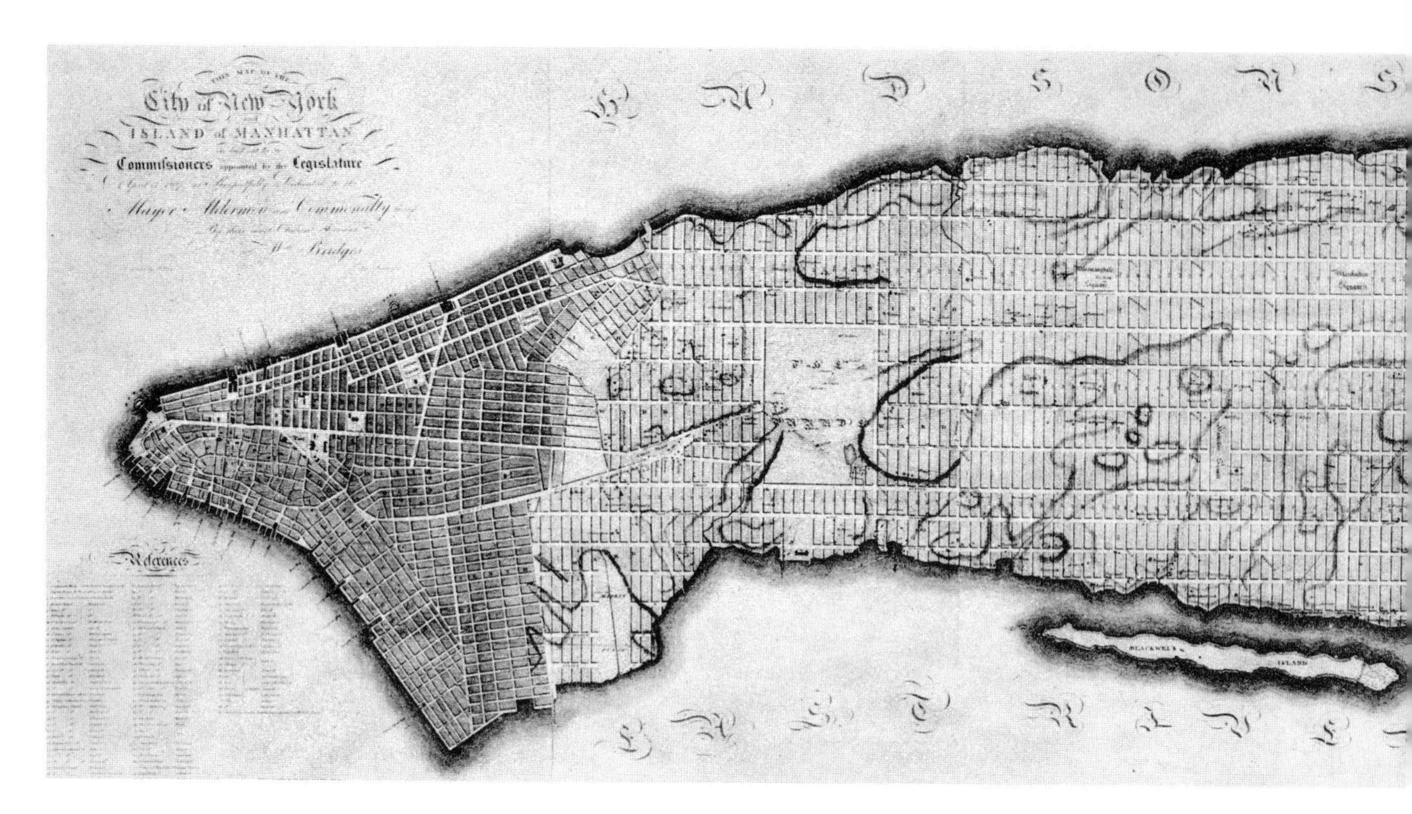

This map of Manhattan Island, laid out in streets by commissioners appointed by the Legislature in 1807, shows the plan which they presented in 1811. The gridiron

Even before James Madison was elected President, Barbary pirates and a warring France and Britain wrought havoc on American shipping and foreign trade. When the President was finally pushed into declaring war on Great Britain, many people labeled the hostilities "Mr. Madison's War."

importer) to pelt-trader, opened the Great Lakes to commerce and then moved westward, his chain of trading posts eventually extending to Astoria at the mouth of the Columbia River in Oregon. By 1810 he was, next to Stephen Girard of Philadelphia, the richest man in the United States.

Astor helped finance the War of 1812 by purchasing millions of dollars' worth of government bonds which he sold at a premium after the war. But embargoes and war turned him from international trade to New York real estate. On his deathbed he said that, if he had his life to live over again, he would never touch furs or pianos or anything but Manhattan land. The Astor family is still one of the most important landlords in the city.

Although the town still clustered around the southern tip of the island and the magnificent new City Hall was adorned with marble on three sides (brownstone was used on the rear, where nobody was ever expected to see it), the undeveloped part of the island to the north was laid out by three commissioners of streets and roads who were appointed in 1807—Gouverneur Morris, Simeon De Witt, and

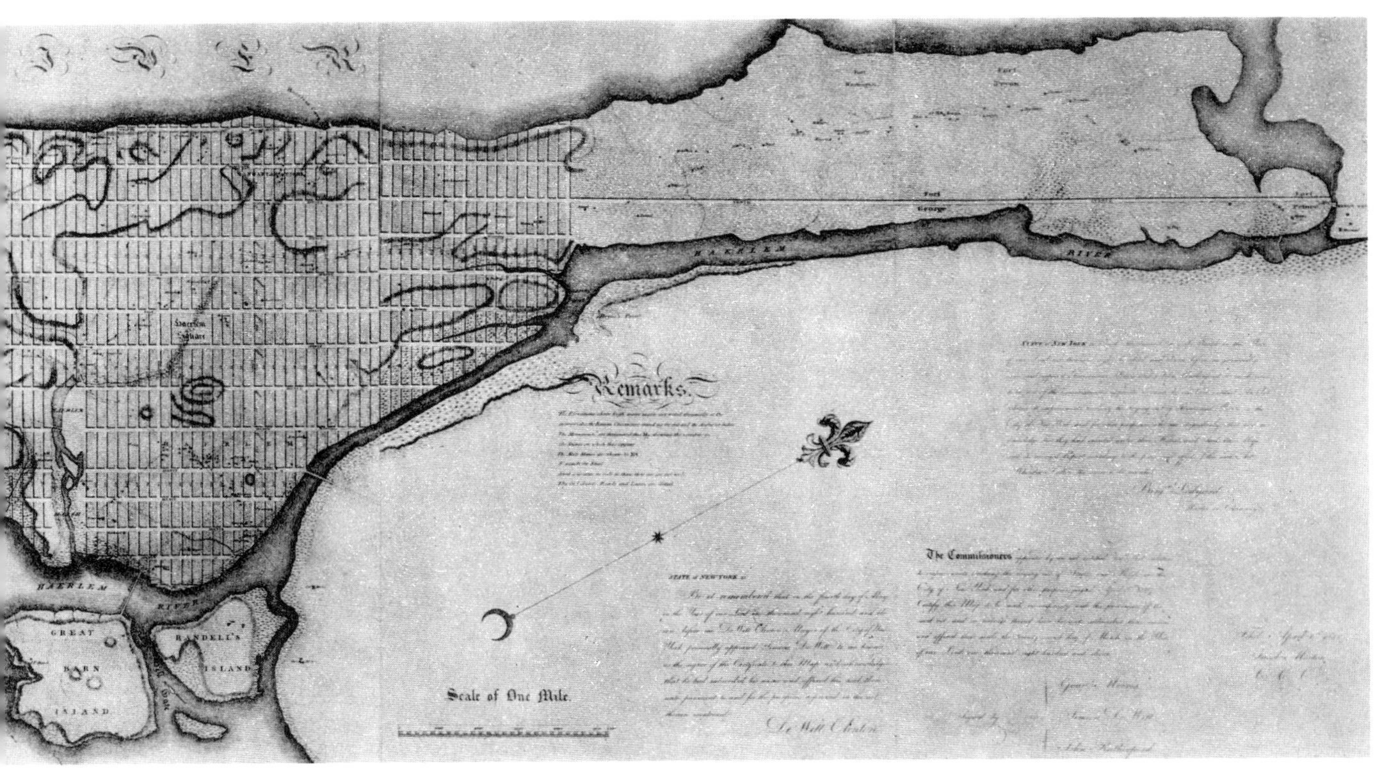

pattern which they decided upon has given the layout of the city's streets a quality of uniform monotony and influenced the plan of almost every other American city.

John Rutherford. In 1811 they made their report and presented their map.

"One of the first objects which claimed their attention," they said, writing in the third person, "was whether they should confine themselves to rectilinear and rectangular streets, or whether they should adopt some of those supposed improvements, circles, ovals and stars which certainly embellish a plan, whatever may be their effects as to convenience and utility. . . . They could not but bear in mind that a city is to be composed principally of the habitations of men, and that strait sided, and right angled houses are the most cheap to build, and the most convenient to live in."

Because the island was surrounded by "large arms of the sea," there was little need for parks or vacant spaces for fresh air, the commissioners claimed. They went on to recommend a large "reservoir, with a copious supply of pure and wholesome water" and a Grand Parade "at the foot of those heights called Inklangberk [Murray Hill]. . . . The City of New-York contains a population already sufficient to place it in the ranks of cities of the second order, and is

John Jacob Ashdore, or Astor, came to the United States from Germany in 1784. Starting out virtually penniless, he built a vast fur-trading empire, and switched to New York real estate during the war of 1812. At his death in 1848 he was considered the wealthiest man in the country.

America's first great author was Washington Irving whose monumental satire, DIEDRICH KNICKERBOCKER'S HISTORY OF NEW YORK, *was written in his brother's law office at Wall and New streets.*

rapidly advancing towards a level with the first. It is perhaps not unreasonable conjecture, that in half a century it will be closely built up to the northern boundary of the Parade, and contain 400,000 souls . . . it may be a subject of merriment that the Commissioners have provided space for a greater population than is collected at any spot on this side of China . . . it is improbable, that [for centuries to come] the grounds north of Haerlem Flat will be covered with houses . . . to have gone further, might have furnished materials to the pernicious spirit of speculation."

The gridiron plan which the commissioners adopted has been followed with only an exception or two—Central Park was a later thought, and the Reservoir was originally to be located east, rather than west of Fifth Avenue. Since the officials envisioned that most of Manhattan traffic would be borne by the new steamboats on the Hudson and the East rivers, with frequent stops along the shore, they made the blocks running north and south short and the crosstown blocks extremely long.

It was too late to remake the old part of the city, but the commissioners gave the unoccupied part of the island a layout which, with the exception of the diagonal sweep of Broadway, has as much personality as a waffle. A further handicap has been the influence this plan was to have on the aspect of other American cities, aside from its insidious influence on architecture. The skyscraper is simply the gridiron city standing on end.

The commissioners cannot be blamed for being swayed by the potential role of the steamboat, for they were appointed the same month that Robert Fulton launched the *North River Steamboat of Clermont*, which had been the subject of much speculation and raillery while its machinery was being installed.

In July, with many skeptical guests aboard, the craft started up the Hudson from the Cortlandt Street pier, stalled to the gratification of the crowds on shore, and then, after Fulton rushed below and adjusted the engine, began to move triumphantly upstream. Belching flame and smoke, the *Clermont* chugged up the Hudson, spreading consternation among the crews of other vessels as it defied adverse wind and current. As it passed the Palisades, a wall of solid rock twenty miles long, the noise and sight of this strange ship so startled one rustic that he ran home to tell his wife he had just seen the devil on his way to Albany in a sawmill.

Fulton made the trip at a speed of about five miles an hour (covering the 150 miles to Albany in thirty-two hours) and shaved two hours off the northbound mark when he churned downriver on his return to New York. Although Fulton was not the first to build a steamship, the *Clermont* was the first steam vessel to complete a journey of such length at a cost low enough to insure a fair profit for its operators, and it was the tested practicality of Fulton's ship on which his fame is largely based.

The *Clermont* was one of the first inventions financed by Wall Street. Chancellor Livingston had previously backed other power-driven boats because of his faith in the potential of the steam engine at sea. In Paris while negotiating the Louisiana Purchase, he met Fulton who was not only an excellent painter of miniatures (he had been in England studying art with Benjamin West), but was also a gunsmith, a civil engineer, and the inventor of a submarine, which he was then trying to sell to Napoleon. Fulton went into partnership with Livingston who, through his strong family and political ties, was able to obtain a monopoly from the New York Legislature for the operation of steam vessels in New York waters. Although he died in 1813 and Fulton died two years later, their company continued to operate ferries to Brooklyn and New Jersey as well as steamers on the Hudson until the monopoly was eventually broken. One of the men who helped to break it was a tough, hulking young steamboat captain named Cornelius Vanderbilt.

Vanderbilt got his start operating a sail-and-rowboat ferry from his birthplace, Staten Island, to Whitehall Slip, where another tough, stubborn Dutchman, Peter Stuyvesant, had lived, 150 years before. In 1812, at the age of eighteen, he was also ferrying supplies under contract to the new military fortifications in New York Bay which were hastily being constructed because of the outbreak of war.

What the people of New York called "Mr. Madison's War" erupted after years of maritime difficulties with an arrogant England and an insolent France. Since the former offered the more intolerable provocations, the fledgling Republic finally declared war on Great Britain. Within four months, twenty-six privateers had been outfitted and dispatched from New York. The brokers and bankers of Wall Street burst into activity reminiscent of Hamilton's day when the government issued bonds to finance the Army and Navy. Investors and entrepreneurs, prevented by the British blockade from sending their funds abroad or expanding their businesses, actively encouraged the creation of new industries at home and the manufacture of goods that were formerly imported. Such great craftsmen as Duncan Phyfe proved that American workmanship could be the equal of European. Phyfe, a cabinetmaker born in Scotland, first worked as a joiner on Broad Street and, in 1795, opened his first shop on Fulton, then known as Partition Street, across from St. Paul's Chapel.

For three years Manhattan resounded with cheers celebrating naval victories on the Great Lakes and on Lake Champlain and with groans of despair over defeats in Canada, at Washington, D.C., and on the Atlantic. In 1814, with Napoleon defeated and in exile, England was able to turn its full attention to the war with the American Republic and waves of apprehension swept through the states for fear that

South Street at Maiden Lane early in the nineteenth century was a forest of ship's masts and prows jutting out over the street, which remained a busy, brawling thoroughfare until after the Civil War, when steam navigation became dominant and new ships began docking along the Hudson River piers.

Many exciting battles during the War of 1812 were fought at sea. The queen of the United States Navy was the CONSTITUTION, *commanded by Commodore William Bainbridge, shown here capturing the British ship* JAVA *in a savage, bloody battle off the coast of Brazil in December, 1812.*

the victorious British would launch a stepped-up attack. But the English were tired of war and peace negotiations were begun at Ghent. New York City in particular was nervous and fearful because of its exposed position, and there was feverish activity to build more forts, recruit additional troops, and launch more ships of war.

Robert Fulton had interested John Paul Jones, Stephen Decatur, Oliver Perry, and other naval officials in a proposed cannon-proof steam frigate which would carry a heavy battery and achieve a speed as fast as four miles an hour. It was to be fitted with furnaces for heating incendiary shot and some of her guns were to be fired from below the waterline. In March, 1814, Congress voted $320,000 for the project and in the fall the *Fulton I* was launched. Its trial run to Sandy Hook and back was a success, but the warship was never used in battle. Nor did the inventor live to see it completed, dying of an illness contracted while supervising the construction of the vessel.

The War of 1812 was foremost a sea war with many exciting naval engagements. Perhaps the most dramatic and spectacular encounter took place between a privateer from New York and a British fleet in a neutral harbor. The *General Armstrong* was commanded by thirty-year-old Captain Samuel Chester Reid, "a man of rare combinations — the courage of a lion, the venturous spirit of a crusader, the taste of a poet, and the tenderness of a woman."

In September, 1814, British boarding parties tried to capture the New York privateer GENERAL ARMSTRONG *at Fayal in the Azores, but were driven off with heavy casualties. The encounter indirectly resulted in delaying the Battle of New Orleans for a month.*

On the evening of September 9, 1814, he successfully ran the British blockade off Sandy Hook, crossed the Atlantic, and entered the harbor of Fayal, one of the Azores, belonging to Portugal, at noon on the 26th. Just before sunset, six British warships, the squadron of Commodore Lloyd, anchored in the roads. The odds were heavily weighted in favor of the British—136 guns and over two thousand men against nine guns and only ninety men.

In defiance of international laws of neutrality, the British commander sent out two boarding parties, the first consisting of four boats and 160 men and the second of fourteen boats and five hundred men. Reid's crew repulsed each of them so savagely that the British lost more than three hundred killed and wounded while only two of the Americans died and seven were wounded. One English officer wrote: "God deliver us from our enemies, if this is the way they fight." At daybreak the *Carnation*, an English brig, opened heavy fire on the American ship, which answered with such a salvo of broadsides that the *Carnation* retired out of range to make repairs. The

Despite the famed admonition of mortally wounded Captain James Lawrence ("Don't give up the ship!"), his vessel, the CHESAPEAKE, *surrendered to the British frigate* SHANNON *in June, 1813. The British returned Lawrence's body with military honors.*

To the south of Trinity Church entrance at Broadway and Wall, surrounded by eight naval guns, a casket-like monument of blackened stone stands over the grave of Captain James Lawrence—a reminder to the passer-by of the heroism and sacrifice of earlier Americans.

town of Fayal was endangered by the battle, and several of its citizens were wounded by shots fired from the *Carnation*. Seeing no hope of saving the *General Armstrong*, Reid scuttled her and brought his men ashore. Commodore Lloyd ordered the Portuguese Governor to surrender the Americans, and when he was met with an unqualified refusal, threatened to land five hundred troops to take them by force. Reid's men retired to an abandoned convent, knocked away the drawbridge, and prepared to give battle on land. The Commodore, however, backed down and spent the next ten days burying his dead, caring for the wounded, and making repairs on his damaged ships.

Finally, upon reaching Jamaica, where the great expedition against New Orleans was anxiously awaiting his flotilla before proceeding against the Americans, Lloyd was severely reprimanded by Admiral Cochrane. The delay permitted General Andrew Jackson to fortify and man the defenses of New Orleans so well that when the crack British Army, conquerors of Napoleon at Waterloo, attacked on January 8, 1815, the motley collection of American troops, militia, buccaneers from Barataria, and mountain men that Jackson had assembled was able to repulse the attack and thoroughly defeat the amazed Britons. The American casualties were only seven killed and six wounded.

Ironically, two weeks earlier, on December 24, 1814, a treaty of peace had been signed in Ghent and was ratified by the British government four days later. On February 11, 1815, the British ship *Favourite* arrived at New York under a flag of truce with the unexpected treaty. It was late on a Saturday evening. The news spread with lightning speed. People rushed into the streets, cannon roared, bells clanged, bonfires were set at every corner, rows upon rows of candles were lighted in thousands of windows —and night in the glowing little city was turned into day.

6

Financial Growth

BY THE TIME that the War of 1812 had come to its end, commerce in the United States had virtually limped to a halt. In 1815, however, business leaped once more to life. Shipyards echoed with the pounding of hammers and the rasping of saws, and new American ships were soon sailing to the far corners of the earth. Employment rose, the population increased rapidly, and the development of the new lands to the west was begun in earnest. For the first time the country was becoming a commercial force, not only beyond the Alleghenies, but abroad.

Imports doubled over previous figures and the British flooded the American market with a tremendous volume of goods at extremely low prices. The British had a dual purpose in this maneuver: to clear English warehouses of the backlog of goods that had piled up during the war and to knock out the competition of the new American industries by selling the same products they manufactured at cheaper prices. Consequently, many importers and merchants overbought British goods, with the result that a financial crisis during 1818–19 caused numerous business failures and a wave of bankruptcies.

The young and growing nation was entering its adolescence, with all the accompanying high spirits, try-anything, know-everything attitudes of youth. Like a gangling boy growing out of his clothes, the country expanded too quickly. Recklessly, great land-development schemes were launched; towns were laid out on well-chosen sites, as well as in trackless forests and on barren plains; canals were promoted and railroads projected; inventions were developed and manufacturing became a major factor in the economy. For every venture that survived and succeeded there were ten failures which wiped out the hopes and money of investors. America grew fast, but not without its share of growing pains.

As a result of the war, outstanding bonds of the United States increased from forty-five million to 123 million dollars. In addition to this, the stockbrokers who had also been dealing in the bonds of the states and "the corporation," as the City of New York was called, found themselves handling new issues. Banks, fire- and marine-insurance firms, and, soon, a canal-development company had their securities listed. In

View down Wall Street from Trinity Church in 1834. Only three copies of this lithograph by Peter Maverick, Jr., after a painting by Hugh Reinagle, are known to exist, one selling for $3,950 in 1916. At the south corner of Broadway was Cummings Exchange and Lottery Office. Snow brought out a complete array of sleighs.

1817, feeling that a more formal organization than the one which met in the Tontine Coffee House was needed, the brokers adopted a constitution and the name of "The New York Stock and Exchange Board." They began meeting in a succession of offices on or near Wall Street, except during the yellow-fever season, when they moved uptown to Washington Hall on Broadway at Reade Street.

The procedure of the early exchange seems quaint today. The members met at 11:30 A.M. and the President "called" the stocks on the list, while the Secretary recorded the quotations and sales, as well as the names of the buyers and sellers. Since, in 1818, there were less than forty issues to be called and on some days no more than eight sales were recorded, it is unlikely that the exchange was in session much more than an hour. The initiation fee was twenty-five dollars and the members were sworn not to divulge the details of their transactions to outsiders. A commission of ¼ per cent was the minimum charged.

The south side of Wall Street from the East River (LEFT) to Broadway. The first Merchants Exchange, completed in 1827, is the building with a cupola in the center. No other building is more than four stories high.

Looking west toward Trinity from present 35 Wall Street, 1825–30. This view shows the Presbyterian Church with tavern still next door. The bookstore at Broad was on the site of the present Stock Exchange Annex. Custom House was replaced by impressive new building in 1842.

Cashing promissory notes rated a fee of ½ per cent, and when mortgage money was obtained, a fee of 1 per cent went to the finder. Wash sales were prohibited, as "no fictitious sale or contract shall be made at this Board. Any Member or Members contravening this article, shall, upon conviction thereof, be expelled." Among the other rules:

> *Any Member leaving the Room during the calling of stocks, without permission of the President, shall be fined Twenty-five cents.*
>
> *Any Member of this Board who shall be guilty of indecorous language or conduct towards another Member while in session, shall, by a vote of two-thirds of the Members present, be suspended from his seat at the Board for no less than one week nor more than one month. . . .*
>
> *Any member interrupting the President while calling the stocks, by speaking or otherwise, shall pay a fine of not less than Six nor more than Twenty-five cents for each offence, at the discretion of the President, from which there shall be no appeal. . . .*
>
> *The fines for non-attendance at the calling of the Stocks shall be six cents, unless sick or out of Town. . . .*

By 1827 the Board was dealing in one New York City, four United States, and three state issues. Also listed were the securities of twelve banks, fourteen fire-insurance companies, five marine-insurance firms,

Sketch of the north side of Wall from Broadway (LEFT) *to South Street shows Presbyterian Church, with tower, and churchyard to Nassau. In the block between Front and South streets is Number 108, still standing today.*

The end of Wall Street at the East River was still called Coffee House Slip although the Merchants and Tontine coffee houses were gone. A half-century later this was to become the center of the United States coffee industry, but after the War of 1812 the slip was used as a dock for swift coastal packets.

New York's Great Man of the period was De Witt Clinton who served for nineteen years as Mayor of the city and Governor of the state. Ardent sponsor of the Erie Canal, he was also a champion of a free public-school system and other civic advances.

the Delaware and Hudson Canal Company, the New York Gas Light Company, and the Merchants Exchange.

The handsome and imposing building of the Merchants Exchange, located at the corner of Hanover with its main entrance on Wall Street, was completed in 1827, and the Board offered to pay a yearly rental of five hundred dollars for Room 43, on the second story, overlooking Exchange Place. A condition of the brokers' offer was "that the doors of the adjoining room No. 41 may be thrown open for the benefit of a circulation of air during the sittings of the Board from eleven to twelve o'clock each day during the extreme hot weather between the months of June and October." The offer was accepted "on condition that the Company may allow the Chamber of Commerce to hold their meetings in the same room after one o'clock P.M. on any days and at such other times as the room may not be required by the Board." The Board moved in on May 1 and the brokers were so pleased with their new quarters that they raised the initiation fee for new members to one hundred dollars.

In 1830 the first railroad stock was listed. This was Mohawk and Hudson, the seventeen-mile line between Albany and Schenectady, which was the first railroad to operate in New York State and the initial link of the New York Central. By 1837 the Delaware and Hudson Canal Company had been transformed into a railroad and was now listed as such along with eight other railroads, twelve banks and trust companies, five of them in the South, and the New Orleans Gas Company.

During these years, New York assumed a commanding lead in American shipping. Before the war, commerce between the United States and Europe was not based on any regular schedule or orderly routine of sailings. In 1817 the Black Ball Line, using four ships, began sending packet boats out of the East River bound for England on the first of every month. Soon the Red Star Line started a regular transatlantic service with sailings on the twenty-fourth of the month. Black Ball added four more ships which sailed on the sixteenth. Then the Swallow Tail Line entered the picture with four new packets which embarked on the eighth. Within three years, New York merchants and travelers could count on a ship sailing to Europe every week in the year.

The regularity of the sailings and the dependability of the service also drew trade and visitors to the city from the rest of the country. Trade with China boomed, American ships in ever greater numbers sailed around the Horn laden with furs and ginseng (highly prized by the Chinese as a medicine) and returned with cargoes of tea. Thus the port of New York enjoyed a phenomenal growth that has never been equaled by any other harbor.

An extremely important factor in this success was the construction of the Erie Canal, which enabled the commerce of the whole Great Lakes area to be channeled through New York harbor. Before the canal was dug it cost $125 a ton to move freight between Albany and Buffalo. After 1825 the cost was reduced to five dollars a ton. It is even less today, and although the canal is no longer the all-important waterway it once was, the yearly tonnage passing through it now is greater than when its usefulness was at its peak.

Arrival of the first boats from Buffalo via the new Erie Canal on November 4, 1825, was the occasion for a Grand Canal Celebration and a massive water parade. A five-mile-long parade was also held on land in which fifty-nine civic and trade groups participated, including firemen on a float whose banner read: "We Raze to Save."

From the bow of the SENECA CHIEF, *Clinton poured Lake Erie water into the Atlantic off Sandy Hook, symbolizing completion of the canal. Behind Clinton is Dr. Samuel L. Mitchill who followed him by emptying bottles of water which he had gathered from the world's principal rivers.*

However, before the Erie Canal was built, there were long years of struggle to bring the dream to life. The project had first been proposed during the Revolutionary War by the Irish-born engineer, Christopher Colles. By 1795 General Philip Schuyler, Alexander Hamilton's father-in-law, had pushed through a three-mile, five-lock canal connecting the Mohawk and Lake Ontario. In 1800 Gouverneur Morris traveled up New York State and into Canada to Montreal, down the St. Lawrence to Lake Ontario, and then by land to Lake Erie. He wrote to a friend: "Hundreds of large ships will, at no distant period, bound on the billows of these inland seas. . . . As yet, we only crawl along the outer shell of our country. . . . One tenth of the expense borne by Britain in the last campaign would enable ships to sail from London through the Hudson River into Lake Erie."

Others took up the idea, and in 1810 the Legislature appointed a commission to explore the route. After suitable action by the state, Morris and De Witt Clinton, the son of James and nephew of

Handsomely carved keg, painted green with gilded hoops and adorned with devices and inscriptions, was one of a pair filled with Lake Erie water sent from Buffalo for the Atlantic Ocean ceremony.

George Clinton, went to Washington to persuade the Federal government to back the canal project. Although Congress was appropriating large sums to build roads in several states, the canal proposal was turned down.

The War of 1812, with much of its land action centered along the Canadian border, had emphasized the need for improved means of transportation in upper New York. After the country began to prosper in peace, De Witt Clinton became the spearhead, the leader, the driving force in making the canal a reality. Clinton was a giant among the officeholders of his era. Through the stormy partisan politics of the early nineteenth century, he was Mayor of New York on three different occasions for a total of ten years and Governor of the state for nine years. His energy, eloquence, and integrity made him a great force in the support of every good cause. Against violent opposition from many quarters, faced by the enormous problems of constructing the longest canal of its day—one of the most difficult engineering feats attempted to that time—Clinton never faltered or lost sight of the grand objective.

Despite the Federal government's refusal to assist financially in the construction of the Erie Canal, New York completed the project, at a cost of $7,602,000, with nothing but good wishes from the other states. When it was finished, "without the interference of Congress," that body was requested, in a polite petition, "not to sanction any such pretension as of late made by some of its revenue officers, that our canal-boats, traversing our hills and valleys in an artificial channel made by ourselves, entirely within our territory, hundreds of miles from the sea, and six or seven hundred feet above its level, were engaged in the coasting trade of the United States—and that they must, therefore, take custom-house licenses, and pay a tax to the general government."

De Witt Clinton's day of triumph came on October 26, 1825, when the waters of Lake Erie were admitted into the canal at Buffalo. The news was transmitted to New York City in the remarkable time of ninety minutes by means of cannon fired in sequence along the route to signal the event. New York City replied in kind, the crash of cannon roaring back up the Hudson and across the state to announce that the message had been received.

Immediately, the *Seneca Chief*, with Clinton and other canal officials aboard, led a parade of canalboats eastward. One vessel, *Noah's Ark*, carried eagles, fawns, a bear, and other birds, beasts, and "creeping things," as well as Indian boys in native dress. Night and day, along the route to Albany, people lined the banks of the canal to cheer the aquatic parade. Cities along the way outdid each other to greet the procession; visitors from New England and Canada arrived in Albany to celebrate the event. There were special prayers, theatrical performances, tableaux and pageants, artillery salutes, and blazing bursts of fireworks at night. At Albany a fleet made up of all the steamboats on the Hudson towed the canalboats down the river to New York, receiving a twenty-four-gun salute at West Point.

On November 4, Manhattan was wakened by the thunder of cannon, the pealing of bells, and the sound of martial music. The canal fleet had arrived. A committee representing the City Council sailed out on the *Washington* to meet the *Seneca Chief* in midstream.

"Where are you from and where are you bound?" one of them called out.

The reply came ringing over the water: "From Lake Erie, bound for Sandy Hook."

After appropriate greetings from the committee, the procession moved on toward the ocean. By nine o'clock the line of vessels comprised twenty-nine steamboats, in addition to schooners, canalboats, barges, and other craft. Crowded with bands and prominent citizens, all the ships and boats were decorated with pennants and bunting. The British Navy sent a squadron to serenade the parade, while the forts in the harbor saluted the vessels as they passed. "The pageant was the most magnificent which America, and perhaps the world, had ever beheld," Martha Lamb wrote. "It was like a bewildering fairy scene." As the fleet formed a circle almost three miles in circumference around the *Seneca Chief*, De Witt Clinton poured Lake Erie water into the ocean from an elegant keg. Then Dr. Samuel Latham Mitchill, who had traveled extensively for the purpose, poured out the contents of bottles containing water from the Nile, Gambia, Thames, Seine, Rhine, Danube, and Elbe rivers, as well as from the Mississippi, the Orinoco, La Plata, and the Amazon.

When the fleet returned to Manhattan, a great parade was held on shore in which all of the city's trades were exhibited in operation on floats, including printers working a pair of new Hoe handpresses,

A tumultuous welcome greeted Lafayette on his visit to the United States when he landed in New York on August 16, 1824. Inside Castle Garden (CENTER) he was cheered by six thousand people. "Through this gay multitude," wrotes James Fenimore Cooper, "the old man slowly passed, giving and receiving the most cordial and affectionate salutations at every step. . . . He appeared to be some venerable and much respected head of a vast family who had come to pass an hour amid their innocent and gay revels. He was like a father among his children."

Marquis de Lafayette, who had left the country as a wealthy youth, returned forty-five years later as an impoverished old man. Everywhere he went he received roaring ovations, grateful gifts of land and gold. This portrait, which is now in City Hall, was painted by Samuel Finley Breese Morse.

When Andrew Jackson arrived at Castle Garden on June 11, 1833, he was mobbed by so many hero-worshipers that the bridge to shore collapsed and hundreds were thrown into the water. Fortunately, the tide was out at the time and the celebrants were all soon fished out of the water.

View of New York from Brooklyn Heights, 1836, shows the East River crowded with sailing vessels and steamships. In the distance, beyond the Hudson, are (LEFT TO RIGHT) *sparsely settled Jersey City, Hoboken, and Weehawken. Above the woman on the balcony is St. Paul's steeple and Holt's Hotel on Fulton Street.*

striking off and passing out copies of an ode written especially for the occasion. After a brilliant fireworks display that night, a sumptuous dinner, and a ball, the celebration—the most elaborate and imposing held up to that time in New York—came to an end. The city fathers then sent to Buffalo "a superb keg containing water of the Atlantic." It bore the city's coat of arms painted in bright colors, over which were the words, in gold leaf, "Neptune's return to Pan." Fifty-one gold medals, designed and cast to commemorate the event, were presented to the crowned heads of Europe and eminent men in America. John Adams and Thomas Jefferson, both of whom lived until the following Fourth of July, accepted theirs with words of praise for New York's achievement in completing what many had thought impossible—the magnificent Erie Canal.

Another celebration had been held the year before when the seventy-seven-year-old Marquis de Lafayette visited the United States as the guest of the government. The slight, bent Frenchman wept at the unexpected ovation he received in New York. Bells rang for an hour and business and traffic were suspended as almost everyone in the city turned out to meet him. There were parades, illuminations, receptions, gifts, dinners, and even a balloon ascension. He then left on a tour of the country which was a continuous triumphal procession. Congress voted the impoverished Marquis two hundred thousand dollars and a grant of land. Since several states and cities also voted him various sums of money, Lafayette, who had fought so valiantly for the American people, was able to live out the last ten years of his life in comfort.

In June, 1833, President Andrew Jackson arrived in New York, landing at Castle Garden, where he mounted a horse and crossed the bridge which then linked the former fort with the mainland. So great was the crowd that, as the people raced after Jackson, the bridge collapsed, throwing everyone into the water. Fortunately it was low tide, and no one was drowned. Broadway, from the Battery to City Hall,

In this Nathaniel Currier print of Broadway, City Hall Park is at the left and the Astor House at the right. St. Paul's is in the center, facing the American Museum. Five blocks south is the spire of Trinity Church. Although Currier did not depict it, this block was the most congested, traffic-jammed street in the city.

A closer view of Trinity in the 1830's, looking south on Broadway from Liberty Street. Omnibus stands in front of the City Hotel; the cupola beyond Trinity is atop Grace Church. Omitted from this scene are the scavenging pigs (estimated to number twenty thousand) which roamed the city and inspired Charles Dickens' satire.

The first railroad chartered in the United States was the forerunner of the New York Central. Authorized by the New York Legislature in 1826, it opened regular service between Albany and Schenectady along the Mohawk and Hudson rivers on September 24, 1831. The locomotive, the DE WITT CLINTON, *made the seventeen-mile trip in one hour and forty-five minutes.*

was a solid mass of men, women, and children, cheering the old warrior with wild enthusiasm, for he was even more popular with the people than Washington had been.

Jackson was also popular in Wall Street because he had broken the power of the second Bank of the United States by refusing to renew its charter and transferring the Federal accounts to other institutions, which were immediately labeled "pet banks." The Bank of the United States was controlled by Nicholas Biddle, a wealthy, aristocratic Philadelphian, who was no match for Jackson and his tough Democratic friends in the White House. On the whole, Biddle had run an efficient national bank after he became its President in 1822 at the age of thirty-seven, although it was felt that he had concentrated too much of the money and the money power of the country in Philadelphia. His bitter feud with Jackson and the administration led to his undoing. In the end, after a series of financial manipulations, the bank went under. Biddle lost his fortune, was indicted, and only escaped a prison term by a technicality of law.

The banks and money managers of Wall Street benefited by Biddle's downfall, and new banking institutions suddenly sprang up throughout the country, many of them unreliable and undercapitalized. A flood of bank notes issued by these institutions and backed by little or no hard cash soon poured into circulation. For the next thirty years a form of financial anarchy plagued the land. It took an expert to know what percentage of face value these bank notes were actually worth, and a transaction depended not only on the price agreed upon, but on what kind of bank notes were involved. To add another complication, a great many of these notes were counterfeit.

The New York branch of the Bank of the United States, erected in 1824, was one of the most graceful buildings on Wall Street. After the failure of the bank in 1836, the building became the Government Assay Office and, for a time, also housed the Sub-Treasury. Next door, on the corner where Federal Hall had stood, were three business buildings. The government purchased the land, tore down the structures, and began to erect the half-million-dollar Custom House, which was completed in 1838.

Castle Garden was the great auditorium of the city, its six thousand seats making it the nation's largest entertainment center, and the Battery was the favorite promenade of the town. Despite the fact that hotels and business buildings were replacing the fine mansions of lower Broadway, it was still a fashionable section, although more people continued to move up to the neighborhood of City Hall Park. Others began to build as far north as the former Potter's Field, now known as Washington Square, after Cornelius Vanderbilt erected a home there.

The New York branch of the second Bank of the United States on Wall Street, completed in 1824, became the United States Assay Office in 1836. When it was taken down in 1914, the Tuckahoe marble front was preserved and is now the façade of the Metropolitan Museum of Art's American Wing.

Broadway was illuminated by gaslight in 1825, and the shops and stores were rather sharply divided both in price and quality. The east side of the street, which had been almost a slum in the Dutch days, was known as the "shilling" side, while the better, west side was referred to as the "dollar" side. Marble was being introduced more widely as a building material, but there was such a prejudice against its use and so few craftsmen capable of handling it that, in order to get an artisan to work on the construction of the American Museum across the street from St. Paul's, the contractor had to pull strings to have a convict released from Sing Sing. The block on Broadway where the American Museum faced St. Paul's was the most traffic-congested street in town, and there were times when it seemed as if all the Broadway stages or omnibuses in the city were trying to squeeze through this one block at the same time. In 1832 the first horse-drawn streetcar company, the Fourth Avenue Line, began making trips uptown from Prince Street. That year, however, after having discovered that the epidemics of yellow fever could be checked by strict quarantine, New York was struck by a serious outbreak of Asiatic cholera.

Wall Street was not only the center of the financial district, but also the gaudy Times Square of that day. A spectacular demonstration of a new fire extinguisher was held in public when a small building was set ablaze and promptly saved from the consuming flames before a thousand admiring witnesses. The inventor of a new locking mechanism, Dr. Solomon Andrews, chained an iron chest containing one thousand dollars to a lamppost and announced that anyone who could pick his lock was welcome to the money. For a month the most skillful safecrackers and the best local locksmiths tried to open Andrews' key-operated combination lock without success. Impressed by this promotional stunt, many banks installed Andrews' locks on their safes and the doctor made a profit of thirty thousand dollars on his patent before the invention of nitroglycerin thirty years later enabled safecrackers to operate profitably again.

In those days Wall Street resounded with the cries of peddlers hawking their wares: "Fine Ripe Strawberries!" "Cat Tails, Cat Tails, to make Beds Going!" "Here's white sand, choice sand, here's your lily white sand, here's your ROCKAWAY beach sand!" "Butter Mil-leck!" "Here's your beauties of Oysters, here's your fine, fat, salt Oysters!" The little "Hot Corn" girl was also to be heard as she moved up and down the street, just as today the "Hot Pretzel" man and the "Genuine Imitation Pearl" peddler announce their bargains along the same sawed-off boulevard.

Another cry first heard in Wall Street about 1833 was that of boys shouting the sensations of the day as they sold their newspapers. Many of the New York publications were born in the vicinity of Wall Street. James Gordon Bennett founded the *Herald* as a penny paper in the basement of 20 Wall Street in 1835. Horace Greeley and two partners attempted to issue a modest penny paper in January, 1833, but it lived only three weeks. The first successful news sheet to sell for one cent was the *Sun*, which Benjamin H. Day started in September, 1833. It was Day who first used boys to hawk his journal in the streets, for until then newspapers were delivered directly to subscribers or purchased at newsstands and at the papers' offices. The *Sun*, a four-page, three-column sheet nine inches deep, with no editorials, no opinions, and no stock-market reports, achieved a circulation of eight

The first fine office building on Wall Street was the graceful, white marble Merchants Exchange, which was finished in 1827. The New York Stock and Exchange Board moved into Room 43 and paid an annual rental of $500.

The oval hall of the Merchants Exchange had a dome forty-five feet above the floor and an Ionic portico twenty-seven feet high. The Hamilton statue did not appear in the original engraving of 1830 on which this print was based, since it was not unveiled until March 28, 1835. In preparing this engraving, two men were blocked out and the statue of Hamilton was inserted.

thousand within two years, making it the most popular paper in the city. Its price remained one cent for a period of thirty years.

Bennett had made a scientific study of the newspaper business and set about improving it with the *Herald*. Independent in politics, it was vigorous and startling in its choice, gathering, and reporting of the news. Although eleven large or "sixpenny sheets" were published daily, Bennett made good his boast that his paper would become the greatest, the best, and most profitable that had appeared up to that time in America.

The *Journal of Commerce*, started in 1827, soon began sending schooners out to sea to intercept New York-bound ships, get the latest news from abroad, and scurry back to the city to report. In 1833 it established a horse-express to Philadelphia. The other papers followed suit. Greeley had better luck with his *Tribune* (now combined with Bennett's *Herald*), which he launched in 1841. The oldest paper still being published is the *Post*, which William Coleman began editing in 1801 as a Federalist organ. One feature of the paper was that it carried the prices of stocks on its front page. The great Federalist, Alexander Hamilton, was one of the paper's founders and its legal adviser. Curiously, it is today the only New York newspaper that generally represents the viewpoint of the Democratic party.

For the next fifty years an average of three new papers a year were started in New York and the mortality rate was overwhelming. The Wall Street neighborhood served as headquarters for most of them, but in the 1840's they began to drift a bit northward to Park Row where they remained for some five decades before scattering farther uptown. The area was also the home of the magazines of the period and the print shop of the Harper brothers, James, John, Joseph, and Fletcher, grew into a magazine and book-publishing colossus at 22 Cliff Street, near Fulton.

Beginning with the postwar boom, goods which arrived by ship, unless consigned directly to a business house, were sold at auction. Both sides of Wall Street, near the Coffee House Slip, were lined with auction rooms where the merchants and other buyers would inspect the day's offerings. Among those who strolled daily along Auctioneer's Row were men whose names are still a part of the business life of the city today. In 1818 the Brooks brothers founded their clothing store on Catharine Street, opposite the

Model of Robert Ball Hughes' statue of Alexander Hamilton which stood in the rotunda of the first Merchants Exchange.

Fish Market. Samuel Lord and George Washington Taylor also started on Catharine Street, in 1825. Messrs. Arnold and Constable began doing business together two years later. Peter Cooper, merchant, inventor, and benefactor, was then, and for fifty years afterward, the first citizen of New York. He made a fortune in the glue business, built the first American locomotive, the *Tom Thumb*, and was so universally respected that when he drove through the town in his open carriage, even the profane, hardbitten Broadway stage drivers respectfully gave him the right of way.

The Merchants Exchange, with its graceful, newly installed statue of Alexander Hamilton in the rotunda, had been in existence less than a decade when, on the bitterly cold night of December 16, 1835, fire broke out across the street on Exchange Place. Although the volunteer fire departments responded at once, the only water available was from the East River, but the hoses quickly froze in the seventeen-degree-below-zero weather. A gale wind drove the flames from building to building, the intense heat melting copper roofs and iron shutters. Valiant attempts were made to rescue the Hamilton statue in the exchange, but the roof caved in and the supposedly fireproof marble structure lit up the city with its blaze.

"Wall after wall was heard tumbling like an avalanche," Mrs. Lamb wrote in her history of the city. "Fiery tongues of flame leaped from roofs and windows along whole streets, and seemed to be making angry dashes at each other. The water of the bay looked like a vast sea of blood. The bells rang for a while and then ceased. Both sides of Pearl Street and Hanover Square were at the same instant in the jaws of the hungry monster."

Spreading wildly, the conflagration reached almost to Broad Street on the north, to Coenties Slip and South Street, the water's edge, on the south and east. The fire was reported in newspapers of the time to have lit up the sky so that it was visible as far away as Philadelphia. It raged until noon of the following day and burned out the principal importers and exporters of the city. Nearly thirteen acres and seven hundred buildings were laid waste. The wholesale district, the Garden Street (Exchange Place) Church, and many other landmarks were destroyed. The loss was between sixteen and twenty million dollars—equivalent to eighty million dollars today. More of the city would have burned had not Charles King volunteered to row across to the Navy Yard for a supply of powder. He returned with a detachment of marines and sailors, and at two in the morning they blew up a number of buildings in the path of the fire and arrested its progress. The fire not only ruined the business houses which were burned out,

The great fire of 1835 as seen from the Bank of America at Wall and William streets. Starting at 9:00 P.M. on December 16, it raged for fifteen hours, destroying about \$20 million in property. Almost 700 buildings on thirteen acres lying south of Wall, east of Broad, and west of South Street were demolished.

The smoking lower end of Manhattan (RIGHT) *as seen at noon, December 17, from Brooklyn Heights (Governor's Island is at left center). This painting has been attributed to Nicolino V. Calyo, who also painted the preceding picture and the view of the ruins at bottom of facing page. The fire was one of Calyo's favorite subjects.*

While the fire still smoldered, merchants had their safes hauled to Hanover Square, where they were opened and their contents examined. The store of Verner, Saloman, and Benson, in the center of the burned-out area, remained unscorched. The firm was promptly named the modern Shadrach, Meshach, and Abednego.

View of the ruins from Exchange Place, looking north and west. South Dutch Church (LEFT) *and the Merchants Exchange* (CENTER) *resisted the flames for four hours. However, all attempts to save the Hamilton statue failed and it was destroyed. Within a year the area was rebuilt, but no trace of the old Dutch houses was left.*

During 1836, Aaron Burr, now a rather obscure lawyer, died at the age of eighty after outliving almost every other figure of the Revolutionary and Federal periods.

but bankrupted all of the New York fire-insurance companies.

Yet this did not hold back Wall Street for long. Within two years the burned-out areas were rebuilt and the last remaining traces of the Dutch town were gone.

On the day after the fire, the members of the Board of the Stock Exchange met and voted to suspend all operations for that week. They appointed a committee to secure temporary quarters, and two days later a room was engaged at Howard's Hotel, 8 Broad Street, for three dollars a day. This was the first time that the exchange met on the property it later acquired as part of the present Stock Exchange site. That day the Board voted "a donation of one hundred dollars, together with the thanks of the Board, to J. R. Mount, a Watchman, who assisted in removing and taking care of the Iron Chest," which presumably contained the records of the exchange. On December 23, the brokers moved again, to the back room of the basement story in John Warren's building, rented from a Mr. Pepoon at the rate of $750 a year, with both parties obliged to give ten days' notice of cancellation.

The next year the Board moved to 43 Wall where speculation in railway shares, as well as those of banks and trust companies, started to increase. State bank currencies were at an inflated level and land values boomed as well. These elements, together with the failure of the Bank of the United States and Jackson's monetary policies, brought on the Panic of 1837, which was marked by a dizzying drop in prices, business paralysis, general suspension of specie payments by banks (the refusal to give gold and silver in return for their own currency), and many business bankruptcies. One Stock Exchange firm failed with liabilities of five million dollars. Many states either repudiated their debts or defaulted on interest payments, and for a while state bonds and bank shares were rated as very hazardous investments. By comparison, railroad stocks were considered both practical and solid.

In this period emerged the first great stock-market operator, Jacob Little, the son of a Newburyport shipbuilder, who came to New York in 1835. For the next twenty years he was the great name in Wall Street, making and losing fortunes, sometimes overnight. Had he started in 1861, he might have been a great builder, like Cornelius Vanderbilt. But the crash of 1837 turned him into a bear and he amassed a fortune of two million dollars by 1846 through his short-selling techniques. Then he attempted a corner in Norwich and Worcester Railroad and lost a million. Little was a nervous perfectionist who personally attended to every detail in the coups he managed to arrange. He was, according to all chroniclers, kind, magnanimous, honorable, and a genius in market maneuvers. Stocks were his life, but he died leaving very little money.

In 1836, at the age of eighty and almost penniless, Aaron Burr died on Staten Island. Even in his last years he scandalized the proper, staid citizens of New York in 1833 by marrying one of the richest widows in America—Madam Betsy Bowen Jumel—when he was seventy-seven years old. A year later she divorced him on charges of infidelity.

7

National Influence

THE INNATE vigor of the rapidly expanding United States revived business and pumped merchandise and money into and out of New York. First the city and then the rest of the country recovered from the temporary economic paralysis brought on by the Panic of 1837. The lower part of Manhattan Island, which had been a place of craggy hills and granite outcroppings, was by now flattened out. There were no longer any bogs and swamps to breed the mosquitoes that had spread the frequent deadly epidemics of former years. But it took another century, punctuated by a dozen more panics, before the economic bogs and swamps and the havoc they spread were finally eliminated.

New York had pushed ahead of Philadelphia by this time, and was now the first city in America, not only in population but as the center of banking, commerce, and speculation. The Stock Exchange, which had been driven out of the Merchants Exchange building by the fire of 1835, was still at 43 Wall in one of the Jauncey Court buildings. These were originally occupied by an English gentleman who lived in great style, the building used by the Board of Brokers having been his stable and the trading room formerly the hayloft. Here they continued to meet for six years.

In 1840 a motion was made to take advantage of depressed real-estate prices and use the twenty-thousand-dollar surplus the Board had accumulated to purchase property on Wall Street for an exchange of its own. However, this proposal was rejected by the membership and, in 1842, the brokers moved into the magnificent new second Merchants Exchange building which covered the whole block from William to Hanover streets on Wall and Exchange Place. This is the same building, with four stories added to the top, now occupied by the First National City Bank. Principal quarters for the stockbrokers was the large hall over the Reading Room, with windows looking out upon William Street. A rival organization, called The Bourse, or New Board, also met in the same building, but like all of the competing organizations except the Curb Exchange, it did not last long. "The memorable crash of that period broke more than two-thirds of its members," said a chronicler in 1848, "and it soon sunk into compara-

The second Merchants Exchange, completed in 1842, has massive columns of blue Massachusetts granite, and occupies the entire block from Wall to Exchange and William to Hanover. The Stock Exchange was located here until 1854, as was the short-lived New Board or "Bourse."

tive insignificance from which it has never recovered. It numbers at present but fifteen or twenty members and they are mostly small potatoes with small means." Shortly afterward most of the New Board members joined the older organization and The Bourse ceased to exist. In those days expenses of the Stock Exchange ran to about ten thousand dollars a year, with receipts averaging at least a thousand dollars higher. Now expenses are over fifty thousand dollars each working day.

In 1854 the brokers moved to the top floor of the Corn Exchange building at William and Beaver streets, but remained there only until 1856, leaving because of the intolerable heat in the summers. It was while they occupied these quarters that the rules of the Board were changed to include annual dues of fifty dollars and less stringent admission regulations, the blackballs necessary to exclude new members being raised from three to five. Also, the presidency became a position of honor and a vice-president, with an annual salary of twenty-five hundred dollars, was elected to announce the issues at the First Board (or Morning Call). A second vice-president was also chosen to conduct the Second Board (or Afternoon Call). His annual salary was fifteen hundred dollars. Both were forbidden to deal in stocks while presiding.

From 1856 until the brokers moved into their own building at the close of the Civil War, the business of the Stock Exchange was conducted at Lord's Court. The exchange was expanding. Here the board room was sixty by forty feet, each member had his regular seat, and the public was barred from all sessions. Lord's Court was a rabbit-warren of buildings which could be reached from 25 William Street, 53 Beaver Street, or 50 Exchange Place. There were so many intricate passages in the route from the street to the exchange that a stranger required a guide to reach it.

In 1838, the new Custom House—which became

the Sub-Treasury twenty-five years later and has been known since 1939 as Federal Hall—was completed and opened on the site at Wall and Broad of the old City-Federal Hall. A replica of an ancient Greek temple, the building was designed to reflect the majesty and permanence of government. For its day it was a huge and grandiose structure, costing over a half million dollars. The huge blocks of marble for the columns were the wonders of the time and required forty yoke of oxen each to draw them from boats on the East River to the building site.

The position of Collector of the Port of New York was one of honor and responsibility. Samuel Swartwout was appointed to the post by President Jackson in 1830. A huge man of amiable countenance, he had been closely associated with Aaron Burr and had been successful for a while in converting the swamps east of Newark into industrial property. While in Europe on private business in 1838, a huge discrepancy (in excess of a million dollars) was discovered in the Custom House accounts. Swartwout remained in Europe, but surrendered all of his assets to the government to cover the loss, although the crime was said to have been committed by subordinates. When he returned to the United States, he was not prosecuted, but for many years afterward every man caught embezzling funds in New York was called a "Swartwouter."

Jackson's edict, ruling that purchasers of public lands must pay for them in hard coin, led to the creation of the Sub-Treasuries which received and stored the money in their vaults. The New York branch was by far the most important, doing more business than all of the others together. The first Assistant Treasurer of the United States for New York, William C. Bouck, took office in 1846. Until 1863 the Sub-Treasury shared quarters with the Assay Office in the former United States Bank building, next door to the Custom House. Although the Sub-Treasury system at first encountered great opposition from the banks, it soon took the place of an official government bank. As the United States borrowed

In the "large hall over the Reading Room," the Old Board convened daily for calling of the stocks by the President and the bidding and asking of seventy-five members. Exchange expenses were $10,000 a year, raised half by admission of new members at $400 each and half by levying fines.

Gold bricks, made on Wall Street in the United States Assay Office, were about twice the size shown here and worth around $5,500.

In the Sub-Treasury, occupying the same building as the Assay Office, expert gold tellers, Birdsall (LEFT) *and John Cisco, Jr., had sensitive ears and fingers and could instantly detect counterfeit gold coins.*

money from individuals, giving gold certificates in exchange, the Sub-Treasury acted as a reservoir which accumulated gold in times of expansion and disbursed it when money became tight.

One of the most annoying problems confronting the Sub-Treasuries was that of counterfeit coins, the manufacture of which was once a thriving industry. But the two tellers at the Sub-Treasury in New York, considered the most expert in the country, boasted that they had never accepted a single disemboweled, spurious, or sweated coin. The spurious pieces were made of some inferior metal and could be detected by the imperfect ringing sound they produced when bounced on a marble counter. There were two methods of disemboweling a coin; it could be sawed in half and the halves scooped out, filled with base metal, and then soldered together again, or a hole could be bored along the edge, the gold hollowed out, and the cavity filled with lead. Using either of these methods, coin disembowelers extracted as much as 60 per cent of the gold content of the money that passed through their hands. Sweating was simply filing down the face or the edges of a coin and then remilling it, saving the gold dust thus obtained. But the Sub-Treasury counting-house men apparently never failed to reject false coins, although

Croton water was introduced with an appropriate New York celebration and parade on October 14, 1842. As the procession passed each square and park, a fountain, such as this one at City Hall, burst into play.

Panoramic view of 1850 shows built-up lower Manhattan (city population, 515,547). To the right of the Battery are Staten Island Ferry, Barge Office, and sailing ships; to the left, Castle Garden and steamships; at Wall Street: the third Trinity Church, Custom House, and Merchants Exchange.

several hundred thousand dollars' worth passed through their hands every day.

"The bulk of the bullion is in the shape of 'bricks,'" reported a writer in *Harper's Weekly* in 1859. "These are solid pieces of metal in the form of small oblong blocks . . . bricks are made of various sizes, down as low, we believe, as $200. These last bricks, which one can take between the finger and thumb and stow away as conveniently as a toothpick in the waistcoat pocket, ought to be more generally used than they are by travellers."

Although the small gold ingots never became popular, the larger bricks were soon copied extensively, if not expensively, and became the stock-in-trade of those fast-talking gentlemen who went about the country disseminating financial knowledge and experience in the rural areas.

The fire of 1835 had pointed up the pressing need for an adequate water supply for the city, whose population had increased to a quarter of a million, and a plan, more ambitious than that of the Roman Aqueduct, was initiated. This involved the creation

On the night of July 19, 1845, fire and explosion in a grocery warehouse on Broad Street blew volunteer fireman Francis Hart, Jr., seen on section of roof (CENTER), *across the street. Miraculously, he was not seriously hurt, but several lives were lost and seventeen stores were blown up, Engine 22 destroyed.*

Bowling Green at the height of the fire. Heroic volunteer firemen, pumping water from the pool of controversial "rip-rap style" fountain, fought bravely to stem the blaze, but did not succeed until more than three hundred buildings were destroyed. This engraving and preceding one were made from colored lithographs by Nathaniel Currier, who amazed the public by the speed with which he produced prints.

of a five-mile-long lake in the Croton hills, forty-five miles from New York, and a complicated system of conduits to bring the water to the city. Completion of the aqueduct required digging sixteen tunnels through rock; the erection of an arch at Sing Sing with an eighty-eight-foot span, seventy feet high; the crossing of twenty-five streams; construction of High Bridge over the Harlem River; building walls for two reservoirs in what was to become Central Park; and the laying down of four hundred miles of iron mains. The Croton Aqueduct took twelve years to build and had the capacity to deliver 115 million gallons of water a day. When the system was at last completed and in operation the fire-insurance companies announced that rates would be cut drastically.

As usual, Manhattan celebrated the arrival of the water from the Croton basin with a military and civic parade. This one, seven miles long, outshone both the great Federal Pageant of 1788 and the Erie Canal celebration in 1825 for sheer grandeur of display. As the parade passed the parks and squares of the city, cascades and silver sprays of water burst forth from beautiful fountains. When the marchers assembled at City Hall Park for the inevitable speechmaking that concluded New York's celebrations, members of the Sacred Music Society stood before the gushing waters of the park fountain and raised their voices in an ode prepared for the occasion by the popular songwriter and editor, George P. Morris:

> Water leaps as if delighted,
> While her conquered foes retire!
> Pale contagion flies affrighted
> With the baffled demon Fire!
> Water shouts a glad hosanna!
> Bubbles up the earth to bless!
> Cheers it like the precious manna
> In the barren wilderness.

But the Croton water was of little avail against the explosion and fire that wiped out the wholesale and part of the financial district around Broad Street on the extremely hot night of July 19, 1845. The damage was only a third of that caused by the previous conflagration in 1835, but the work of the valiant volunteer firemen did not check the blaze until 345 buildings had gone up in smoke.

George Templeton Strong, then a fledgling Wall Street lawyer who lived on Greenwich Street west of Trinity, wrote in his diary that he was awakened at 3:30 A.M. by a series of explosions that shook the house like an earthquake and must have blown him out of bed. To the east, he could see "red flames which made the moon look pale." As he hurried toward his office, "everything in New Street as I looked down from Wall seemed withering away and melting down in absolute heat . . . all Broad Street on both sides from about Number 20 down was one grand solid substantial flame, most glorious and terrible to look at . . . the engines were playing on the West side of Broadway where the house fronts were hissing hot already."

One of the casualties of the fire was the fountain at Bowling Green, a loss not mourned by the more esthetic members of the community. Edgar Allan Poe, writing in the *Columbia Spy* a year before, labeled it an absurdity. "The whole has much the air of a small country jail in a hard thunder shower."

The annexation of Texas was the major political issue in the presidential campaign of 1844, and when James K. Polk, the Democratic candidate emerged the victor, the eight-year-old Republic was added to the Union. This upset the balance between free and slave states and also angered Mexico, which was involved in a border quarrel with Texas. General Zachary Taylor, leading an army of more than three thousand troops, was ordered to the disputed border territory. When Mexican troops arrived to occupy the same space, the Mexican War began. This was in April, 1846, and "Old Rough and Ready" Taylor and "Old Fuss and Feathers" Winfield Scott proceeded to invade the country. A number of United States victories brought Mexico to its knees. Philip Kearny, a dashing New York officer, was the first man to enter the city of Mexico, losing his left arm in the fight at the San Antonio Gate. His uncle, Stephen Watts Kearny, beat the Mexicans in California, where, on March 1, 1847, he established a provincial government with himself as first Governor. Another New Yorker who settled early in California was Leland Stanford, the railroad builder, who served as Governor of the state from 1861 to 1863. By the terms of the Treaty of Guadalupe Hidalgo, signed in February, 1848, all of New Mexico and California was ceded to the United States. In the same month, gold was discovered at Sutter's Fort and the Rush was on. In New York the yellow metal was a magnet which drew men away from their jobs and businesses to undertake the difficult

Sunday, April 22, 1838, marked the completion of the first all-steam voyage from Europe to New York. The vessel was the 178-foot-long English packet SIRIUS *of Dublin, which made crossing from Cork in 16½ days. This illustration is reproduced from a souvenir silk handkerchief painted by Napoleon Sarony.*

On Monday, less than twenty-four hours later, New Yorkers at the Battery and Castle Garden hailed the arrival of the GREAT WESTERN *which completed the voyage in fifteen days from England. The figures in the foreground resemble characters taken from the novels of Dickens.*

and hazardous journey to the fabled West across the continent, around Cape Horn, or over the Isthmus of Nicaragua or Panama. Thousands of fathers, husbands, sons, and brothers kissed their families goodbye and departed by covered wagon, clipper ship, or one of the steamers operated by Commodore Vanderbilt's Accessory Transit Company.

Steam transportation was forging ahead with great

rapidity. The first all-steam vessel to cross the Atlantic had been the English packet *Sirius* of Dublin which arrived in New York harbor from Cork on April 22, 1838, to be followed one day later by the *Great Western* from Bristol. Although the American ship *Savannah*, which utilized both sail and steam, had made the crossing twenty years before, the *Sirius* and the *Great Western* were the first to complete the Atlantic voyage under steam power alone. Ocean-going steamships continued to improve in performance and were built even larger, but they did not crowd sail off the seas for another half century, principally because of the development of a type of vessel which, for sheer grace and beauty, has never been surpassed—the clipper ship.

After the original clipper, the *Ann McKim*, was built in Baltimore in 1832, New York rapidly became the headquarters and Atlantic terminus of the majority of these ocean greyhounds. The most famous and fastest was the *Flying Cloud*, owned by the New York firm of Grinnell, Minturn and Company. She made the fifteen-thousand-mile run from New York to the Golden Gate in eighty-nine days, during which she logged 374 miles in twenty-four hours, the fastest day's run under sail or steam up to that time. Designed primarily for use in the China tea trade, the clippers were built for speed because every day saved on the voyage was an advantage, since the tea tended to deteriorate during the ocean trip. After the discovery of gold in California, the clippers were assured of passengers and freight at the highest rates for half the journey out and back by breaking their voyages at San Francisco.

While steam vessels were proving practical, swifter sailing ships were being built for the China tea trade, such as the famous clipper FLYING CLOUD, *which broke all previous records on a run from New York to San Francisco.*

The first street railway in the world was the New York and Harlem Line, which was chartered in 1831 and began operations the following year by running from Prince Street to the Harlem Bridge. Drawn by horses, the first cars resembled double stagecoaches on rails, with three compartments to each, the whole balanced or "sprung" on leather straps. By 1839 steam cars were installed and the lower terminus had been moved southward to Tryon Row, where the present Municipal building stands.

Another and most far-reaching invention was the telegraph, developed by one of Manhattan's most talented residents—Samuel Finley Breese Morse, a celebrated artist, founder and first President of the National Academy of Design, scientist, and professor at New York University. After he perfected his electromagnetic transmitting and recording apparatus, it took six years before he could get a thirty-thousand-dollar appropriation from Congress to install telegraphic connections between Washington and Baltimore. The first line was enclosed in lead pipes and buried in a trench. After ten miles of trench, the pipes were abandoned and the wires were strung aloft from poles. On May, 24, 1844, the first successful telegraph system was completed, and the first message tapping out the words "What hath God wrought!" was sent and received.

The telegraph was the first of four inventions which were to assure the ascendant destiny of Wall Street. By providing a means of swift communication, it kept the securities market centralized in New

The railroad reached the Wall Street district when the New York and Harlem built the first terminal of the road at Tryon Row in 1839. The station was located where the south portion of the Municipal building now stands. The railroad was another early link in the chain of small lines which became the New York Central.

The first Otis elevator was displayed at the Crystal Palace Exposition in 1853 by Elisha Otis, who, after being hoisted to the ceiling, had the rope cut and descended safely.

The original typewriting machine, which won a gold medal at the American Institute Fair in 1856, was intended by its inventor, Alfred Ely Beach, to print embossed letters for the use of the blind.

This photograph of Mathew Brady shows the slight, five-foot, six-inch photographer as a young man. Brady was a bundle of energy, but his eyes were weak and he required assistants to help him focus his camera.

Samuel F. B. Morse, painter, scientist, and inventor, shown with his early telegraph instrument. The father of American photography, Morse taught the technique to Mathew Brady, who took this fine portrait.

York. The second invention was the typewriter of Christopher Sholes which made it possible for a comparatively small number of girls to handle correspondence that formerly engaged the full time and energy of armies of male clerks. The adding machine, invented by William Seward Burroughs, eliminated another mass of male bookkeepers and considerably speeded the computations and calculations so vital to the business of Wall Street. The fourth invention, which kept Wall Street from spreading out all over Manhattan Island, was Elisha Otis' safety elevator, a device that permitted buildings to rise vertically and soar to previously undreamed-of heights.

Morse also introduced another invention to the United States — the daguerreotype, the first truly effective photographic process. Invented in France by Louis Jacques Daguerre (who hated to have his own picture taken), the daguerreotype was brought to this country by the artist-inventor on September 20, 1839, after one of his fruitless attempts to interest foreign governments in his telegraph. It created an immediate sensation in America.

A young portrait artist named Mathew Brady, who left Saratoga and painted his way to New York, met Morse that year, but instead of enrolling in a painting class, joined one devoted to learning the daguerreotype process. Brady made himself an expert in all of the ramifications of the process, from lenses to chemicals, and his sense of pictorial composition and drama lent distinction to his work. Starting in 1841, Brady operated a factory which manufactured fancy leather cases for mounting daguerreotypes, earning enough money to open a portrait studio on Chambers Street. This venture was so successful that he was able to move to a grand salon with a skylight studio at Fulton and Broadway, across the street from St. Paul's, and cater-corner to Mr. Phineas T. Barnum's American Museum. Brady's work was so brilliant that he found it easy to persuade the celebrities of the period to sit for him, thus collecting a gallery of notable photographs.

From aged John Quincy Adams who sat for him in 1847 to William McKinley, Brady took pictures of all the presidents and many government officials.

In 1844, at the age of twenty-one, Brady opened his studio at Broadway and Fulton and began photographing many celebrities. In 1853 he opened his new gallery further up on Broadway. Luxuriously decorated with satin draperies, gold paper, and velvet tapestry carpet, its walls were covered with photographs of presidents, generals, statesmen, and visiting royalty.

His salon, which he advertised in the newspapers, came to be one of the leading sight-seeing objectives in New York. Of course, the visitors frequently remained at the establishment to have their own pictures taken. Brady not only photographed politicians and generals, but also leading professional people, actors and actresses, opera stars, and even champion chess players. Aside from the camera, his most important piece of equipment was the head clamp which held his subjects rigidly immobilized. George Templeton Strong, who had himself daguerreotyped, recorded that he had to remain frozen for two minutes and found the experience "very boring."

When he abandoned the daguerreotype in favor of the wet-plate process known as ambrotype, he began to photograph life-sized heads, often colored by artists on his staff, which were sold for more than the oil paintings of the day. For the ordinary visitor with two dollars in his pocket, the Brady staff would turn out popular *cartes de visite* portraits. From Fulton Street, Brady moved up Broadway, first to 359, over Thompson's Saloon, where a huge model of a camera served as a sign, and then to the corner of Tenth Street where he photographed the Prince of Wales during his visit to this country.

"One photograph that Brady himself took on February 27, 1860, changed the entire course of his life," wrote Peter Pollack in *The Picture History of Photography*. "Abraham Lincoln said of this picture two years later, 'Brady and the Cooper Union speech made me President of the United States.' Brady's portrait of the tall, unbearded lawyer introduced Lincoln, through the illustrated press and Currier and Ives prints, as a man of profound dignity and inner strength. This was only the first of many sittings Lincoln was to give Brady."

A dedicated man, Brady became obsessed with the idea of photographing the Civil War. Armed with permits to accompany the Union troops, he abandoned his profitable business and, aided by a corps of assistants, covered the battlefields with the cumbersome cameras of the period and darkrooms set up in horse-drawn vehicles which were called "What-Is-It?" wagons by the soldiers. Brady was the first American combat photographer, but his achievement led to his bankruptcy, for he photographed every aspect of the entire war without official help or funds of any kind. By the time he returned to New York to resume his business, he was unable to regain his eminence as a leading portrait photographer. Nevertheless, the magnificent pictorial record of the Civil War which he left is a monument to Brady that towers over any he could have possibly earned as a fashionable photographer.

Another famous graphic enterprise that had its start in lower Manhattan was the firm of N. Currier which was opened at 1 Wall Street in 1835 by handsome, twenty-two-year-old Nathaniel Currier, whose first two lithographs were "The Ruins of the Merchants Exchange" and "The Fire of New Orleans." Aloys Senefelder invented lithography in 1796 and discovered that the limestone tiles of Solenhofen in his native Bavaria made ideal printing plates. Within less than forty years Currier put lithography to its most widespread use, for it is generally acknowledged that he laid the basis for folk art and pictorial journalism in America. Recognizing the possibility of publishing lithographs about newsworthy subjects and people, he found a dramatic subject at hand almost as soon as he went into business. When the Merchants Exchange print came off the press hot on the heels of the great fire of 1835, the new era of pictorial reporting had begun.

Joined in 1852 by James Ives, who became a full partner five years later, the firm struck off pictures of every major event and disaster, all the most prominent and notorious people, the popular pastimes of the day, the most interesting scenic views, and recreations of historical events. In addition, there were comedy scenes—the most successful cartoons of their

New York, looking southeast from the steeple of St. Paul's, 1848. Brady's first "Daguerrian Miniature Gallery" is across Fulton Street. Barnum's Museum is at the corner of Ann; Genin the Hatter is the second door south. The print store of Nathaniel Currier was on Nassau Street to the right of the American flag at the rear of the Barnum building.

Nathaniel Currier popularized folk art by selling prints at wholesale for one or two cents each. Originals of the rarest of these lithographs sell now for thousands of dollars.

James Merritt Ives, who joined the firm in 1852, was related to Currier through marriage. Currier and Ives produced and distributed millions of prints from 1835 to 1894.

The front of Currier and Ives' shop at 115 Nassau Street at the time of President Grant's funeral (1885). Sales manager Daniel W. Logan, Sr., stands at the right.

time — and several series on sailing ships, railroad trains, family life, and firemen. The second Currier and Ives shop was located at 115 Nassau Street around the corner from Mathew Brady's studio. It remained at this address for forty-eight years, but around another corner, on Spruce Street, several hundred people were kept occupied in large lofts with the assembly-line job of coloring the prints.

When the Nassau Street store opened in the morning, a crowd of lithograph hucksters was already waiting to dash in and ransack the bins where the prints were stored. They bought them for one or two cents apiece and sold them everywhere in the United States for prices ranging from ten to twelve and a half cents each.

The firm prospered for many years because mass production enabled it to sell millions of colorful, inexpensive prints. On the other hand, Brady's daguerreotypes and photographs could not be reproduced until the process of photoengraving was invented near the end of the century. However, the Brady photographs served as the originals from which wood-engravings were made to be printed in the daily and weekly newspapers and books of the time. The credit line, "From a Daguerreotype by Brady," was the most familiar one encountered under an illustration for twenty-five years.

Walt Whitman, known then only as a former editor of the *Brooklyn Eagle*, had his *Leaves of Grass* privately published in 1855. Concerning these poems and their intimate link to the life of lower Manhattan, he wrote: "I suppose the critics will laugh heartily, but the influence of those Broadway omnibus jaunts and drivers and declamations and escapades undoubtedly enter'd into the gestation of 'Leaves of Grass.' " Lower Broadway, the pulsing, crowded artery of the city's heart, was described by Whitman in *Broadway Sights:*

> *Off and on for years, I knew and frequented Broadway — that noted avenue of New York's crowded and mixed humanity, and of so many notables. Here I saw, during those times, Andrew Jackson, Webster, Clay, Seward, Martin Van Buren, filibuster Walker, Kossuth, Fitz Greene Halleck, Bryant, the Prince of Wales, Charles Dickens, the first Japanese ambassadors, and lots of other celebrities of the time. Always something novel or inspiriting. . . . I remember seeing James Fenimore Cooper in a court-room in Chambers Street. . . . I also remember seeing Edgar A. Poe*

Happy part of a popular pair of Currier prints is entitled STOCKS UP.

Second of the pair is STOCKS DOWN. *These prints were issued in 1849 when the country at large was beginning to learn how to play the market. Speculator Jacob Little had changed the Stock Exchange from a dull trading mart to a battlefield for daring men.*

New York from Governor's Island in the 1840's. This Mathew Brady photograph, found in the National Archives and heretofore unpublished, shows sailing ships at the toe of Manhattan, spire of Trinity and dome of the Merchants Exchange above cabin of the barge in foreground.

An aquatint sketch that almost matches the view in Brady's photograph bears the caption: "New York. Taken from the Northwest angle of Fort Columbus, Governor's Island." Dated 1846, it is far more romantic than Brady's picture. Added are the parade ground, soldiers, and fishermen; it also depicts similar Trinity spire, Merchants Exchange dome, and poplars at right.

An early photograph of Wall Street, looking west from between Pearl and Hanover, shows Du Pont's Gunpowder office at lower right. The realism of the photograph contrasts sharply with the romanticized version below.

and having a short interview with him. . . . Poe was very cordial, in a quiet way, appear'd well in person, dress, &c. I have a distinct and pleasing remembrance of his looks, voice, manner and matter; very kindly and human, but subdued, perhaps a little jaded. . . . I once saw a bent, feeble but stout-built very old man, bearded, swathed in rich furs, with a great ermine cap on his head, led and assisted, almost carried, down the steps of his high front stoop and then lifted and tuck'd in a gorgeous sleigh, envelop'd in other furs, for a ride. The sleigh was drawn by as fine a team of horses as I ever saw. Well, I, a boy of perhaps 13 or 14, stopp'd, gazed long on the spectacle of that fur-swathed old man, surrounded by friends and servants, and the careful seating of him in the sleigh. . . . The old man, the subject of so much attention, I can almost see now. It was John Jacob Astor.

The great architectural addition to Broadway in this period was the third Trinity Church. Consecrated on May 21, 1846, it replaced the more graceful and delicately designed second Trinity, which was torn down in 1840 after the heavy snows of the previous winter had ruined its roof and caused the supporting columns to buckle. In his diary entry for June 2, 1839, when an attempt was being made to

Artist's view up Wall from William Street in 1850 makes the street three times as wide, level instead of sloping, smoothly paved rather than cobbled, lined with handsome structures, and peopled with pedestrians in elegant attire.

Photograph of the river end of Wall Street, east from Pearl, shows ferry to Brooklyn, masts of the REMORNE, *signs advertising sailings of the clippers* UNDAUNTED *and* ZOUAVE. *The office for Australia packets is at 108 Wall.*

overhaul the weakened edifice, George Templeton Strong wrote: "They ought to pull it down and build a big cathedral in its place, if only to sanctify Wall Street; a fine building on that situation would show to very great advantage. . . ."

This proved to be the case, for the new Trinity Church was an outstanding landmark, especially for ships which took their bearings from the 280-foot, five-inch spire, until it was completely engulfed by surrounding skyscrapers fifty years later. "Now," according to Charles Townsend Harris, "if you want to see Trinity Church, you have to get a search warrant." The builder of Trinity was Richard Upjohn, one of the foremost ecclesiastical architects of the nineteenth century, and Trinity is considered an outstanding example of his work. For this building, he set up a small glassworks on the grounds where the first stained glass in America was fabricated for the windows. The style of the church has been described as "English Perpendicular Gothic."

On March 10, 1846, the chimes were first rung at the new Trinity "much to the delight and astonishment of the giddy and excitable populace, who stood and stared at the church steeple with eyes and mouths in a state of dilation," as Strong wrote in his diary. Strong was a keen observer of the New York scene, and his descriptions of his contemporaries could be caustic and biting. He called Gouverneur

Artist's sketch of the same scene, viewed from street level instead of the third floor, depicts a much wider street, but the carts, barrels, and three-masters at both sides of the Wall Street Ferry building almost duplicate those in the photograph.

Morris Ogden "that dense, impenetrable and dangerous King of the Pachyderms," and referred to the Secretary of State and his family as "Hamilton Fish and his whole ichthyological collection." On March 16, 1849, he wrote: "Friday. Curious attempt to extort $50,000 from William B. Astor—as arduous an undertaking as extorting its hide and tallow from a flint. A genius in rascality, a Michael Angelo of swindlers, could have conceived so sublime an idea. . . ." Of *Jane Eyre*, he wrote: "Queer novel . . . not a book I *like* at all, but very full of cleverness and character." And about Thackeray's *Vanity Fair*: "Not a superior work of genius as some people call it, by any means, but a remarkable book written on a new principle—the exclusion of any sort of *idealism*—a novel without a hero." When he read a novel with four heroes, his comment was: "November 20, 1848, *Trois Mousquitaires*—amusing trash." Among his legal clients at the Wall Street office where he sometimes "did nothing all day but look sagacious" was Elizabeth Schuyler Hamilton, the widow of Alexander Hamilton. After she had called on him one day, his entry read: "I don't believe that old lady has the slightest intention of ever going to a better world: such a specimen of juvenile antediluvianism I never en-

This previously unpublished photograph of Broad Street north to the Custom House is from the Mathew Brady Collection at the Library of Congress. It was taken in the early 1850's from where the Stock Exchange now stands.

The same scene "drawn from nature and on stone" is by Robert Kerr, who was the architect of the Custom House. Note oyster stand at the Morgan corner, country Jake (LEFT), *and urchin smoking* (CENTER). *The sign carried by man* (RIGHT) *announces a concert of Ole Bull, celebrated Norwegian violinist.*

View up Nassau Street, other side of Wall from preceding scene, the Custom House (RIGHT) *and the Post Office* (CENTER). *The Delaware and Hudson Canal Company* (TOP LEFT) *had been listed as a railroad on the Stock Exchange since 1837.*

countered." However, Mrs. Hamilton did go to a better world, exactly six years and three days later.

In 1848, the year Karl Marx published his *Communist Manifesto*, a new word — millionaire — became current in Wall Street. Soon after, the sky above the city was often darkened by the soot and smoke produced by the burning of soft coal in homes and factories. Knox was making and selling men's hats. The Great Atlantic and Pacific Tea Company opened the first of its chain of red-and-gold-fronted retail stores. The attire of a lady of fashion contained about 130 yards of material, but the introduction of the hoop skirt in 1856 resulted in the loss of sixty yards. The trees of the city were so infested by caterpillars in 1858 that English sparrows were imported to get rid of them. The birds were successful and multiplied so rapidly that no way has yet been found to reduce their numbers.

More than a half million people were living in New York City in 1850, and during that decade the population increased by over three hundred thousand. Since most business was concentrated below City Hall Park, the torrent of traffic on lower Broadway was so dense that it sometimes took twenty

The City Post Office, converted in 1844 from the old (1731) Middle Dutch Church, had a special mail window marked "Ladies." This engraving borrowed scene from a Currier print in which the wagon (RIGHT) *was marked "Adams & Company, Express, 10 Wall St."*

Jenny Lind made her American debut at Castle Garden on September 11, 1850. She donated receipts of $26,238 to charity. The first ticket was auctioned by Barnum to Genin the Hatter for $625.

or thirty minutes to cross from the "shilling" side to the "dollar" side of the street. Along with the jam, there was the smell ("the whole city's one huge pigsty, only it would have to be cleaned up before a prudent farmer would let his pigs into it for fear of them catching the plague," wrote Strong) and the noise. The continuous rumble of omnibus wheels and the clatter of horses' hoofs on the cobblestones never stilled. Walt Whitman described it as ". . . tumultuous New York [with its] heavy, low musical roar, hardly ever intermitted, even at night."

The principal places of entertainment were situated on Broadway. In 1842 Phineas T. Barnum purchased the American Museum and established the techniques of clever advertising and publicity known ever since as "showmanship." In 1850 he imported the Swedish soprano, Jenny Lind, and applied his methods so successfully that the country went wild in a fever of adulation which he promptly named "Lindomania." The lady lived up to Barnum's advance billing and captivated the American public, not only with her bell-like tones, but with her charity, circumspection, and strict moral code. She had abandoned a career in opera because of some of the wanton roles she was called on to play.

In 1853 a World's Fair was celebrated in a gigantic greenhouse, the Crystal Palace, erected at Forty-second Street and Fifth Avenue. The site of Central Park was purchased in 1856 for $5,500,000 in spite of protests by conservative taxpayers who would have been a great deal more vigorous in their opposition had they known that the cost of landscaping alone was to be an additional ten million dollars, much of which went into the pockets of Boss Tweed.

"2:30 P.M. Oct. 13, 1857, Panic on Wall Street"—an unusual artistic collaboration by two painters, James Cafferty, N. A. (buildings) and Charles G. Rosenberg (portraits). The scene, in front of the Merchants Exchange, shows a number of financial leaders, including Cornelius Vanderbilt (RIGHT) *in gutter and Jacob Little in light coat.*

Panic scene on Wall Street, from HARPER'S WEEKLY, *accompanied a front-page report which began as an attack on usurers who took advantage of the tight money situation, but switched to a denunciation of respectable wealthy people who refused to lend money under any circumstance.*

But the creation of the park, out of what had been mostly squatters' slums, was to provide jobs in 1857 when they were desperately needed. For in that year New York fell on hard times—blamed, with justification, on Wall Street and many of the corporations in whose shares Wall Street dealt.

From 1830 on the corporation had become the major instrument of economic expansion. Existing as an individual entity, the corporation cut the personal risk and liability of the investor, providing him, through the stock markets, with a quick opportunity to buy into or withdraw from an investment. In addition to New York, there were exchanges in Boston and Philadelphia, and people throughout the country had been educated in the mysteries of "playing the market," the new network of telegraph wires making it possible for them to lose their money on speculations rumored from afar.

The rise of the corporation was accompanied by the most barefaced abuses that dishonest promoters were able to invent and put into practice. Fat dividends were often paid out of capital to boost prices, and, when the public was burdened with expensive stock, the price was then driven down by rumors circulated by manipulators, frequently the officers of the company involved, on short-selling sprees. Even outright thievery was not uncommon. In 1854 Robert Schuyler, President of the New York and New Haven Railroad, sold twenty thousand shares in his own company for two million dollars. These were shares for which there was no authorization, other than that given by Schuyler to some obliging printer. The same year Alexander Kyle, Secretary of the Harlem Railroad, pocketed three hundred thousand dollars as the proceeds of forged shares he issued. The officials of the Parker Vein Coal Company inundated the market with five times as many shares as they were authorized to sell. Edward Crane, President of the Vermont Central Railroad, hatched and sold ten thousand illegitimate shares for his own profit, scattering them so widely about the country that they could not be recalled. Finally the Legislature had to increase the authorized capitalization of the railroad in order to save the victims. The flood of these illegitimate shares was largely responsible for precipitating the Panic of 1854 and the more severe crisis of 1857. Most of the up-and-down movement was in railroad stocks. Since they required the most capital and promised the highest returns, they dominated the action on the exchanges.

A railroad charter was often used as a license to steal. State legislatures were persuaded to grant charters, buy bonds, and donate enormous strips or checkerboards of land to these enterprises. In order to be "on the main line," cities and counties bought railroad securities and granted liberal cash subsidies. Then the promoters would form construction companies of their own, award themselves contracts at high rates, build ramshackle lines, and buy overpriced, but dangerous or inefficient, equipment. This would inevitably be followed by attempts to eliminate any rivals through ruinous rate wars.

Many public officials, far from trying to regulate or curb this felonious skulduggery, co-operated eagerly, for they shared in the loot. Only the most flagrant thieves were brought to justice, while many of the others were not only objects of deference, but of public admiration, which was expressed in the philosophy of the times: "He got away with it." The frequent losses of investors did not discourage them, for playing the market gave many prosperous merchants a zest and excitement which was lacking in their otherwise drab lives. As one said: "Gambling in stocks, after following a legitimate business, is like quaffing brandy after sipping claret." But the outside investor had the cards stacked against him. If he survived the pools, the rigging, the rumors, the manipulation, and the water pumped into his stock, there was always the chance that his broker would fail.

What happened in 1857 was that promoters had loaded the railroads and land companies with stocks so saturated with water, or so unreasonably inflated, that these securities had neither assets nor dividends

After the Atlantic telegraph cable was completed in 1858, the hero of the hour was Cyrus W. Field, who had raised the money to finance the project in a single half-hour session with a half-dozen rich sponsors.

to support the prevailing prices. There were more cities on paper in Kansas than actually existed in all the Midwest and the Northern states combined. So much money and time were consumed in financing and promoting that little was left for building and cultivating.

"The Western Blizzard," as Henry Clews called the Panic of 1857, came with terrifying swiftness on August 24 when the New York branch of the Ohio Life Insurance and Trust Company failed. All business came to a standstill, first on Wall Street, then everywhere else in the country. Some of the richest men became paupers in one day. By December, 985 merchants in New York had failed, losing a total of $120,000,000. The working people were soon destitute. In New York, twenty-five thousand men were jobless and the winter was severe. Ten thousand people were fed in one Manhattan district on one cold day. Crowds seized bakers' wagons and invaded food shops. Many people died of starvation. United States troops were brought in to guard the Custom House and the Sub-Treasury. Fortunately, the banks resumed business at this time and, with the coming of spring, commerce slowly revived.

The year 1858 was marked by the celebration of the completion of the Atlantic Cable. Like so many other progressive ideas, this one originated in New York and was first promoted by Cyrus W. Field, a former rag and junk dealer. Field interested Peter Cooper, Moses Taylor, the banker, and other wealthy New Yorkers in the project and was so persuasive that, in a half hour, $1,500,000 was subscribed to finance it. After three years the cable was laid, and on August 16, 1858, Queen Victoria sent a telegraphic message to President Buchanan, to which he responded within a few brief minutes. This was a signal for New York to launch one of its protracted celebrations. There was a parade, with a hundred guns booming and all the bells in town clanging. The bands played, the flags snapped in the summer breeze, and it seemed that everyone in the city either marched in the parade or looked on to cheer it as it passed. The festivities continued long into the night and there was great rivalry between business buildings and private homes in creating the most elaborate and beautifully illuminated façades. Everyone agreed that the prize, if one were awarded, should have gone to City Hall, where a grand display of fireworks set fire to the cupola, which went up in a spectacular,

Parades and fireworks honored the transmission of the first cable messages between Queen Victoria and President Buchanan. New Yorkers agreed that the high point of the festivities was the illumination of City Hall.

The populace witnessed an even more thrilling spectacle than it had anticipated when the cupola of the City Hall was set aflame by fireworks discharged earlier in the evening. Three weeks later, the cable parted and Field became an object of ridicule. Not until 1866 did he succeed in laying a new transatlantic cable.

Edward, Prince of Wales, visited the city in October, 1860, and his reception was as enthusiastic as that given Jenny Lind and Lafayette. At a Grand Ball in the Academy of Music, the nineteen-year-old Prince (CENTER) *danced with the wife of Governor Edwin D. Morgan.*

but unscheduled, blaze of flame, sparks, and smoke.

Cyrus Field was the lion of the hour, until the cable suddenly snapped three weeks later and there was nothing but silence on both sides of the Atlantic. Then he became the butt of every joke and wisecrack the cynics could think up, and the more backward citizens refused to believe that any message had ever been transmitted. It took Field eight more years—years made more agonizing because he had been momentarily successful—before he succeeded in laying a new, improved transatlantic cable that once more made speedy communication possible between Europe and America.

Although 1860 was marked by mounting bitterness between the two political parties and between the North and the South, there was one bright event in which everyone was interested: the visit of the handsome nineteen-year-old Prince of Wales, later King Edward VII, who, like his grandson during 1919, traveled incognito as Baron Renfrew. He was given a typical tumultuous New York welcome, a grand tour which included the Deaf and Dumb Asylum, several parades and military reviews, and a ball at the Academy of Music on October 12 which would have been the most celebrated social event ever held in Manhattan, except that it was an unmanageable crush plagued by an unfortunate series of accidents. Huge vases of flowers were tipped over and smashed, and parts of the dance floor gave way in three places under the combined weight of the crowd. The elite of New York vied with each other in elaborateness of dress and display of jewels, but since their very numbers jammed them so tightly together, little of their finery could be seen. The Prince wearily gave up the struggle at four-thirty in the morning; the other guests followed at five.

8

The Second Revolution

THE CIVIL WAR, the South's revolution against the otherwise united states, was not only an attempt to retain the institution of slavery at home, but to some extent a rebellion against its own economic enslavement. For New York controlled the cotton crop and the commerce of the South, and everything coming from and going to that region had to pass through the port of New York. This situation existed because the Southern planter was always in pawn to the cotton broker, banker, merchant, or shipowner of Wall Street, and this year's bales paid last year's bills. The South, in its desperate attempt to break away, hoped once and for all to eliminate the control of the middleman.

Naturally, New York had no desire to lose its most valuable customer and those businessmen who were not pro-South were at least in favor of conciliation. In January, 1861, fifty thousand people signed petitions to Congress praying for a compromise. But secession was in the air and even infected the crafty, crooked Mayor, Fernando Wood, who made the amazing proposal that Manhattan, Staten, and Long islands become a separate nation to be called Tri-Insula. In his annual message to the Common Council on January 7, His Honor said:

> *Why should not New York City, instead of supporting by her contributions in revenues, two thirds of the expenses of the United States, become also equally independent? As a free city, with but a nominal duty on imports, her local government could be supported without taxes upon her people. Thus we could live free from taxes, and have cheap goods nearly duty free. . . . When disunion has become a fixed and certain fact, why may not New York disrupt the bonds which bind her to a corrupt and venal master?*

The Common Council, as fine a legislative body as money could buy, thought so well of this treasonable document that it ordered three thousand copies printed for general circulation. However, the proposal received as little serious attention as the more recent attempts of the city to break away from the state.

When, on April 12, Fort Sumter was fired on, a transformation in public sentiment began. Slowly at first, then with increasing speed, the city swung to the Northern cause. The militia regiments assem-

On February 19, 1861, on his way to Washington, President-elect Lincoln spoke to a crowd on Broadway from the Astor House balcony. It was on this trip that Allan Pinkerton discovered a Southern plot to kill Lincoln in Baltimore and had the train speed through the scheduled stop there.

bled, patriotic citizens helped equip them, the Stock Exchange gave one thousand dollars to the silk-stocking Seventh Regiment, the Assay Office was crowded with citizens exchanging their gold for war bonds, and Commodore Cornelius Vanderbilt lent his enormous yacht, the *North Star,* to the Navy—and never got it back.

Of all the horrible growing pains the United States has experienced, the Civil War was the most excruciating. It brought forth not only all that was noble, but also all that was detestable, in the people of Wall Street. While many young men of Wall Street were dying or bleeding or starving for the Union, there were others, shrewd operators who gloated over the opportunities that war threw in their paths. This was going to be an El Dorado, they felt, a new Gold Rush right in the heart of Wall Street.

At first this prospect of riches did not appear likely. When war was declared stocks fell off 20 per cent in three days. The market lapsed into a sluggishness from which it did not recover until 1862. Then, as industry boomed, so did stocks, and the greatest era of speculation the world had yet seen began. When the war started, only three men in America were worth a million dollars. When it ended, there were hundreds.

Many other changes took place. The tempo of the Street quickened as the frenzied stockjobbing increased. Gone, never to return, was the leisurely pace, the courtly manner, the relaxed business deal. With volume skyrocketing, the New York Stock Exchange had to change its methods, enlarge its membership, and move into new quarters. Other stock markets opened—the Public Stock Board in the "Coal Hole" at 23 William Street, and the Open Board of Stock Brokers. Informal stock-trading took place in the street, on the curb, among the crowds around the exchanges from eight in the morning until dark and was then continued during the evening at the Fifth Avenue Hotel at Twenty-third Street as well as at the Evening Exchange until midnight.

The most frenzied trading was in gold. After the government and the banks suspended specie payments, speculation in the yellow metal began, and the price fluctuations caused by the events of the war made and wiped out fortunes of plungers in a matter of days or even hours. Rumors of peace sent the price of gold down. Northern defeats boomed it up and then the jubilant winners would sing "Dixie" in the Gold Room. In no other war did so many people of the Street behave as selfishly, as callously, or as treasonably. Attempts to legislate against gold-

On Wednesday, the 20th, Lincoln was received by Mayor Fernando Wood in the Governors' Room at City Hall. Six weeks before, Wood had urged secession of New York from the Union. Between the two men is the desk on which George Washington had written his Inaugural Address.

Many free New York Negroes enlisted to fight against the South. A total of 178,975 Negroes served in the Army of the North and 36,847 were listed as killed, wounded, or missing. Here the Twentieth U.S. Colored Infantry is being presented with its colors at the Union League Club.

trading failed, and a desperate crew, made up of speculators forced out of other businesses by the war, of Southerners eager to profit at Union expense, and war profiteers bent on further gains, filled the halls and streets with excitement. Few if any attempts were made on the part of the old leaders of Wall Street to discourage or regulate the speculators. Perhaps they were powerless, or perhaps they were only interested in gathering to themselves some of the fresh money that poured into the market from all over the country, for a "stock-market mania" accompanied the wartime prosperity.

The wild excesses, the rigged price movements, and the blatant dishonesty displayed during the war and postwar decades gave Wall Street the black name it bore for almost eighty years. Before that time the rest of the country distrusted New York City. But what happened in the Street, starting in 1862, localized and gave focus to the hatred of the hinterland. After that, "Wall Street" was blamed for every bank failure, every closed factory and lost job, every meal skipped and every family evicted. "Wall Street" became the fountainhead of all financial evil and the whipping boy of the reformers. In many cases, the Street was directly responsible for panics and depressions, but sometimes a disaster hundreds or thousands of miles away would start the avalanche rolling. Oil-well promoting began in Pennsylvania, the railroad-building scandals were initiated in Boston, and the Crédit Mobilier fraud was hatched in Washington, D.C.—yet Wall Street was always blamed.

Contributing to the unsavory image of the Street were the great railroad battles which began with the first Harlem Corner in 1863. Cornelius Vanderbilt, sixty-nine years old at the time, had bought control of his first railroad, the New York and Harlem Line, the previous year. The stock, which had sold at nine dollars, reached fifty dollars in April, 1863, and when the Common Council gave Vanderbilt a franchise to lay streetcar tracks from Fourth Avenue down Broadway to the Battery, the stock went up to one hundred dollars on May 19. The Council members took their profit, turned around, and started selling Harlem short, then rescinded the franchise. But as they sold, Vanderbilt kept buying, until he owned much more stock than had been issued and the price was $179. The Councilmen were ruined. So, almost, was their adviser, Daniel Drew, the old drover credited with inventing "watered stock," a term first applied to cattle that had been fed salt and then allowed to drink their fill of water before being driven to the butchers' scales.

Reaching out for other lines, the Commodore bought a major interest in the New York and Hudson that fall. Then he went to Albany to get permission from the Legislature to combine the two roads. That august body thought it could succeed where the New York Common Council had failed. They held out promise of permission and the stock climbed from twenty-five to 150. Then they proceeded to take their winnings and sell New York and Hudson short. They managed to drive it down to ninety, but could not get it below because Vanderbilt kept buying. He bought twenty-seven thousand more shares than had been issued, pushing the price up to 285 and bankrupting the legislators. Daniel Drew, again the "brains" behind the officials, got off easy—he paid

The elite Seventh Regiment, original unit to be called "The National Guard," marches down Broadway in April, 1861, to embark for Washington and the war. Building at Number 501 (LEFT) *was occupied until 1959 by Francis Bannerman Sons, Inc., dealers in surplus Army and Navy goods of Civil War.*

Temporary troop barracks were erected in City Hall Park, where both American and British soldiers were quartered during the Revolution. Later, Confederate prisoners-of-war were confined here and did a thriving business counterfeiting Confederate Army buttons to sell to curious visitors.

Vanderbilt a million dollars in settlement. Drew, a sanctimonious raider and looter of railroads, was an old Vanderbilt antagonist from steamboating days. He was to mulct the Commodore in the famous Erie War, only eventually to lose out again, but each time he would come to Vanderbilt contrite and begging forgiveness and, for some reason, the tough old Commodore would let him off at bargain rates.

With the money market a place of frenzied speculation, an investment as stodgy as government bonds appealed to few buyers. At first, Secretary of the Treasury Salmon P. Chase and the New York banks co-operated well and the government borrowed $150,000,000. But at the end of 1861 they disagreed as to where the money was to be kept as well as on other matters, and the government then, for the first time in its history, issued paper currency of its own—$450,000,000 in greenbacks. In March, 1863, Chase hired Jay Cooke of Philadelphia, the first high-pressure security salesman, to market government bonds. Cooke soon organized a nationwide sales force to sell bonds at almost every rural crossroads and city square. He introduced the idea of securities to all classes of people and was so successful that he once oversold an issue by eleven million dollars, which Congress quickly ratified. When there was a loud public outcry against the huge commissions Cooke earned, Chase had to withdraw him. Then sales fell off sharply and Cooke was rehired. The high-pressure campaign was resumed, and on his biggest day, Cooke and his staff sold $30,500,000 worth of bonds.

It was during the war that the National Banking System was created. This was another triumph for Chase, although he was replaced as Secretary of the

Balloon proposed for Atlantic flight by Thaddeus Lowe was designed to carry a small steamboat, should the bag deflate in midocean. It was never built, but Lowe became a famous Union observation balloonist.

Treasury in July, 1864, after unsuccessfully attempting to stop speculation in gold. Before the inauguration of the system, seven thousand different kinds of bank bills, issued by state banks, were in existence. Many of these were of dubious value and were backed by varying amounts of hard cash. This money circulated so widely that there was a thriving business in the sale of "bill directories," which attempted to give the value of bank notes everywhere, a value that might range from two cents on the dollar to par. The National Banking Act, passed in 1862 and reenacted with important modifications in 1864, created a system of banks with a definite relationship to the Federal government. While the worst of the wildcat banking era had passed, many shaky banking institutions remained, as well as a hodgepodge of state banking laws. Now, a National Bank was required to deposit a third of its capital in government bonds, against which it could issue notes up to 90 per cent of the deposit. These notes, printed by the government, became legal tender. The old state bank notes were doomed in March, 1865, when a Federal law was passed, placing a 10 per cent tax on any of this currency still in circulation in July, 1866.

In the first year of the war Western Union completed the first transcontinental telegraph line—just seventeen months after the Pony Express began delivering messages in the incredibly swift time of eight days between St. Joseph, Missouri, and Sacra-

The Public Board, a wildcat exchange, opened in the "Coal Hole" at 23 William Street in 1862. Here there was heavy speculation in gold, which fluctuated wildly in price with news of Union victories and defeats. Millionaires, lottery-ticket men, shopkeepers, clerks, "old clo's men," cooks, waiters—everyone plunged.

The gold market moved to its own Gold Room at William and Beaver streets in October, 1864. The membership fee of $200 a year was soon raised to $2,500. Among the hundred members were J. P. Morgan, Fisk and Hatch, Livermore, Clews and Company, Drexel and Company, and Brown Brothers. Although the supply of gold was small, speculation was enormous.

This cartoon is entitled "An Exciting Day in the Board of Brokers—'On the Rise.' Performances by the Whole Stock Company. 1862." The room depicted was in old Lord's Court. In December, 1865, the newly renamed New York Stock Exchange moved into the new building it had constructed on Broad Street.

Gambling in stocks became so frenzied that the regular exchange and curb hours were not enough for fanatical plungers. Evening exchanges sprang up, such as this one operated by R. H. Gallaher in the Fifth Avenue Hotel. In 1865 Gallaher built a handsome new building and charged $250 a year, but was frozen out in four months.

Since the days of the buttonwood tree, exchange members and free-lance brokers traded on the curb outside the Board room before and after official hours. During the Civil War the outdoor securities market was along William between Exchange and Beaver. The portico of the Delmonico Restaurant is at right.

The Draft Riot battle on Second Avenue. When the Federal Draft Act selected family men too poor to buy their way out of military service, while others could do so for $300, mobs wrecked the draft office, pillaged the city, lynched Negroes, and fought the police as well as soldiers diverted from the front lines to restore order.

mento. In 1862, fourteen-year-old Edward Henry Harriman of Jersey City found a job on Wall Street as an office boy. Seven years later he owned a seat on the Stock Exchange. J. P. Morgan, Sr., twenty-four years old when the war started, had already been employed for a year as the agent for George Peabody and Company, the firm of Boston and London financiers. Jay Gould, born in Roxbury, New York, was a year older and already a consolidator of small railroads. Alfred Nobel was a twenty-eight-year-old

The sacking of Brooks Brothers Clothing Store at Catharine and Cherry streets. "Gorillas," as the August 1, 1863, issue of HARPER'S WEEKLY *called them, looted the store which supplied President Lincoln with the coat worn at his inauguration.*

The rioters were finally turned back at the TRIBUNE *office in Printing House Square and never reached the well-guarded Wall Street area. The four days of rioting brought death to over a thousand people and caused millions of dollars in property damage. Southern papers, trying to counteract depressing war news, hailed the Riots as the beginning of a Northern revolt against the Union.*

engineer assisting another native of Sweden, John Ericsson in building the *Monitor* at Greenpoint across the East River from Manhattan. And at the Brooklyn Navy Yard, the *Intelligent Whale*, a new type of submarine, was under construction, but it was not completed until 1866, and never saw action against the Confederate Navy.

Charles Dickens wrote about "Broadway . . . with its wiry merchants, its sallow-faced and dyspeptic clerks, its hairy rowdies, its Californian itinerants and its staring, woe-begone emigrants." On Broadway you could also see the explorer Paul Du Chaillu, who captured the first gorilla ever exhibited in America, General Santa Ana, erstwhile "Butcher of the Alamo," the Italian expatriate Giuseppe Garibaldi, who got the idea for the uniform later worn by his revolutionary forces from the red shirts of the "paid fire department," or perhaps the gang leader Danny Deever, whose name at least is said to have been borrowed by Rudyard Kipling for his poem containing the line, "An' they're hangin' Danny Deever in the mornin'."

In March, 1863, the Federal government passed the first draft act in United States history, although the Confederacy had begun national conscription a year earlier. By paying the government three hundred dollars or by providing a substitute who would enlist for three years, an eligible young man could purchase commutation or exemption. "It's the rich man's war, but the poor man's fight," said George Fort Milton, and many agreed. Allowing no provision for the exemption of married men or fathers, the draft law was not enforced until after the Battle of Gettysburg, when New York was picked as the first place where drawings were to be held. The draft was made on Saturday, July 11, 1863, and the lists of selected names appeared in the Sunday newspapers. On Monday morning the Danny Deevers took over. Groups of people from the West Side tenement district gathered near Central Park and swept down Sixth and Seventh avenues to Forty-sixth and Forty-seventh streets. Then they turned east and made for the office of the draft on Third Avenue. Here they destroyed all draft paraphernalia and records and set fire to the building. Adjoining buildings also burned as the flames spread, and when John Kennedy, head of the Metropolitan Police, appeared, he was beaten savagely by the mob. Troops were called from Central Park to quell the riot, but were driven back by the angry crowds. Ordinary

"Reading the War News on Broadway" shows a fake country Jake picking the pocket of the man in silk topper, absorbed in dispatches, while a Negro (LEFT) *reaches for picker's pocket.*

Photographic version of "Reading the War News" was taken in front of the EVENING POST *building where hand-lettered bulletins were pasted, announcing the latest events in the Peninsula Campaign.*

working people who had been stirred up to protest against an unfair draft act had turned into mobs of looters, murderers, and arsonists. Every thug and saloon fighter in New York also came out to have his day against the police and the corps of volunteer specials who were organized to co-operate with the uniformed force.

By noon, Third Avenue, from the Bowery to the burning draft office at Forty-sixth Street, was choked with swarms of milling, shouting, defiant rioters. Horsecars were overturned and stores were gutted as the fires began to spread. Part of the mob attacked a gun factory at Twentieth Street and Second Avenue and here the first man to swing a sledge hammer at the heavily bolted door was the first to be killed. Just how many more joined him before the riots subsided is unknown to this day. Estimates range from twelve hundred to over three thousand. Many were Negroes beaten to death or hanged from the nearest tree, simply because they were the most convenient reminders of the cause of the war and the draft. The mob reached its peak of animal frenzy when it sacked and fired the Negro Orphan Asylum.

Cannon and infantry were finally brought in against the rioters, who set up barricades throughout the city. By Wednesday pitched battles between Army units and rioters were taking place at Seventh Avenue and Thirty-second Street, at First Avenue between Eighteenth and Nineteenth streets, at Second Avenue and Thirty-first Street, on the lower East Side, and at many other points. Slowly the force of arms crushed the worst mob uprising America has ever known. After four foul, bloody days the Common Council voted nine million dollars to pay the draft-exemption fees of poor men with dependents. Quiet once again descended on the torn, stricken city.

One of the strangest incidents of the war occurred on November 25 of the following year when a group of Confederate officers trickled down to New York

City from Canada and attempted a "fire raid" on the town. They registered at different hotels and, at an appointed time, all set fire to their rooms, hoping to start a conflagration that would send the city up in smoke. The fires were checked with little damage.

During the war, the Sub-Treasury outgrew its quarters in the Assay Office and arrangements were made to take over the Custom House next door. This was possible because the Merchants Exchange, a block away at Wall and William, was available as the new Custom House. The Federal government rented the exchange and later exercised its option to purchase for a million dollars. The Assay Office, which had originally been the United States Bank building, remained open until 1914. Its façade now graces the American Wing of the Metropolitan Museum of Art.

After the summer and winter of 1864, when the war might have been won had General William F. Smith pushed through to Petersburg on June 17 instead of sitting back and waiting until Beauregard filled the deserted trenches with Confederate troops, General Robert E. Lee surrendered to Grant at Appomattox Court House on April 9, 1865. News of the surrender of the Army of Northern Virginia reached New York at 11:30 P.M. On the following day the city was gaily decorated with flags and bunting, Trinity celebrated with a grand "Te Deum;" cannon boomed, the streets were filled with happy, singing people, and the Governor fixed April 20 as a grand and patriotic day of jubilee. But this was not to take place, for on the evening of the 14th, Abraham Lincoln, viewing *Our American Cousin* in Ford's Theater in Washington, was shot by John Wilkes Booth. On Saturday, April 15, all of New York went into deep mourning, business was suspended, and the city waited for the funeral cortege, which left Washington on the 19th and reached New

Celebration in New York after the surrender at Appomattox Court House depicts returning troops marching south on Broadway, then around City Hall Park into Park Row. At right is Barnum's American Museum; portico of the Astor House (LEFT) *is where Lincoln spoke just before the war.*

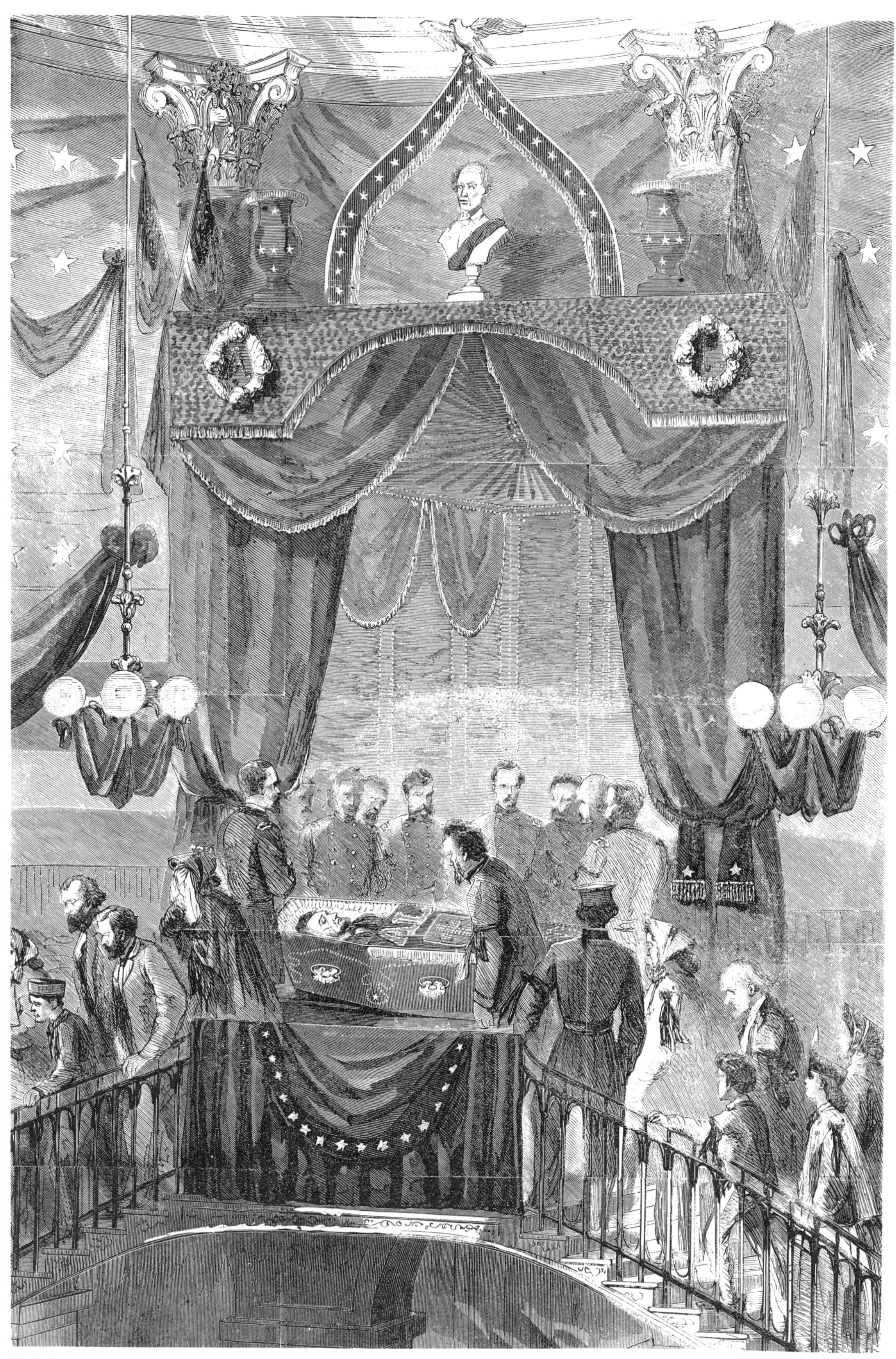

Jubilation over the end of the war gave way to national mourning when Lincoln was assassinated. On April 24, the funeral cortege stopped in New York on its journey to Springfield. The President's body lay in state at the head of the staircase in City Hall. At least 120,000 people came to pay their respects.

The following day the funeral procession departed up Broadway for the railroad station. The catafalque was drawn by sixteen gray horses and was escorted by long ranks of soldiers who marched slowly past the solemn crowds of people lining the street. "Not a building but assumed the garb of sorrow," reported the HERALD.

York on the 24th. Escorted by the Seventh Regiment, the cortege proceeded to City Hall where Lincoln's body lay in state for twenty-four hours. Up the graceful staircase came the people, 120,000 of them, to have one last look at the martyred President. Then the funeral procession resumed its mournful journey across America, stopping at countless towns and cities to allow millions to pay their final respects to Lincoln before his burial in Springfield, Illinois.

On December 9 of that year, the Stock Exchange moved from Lord's Court into the new building at 10 and 12 Broad Street which had been constructed especially for its use. One tart comment on the architecture was: "It looks like it was designed by a pastry chef with orders to be lavish." The Regular Board occupied a hall, seventy-five feet long by fifty-three feet wide, on the second floor. George W. McLean and his associates leased the ground floor where they operated the "Long Room" so that brokers and nonmembers could trade between calls upstairs. This room was 145 feet long and forty feet wide and was serviced by telegraph offices near the Broad Street entrance. At 16 and 18 Broad Street the Open Board of Stock Brokers, organized in 1864, held its sessions. The New York Gold Exchange stood next to the Stock Exchange on New Street. Thus, within a year, the center of market activity moved from William Street to Broad. Here it has remained ever since, with additions beginning fifteen years later and continuing until the Stock Exchange now covers most of the block between Wall and Exchange Place and Broad and New streets.

The phenomenon of evening exchanges began when the Fifth Avenue Hotel was overrun by traders in stocks and gold. In late 1862 the first attempt at a formal evening market was made when one of the dealers rented the northwest corner of Fifth Avenue and Twenty-third Street, but since the other traders

Aftermath of the Rebellion—the burned-out shell of the Gallego Sugar Mill at Richmond, seen from across the James River Canal after capture of the city by Union forces. This picture is from the monumental photographic record of the Civil War made by Mathew Brady and his staff.

preferred the halls of the hotel, this was abandoned in January, 1863. As trade volume grew larger—frequently much heavier than at the day exchanges—the hotel was forced to post a printed notice: "Gentlemen are requested not to buy or sell stocks or gold in these rooms." It was the only way the hotel could remain in the hotel business. Then another night market was set up in the basement of the building that had housed the first one, and this continued in operation until March, 1864, when R. H. Gallaher leased what had been Republican party headquarters on the southeast corner of the same street. The market followed him and the venture was so successful that Gallaher built a handsome, elaborate Evening Exchange building behind the Fifth Avenue Hotel on Twenty-fourth Street. The new exchange was opened in April, 1865, and charged $250 annually for membership. Before that, the only charge had been fifty cents for a single admission. Attendance ranged from several hundred to a thousand traders an evening and here volume, it was claimed, continually topped business on the day exchanges.

By 1865 gold certificates were used for gold-trading and when E. B. Ketchum, a speculator in the precious metal, ran into a series of unlucky breaks, he forged several million dollars' worth of the certificates and floated them in an effort to recoup his losses. But his bad luck still held and on August 15 he slipped quietly away.

The forgeries were soon discovered and on August 23 the Stock Exchange adopted the following resolution:

> *Any member who shall be present at or indirectly send orders to be executed at what is commonly designated as the Evening Stock Exchange, shall cease to be a member of this Board.*

The Open Board and the Gold Exchange took similar action the next day, with the result that the Evening Exchange was forced to shut down. Business picked up remarkably at the other spots.

9

Turmoil and Panic

THE RIOTOUS speculation that marked the Civil War period on Wall Street was only a prelude to the financial anarchy and tumult of the next eight years—a span which has been labeled "The Age of Flash," mainly in honor of the most flamboyant figure of the era, Colonel Jim Fisk, Jr. Fisk's position in economic history is unique. At once a vain, pompous clown and prodigal spender, he was also a great salesman, wily schemer, and ruthless stock-market operator.

His career began as a Yankee peddler working for his father. Once, when a woman customer accused the elder Fisk of misrepresenting a piece of calico worth twelve and a half cents, young Jim said: "Well, now, I don't think Father would tell a lie for twelve and a half cents . . . though he might tell eight of 'em for a dollar." Jim died at the height of his glory and infamy when he was shot down by the man who had stolen his girlfriend. In this sense, "The Age of Flash" had an ironic consistency. If there was no justice for Fisk's victims, neither was there any for him.

It was the day of the dashing horse turnout, the brownstone front, the bustle, and the polished brass spittoon. Saratoga was the resort of the smart set—the elegant spa for the elite to relax and sip health-giving waters. As Henry Collins Brown wrote in *Brownstone Fronts:*

> *Before the war, Saratoga had been the favorite mecca for the Southern aristocracy, fleeing from the miasma of the old Kentucky home, the Swanee River and similar delectable resorts of the cholera, yellow fever and malaria . . . so the First Families of Virginia and the Georgia Crackers and Dixie in general came there periodically to wash out the winter's quinine. . . . War changed that and now came the war "contractors," the speculators, the railroad men, all bloated and ready to spend it. Mr. [Alexander T.] Stewart put up the Grand Union Hotel on a scale to dumfound Baden-Baden and Aix-le-Bains and all Wall Street crowded its parlors to look at an enormous allegorical painting as big as the drop-curtain of the Grand Opera House, depicting America shaking out a cornucopia to the assembled nations of the world. It was one of those pictures that cost $150,000 to paint and brings $49.75 at auction. . . . You couldn't walk along one of those verandas without stumbling over*

The biggest sensation of its sensational career was the burning of Barnum's Museum on July 13, 1865. A dead whale lay in the street for two days and a marble statue of Queen Victoria was heaped on the smoking ruins. Previous fires, including one set in 1864 by Confederate agents, had been quickly extinguished.

the boots of a Vanderbilt, a Jerome, a Gould or someone else positively filthy with money, seated in a rocking chair, discussing the water-holding capacity of a new railroad along the Ashtabula River.

It was a day when the young speculator, Jay Gould, offered to buy the Pennsylvania Railroad and split the profits with Andrew Carnegie, then superintendent of the Philadelphia division, if the thirty-year-old Carnegie would operate it for him. P. T. Barnum attracted crowds to his American Museum by advertising a "Cherry Colored Cat" (black cherry colored, at it turned out) and then achieved a record turnover of patronage by posting huge signs and arrows reading: "This Way to the Egress!" The imposing Western Union building was erected, its flagpole sporting a wooden ball at its top which was dropped precisely at noon every day, tying up traffic as everyone stopped to set and wind his watch. Lorenzo Delmonico put his niece to work as cashier of his restaurant and the town clucked, for there was hardly another female employee in the district.

William Marcy Tweed, son of a respected chairmaker, climbed into a commanding position in local politics by devious stages, starting with service in a volunteer fire company, and eventually achieved the acme in municipal rascality. Much of the later civic corruption uncovered in New York has been dismissed as being on a piddling scale when compared with what went on during the reign of the first Boss. Although he was undoubtedly kind to the poor, he managed to double the city's debt every couple of years and build the Hall of Records for ten times the original estimate (some of the little extras—forty thousand dollars for brooms and over seven thousand dollars for thermometers). All in all, he swindled the treasury of New York out of seventy-five million dollars (some historians place the figure at almost two hundred million). Of course, even so energetic a man as Tweed could not accomplish this larceny entirely on his own. He had a lot of willing helpers, some of whom later found themselves at his side in jail. The *Times* and *Harper's Weekly* constantly fought the Tweed Ring. Thomas Nast's savage and challenging cartoons of the Boss, which appeared in *Harper's*, not only hastened Tweed's downfall, but,

The worst traffic jams in the city were at Broadway and Fulton where it sometimes took twenty minutes to get across the street. The solution, proposed by Genin the Hatter and others, was to construct a bridge over the street. After fifteen years of agitation and delay, the Loew Footbridge was opened on May 16, 1867.

The footbridge, which cost $24,000, was a boon to pedestrians. However, it was closed on December 24, 1868, and demolished, after Knox the Hatter, claiming it blocked his light and air, sued to have it removed.

The nightstick or baton was the principal weapon carried by patrolmen. New recruits were given thirty days instruction in its use. According to police experience in the Draft Riots of 1863, this was supposed to make them equal to twenty times their number in a street brawl.

ironically, served to identify him to the Spanish police when he fled New York after his arrest and tried to enter Spain.

Tweed flourished in an era when people adored the "rags-to-riches" hero and paid homage to "the bitch-goddess, Success." False weights and measures, adulterated food, widespread drunkenness, and only one type of employment open to women, aside from domestic service, were typical of the times. Tweed stayed in power in the 1860's by being ingeniously efficient in his rapacity. Just before election he would stage the wholesale naturalization of immigrants for voting purposes. On one occasion, at Tweed's behest, Judge George G. Barnard manufactured sixty-thousand new citizens in twenty days.

On July 8, 1871, the *Times* began running transcripts from the account books of Comptroller Richard B. Connolly, and never were bookkeeping

While the preceding sketch from a New York journal depicted the police as a group of clean-cut public servants, the LONDON GRAPHIC *saw them as tobacco-juice spitting Cossacks exiting from a store featuring "Lorilard's Long Cut."*

The first Stock Exchange building on Broad Street (LEFT CENTER) *occupied part of its present site. Despite its impressive marble façade, it sank on the New Street side to a modest two-story brick rear, "emblematical of stately fortunes which enter stately front, issue diminished from that diminished rear."*

figures read with such avid interest. When John Jacob Astor III, head of the committee formed to investigate the city's finances, turned in a report that whitewashed the administration, Thomas Nast drew a cartoon of a sneering "Tweedy" Tammany tiger standing over a prostrate maiden labeled "New York." The caption read: "Well, what are you going to do about it?" A mass meeting of aroused citizens, held at Cooper Union, finally led to grand-jury indictments and the eventual smashing of the Ring.

In 1873, H. W. Johns, who conceived the idea of using asbestos mined on Staten Island as a roofing material, moved to 87 Maiden Lane from a Brooklyn basement. (The firm was merged in 1901 with the Manville Covering Company of Milwaukee to form Johns-Manville.) Borden's milk, Singer sewing machines, Macy's department store, the Chase National Bank, and Babbitt's cleanser appeared on the scene. An early form of jazz was heard in New York, introduced by the freed slaves who flocked to the city after adoption of the Thirteenth Amendment. At Promontory Point, Utah, on May 10, 1869, at the ceremony linking the Union Pacific and the Central

Instead of subsiding after the war, the stock-gambling craze became more frenzied. It attracted people from all walks of life and every section of the country, bringing many diverse types to Wall Street brokerage offices.

Of all the market riggers and speculators, the most daring, conniving, and ruthless was Jay Gould (CENTER) *who plotted a corner on gold in 1869 with his partner, Jim Fisk* (LEFT) *and broker William Belden* (RIGHT).

Next door to the exchange on New Street was the Gold Room where, on Black Friday, Gould and Fisk bought millions of dollars' worth of gold and squeezed frantic short-sellers by demanding immediate settlement.

At the height of the squeeze, James A. Garfield, Chairman of the House Banking Committee, announced from the steps of the exchange: "Fellow Citizens! God reigns and the government at Washington still lives! I am instructed to inform you that the Secretary of the Treasury has placed ten million dollars in gold upon the market." The tension was broken and the price of gold fell.

Pacific lines, Governor Leland Stanford of California, given the honor of driving in the last, golden spike (which was removed immediately after), lifted his head on the backswing, missed the spike entirely, and fell flat on his face in the mud. An alert telegrapher simulated the blow with his key, nevertheless, and a waiting multitude on both coasts, including the members of the Stock Exchange, cheered the completion of the first transcontinental railroad span.

While the Exchange volume grew steadily larger because of the increased trading in railroad shares, business in the Gold Exchange, next door on New Street was also booming. *Harper's Weekly* described the Gold Room as

> *. . . a hippotheatron, with a little fountain in the centre. The centre of the fountain is a bronze Cupid with a dolphin in its arms. From the head of Cupid arises a tiny silver stream which falls in jets into the basin below. Fancy an iron railing ninety feet in circumference about this basin, then a space of some twenty feet between the walls and the fountain, and you have a rough idea of the Gold Room. On one side there are two galleries—the lower for the errand boys, and the upper for the spectators. Beyond the fountain, with his back toward New Street, stands the Secretary, recording the sales which he catches by his ear. Near him is the telegraph operator. Wires run from his machine to nearly five hundred brokers' offices, who are thus instantly informed of the state of the market, and are enabled to make their bids undisturbed by the furious excitement which rules in the Gold Room on important occasions.*

In this setting on September 24, 1869, an unprecedented drama was enacted—a drama that would ever after be remembered as "Black Friday." Jay Gould, using Jim Fisk as a front, attempted to send the price of gold so high that he would make a quick killing of many millions. The two men had cornered all of the gold in New York—twenty-five million dollars' worth, on margin—except what the government had on deposit in the Sub-Treasury. Gould confidently believed that this gold was safely "frozen," since the

Tennie C. (or Tennessee) Claflin was the hoyden partner of her queenly sister, Victoria Woodhull, in the first brokerage house operated by women.

Commodore Cornelius Vanderbilt was seventy-five when he fell under the spell of the spiritualist Claflin sisters and sponsored their short careers on Wall Street.

Victoria Woodhull was an incredible figure in a period when women had just won the right to open bank accounts. She advocated free love, ran for President, was the first in America to publish Karl Marx' MANIFESTO. Here she is being rebuffed when she and Tennie tried to vote in the elections of 1871.

After acquiring St. John's Park from Trinity Church, Vanderbilt constructed a giant freight depot for his Hudson River Railroad. The structure was topped with a sculptured pediment centered on a heroic bronze statue of himself. When the depot was razed, the statue was moved to Grand Central Station and now faces the automobile ramp on the Forty-second Street side.

appointment of Daniel Butterfield as Assistant Treasurer, in charge of the New York Sub-Treasury, had been arranged by him through Abel R. Corbin, a Wall Street operator who was married to a sister of President Grant's wife. It was also understood that Corbin was to use his influence with the President to keep the government out of the gold-selling business. However, when Gould and Fisk pushed the price to 160 and many of the short-sellers were ruined (several went insane and others committed suicide), pressure on the Treasury and Grant's disavowal of the scheme broke the corner. Butterfield was ordered to sell four million dollars' worth of gold. The Assistant Treasurer first sold his own gold, then gave Gould half an hour's grace, enabling him to get out of the market, which he did without bothering to pass the information on to Fisk. Then Butterfield took the pressure off the short-sellers by supplying them with government gold. The brokers who were acting on orders from the pair of scoundrels were repudiated and went bankrupt.

Not everyone lost on Black Friday. Two who first tasted a profit on the market that day were Victoria Woodhull and her sister, Tennie C. (or sometimes Tennessee) Claflin, who were guided by a tip from Commodore Vanderbilt. For almost ten years these almost illiterate young women (Victoria was thirty-two and Tennie twenty-five) were to be the talk of Wall Street and the entire country. Born in the Midwest, they had been married and divorced, and lived at various times in every section of the country. They made the acquaintance of the seventy-five-year-old Vanderbilt when they were introduced to him as exceptionally skillful spiritualists and faith-healers. Otherwise tough and realistic, the Commodore had an almost childlike faith in faith-healers. Perhaps he

The great fire at Chicago, which raged from October 8 to 10, 1871, destroyed property worth $196 million, drove stock prices down as fire-insurance firms were forced to liquidate, and caused seven brokerage failures. On November 9, 1872, the Boston fire caused $80 million damage and seven more failures.

believed in miracles, for his life certainly seemed to be one long stream of miracles. Starting out with only one rowboat ferry, he had acquired a fleet of twenty steamships and forty river craft. Then, at seventy, he had invaded the railroad field and was starting to dominate that, too. Now the magnetic Victoria and her pert, vivacious sister seemed to offer him a new lease on life. He gave them a check for seven thousand dollars and they plunged into the stock market.

Not content to take a profit and retire from the field, they opened a brokerage office on January 20, 1870, at 44 Broad—the first in the world to be operated, or, rather, fronted, by females. Because of the tremendous publicity they received, and because Wall Street thought Vanderbilt was backing them, all the financial houses of the district sent representatives and the crush of callers caused the sisters to put up a sign: "All gentlemen will state their business and then retire at once." According to Emanie Sachs in *The Terrible Siren, Victoria Woodhull:* "She inevitably confused amazement with the admiration she craved." Amazement was always the reaction to Victoria Woodhull. She demanded that women be granted the same freedom and the right to vote that had been given to the slaves; she advocated free love and practiced it; she was the first woman to address the United States Senate; she ran for President of the United States as the candidate of the Equal Rights party, with Frederick Douglass, the Negro lecturer and writer, as her running mate, and she was elected President of the National Society of Spiritualists at Troy, New York.

Once the ladies achieved fame, their names were constantly on the front pages. However, their vogue as the bewitching brokers of Broad Street soon passed; their office rental was quadrupled and their landlord demanded payment for a full year in advance. They next turned their attention to editing their newspaper, *Woodhull and Claflin's Weekly*, which began with the loftiest of principles and wound up by being the first to publish the most sensational scandal of the century—a detailed, lurid exposé of the Reverend Henry Ward Beecher's intimacies with his editor's wife.

Because the sisters published this scandal they were flung into the Ludlow Street Jail on charges brought by the self-appointed guardian of New York's morals, Anthony Comstock, of sending obscene material through the mails. They were in and out of jail several times after this. While enjoying one of her periods of freedom between incarcerations, it was advertised that Victoria would speak at the Cooper Union Institute on January 9, 1873, on the subject "The Naked Truth." Comstock obtained an order for her arrest and posted marshals at all the doors to prevent her from speaking. They overlooked an "old Quaker lady" who stood behind a pillar until the hall was filled. She suddenly raced down the aisle, pulled off her bonnet, mounted the rostrum, and

The Stock Exchange was thrown into an uproar of hysterical excitement on March 25, 1872, when Erie Railroad stock climbed to fantastic new highs.

Ticker-tape indicators spread stock-market reports instantly, enabling speculators throughout the country to lose or make money without inconvenience. Here traders in Erie stock neglect luncheon at the Delmonico Restaurant on Broad Street to study the ticker, recently improved by young Thomas A. Edison.

Behind the Erie excitement were Jay Gould and Daniel Drew (with feet up). To Drew the Erie was a money-making toy which he manipulated and played with for fifteen years. The former drover, who delighted in robbing investors during the week, sang psalms in church on Sundays, and welshed on the seminary he endowed.

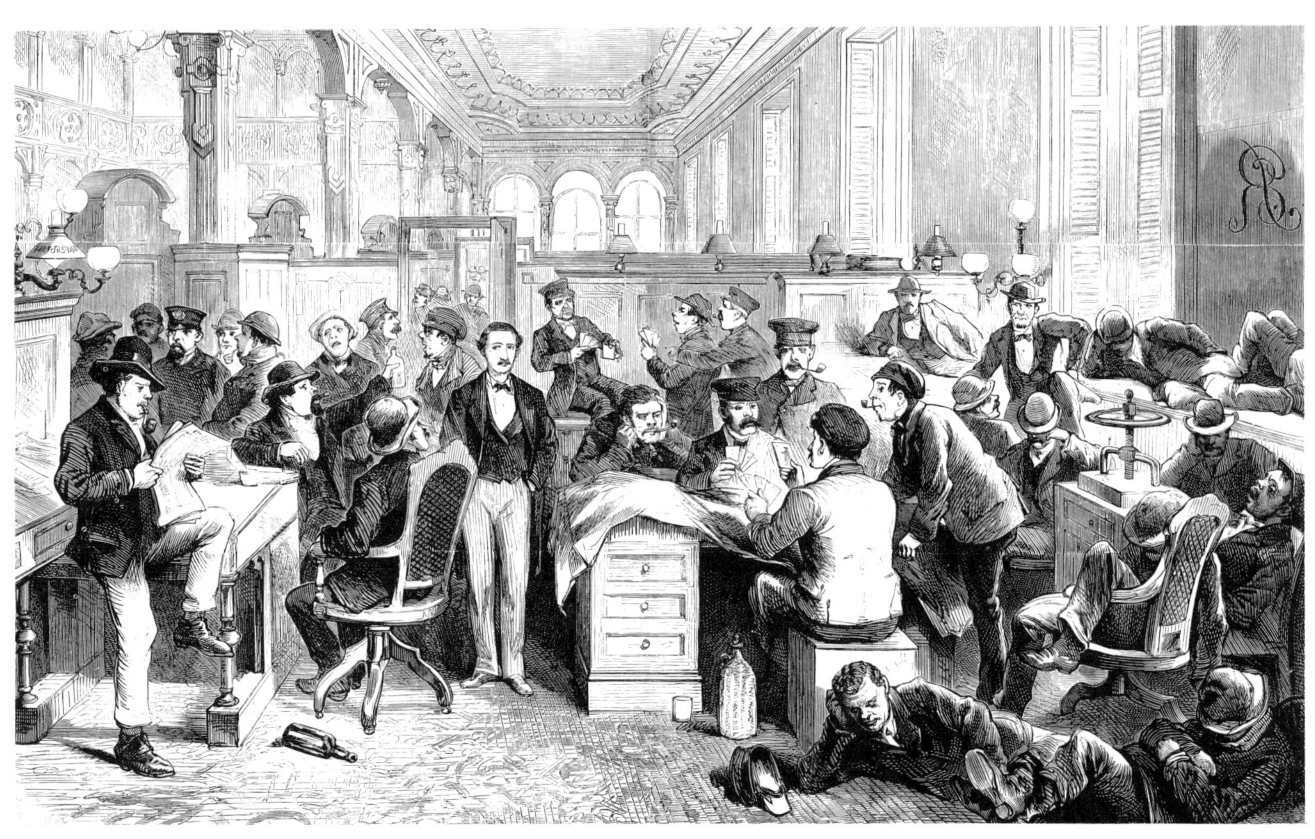

No melodrama ever played at the Grand Opera House had so many thrills as the Erie War, when Jay Gould, surrounded by a private army of thugs, defied stockholders and court orders. Jim Fisk, using Erie funds, had bought the theater as a plaything and had the railroad's offices located in the building.

After selling Vanderbilt unauthorized Erie stock, Gould and Fisk escaped to New Jersey in a rowboat when the law came after them. Later, the Legislature made the stock legal.

held the audience spellbound for an hour and a half. Not a marshal moved.

The sisters were unconventional, raffish, unprincipled by ordinary standards, and did many things in public which are still not generally accepted. But they were also courageous, fighting pioneers — not only for sexual equality but for social justice. Their names might have been hallowed as leaders of the feminist cause had they not insisted in exploiting the Beecher scandal and had persevered in their crusading efforts. In 1877 they went to England where both married rich men—Tennie C. becoming the wife of Sir Francis Cook, in October, 1885, two years after Victoria became Mrs. John Biddulph Martin. Each lived prosperously to a ripe old age. Tennie C. died in 1923, after sitting up in a chair the last four years of her life for fear she would die if she went to bed. Victoria, the lady of the manor at Bredon's Norton, offered a trophy and a prize of five thousand dollars to the first man who would fly the Atlantic. This was in 1912. She died in her ninetieth year, on June 10, 1927, when the furor over Lindbergh's solo flight pushed her obituary notice off the front page.

It was said when Victoria and Tennie C. left for England that they were whisked out of the country so that they could not testify in the case arising out of the contest over Cornelius Vanderbilt's will. He had died in 1877 at the age of eighty-three with the satisfaction of knowing that his last ten years had been the most exciting of an extremely eventful life. For one thing he became involved with the Erie Railroad, which had more ups and downs than a good roller coaster and not much more trackage. For years it had been the pet vehicle of Daniel Drew who milked it, pushed up the price of its stock, pulled it down at will, robbed it blind, lent it millions, and did whatever his avaricious fancy dictated in issuing new securities.

Drew took on two young partners in 1867 — Jim Fisk and Jay Gould. He needed active assistants because a new Mother Lode had opened up in the person of Vanderbilt, who now controlled New York Central and wanted to eliminate competition by purchasing Erie. Vanderbilt began buying Erie stock and Drew started selling it to him through the expansive Fisk and the secretive Gould. It did not take the Commodore long to acquire the stock which should have given him control. But he found that as fast as he bought shares, more poured into the

Gaudy, happy, ruthless Jim Fisk was shot to death, not by a ruined victim of a stock deal or love affair, but by a friend who had betrayed him.

market. "If this printing press doesn't break down," Fisk said, "I'll be damned if I don't give the old hog all he wants of Erie."

Then, when the Commodore discovered that the ink was hardly dry and the stock was not authorized, he obtained an order from a New York court for the arrest of Gould and Fisk. Tipped off as they were dining at Delmonico's, the pair dashed up to Canal Street, got into a rowboat from one of Fisk's steamers, and started across to New Jersey, carrying the Erie books and about six million dollars in greenbacks. Setting up headquarters in "Fort Taylor," as they called their thug-guarded Jersey City hotel, they were joined by Uncle Dan Drew and planned their next move—which proved both simple and effective. Gould lugged a bag crammed with greenbacks to Albany and bribed members of the New York Legislature to legalize not only the stock unloaded on Vanderbilt, but a great deal more besides. Drew scuttled off to make his peace with Vanderbilt, while Fisk and Gould returned to town in triumph. They opened luxurious offices in Pike's Opera House, at Twenty-third Street and Eighth Avenue, which Fisk purchased and renamed the Grand Opera House. Here he produced the merriest, rowdiest musical shows of the time.

While Gould was small, egg-skulled and somberly bearded, nervous and timid in manner, Fisk, who was a year older (Gould was 32 in 1868), has been described in many ways. "Blonde, bustling and rollicking," one commentator wrote, "[a man] who came bounding into the Wall Street circus, like a star-acrobat, fresh, exuberant, glittering with spangles, and turning double summersets, apparently as much for his own amusement as for that of a large circle of spectators." "A more obnoxious person never imposed himself on the stage," wrote William Winter, the critic, who had icily rejected a retainer of $2,500 a year to "drop into the paper an occasional paragraph about him—anything pleasantly personal." Fisk loved to dress up as colonel of the Ninth Militia, or as admiral of the fleet of Fall River liners he operated. He would take actresses fresh from Paris for carriage rides through Central Park and tell them it was his estate—until one of them said in that case she was striking for a larger salary. He gave away and spent his money with the liberality of a drunken sailor—and among his long catalog of weaknesses the greatest was for Mrs. Helen Josephine Mansfield Lawlor, better known as Josie Mansfield.

Whenever Fisk was busy and Miss Mansfield pouted and felt neglected, he would send Edward S. Stokes, the handsome young Treasurer of the Brooklyn Oil Refining Company which Jubilee Jim had bought and revived, to divert her. Soon Stokes was assuaging Josie without any prompting from Fisk. He also was twenty-seven thousand dollars short in his accounts at the refinery when Jim caught up with him. Then Josie and Ed began legal action for fancied damages, while collecting blackmail from Fisk. Pushed into a corner, the long-suffering Fisk began to fight at last. He had the two of them indicted for blackmail. The news came an hour after both Josie and Stokes had fared badly on the witness stand in *their* suit against Fisk. Stokes was so enraged that he ambushed Jim on the marble staircase of the Grand Central Hotel—now the Broadway Central

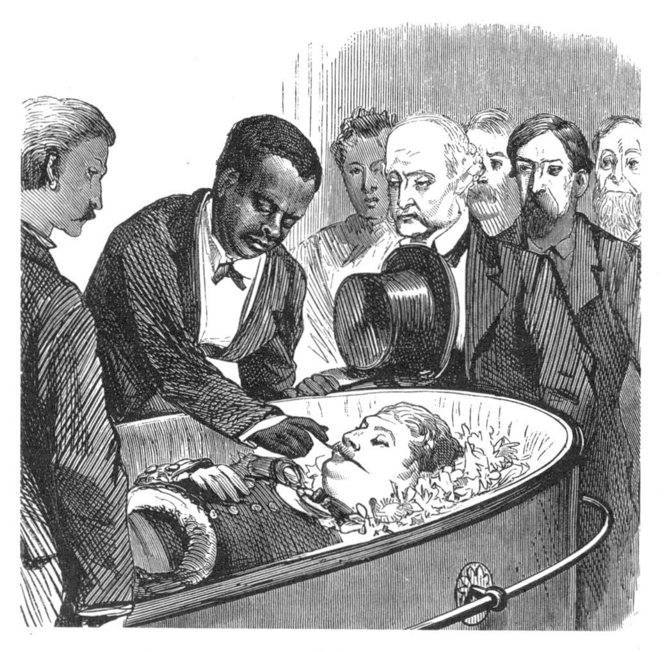

THE BARBER'S FAREWELL. *"One more twirl, dearest of friends, for the last time" read the caption of this picture in a popular journal. Fisk's body, attired in his colonel's uniform, lay in state in the Grand Opera House before his funeral.*

Hotel—and shot him down. Fisk died the next day, January 7, 1872, and, oddly enough, his passing was mourned by many. Stokes was tried, found guilty, and condemned to hang. However, he won a new trial and was sentenced to a term of six years for manslaughter. After serving four years, he was released and became the proprietor of the Hoffman House, the city's leading saloon. Josie Mansfield lived on for another sixty years and died after collapsing during a shopping tour in a Paris department store.

Unfortunately for Gould, Drew, and their pack, Fisk was not on hand to take the blame for the deplorable condition of the Erie Railroad. The result was that Gould was dropped as President, Treasurer, and Director. Acting on information supplied by disgruntled former partners in Gould's brokerage house, the new management of the Erie sued him for $9,700,000, which they claimed he had taken from the road by fraud. Of this sum, it was alleged, about $4,500,000 had been realized by Gould out of sales of forty million dollars' worth of unauthorized stock. Another three million dollars of Erie funds were transferred by Gould for his own use to repay

A FINANCIER'S GRIEF. *Jay Gould weeping beside Fisk's coffin. Gould, himself, was to die at fifty-six of tuberculosis, the workingman's disease.*

Boss Tweed attending to the removal of Fisk's body from the Grand Central Hotel. Tweed and crooked judges helped keep Fisk and Gould out of jail.

After the fire in 1865, Barnum moved his Museum to Broadway near Spring Street. Another fire broke out on the night of March 2, 1868. P.T. wrote: "The cold was so intense that the water froze almost as soon as it left the hose. . . . Thousands congregated daily to get a view of the magnificent ruins."

his losses in gold speculation in 1869. Then there were other charges of fraudulent embezzlement and misappropriation which made up the sum total of $9,700,000. In December, 1872, Gould made restitution, surrendering assets supposed to be worth nine million dollars, saying: "I do this for the sake of peace, because any litigation of such questions is more annoying than the loss of the money involved."

The Erie situation was about the worst, but few railroads were in a state of good health in 1873. Construction had progressed with far more rapidity than business conditions warranted, bankers had been advancing large sums to the roads even before construction bonds were sold, and now the market was unable to absorb all the new securities offered.

Jay Cooke and Company, the financial heroes of the Civil War and the promoters of the Northern Pacific Railroad, failed on September 18, 1873. Many other bank failures followed. Stocks declined, money tightened and disappeared. On Saturday, the 20th, the Governing Committee of the Stock Exchange ordered trading suspended at noon until further notice, for the best stocks had been unsalable at any price all morning. Ten days later the exchange reopened, but between September 18 and the end of the year, fifty-seven exchange firms failed. In addition, the Union Trust Company, the Bank of the Commonwealth, and many other financial institutions closed down. It was almost six years before Wall Street recovered.

10

The Age That Had Everything

THE LAST QUARTER of the nineteenth century has often been called "The 'Gilded' Age," but it can also be described as "The Age That Had Everything." It was an age crowded with celebrations and disasters, economic peaks and depths, good times and hard, improvements and inventions, the creation of new landmarks and the passing of old—and a continuous parade of great men, strange characters, and talented swindlers.

Skyscrapers, rapid transit, electric lighting, the telephone, and the automobile were introduced in these years. Wall Street was rocked by the blast of a second deadly explosion; the country fought a brief and profitable war; and New Yorkers battled *the* blizzard to which every other storm will always be compared. The giant Statue of Liberty was unveiled in New York harbor and the monumental bronze figure of George Washington was set on its pedestal in front of the Sub-Treasury, but the age had its living giants, too—J. P. Morgan, Willy Vanderbilt, the Rockefellers, Thomas A. Edison, and Andrew Carnegie.

Panics and booms alternated in swift cycles. President Garfield was assassinated; the Johnstown Flood almost wiped out an entire town; the Brooklyn Bridge was completed; the bicycle craze swept the country; and a rash of lockouts and strikes, marked for the first time by bloodshed and killings, erupted in various industrial and mining areas. It was an age that saw the rise and fall of the mustache and the bustle, the age of such celebrities as Lillian Russell, "Diamond Jim" Brady, and Steve Brodie. The term "Four Hundred" was coined, and a riot of vulgar, ostentatious spending by the new-rich stood out in shameful contrast to the bleak misery and semi-starvation of the poor. And the kitchen sink was introduced.

Bankers in those days did not try to beguile ordinary citizens into accepting loans. They were for the most part taciturn and conservative, tending to avoid any kind of publicity. When James Stillman and Henry C. Frick were besieged by reporters seeking a statement on a day the stock market was turning cartwheels, they kept the newspapermen waiting in an anteroom for an hour. Then Stillman's secretary handed the reporters the following statement:

Bird's-eye view of the port of New York in 1878, south from the Battery, with land filled in to the Castle Garden Emigrant Depot. LEFT *(bottom to top): Sound steamers, Governor's Island, Buttermilk Channel, Brooklyn, Gowanus Bay, Red Hook Point, Gravesend Bay, Coney Island.* CENTER: *the Narrows.* RIGHT: *Hudson boats, Bedloe's Island, Bayonne, Kill Van Kull, Staten Island.*

The United States of America is a great and growing country.

SIGNED, *James Stillman*
Henry C. Frick

This is confidential and not for publication unless names are omitted.

The United States was indeed great and growing at a tremendous pace mainly because of the heavy flow of immigration and the settlement of the West. The population of New York City doubled during the twenty-five years ending in 1900, reaching a figure of 3,437,202, while a total of ten million immigrants arrived from Europe, most of them passing through the port of New York.

The number of immigrants who remained in New York made it necessary to push the settled part of the city north. The empty lots around Central Park and to the rivers on either side were first dotted with squatters' shanties which eventually gave way to rows of brownstone-fronted houses. The salt marshes edging the East River, which sometimes flooded as far west as Third Avenue, were filled in and provided additional ground on which to build. The erection of the palatial Dakota on Central Park West and other "French Flats" started the vogue of apartment living for the well-to-do. Solid blocks of huge tenements were erected for the poorer classes, and the population density reached a third of a million per square mile in the crowded Tenth Ward. This area became the center for the manufacture of artificial flowers, cigars, and clothing which were priced at incredibly low figures. "One Bowery store sold 15,000 of its suits a year at $1.95 apiece," Smith Hart wrote in *The New Yorkers*. Sweatshops, piecework at home, and child labor in factories, where a twelve-hour a day, six-day week was routine, were prevalent as the industrial era came of age.

While manufacturing flourished in that part of Manhattan north of City Hall, shipping along the East River gradually fell off and almost stopped completely in the years between the Civil War and 1900. The war delivered the first blow to the American mercantile marine, which relied heavily on sail and was therefore unable to meet the increasing competition of European countries, especially England, with their fleets of superior steamships. The new ocean liners began to dock at the piers along the Hudson, while South Street, along the East River, remained the last haven of the freighters of the sea—the worn-out clippers and packet boats—as well as of the suppliers of slop chest, galley, and cabin; the rope-dealers, figurehead carvers, and block-makers; the sail lofts, the chronometer dealer at the corner of Wall, the commission merchants, ship agents and brokers who occupied the old buildings that stood facing the old wooden vessels.

Today in India House, the private club on Hanover Square, the classic feminine figure which graced the prow of the *Glory of the Seas*, last of the great clippers built by Donald McKay, looks down from the head of the stairs, reminding the shipping executives who gather there at lunch of a South Street which was once dominated by ships of wood and men of steel.

The great man of steel of the period was a sailor only in the sense that he owned the yacht *Corsair* and was Commodore of the New York Yacht Club. This was John Pierpont Morgan, son of Junius Spencer Morgan, a Connecticut merchant who went into the fire-insurance business and established a great reputation for his company by arriving in New York immediately after the fire of 1835 with a satchel of currency and promptly paying off all claims. J. P. Morgan—grandson of the Reverend John Pierpont, a crusading Boston clergyman, and Joseph Morgan, a Hartford tavern- and hotel-keeper—was born in his paternal grandfather's house in Hartford on April 17, 1837. He received a generally standard education, embellished, however, by a year of study at the University of Göttingen in Germany. Returning to America, he came to Wall Street to serve an apprenticeship as a junior accountant just in time to exper-

South Street in 1878 was all masts, horse-drawn drays, buildings filled with nautical instrument stores and sail lofts. In the distance are cables and the Manhattan pier of the Brooklyn Bridge, then under construction.

ience the Panic of 1857. Soon after, he became the American representative for the firm of George Peabody and Company of London, in which his father, Junius, was a partner. In 1861 he was married, but his wife died only four months later. The following year he went into business under his own name and prospered during the Civil War, although he became entangled with two unscrupulous speculators. In the Hall Carbine Affair he lent twenty thousand dollars to Simon Stevens, who used the money to buy outmoded guns, previously purchased from the War Department, for $3.50 apiece and then sold them right back to General John Frémont at a price of twenty-two dollars each. Morgan was cleared of any implication in this scandal except that of acting as moneylender. During 1863 he joined Edward B. Ketchum to run up the price of gold and split a $160,000 profit. The act might have gone unnoticed, except that his partner in the deal was the same Ketchum who, two years later, forged the gold certifi-

The House of Drexel, erected by the Philadelphia banking firm at Wall and Broad in 1871, was soon dominated by imperious New York partner, John Pierpont Morgan. In the 1890's the building became known as the House of Morgan.

J. P. Morgan once said he was a descendant of Sir Henry Morgan, the corsair. Each of the Wall Street Morgan's yachts was painted black and named CORSAIR.

Photographed in Paris at thirty-one, Morgan was a tall, dashing figure, with piercing eyes that made him look the part of a powerful financial leader.

cates that led, indirectly, to the closing of the Evening Exchange.

Representing his father's firm and its anxious English clients during the Civil War and afterward, as well as transacting a general private banking business, J. P. continued to prosper mightily. He married again and built a home at Thirty-sixth Street and Madison Avenue, then practically the northern outskirts of the city. He also participated in the "Susquehanna War" for control of the Albany and Susquehanna Railroad as principal aide to the management against the efforts of Jay Gould and Jim Fisk to take it over, although the story that he personally threw Fisk down a flight of stairs at a stockholders' meeting appears to be purely apocryphal.

Largely as a result of Morgan's efforts, the Gould-Fisk gang were defeated in their raid on the Albany and Susquehanna, and Morgan's reputation was enhanced. Perhaps the rough-and-tumble of the battle, the chaos of unrestrained competition, made young Morgan the staunch advocate of monopoly and combination which he was to become. As Frederick Lewis Allen wrote in *The Great Pierpont Morgan:* "It is hardly an accident that most of the Americans who at the beginning of the twentieth century were charged with being monopolists had got a good look in their youth at competition at its savage and unbridled worst, and had decided to try to do something about it."

In London his father floated a fifty-million-dollar loan to the beleaguered French government during the darkest days of the Franco-Prussian War. This worked out so successfully that after Peabody died the firm name was changed to Junius Spencer Morgan and Company. Junius also began the negotiations which resulted in his son joining with Anthony J. Drexel's Philadelphia firm in forming Drexel, Morgan and Company of New York on July 1, 1871. Within two years young Morgan was able to break into Jay Cooke's monopoly in distributing United States bond issues. When the Cooke firm led the avalanche of failures which set off the Panic of 1873, he quickly assumed the lead in this field, for he was able to sell bonds abroad, where a great deal of money was available, not only through his father in London, but also through Drexel, Harjes and Company in Paris and, in alliance with the firm of Levi Morton, who was to become Harrison's Vice-President in 1889, through the huge Rothschild banking empire. In spite of the depression of the times, in the

Looking northwest on Wall from William Street in 1883. Trinity Church still towered over the city. The building with Neptune above the door and the one with two columns were replaced by the Bank of Manhattan building the next year.

first five years of the firm's operation, Morgan left in the business over a million and a half dollars of his share of the profits.

The firm of Drexel, Morgan and Company had its headquarters in an imposing six-story building of white marble at 23 Wall, across the street from both the Sub-Treasury corner and the Stock Exchange which was built just before the partnership was established—a site that was to be rocked only seven years after J. P.'s death by one of the most dreadful incidents in Wall Street history.

Before joining with the Drexels, the thirty-three-year-old Morgan had given serious consideration to retiring from business altogether because of his health. For years he had suffered from fainting spells, massive headaches, and insomnia. He was also afflicted with a chronic facial rash that centered about his nose. As time went on this *acne rosacea* became increasingly severe, distorting his nose and features toward the end of his life so that his face seemed to take on the cast of a gross caricature that no caricaturist dared copy. This condition made him so self-conscious that he was often pugnacious toward photographers and tended to withdraw from public appearances. For although he had become the outspoken dictator of the financial world, John Pierpont Morgan was a shy, aloof, and often withdrawn man. Leading a rather solitary life, he would slip into his church to sit alone and thunder out hymns in his unmusical voice, or go for rambling, lonely walks with his dog at Cragston, his summer place on the Hudson, just below West Point. In the evenings, he kept to himself, playing long sessions of solitaire in his library.

Morgan went into railroad financing in 1879 when William Henry Vanderbilt decided to cut his 87 per

On Monday, November 26, 1883, in a heavy storm, Governor Grover Cleveland and President Chester A. Arthur unveiled the thirteen-foot statue of George Washington on the very spot where he was inaugurated.

cent ownership in New York Central in half without upsetting the market. Morgan discreetly disposed of the stock among English investors and, as holder of their proxies, he became a powerful member of the board of the New York Central. In this position he was able to bring some order and stability into the chaotic railroad picture. First he persuaded the heads of the Pennsylvania Railroad and the New York Central to stop cutting rates and building competitive lines. This led to an increase in first-class fares to Chicago from seven dollars to twenty. Next he gathered the coal carriers, who controlled the hard-coal mines, and got them to limit production, thus raising the price of coal twenty-five cents a ton.

Then he set out to consolidate his new power. Backed by Kidder, Peabody and Company, Brown Brothers and Company, and the London firms of his father and Baring Brothers, he demanded, in the name of the foreign and domestic security-holders they represented, the immediate cessation of railroad wars, the elimination of ruinous competition, no more construction of rival routes, and the curbing of speculative expansion. Although Morgan had a competitor for power in the new Interstate Commerce

A PUCK *cartoon of Washington's statue at Broad and Wall, across the street from Morgan's bank, was captioned "In Bad Company." The fourth building toward Trinity Church had been torn down to make way for the Stock Exchange Annex.*

Commission, he proved to be much the stronger during the first eighteen years of that body's life. Of the cases appealed from the commission's rulings which reached the Supreme Court, the railroads won fifteen out of sixteen times against the complaints of shippers and other customers.

No wonder that when he purchased George Washington's sword, the *New York World* published a cartoon titled "The New Commander," showing Morgan, sword in one hand and checkbook in the other, with hard-winged collar, Ascot tie, and plug hat, standing in Washington's place on the pedestal before the Sub-Treasury. Washington's name has been crossed out and in its place is "J. Pierpont Morgan, General of Industry," while "The Father of His Country" has been relabeled "The Father of Wall Street."

Earlier, the comic magazine, *Puck*, printed a cartoon of Washington's proposed statue at the crossroads of Wall and Broad surrounded by well-dressed thieves stripping the unwary. The caption read: "In Bad Company." But Morgan, who had the choicest seat, across the street, for both the dedication of the John Quincy Adams Ward statue in 1883 and the centennial celebration of Washington's first inaugu-

On September 4, 1882, three years after Edison had invented the first electric light, he opened the Pearl Street generating station and began service to fifty-nine customers in the financial area.

The dynamos in the Pearl Street station had a total capacity of 540 kilowatts, compared to Consolidated Edison's current 3½ million. Lines have grown from fifteen miles to 67,000 and customers have increased by 2,500,000.

The dedication of the Statue of Liberty on October 28 was a big event of 1886. This painting is owned by Mrs. Seton Henry, daughter of Joseph Drexel, a Morgan partner and chairman of the pedestal fund committee. She remembers how her mother combed New York for frog legs to serve the French sculptor Bartholdi, who said they were delicious and also that it was the first time he had ever eaten them.

ration six years later, was a leader who brought back honesty and ethics, not so much to the Street as to the great industries whose securities were marketed there. His moral values were not those of today, for his responsibility was first to himself, then to his investors, and not to the consumer or public. But in comparison to the ethical code, or lack of one, of the successful operators around him, his was high-minded and righteous and conservative. Before he could enforce his code, he had to put the fear of J. P. Morgan into the people with whom he dealt, sometimes waiting a year for the proper moment to wipe out a man or group who had double-crossed him or reneged on an agreement. But he prevailed and predominated, and after he had been called in to clear up the wreckage of the roads in the Panic of 1893, "Morgan occupied a position unprecedented in American railroading," as Frederick Lewis Allen wrote in his biography of the banker. "He had long been influential in the councils of the New York Central; now he was at least influential, if not dominant in those of the Erie, the New Haven, the Reading, the Norfolk & Western, the Southern Railway System, and the Lehigh Valley. . . . In alliance with James J. Hill, he was influential in the Northern Pacific, the Baltimore & Ohio, and Hill's own Great Northern. The Jersey Central was dominated by his close ally, George F. Baker of the First National Bank. And the Pennsylvania, Lackawanna, and Delaware & Hudson were all in hands generally friendly. . . . In short, the managements of most of the leading railroads of the East were at least deferential to his wishes, and through the Great Northern and the Northern Pacific his sphere of influence reached all the way to the West Coast."

Morgan's rise in the railroad field made him the dominant American banker, so much so that when the nation's financial structure was on the verge of collapse because of the withdrawal of gold to Europe at the beginning of 1895, it was to him and August Belmont that the government turned to halt the flow and shore up the gold reserves. There was much bargaining over interest rates and a loud outcry against the bankers by the Democratic press, but Morgan found a Civil War statute which provided the method of financing. He insisted on seeing President Cleveland face to face in order to explain. For some days Cleveland refused, but when they met, Cleveland later said: "I had a feeling, not of suspicion, but of watchfulness. . . . I had not gone far, however, before my doubts disappeared. I found I was in negotiation with a man of large business comprehension and of remarkable knowledge and prescience . . . of clear-sighted, far-seeing patriotism."

On his side, Morgan guaranteed that the gold received by the United States would not be siphoned out of the country during the time of the contract. This was a reckless promise to make, but he accomplished the feat, at considerable expense to the syndicate.

Regarded universally as the symbol of conservatism, Morgan was most radical in his approach, not only in the way he combined corporations, but in his creation and development of new industries. He was one of the first investors in Thomas A. Edison's Electric Light Company, supplying funds four years before Edison lighted a hundred buildings in lower Manhattan from his power station on Pearl Street. At 5:00 P.M., September 4, 1882, while a vast crowd of people waited in anticipation, the switch was

Wall Street political parade in the Cleveland-Harrison campaign of 1888 received ticker-tape greeting from the windows of the Stock Exchange Annex. Although President Cleveland polled a greater popular vote, Harrison was elected. Four years later Cleveland came back to win his second term.

The Panic of 1884. In May the failures of Grant and Ward (in which the former President had a small interest) and the Marine Bank had a slight effect on the stock market, but the subsequent closing of the Metropolitan Bank started a panic that resulted in fifteen more Stock Exchange bankruptcies.

National pride over the driving of the Golden Spike at Promontory, Utah, marking the opening of a transcontinental railroad, was slightly soured by news that the Union Pacific had been secretly acquired by Jay Gould.

Cornelius Vanderbilt had called Gould the "smartest man in America," but in the Panic of 1884 he barely squeaked through while the Commodore's son sat on $40 million in United States bonds.

William Henry ("the public be damned") Vanderbilt outlived his father by only eight years, but he more than doubled the $90 million inheritance that Cornelius had left him and contributed to many philanthropies and educational institutions.

John D. Rockefeller (seen here at age thirty-three in 1872) made a billion dollars by eliminating competition from the oil industry. Said Mark Hanna: "He is sane in every respect save one. He is money mad."

John D. was sane about money compared to the most colorful Wall Street character of all—Hetty Green, who ran her inherited million up to $90 million and "went to court like other women go to the opera."

thrown and thousands of incandescent lamps suddenly glowed in half a hundred buildings. One was Sweet's Restaurant at Fulton and South streets, where little has been changed since except the bulbs. Another was the Drexel building where Edison came to switch on the lights himself, bringing five associates, including his secretary, Samuel Insull.

Morgan's house, uptown, at 219 Madison Avenue, was also wired for electricity, necessitating the installation of a small steam plant to turn the generator which supplied the current. This required the service of a full-time engineer to fire the boiler, check the short circuits, and keep the lights burning. In spite of accidents beforehand, the system found favor among the hundreds of guests at a reception given to show off its advantages. The next morning, when Darius O. Mills, the California mining magnate, came to 23 Wall to buy a thousand shares of Edison stock, Morgan told him that he was matching every purchase with one of his own. When an uptown power station was to be built, providing current for the house on Madison, Morgan himself subscribed half of the million dollars needed.

Although the ferry ride from Fulton Street, Manhattan, to Fulton Street, Brooklyn, took less than five minutes and cost less than five cents, frequent accidents and collisions such as this one in 1868, were factors in advancing the plan to span the East River with a bridge so high that the tallest ship's masts could pass easily underneath.

William Henry Vanderbilt, who gave Morgan his great push up when he sold half of his New York Central stock, was a living fulfillment of the biblical prophecy that the meek shall inherit the earth. He was a sickly, passive Staten Island farmer and a great disappointment to his father, the hearty, forceful Commodore. Willy did nothing which either crossed or pleased his father until he was over forty, when he persuaded old Cornelius to have him appointed receiver of the thirteen-mile-long, debt-ridden Staten Island Railroad. To everyone's surprise, especially his father's, William Henry proved to be a shrewd railroad operator, for, within five years, he sent the stock up to 175. This opened the Commodore's eyes to the potentials of rail expansion and turned him away from water transportation. When the old man died, on January 3, 1877, at the age of eighty-three, he left ninety of his 105 million dollars to William, who lived another eight years and, despite panics and strikes, doubled the Vanderbilt fortune.

The meek William Henry, richest man in the world, summoned the nerve to speak out boldly at least on one occasion. It was a mistake, because only one devastating phrase was quoted and repeated, and even this was wrongly attributed. On October 8, 1882, two reporters were interviewing him in his private car near Chicago. Vanderbilt said that the New York Central was only running its new crack, fast train between Chicago and New York because of competition with the Pennsylvania Railroad. "But don't you run it for the public benefit?" he was asked. "The public be damned!" exclaimed Vanderbilt. "What does the public care for the railroads except to get as much out of them for as little consideration as possible?" All the public ever heard of that outburst was that Vanderbilt had decreed it was to be damned—and most people believed it was the crusty old Cornelius, rather than meek Willy, who made the remark.

The Vanderbilts' Harlem road, the first steam system in New York, was joined by a network of urban railways, elevated above the streets. The Ninth Avenue Line ran along Greenwich Street downtown. The Third Avenue Line, opened in 1878 between City Hall Park and Forty-second Street, was extended to Harlem in 1880. By then the steam cars were carrying a total of 130 million passengers. Almost as many were handled annually by the ferries on the East and Hudson rivers. The owners of the East River ferries fought savagely against the building of the Great East River Bridge, as the proposed link to Brooklyn was first called, but the perseverance of its creator, John A. Roebling, surmounted far greater opposition and difficulties than this.

A million people saw the first fuse of Brooklyn Bridge pyrotechnics touched off, releasing fifty giant rockets, at 8:00 P.M. on May 24, 1883. In moments Manhattan and Brooklyn were bathed in the glow of red, gold, blue, and green bursts as fireworks balloons, rockets, and clusters painted the sky.

The Roebling story is one of triumph and tragedy. He was a Prussian-born engineer who perfected methods of manufacturing wire rope in Pittsburgh and built several suspension bridges there as well as the great suspension bridge across the Niagara, which was finished in 1855. In 1857 he moved his factory to Trenton and proposed to span the East River with a soaring high arch under which the tallest ships could sail. Because of the Civil War and the usual civic delays it was not until April 16, 1867, that the Legislature passed an act permitting erection of the bridge and granted a charter to the New York Bridge Company. On June 21, 1869, the War Department approved the plan and location of the bridge. Then, on June 28, while standing on some piles at Fulton Ferry Slip, engrossed in a survey he was making across the river, Roebling failed to observe the approach of a ferryboat. Entering the slip, the ferry crashed into a fender which was driven into the piles, crushing Roebling's foot. His toes had to be amputated, but tetanus developed, and he died on July 22.

However, Roebling had trained an able assistant, his son, Colonel Washington A. Roebling, who went ahead with the actual construction of the bridge. The sinking of the two caissons for the foundation of the towers of the bridge was a hazardous undertaking. Compressed air was used extensively for the first time and this made the project doubly dangerous. In 1871 an accident almost snuffed out the lives of the men in one working chamber when two air-supply shafts blew out and the pressure dropped from fifteen pounds to four. But the younger Roebling, who was one of those trapped, took charge and succeeded in restoring full pressure in a quarter of an hour. This is thought to have contributed to the wrecking of his health. Actually, he spent more hours in the caissons, directing the work, than anyone else. Early in the summer of 1872 he was brought out with an attack of "caisson disease," or the "bends," and although he tried to go back, he again collapsed and was forced to supervise the rest of the construction from an invalid's bed on Columbia Heights, overlooking the bridge from Brooklyn. At the age of thirty-five, Washington Roebling was doomed to a life of paralysis, pain, and progressive loss of his sight, hearing, and speech. The bridge cost the lives of twenty other men during the thirteen years it took to erect.

"The great work was finished," wrote D. B. Steinman in *The Builders of the Bridge*. "The two master builders had paid their price—one with his life, the other with a crippled body. The father had dreamed the Bridge. The son, with gallant fighting spirit, had carried that dream to fulfillment. No inspired builder of a medieval cathedral brought to his work a greater singleness of purpose, a more selfless devotion, than the two Roeblings lavished on their master bridge. The best in their characters went into its building. Of granite and steel and dreams, the Bridge was built."

"It was a glorious spring day," Steinman went on as he described the official opening of the bridge in 1883. "Dawn revealed the twin cities resplendent with waving banners and streaming colors. From windows and roofs, from the forests of shipping along the wharves and from the vessels riding the sparkling waters of the bay, flags were floating proudly in the breeze; while high above all, from the massive, time-defying towers of the Bridge, the Stars and Stripes signaled to the world—from the gateway of the continent—the arrival of the long-awaited day."

It was a holiday such as New York had always loved. Business was suspended and hundreds of thousands of people streamed toward "Roebling's Eighth Wonder of the World." Along the river decorations of every description festooned boats of every kind, from the ferries to the warships of the

Photograph of Roebling's "Eighth Wonder of the World" taken from the tower of the Produce Exchange shows ferries still in service ten years after the bridge was opened. The Hanover Square station of the Third Avenue El can be seen at lower left, to the right of the Coffee Exchange building.

The Brooklyn Bridge has always been a favorite subject of artists and photographers, often with inspired results. This unusual photograph by John Francis Strauss, published in 1903 in a pioneer magazine, CAMERA WORK, *bore the legend: "A photogravure made from the unmanipulated and unfaked negative."*

A terrible tragedy on the bridge occurred six days after it opened when sight-seers, who paid a penny to walk across, were stampeded when a woman fell down the steps. Ten people were crushed to death.

North Atlantic Squadron, making "the waters of the river [to] run with colors, like a dye vat."

At the Fifth Avenue Hotel, President Chester Alan Arthur, who had been Collector of the Port of New York from 1871 to 1879, and Governor Grover Cleveland, who was to succeed Arthur as President two years later, climbed into their open carriages. Escorted by military bands and the entire Seventh Regiment in gray-and-white dress uniforms, they proceeded to City Hall where they picked up Mayor Franklin Edson and the assembled city fathers. They then drove onto the bridge as far as the New York tower. Here they were met by officials and a military delegation from Brooklyn. The President, Governor, and Mayor left their carriages, the bands began to play, and the officials started to walk across the span between two lines of soldiers in their finest parade dress. Now all the cannon on Governor's Island let loose with salvos, answered by the heavy guns of the Brooklyn Navy Yard and repeated by the battery at Fort Greene. The ships

The first working model of a practical typewriter was demonstrated by Lillian Sholes, daughter of the inventor, Christopher Sholes, who sold the patent on the machine to Remington in 1872.

While Sholes eliminated clerks with copperplate handwriting, William Seward Burroughs cut the number of bookkeepers in counting houses by inventing the first successful adding machine in 1884.

Perfection of the passenger elevator permitted buildings to soar skyward. This is a "Metropolitan Steam Safety Elevator" installed by Elisha Otis' company in Lord and Taylor's five-story building in 1870.

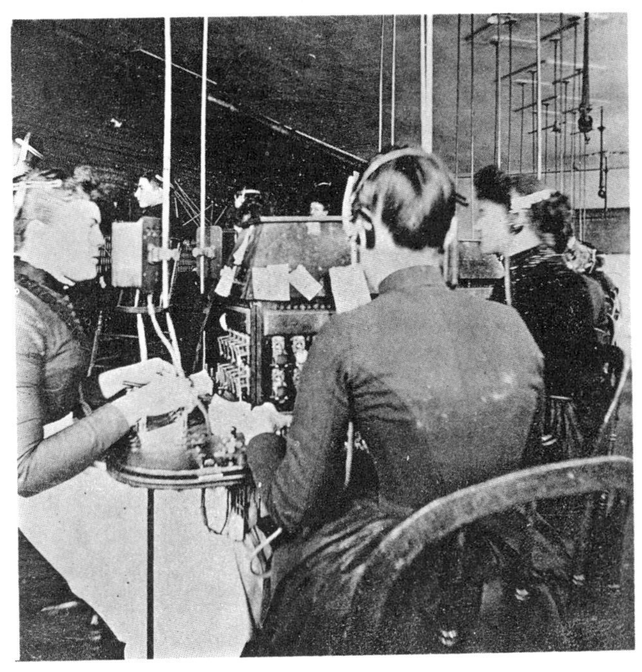

The development of the telephone was rapid in the Wall Street area, where service was at first linked with a burglar-alarm system. Bell boys worked at wall panels while be-bustled girl operators sat at square boards.

tied down their sirens and horns to unleash a steady din, the church bells rang out, and the factories blew their whistles while an estimated million onlookers on both sides of the river cheered themselves hoarse.

At the Brooklyn end of the bridge ten thousand ticket-holders tried to get into the two thousand seats set up in the terminal. Another huge crowd tried to break through the police lines to hear the speakers. The speeches were made and the tributes offered and then, as the celebration and jubilation went on in both cities far into the night, the President, the Governor, the orators, and the trustees marched through the streets of Brooklyn to the house of Washington A. Roebling to congratulate the stricken man and his devoted wife.

Even before the bridge was completed, a cable of Alexander Graham Bell's new telephone was strung across it during the winter of 1877–78. Bell had delivered a lecture on his invention before a large group of interested New Yorkers on the evening of Friday,

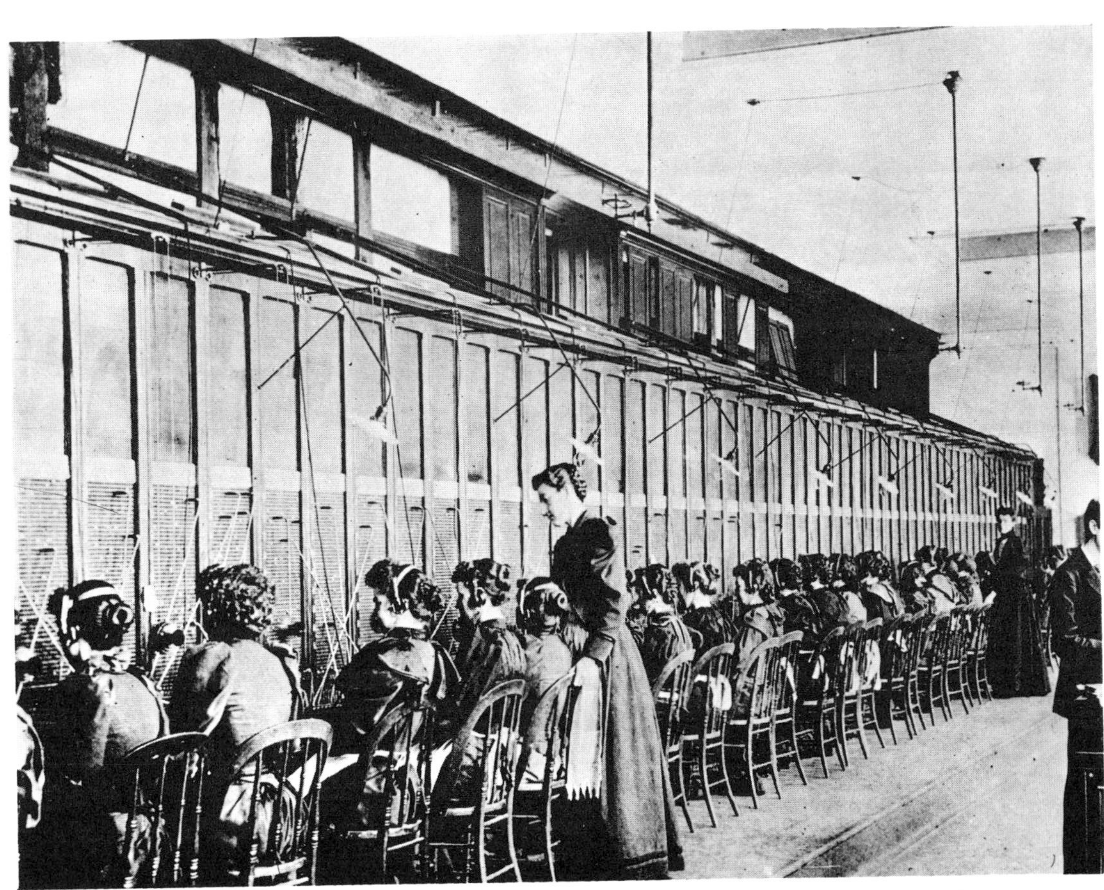

The world's largest, busiest, and most modern telephone exchange—in 1889—was the Cortlandt central office, which served the financial district. The staff totaled almost 300, including a small night shift of male operators.

Broad Street in the 1880's, looking north to the Sub-Treasury, was becoming cluttered with a crisscross of wires belonging to cable, telegraph, burglar-alarm, and telephone companies. Down the middle of the wide street was a row of private carriages and cabs waiting for fares.

May 11, 1877, which concluded with a demonstration of the device—a musician playing a cornet into a transmitter set up in a telegraph office in Brooklyn. Hilborne L. Roosevelt and Charles A. Cheever obtained the New York franchise and went into business as the Telephone Company of New York on August 29 of that year. That winter the Brooklyn cable was installed on the bridge to connect the office of J. L. Haight in New York with his factory in Brooklyn. Apparently, the composition of the cable was faulty, because talk leaked from one wire to another. Thomas A. Watson, superintendent of the Bell Telephone Company in Boston, tried to solve the problem, but without success. Commenting fifty years later, he said: "For the workers in those early days it was like traveling through a tangled jungle—no paths at all, and plenty of thorns to scratch us."

Roosevelt and Cheever rented a floor on Broadway near Fulton, and Thomas Edison subleased space from them to demonstrate and work on his new Talking Machine. The telephone company was undercapitalized and beset with insurmountable technical problems. Roosevelt went back to his organ factory and Cheever joined Edison in the phonograph business. A new telephone company was formed on August 14, 1878, with Edwin Holmes, owner of an electrical burglar-alarm system, as President. Holmes had a number of burglar-alarm exchanges in lower Manhattan, and one of these was utilized as the first telephone exchange. Connecting subscribers with each other was a complicated process which cut off the burglar alarms at both ends. But the popularity and convenience of the telephone led to its being divorced from the alarm system. Soon the "bell" boys who worked at a long panel board connecting and disconnecting lines gave way to the be-bustled lady operators, just as the original greeting, "Ahoy! Ahoy!" gave way to "Hello!"

The new lines strung up by the telephone company only added to the bewildering maze of wires that were draped from pole to pole along the streets of the financial district. Each year new cross-arms were added to the telephone poles, which were constantly being replaced with taller ones. Cartoons of the period pictured a Manhattan of the future with wires strung from three feet above the ground to as high as the eye could see. This prediction was not to come true, but others made humorously at the time actually appeared later. In 1878 *The Century Magazine* de-

The wire situation was especially acute on lower Broadway where poles carried fifteen and even twenty-five crossarms with ten lines strung on each. Horsecars, which had replaced omnibuses, were soon to give way to cable cars.

The most devastating snowstorm in the history of New York was the blizzard of 1888, which left George Washington wearing a white cap and gown, piled drifts twenty feet high as the wind reached hurricane speeds and the temperature dropped to four degrees below zero. It was estimated that more than 400 people died and more than $20 million was lost in property damage.

picted a practical-looking flying saucer; Thomas Nast, in an 1881 issue of *Harper's Weekly*, drew a Trinity Church engulfed by tall buildings twelve years before the first seventeen-story structure was erected on Broadway; *Puck*, in 1878, predicted that military officers of the future would direct their soldiers in war by means of telephones far from the scene of battle.

The advertisements—which Thomas Jefferson had called the only truthful portion of any paper—furnish a link with today and a glimpse of life at the end of the century. In *Harper's Weekly*, Brown Brothers and Company advertised "Commercial and Travellers' Letters of Credit"; W. L. Douglas announced that his three-dollar shoe "is the best—No Squeaking"; the Inter-State Casualty Company of 62 William Street offered to insure *women*; Walter Baker and Company proclaimed that their breakfast cocoa "is made without the use of Alkalies or other Chemicals or Dyes"; the Remington typewriter offered the Wahl Adding and Subtracting Attachment; G. F. Heublein and Brother sold Club Cocktails, "a bottled delight"; Hunter Baltimore Rye "exhilarates the spirit and restores the tone of languid nature"; Beecham's Pills were "worth a guinea a box," and cured swimming in the head, wind, spasms at the stomach and flying pains in the body; Colgate and Company's Cashmere Bouquet Perfume was "for the handkerchief"; Chickering and Son manufactured plain and overstrung pianofortes, while Steinway and Sons warranted their patent overstrung grands and square pianos for five years; Harrington and Richards advertised a "belly-gun" and Colt and Savage offered pocket-sized automatics which delivered eight to ten steel-jacketed bullets in a couple of seconds. Burnett's Cocaine was intended for the hair, but T. E. Clarke, M.D., of Mount Vernon, Ohio, cured Opium Eaters of the habit. Singer's No. 2 Sewing Machine sold for one hundred dollars and a Beatty Parlor Organ for eighty-five dollars.

Wild geese were flying north on Sunday, March 11, 1888, and the weather fluctuated between thirty-four and forty-six degrees. The Weather Bureau atop the five-story Equitable Life Assurance building predicted "fair and warmer" for the next day. However, a cold-wave banner was put up around seven that night because it was reported that a great line-squall over a thousand miles long, extending from the Great Lakes to Cuba, was moving east at the rate of six hundred miles a day. The rain which had been falling all that Sunday turned to snow after midnight—snow that was to continue for more than two days and nights. The temperature began to drop as the wind gathered speed. Before the storm was over the temperature dipped to four degrees below zero and the wind raged at eighty-four miles an hour. Almost twenty-one inches of snow fell, twice as much as had fallen all winter, but the wind flung it into banks fifteen and twenty feet high and turned it into fine, cutting sleet. Getting anywhere, doing anything, became impossible. There was no electric light and no transportation aside from a few hackies who fed their horses whiskey and charged whatever the traffic would bear. Elevated trains were stalled and passengers made their way down ladders to the street. Horsecars were abandoned and became smoking rooms by day and sleeping places at night. At

New Street north to Wall in the big blizzard. Many wires and poles were down and messages to Boston had to be routed via London by cable. After the storm, the city ordered all wires to be laid underground.

Madison Square someone stuck a bouquet of flowers in a snow bank and a sign beside it: "The Flowers That Bloom in the Snow, Ha! Ha!" Someone else at Sixth Avenue and Fourteenth Street had hollowed out a tunnel and placarded it: "This Way to Canada." Steve Brodie hung a sign outside of his bar at 114 The Bowery: "A free drink of whiskey to anybody that needs it and has not got the money to pay for it."

When Chauncey Depew was asked if the New York Central was still going to run trains, he replied: "Trains! Why, we don't even know if we've got a railroad left!" Hundreds slept in the first Grand Central Depot; hundreds more slept in Macy's where the stock of bedclothing and mattresses were spread all over the store; outside, earmuffs were sold at five dollars a pair and milk at one dollar a quart, when it could be obtained. The troublesome telegraph and telephone wires were down everywhere — down to stay—and messages to Boston had to be sent via cable to London and relayed back across the Atlantic to Massachusetts. P. T. Barnum had paraded his circus through the streets on Saturday and was ready to open Monday night at the old Madison Square Garden. A group of newspapermen, well fortified with alcohol, actually arrived for the performance. The showman kept them warmed with further potations and ordered the show presented for their amusement. "But before the night was over many of the professional clowns were in the spectators' seats watching the newspapermen, who did things in the ring," wrote Donald Barr Chidsey. "Tuesday was much the same as Monday. Nothing moved. Here and there somebody struggled home, or to another bar. . . . On Wednesday there was a little sunlight. . . . Thursday was warmer and the snow had ceased. . . . Friday there was a blessed thaw. And by Saturday, which was St. Patrick's Day, things were almost normal, except for the conversation. The Blizzard cost some twenty or twenty-five millions of dollars in property damage. Twenty persons were frozen in New York City." An indirect casualty was the former United States Senator and power behind the throne of the Grant administration, Roscoe Conkling.

Conkling had arrived at his law office on Monday and found the lower Broadway section all but deserted. Only thirty out of more than a thousand members of the Stock Exchange had shown up that morning and most of these were residents of Brooklyn Heights who walked to Manhattan across the solidly frozen East River. At five that evening, Conkling refused the offer of a hackie to drive him home for fifty dollars and began trudging up Broadway. At eight he stumbled into the New York Club at Broadway and Twenty-fifth Street and fell flat on his face. Three weeks later he took to his bed with an abscessed ear, believed to have been caused by his walk in the blizzard. Two weeks after that he was dead.

The following spring New York celebrated the centennial of Washington's inauguration with three days of such fervid and fulsome festivities that it was probably the high point in the rich collection of such Manhattan events. The moving spirit behind the celebration was J. E. Peyton, an Englishman by birth who lived in Haddenfield, New Jersey. It was he who induced the Tennessee Legislature to pass a resolution petitioning Congress in Washington to "encourage an appropriate celebration of the inauguration of President Washington in New York in 1889." Peyton's hobby was proposing centennials. He had previously given impetus to the 1876 Centennial Exhibition at Philadelphia and the Yorktown centennial festival. The New-York Historical Society resolved to celebrate the occasion, the Chamber of Commerce nudged Congress, and by December, 1887, a committee of fifty-nine had been appointed by Mayor Abram S. Hewitt, son-in-law of Peter Cooper. They worked for more than a year and the results were almost overpowering.

For three days before the celebration was scheduled to begin it rained violently most of the time, filling New Yorkers with uneasiness, and "cleaning the streets to a degree that made them one of the principal glories of the occasion," as Julian Ralph wrote in *Harper's Weekly* of May 11, 1889. On Monday morning the sky was overcast and a chill wind blew from the west. President Benjamin Harrison arrived in Elizabeth, New Jersey, just as Washington had done a hundred years before. Harrison, however, came from Washington, D. C., in a magnificent train of special cars on the Pennsylvania Railroad to an Elizabeth which had the same population, about forty thousand, as New York City had in Washington's time. He was greeted by a distinguished welcoming committee, then escorted by a military parade (with many of the marchers in Revolutionary costumes) and a double line of troops all the way to

Elizabethport, where he passed under a "living arch" of beautiful young girls in white, carrying banners representing the states and territories. "They flung down upon the President's carriage a shower of roses in bud and blossom," Ralph reported.

Crossing the bay, Harrison's party witnessed a great naval parade and spectacle. Every sort of steam vessel afloat, a thousand in all, comprising passenger ships, lighters, nine Navy ships of war, five revenue cutters, and a multitude of tugs towing barges, was in the line, each decorated with rainbows of flags. There were at least seventy thousand people aboard the ships on the water, and every tall building on lower Manhattan was "fluttering with bunting, and fretted with the forms of tens of thousands of men and women looking down upon the water" from grandstands built on the roofs, not only of the big buildings, but on Castle Garden and at the ends of the wharves. "The usual forests of masts that hem the city's sides were now ornamented not only with bunting, but with fence-like lines of sailors, standing hand in hand upon the yards . . . of the men-of-war . . . [and] looked, from the airy distance of a thirteen-story building, as clothes-pins do on clothes-lines."

Thirteen sea captains from the New York Marine Society again rowed the President ashore to the foot of Wall Street, but this time they were dressed in black broadcloth and silk hats, as Harrison was attired. Again Wall Street was decorated, a great deal more elaborately this time, for the buildings were taller and almost hidden behind bunting. There was an arch at Pearl Street and from there to Trinity the street was "a fluttering mass of gay color." At the Sub-Treasury the decorations were especially ornate and a temporary platform and grandstand had been set up for the oratorical exercises that would take place the next day. Harrison was escorted past saluting detachments of Civil War veterans to the block-square Equitable building at Broadway and Pine where he lunched in a private room of the Lawyers

To mark the one hundredth anniversary of the first presidential inauguration, President Harrison re-enacted Washington's triumphant journey to New York. In this engraving after a drawing by Frederic Remington, he is shown reviewing the G.A.R., led by a Zouave drum-and-fife corps, in Elizabeth, New Jersey.

Thirteen silk-hatted shipmasters, members of the New York Marine Society, rowed Harrison and Vice-President Levi P. Morton to a decorated landing at the foot of Wall Street where a huge crowd was on hand to greet them. The President and his party then repeated Washington's stroll up the street.

Club. The table was described as "the most beautifully decorated ever seen in this country, if not in the world." It should have been: the decorations cost $4,500. Nestled among the great banks of roses were electric lights covered with pink silk. The centerpiece was a tremendous century-plant adorned with orchids and more pink electric lights.

After lunch the President, accompanied by Gilmore's and Cappa's bands playing "Old Hundred," proceeded between packed Broadway crowds to City Hall. Here he received about 2,500 of New York's leading citizens and then went on to the Fifth Avenue mansion of his Vice-President, Levi Morton, where he stayed during his New York visit. He had dinner at the Stuyvesant Fish house on Gramercy Park and then attended the Great Ball, held in the Metropolitan Opera House, which had been erected only six years before. The décor of the huge auditorium (a flat floor had been laid over the orchestra seats) included flowers of Washington's time, flags and shields of the states, broad silk bands of red, white, and blue, a hundred stuffed doves seeming to fly high above the stage—and, of course, a dazzling display of diamonds worn by the most prominent ladies of New York. Outside the Opera House, on Thirty-ninth Street, a temporary supper room had been constructed with a wine counter three hundred feet long, equipped with five thousand magnums of champagne. Supper was catered by the Hoffman House, whose proprietor, Edward S. Stokes, had been responsible for the early demise of Jim Fisk.

On Tuesday, the actual centennial day, a mammoth military parade wound all the way up to Central Park, with a million people massed along the route. This had been preceded by services at St. Paul's (where George Washington had worshiped) and a gust of oratory at Wall and Broad streets where Chauncey Depew delivered a twenty-five-minute address and the President followed with a brief speech. In the evening a banquet for eight hundred was held at the Metropolitan Opera House, where five thousand people were admitted to the tiers of seats in the mezzanine and balcony to watch the elaborate feast consumed on the main floor below. Among those attending the banquet were former Presidents Rutherford B. Hayes and Grover Cleveland. The latter, who had been defeated by Harrison in the election of 1888 (although he had received a greater popular vote) would within three years triumph over his Republican opponent by winning the contest of 1892.

In the fourth month of Cleveland's second term as President, on June 30, 1893, he was taken secretly aboard the *Oneida*, anchored off the Battery, and the yacht, belonging to E. C. Benedict, then steamed off on an extremely mysterious trip. Dr. Joseph Bryan admonished the captain: "If you hit a rock, hit it good and hard so that we'll all go to the bottom." Aboard the yacht were five other surgeons who, acting as a team, removed the President's entire upper left jaw, which was being consumed by cancer. Not until he was well on the road to recovery did the news of this operation leak out. Cleveland not only served out his term, but lived on for another fifteen years, dying at the age of seventy-one.

What might be called the Second Great Wall Street Explosion occurred in December, 1891, at the

Harrison addressing multitude from a stand erected on the Sub-Treasury steps with a wreathed Washington dominating the scene. Man in slouch hat, hand on hip, standing just above man (CENTER) *with arm over the rail, has been identified as Civil Service Commissioner Theodore Roosevelt.*

In this building at the corner of Broadway and Rector, a young man entered the second-floor office of Russell Sage on December 4, 1891, and demanded a huge sum of money. When the multimillionaire moneylender refused, the man dropped a bag of dynamite, blowing himself up, killing a bystander and injuring several others. Sage, who used a clerk as a shield, escaped unscathed.

View up Wall from South Street in the 1890's shows American Express wagon (LEFT); *Ansonia Clock truck* (CENTER); *El train passing on Pearl Street. Newer buildings are beginning to overshadow Trinity Church at the west end of the street.*

Arcade building on Broadway at Rector Street, across from Trinity. A well-dressed, bearded young man, later identified as Henry L. Norcross, a Boston broker, entered the office of Russell Sage, the millionaire moneylender. He told the clerk at the gate that the carpetbag he was carrying contained bonds he was to deliver to Sage from John D. Rockefeller. When he was ushered into the inner office, he handed Sage a typewritten note.

"I hold in my hands ten pounds of dynamite," it read. "If I drop it on the floor it will tear the building to pieces and everyone with it. For $1,250,000 it shall not drop. Yes or no?"

Sage did what might have been expected of America's tightest multimillionaire. He pushed a twenty-dollar-a-week clerk, named Laidlaw, at the extortionist and made a dash for the door. This must have been construed as a "No" by the stranger who then dashed the bag to the floor. The resulting explosion killed two people, seriously injured five others, including Laidlaw, and filled Trinity Churchyard with a litter of papers and debris. Laidlaw sued Sage, won a judgment of forty thousand dollars in a bitter court battle, but lost when Sage appealed. The higher court ruled that the trial court had erred in submitting to the jury the question of substantial damages, "there being no evidence tending to show that the plaintiff would not have been injured so badly if his position in the room had not been changed."

During this "gilded" age, there were five panics—in 1884, 1889–90, 1893, 1895, and 1899. The sinking of the *Maine* in Havana harbor in February, 1898, hit stocks hard, but during the year of the Spanish-American War, security values went up more than two billion dollars. Then on Saturday morning, May 14, came the "Ice Water Panic."

On the previous day the former Governor of New York, Roswell P. Flower, felt tired and decided to leave his Wall Street office early and spend the weekend fishing at the Long Island Country Club. That night he ate a hearty dinner, which included ham and radishes, and then partook of an immoderate amount of ice water. At least these were the factors which his physicians claimed led to a heart attack and death. Flower, who endowed the hospital of that name in New York, had been a utilities company operator of great competence and had acquired an enormous following. During the night, the news

Flags flew from almost every building in Wall Street at the time of the Spanish-American War. The First National Bank stood at the northeast corner of Broadway (LEFT). *Tracks were used by Broadway cable cars.*

Roswell P. Flower, a country boy who became Governor of New York, was an expert in doctoring sick stocks, drank too much ice water, started a panic.

By 1893 the hall of the Stock Exchange had been enlarged in all directions, with posts for each stock and three visitors' galleries. There were many exciting flurries of trading, but 1893 was not a good year. When European investors sold off United States securities and withdrew gold, many banks, railroads, and factories failed.

of his death was spread, and before the Stock Exchange opened on Saturday morning its galleries and nearby brokerage offices were jammed with investors and traders discussing the coming price break in such issues as Brooklyn Rapid Transit, Peoples Gas, Rock Island, Federal Steel, New York Air Brake, Atchison, and International Paper—all Flower stocks.

There was little reason for a collapse. The companies had lost nothing tangible by the financier's death. Nevertheless, an epidemic of selling swept the market when it opened. "A hundred or more brokers were struggling to get at each other and apparently overwhelm their associates with something that they wanted to get rid of," reported the *New York Herald* on Sunday morning. "For a few minutes there was an indescribable din, as if a storm had expended its energy upon the mass of brokers, and they were too dazed to extricate themselves. The howling on the floor was taken up by the teeming humanity in the balcony, and the latter jumped and gesticulated as if they were taking part in the actual performance." During the short two-hour Saturday session, four hundred thousand shares of Flower stocks were traded—at a shrinkage in market value of almost nineteen million dollars. But another 350,000 shares of stocks, having nothing to do with the dead man or any of his interests, were traded for a loss of another hundred million dollars!

The position of the Flower brokerage house was solid, there were no speculative accounts on margin to worry about, and the panic was of short duration. Actually, most of the Flower stocks thrown overboard by a nervous public were picked up by brokers for the Vanderbilts, Rockefellers, J. P. Morgan and Company, and Darius O. Mills. When the small, scared traders saw that prices were not continuing to slide down, there was a gradual recovery during the last half-hour of trading. But a total of $120,000,000 had been squeezed out of the value of stocks in two hours—simply because one man had gulped one too many glasses of ice water.

II

Titans, Trusts, and T.R.

THE TWENTIETH CENTURY opened a bright new day. There was promise and fulfillment in the air—great promise for everyone. The mighty men of money looked forward to consolidating all commercial activities into huge, efficient combinations and monopolies, while the radicals, the reformers, and the muckrakers rolled up their sleeves to set about the task of cutting the capitalists down.

A conservative's conservative, William McKinley, was in the White House, elected by Mark Hanna who had objected strenuously to Teddy Roosevelt as Vice-President. When President McKinley was assassinated in 1901, Wall Street went into mourning and Hanna bitterly exclaimed: "And now look—that damned cowboy is President of the United States!" If Wall Street had known what Roosevelt was going to do, the crepe would have been twice as thick.

Yet J. P. Morgan whipped together the billion-dollar United States Steel trust, James J. Hill and Edward H. Harriman staged the wild Northern Pacific Corner, the panics of 1903 and 1907 built up and ran their course, and it was the golden — not "gilded"—age of the Rockefellers, Jacob H. Schiff, George F. Baker, Thomas Fortune Ryan, the Whitneys, the Guggenheims, Charles Schwab, the Lewisohns, John W. "Bet-a-Million" Gates, the Huntingtons, and the Vanderbilts.

Marconi sent the first radio signal across the Atlantic and Orville Wright flew an airplane 120 feet in twelve seconds. Oldsmobile advertised that it was cheaper to buy a car than stable and feed a horse. The pioneer company owner or his heir gave way to the up-from-the-ranks manager. The age of free enterprise was waning. With Roosevelt not only swinging a "big stick" in international diplomacy but on the economic front as well, the Supreme Court dissolved Rockefeller's Standard Oil and James Duke's American Tobacco trusts in May, 1911. Four years before that, Federal Judge Kenesaw Mountain Landis (later czar of baseball) fined Standard Oil $29,240,000 for violating the law against granting rebates to favored customers.

In the end, however, Standard Oil paid nothing. The higher courts set the penalty aside.

Rockefeller's Standard Oil building which went

Assemblyman, crusading Police Commissioner, Assistant Secretary of the Navy, Rough Rider, Governor, and Vice-President, Theodore Roosevelt was a descendant of Claes van Rosenvelt who came to New York in 1650. Only forty-three when an assassin shot McKinley, he became the youngest President on September 14, 1901.

up at the foot of Broadway, across from Bowling Green, was part of the great race into the sky which took place in this era. The problem of the curve of the street led Carrère and Hastings, the architects, to adapt the façade from a palace of papal Rome. The first "skyscraper" (the word had been applied to the tallest mast of the clipper ships) in New York was three doors up—the thirteen-story Tower building at 50 Broadway, built by Bradford Gilbert in 1888–89. The man next door sold out and moved away in fear that it would topple over on him, and Gilbert occupied the top floor himself to prove it was safe. The building was demolished in 1913 to make way for a bigger one. In 1893 the Manhattan Life Insurance building had shot up 344 feet and by 1898 the Park Row building was "the largest office building in the world," twenty-six stories and three tower floors high. The Singer building, forty-seven stories, was completed in 1908 and had the distinction for eighteen months of being the world's tallest. (The impresario Gatti-Casazza, shown the Manhattan skyline, thought that the Singer building was an opera house.) The Metropolitan Life Insurance building was the next champion, topped in 1914 by the Woolworth building. Some reports said that Frank Woolworth had the structure erected because he had once been refused a loan by Metropolitan. Described as being spun of "lace in stone," achieved by using white terra cotta, it is 792 feet high and remains to this day one of the most beautiful skyscrapers in the world. Cass Gilbert, the architect, mounted a twenty-five-story tower on a thirty-five-story base and accented the vertical lines and the soaring height with Gothic pilasters and molding. Today it still retains an aristocratic supremacy over the surrounding buildings. "Father was able to achieve what he did because he was an architect, not an engineer," his son said recently. Two other admirable and age-defying structures designed by Gilbert were the Custom House, completed a few years earlier on almost the exact location of the original Fort, and the George Washington Bridge. Aside from the Eiffel Tower, once defined as "a skyscraper after taxes," the Woolworth building was to remain the highest in the world for more than twenty years.

As the tall skyscrapers reached upward, they did not succeed in dwarfing the old Sub-Treasury building or the two new, low buildings which were

Mark Hanna called Roosevelt "that damned cowboy," while HARPER'S WEEKLY *stated that "Bronco Busting . . . amuses us and don't hurt the horse." Despite criticism, Teddy tamed the trusts and helped make capitalism more democratic.*

At the beginning of the century the race to build the tallest skyscraper began in lower Manhattan. Caissons at Vesey Street were etched by Joseph Pennell, who called New York "the Unbelievable City."

constructed across the street on Broad. These were the imposing New York Stock Exchange building, opened in 1903, and the new Morgan building. The great wealth that each represented and the luxurious waste of space in a sector where land was the most valuable in the world gave these institutions far greater standing than any others on the Street.

The new home of the Stock Exchange, on the site formerly occupied by Western Union, the old exchange, and several other buildings, cost two million dollars to construct. Since that time the entire block has been acquired by the exchange and its activities take place in all four of the buildings occupying the site. The main trading building is an impressive, handsome temple with a pediment supported by seven white marble columns and seven small entrances which, from a distance, resemble the starting gates of a dog track.

By the beginning of the twentieth century, operations on the Stock Exchange had come a long way from the unrestrained speculation of the Fisk-Gould-Erie days. The Long Room had been eliminated and the Open Board consolidated with the Big Board in 1869. In that year stocks were required to be registered, and when Erie refused to give an account of the number of shares issued, it was stricken from the list. Directors of the road then organized the "Na-

First occupied in 1907, the Custom House, which cost $8 million, stands on the site of New Amsterdam's original Fort. Designed by Cass Gilbert, it is adorned by more sculptures and paintings than any other building in the Wall Street area.

Daniel Chester French was the sculptor of the monumental Custom House groups. CENTER: *America, holding torch of progress, sheaves of grain, protecting Labor;* RIGHT: *Asia, with kneeling Hindu and Chinese coolies. In the background was the massive Produce Exchange, where Number 2 Broadway now stands.*

tional Stock Exchange," known as the Erie Board, which lasted six months before the company met the Stock Exchange requirements and was readmitted. A committee on admissions replaced the blackball procedure for new members and memberships became salable. The price of a seat fluctuated between a low of $2,750 in 1871 and a high of thirty-four thousand dollars in 1885, plus a thousand-dollar initiation fee.

By 1881 it became too difficult to page members by voice and the first electric annunciator was installed. Telephones were introduced in 1879, and in May, 1894, the exchange took over control of the telegraph stock-quotation ticker system, enabling it to refuse service to and thus cut down on the operations of "bucket-shops" and bogus brokers. The old method of "calling stocks" gave way to the trading of securities at specified locations by setting up posts where specialists dealt in a specific list of stocks. After several false starts, a stock clearing-house company

The old Custom House (Merchants Exchange of 1842) was sold by the government and became the National City Bank building after its dome was removed and four "harmonious stories" were added at a cost of $1.5 million.

The last day of the New York Stock Exchange in its old building was April 26, 1901, when everyone stood motionless for this picture. Until the new building was finished on the same site as the old one, the Big Board occupied part of the vast Produce Exchange floor at Bowling Green and Beaver Street.

was created, which soon became an integral part of the exchange's functions. The one thousand safety-deposit bins in the vaults under the trading floor were considered the very last word in impregnable security.

Like hornets swarming around a hive, the speculators and free-lance brokers, who had always clung to the fringes of the Stock Exchange, followed and hovered outside each home of the Big Board. Sometimes, during the Civil War, for example, more business was done outside the exchange than in, and often only darkness halted the transactions out on the street. Prices fluctuated more in the open-air market than they did on the more decorous trading floor, which could pile chaos onto pandemonium mixed with frenzy topped with hysteria if the occasion demanded. The Curb, a misnomer since it overflowed all the way across the street, was far more hazardous, because there was no gentleman's agreement where a man honored his word. Frequently, some rascal got in on the bidding, but when it came time to pay up, he had retired from the crowd and business. Such chicaneries and dozens of other deceits led the honest brokers to become clannish and wary in their dealings. By 1912, therefore, a regular organization, the New York Curb Exchange, was functioning, with the members pledged to deal only with each other and only in registered stocks.

Because it was an *al fresco* market, with all the disadvantages and uncertainties of a roofless existence, the Curb was more colorful, providing more fun and more headaches, than the more comfortably housed Big Board. As Curb brokers attracted regular customers, they opened offices and hired runners to bring messages and orders to them on the street. Then one of them ran a telephone line into a second-story room overlooking the milling throng below, won a slight time advantage, and runners were re-

The cornerstone of the new Stock Exchange building was laid on September 10, 1901, but out of respect for dying President McKinley, who was shot five days before, "jollification" was canceled.

Dedication ceremonies of the present Stock Exchange, constructed of white marble and steel at a cost of $2 million, were held on April 23, 1903. The new hall is one of the largest and highest rooms in the world, but the first trading posts were the same as those that had been used in the old building.

While the Big Board had new quarters, outdoor trading continued in Broad Street below Exchange Place. But the brokers organized as the Curb Agency in 1908, adding offices and a listing department in 1911.

The same Curb scene viewed from a broker's phone room. Offices facing the Curb Market were in great demand as signal posts from which clerks could finger-talk to their bosses in the street below.

The code was a one-handed sign language. For some time the brokers wore bizarre hats, blazers, and other distinctive haberdashery so that clerks could spot them easily and get their attention by whistling or clapping.

Any available cubbyhole, ledge, or window was used as a vantage post by clerks who were in communication by phone with the home office and relayed messages back and forth with traders on the street.

placed by telephone boys shouting messages and orders from windows. The constant din of booming voices made shouting impractical, and it was replaced by a system of hand signals, a form of sign language, which is still used today. Because of the difficulty of being spotted in the crowd of competing traders, the brokers began to wear strange and vividly colored hats, so that the men in the windows could more easily identify them in the street below. Through all these evolutions and changes, business went on, every trading day, no matter what the weather.

Customers' rooms, or "funeral parlors" as they were termed in the trade, were outfitted more elaborately by the commission members of the Stock Exchange, while the advent of the lady plunger led to private rooms set aside for them, although women were not considered equipped with the steady nerves and resolute temperament required of good speculators. An exception that proved the rule was Hetty Green, who began her career with a million dollars cash she inherited and ran it up to ninety million dollars by a combination of shrewdness and boldness in speculation, mortgage holdings, and investments in real estate. Hetty's personal penny-pinching, her weedy old clothes, and nomadic life of tax-dodging earned her the newspaper sobriquet of "The Witch of Wall Street." Fearful that a fortune-hunter would marry her daughter, Sylvia, Hetty waited until the girl was thirty-seven before she allowed her to marry. The rich but elderly Matthew Astor Wilks, whose Wilks building at Wall and Broad gave way in 1920 to the Stock Exchange structure on that site, was the groom. Wilks, who was sixty-four years old when he married Sylvia, died in 1926, leaving an estate that was appraised at seventeen and a half million dollars. Hetty died on July 3, 1916, without making any public or charitable bequest.

Sylvia's brother, Colonel Edward Henry R. Green, made up as best he could for the amputation of his leg, resulting from his mother's niggardly attempt to save a doctor's fee when it was infected, by spending twenty million dollars on a gem collection and ten million dollars to build his Round Hill estate. He was a delightful, mildly eccentric man who left ninety million dollars after taxes to sixty-three charitable organizations when he died in 1937. Sylvia tried to break the will, although she was already one of the richest women in the world, having between thirty

Winter snow, scorching sun, or rain had little effect on the number of traders or the prices of stocks. Like the Big Board, the Curb had specialists who traded in specific stocks at invisible, but regular posts. The Curb, now the American Stock Exchange, was always famous for the speed of transactions.

"The strain of frenzied finance in Wall Street," stated the caption of this LESLIE'S WEEKLY *illustration in 1905. "Anxious speculators watching the quotation-board in one of the many brokers' offices during a slump in stocks." Note the calm "Uncle Sam" who appeared often in brokerage scenes.*

Gambling in stocks was a new fad for the ladies, reported MUNSEY'S MAGAZINE. *Some legitimate brokerage firms and bucket shops had private rooms for women.*

and forty-five million dollars in New York City mortgages, ten million in real estate in various cities, between forty and sixty million in non-taxable municipal bonds and other securities, and ten million in farming, oil, and miscellaneous properties.

Russell Sage, who could be termed the "Miser of Manhattan," died in 1906, leaving his widow seventy million dollars. Edward Bok, editor of the *Ladies' Home Journal,* told Clarence W. Barron, publisher of the *Wall Street Journal,* that when he was a young man working in the offices of Western Union, "Russell Sage was a director. He used to send me out at noon for two apples for four cents, and carefully take back the odd cent and deposit it in the center of his well-filled leather wallet, wound about with a leather strap. I shall never forget the day I spent five cents when the two-cent apples were bad. Mr. Sage delivered me a lecture for ten minutes. . . . The next day I bought two two-cent apples and returned one cent."

But the old skinflint was transformed within less than a generation from one of the most detested

Multimillionaire Russell Sage, Wall Street's meanest, shabbiest moneylender, haggled over the price of bruised fruit. He died at the age of ninety.

Mrs. Russell Sage took $70 million, left her by her husband, and established a foundation in his memory. It has done so much intelligent good work that the name of Sage is now illustrious.

characters in the land to a shining example of intelligent benefaction. This new image was created for him by his widow when she established the Russell Sage Foundation.

In 1901 J. Pierpont Morgan put together the United States Steel Corporation with a capitalization of a billion and a half dollars on less than eight hundred million dollars' worth of assets. His house's share of the fee for this waterlogged coup was eleven and a half million dollars, only 1½ per cent of the inflation that was passed on to stockholders. A month later he sailed for Europe where a cable from James J. Hill informed him that they were about to lose control of their Northern Pacific Railroad to Edward H. Harriman, head of the Union Pacific.

Both Union Pacific and Northern Pacific had tried to buy the Burlington Railroad in order to get access into Chicago. Hill and Morgan had won. Harriman, however, would not give up. With the backing of Jacob H. Schiff he went after the majority stock of Northern Pacific, which was controlled by Hill and Morgan through a minority holding. He had almost

"The Witch of Wall Street." In her later years Hetty Green wore mourning and men's underwear, inked holes in her gloves, and waged war on tax collectors.

The great San Francisco fire, started by an earthquake on April 18, 1906, continued to burn for days. The fire weakened the stock market and helped lead to the Panic of 1907 when insurance companies were forced to sell securities to pay claims.

succeeded when Hill, on the Pacific coast, got wind of the raid. He broke all speed records coming east in a special train only to be told by Schiff that he and Harriman had already succeeded in buying control of Northern Pacific. Actually, they now owned 420,000 out of 750,000 shares of preferred, but only a little more than 370,000 of the 800,000 shares of common. This gave them over 50 per cent—790,000 out of 1,550,000. But the rub was that while both classes of stock had voting privileges, the preferred was subject to retirement. Orders came from Morgan: buy 150,000 shares of common, which would give them control. On Monday 127,000 shares were purchased and Northern Pacific went to 127½. By Tuesday it hit 149¾. Morgan stopped buying on Wednesday, but the price went up to 180. By Thursday, when the short-sellers who thought they had a soft touch on Monday now found they could not beg, borrow, or buy a share of Northern Pacific, the price had skyrocketed to one thousand.

Bernard Baruch, thirty-three years old at the time and a member of the exchange, had been warned by Talbot Taylor, son-in-law of James Keene who was the behind-the-scenes operator for Morgan, to keep out of Northern Pacific. He foresaw what would happen and began selling other stocks short. "With Northern Pacific soaring, the rest of the list collapsed, losing up to 60 points as stocks were thrown over at any price," he relates in *Baruch: My Own Story*. "Call money loaned by banks to brokers opened at 40 per cent and touched 60. All sense of value and sanity was gone. . . . The wildest rumors sped to and fro. . . . Scenes in the brokerage offices were as heartrending as those on the floor. . . . Two-fifteen was the deadline when the shorts had to put up the stock certificates to cover their sales of the previous day. A few minutes before, Al Stern, the Kuhn, Loeb [Schiff] emissary, came onto the floor. Mounting a chair and shouting to make himself heard, he announced that his firm would not enforce delivery. . . . Stern was followed by Eddie Norton [the Morgan floor man], who announced that his firm as well would not demand delivery. . . . The crisis was over. Northern Pacific sold off to 300. The general list steadied."

During panics (such as this in 1907), Wall Street attracted crowds of unmoneyed but morbidly curious people, as well as bargain seekers and depositors trying to withdraw money before the shaky banks shut.

What had happened was that the Morgan and Harriman camps had reached an agreement to save the short-sellers from ruin. They would provide stock for them at 150, much easier terms than most of the shorts had anticipated. The warring factions compromised their differences, too. Harriman was to get some places on the Northern Pacific board, and a newly formed New Jersey company, Northern Securities, would hold the shares of both Northern Pacific and Hill's Great Northern, giving it indirect control of Burlington, with Harriman represented as well as Morgan and Hill.

That September 14, President McKinley was dead and Theodore Roosevelt, the "trust-buster," was firmly entrenched in the executive mansion. Five months later Morgan was informed that the Attorney-General of the United States was prosecuting the Northern Securities Company for breach of the Sherman Anti-Trust Act.

"Morgan turned from the telephone to his associates at the dinner table, his countenance showing appalled dismay, but little anger," Mark Sullivan wrote. "In telling the news to his guests he dwelt on what he felt was the unfairness of Roosevelt's action. Roosevelt, he said, ought to have told him, ought to have given him a chance to make over the Northern Securities Company, if necessary, so as to conform with whatever Roosevelt thought was right. Or, if the company must be dissolved, Roosevelt ought to have given him an opportunity to dissolve it voluntarily. . . . He had regarded Roosevelt as a gentleman."

But when Morgan went to Washington and saw Roosevelt, he found that the government was not interested in making over the holding company. Roosevelt wanted the suit prosecuted—and so it was. Two years later the Supreme Court reversed its former position on holding companies and declared that Northern Securities was illegal.

There was a strike of hard-coal miners in 1902 and

The run on the United States Trust Company and the Trust Company of America during the Panic of 1907 as seen from the north side of Wall Street.

Dishonest, slipshod banking methods that led to bank failures and losses to trusting depositors, high prices resulting from the formation of monopolistic "trusts," and low wages paid to labor were criticized in this cartoon which was characteristic of increasing public demands for reforms and government supervision.

George F. Baer, whom Morgan had appointed President of the Reading Railroad, which controlled many mines, attacked the brilliant and admired John Mitchell, leader of the United Mine Workers, with one of the most ill-advised statements in the history of labor relations. He said: "The rights and interests of the laboring man will be cared for, not by the labor agitators, but by the Christian men to whom God in His infinite wisdom has given control of the property interests of the country."

The situation did not improve after Baer's pronouncement and, with winter coming on, the President demanded that the strike be settled. The operators demanded that the men return to the mines first. Morgan visited the White House again and he and Roosevelt reached accord on an arbitration commission which gave the miners better working conditions and a 10 per cent raise in pay.

The trust company was a new type of bank and some of them were in the hands of people who invested in speculative enterprises. In 1907 F. Augustus Heinze, a speculator and President of the Mercantile National Bank, attempted to corner United Copper and was wiped out. Rumors that the bank was involved in the disaster made swift headway and a run began. Two more banks, headed by speculators who had been associated with Heinze, Charles W. Morse and Edward R. Thomas, were also targets. The Clearing House was appealed to for cash, but not until the three presidents were forced to resign did it announce that the banks were sound. By now the faith of depositors was severely shaken and all trust companies were crowded with people withdrawing funds. Loans were called, stocks were sold out, panic seized those with money.

The Knickerbocker Trust Company was next to be hit. Rumors redoubled because its President, Charles T. Barney, had been associated with Heinze and Morse. A committee of directors came from the Knickerbocker office at Thirty-fourth Street and Fifth Avenue to appeal to J. P. Morgan for help, but met with no success. On the morning of October 22, the run on the Knickerbocker began. By 2:00 P.M. the bank had no more cash on hand, was forced to suspend payment, and consequently failed. Now every bank in New York felt uneasy and they all

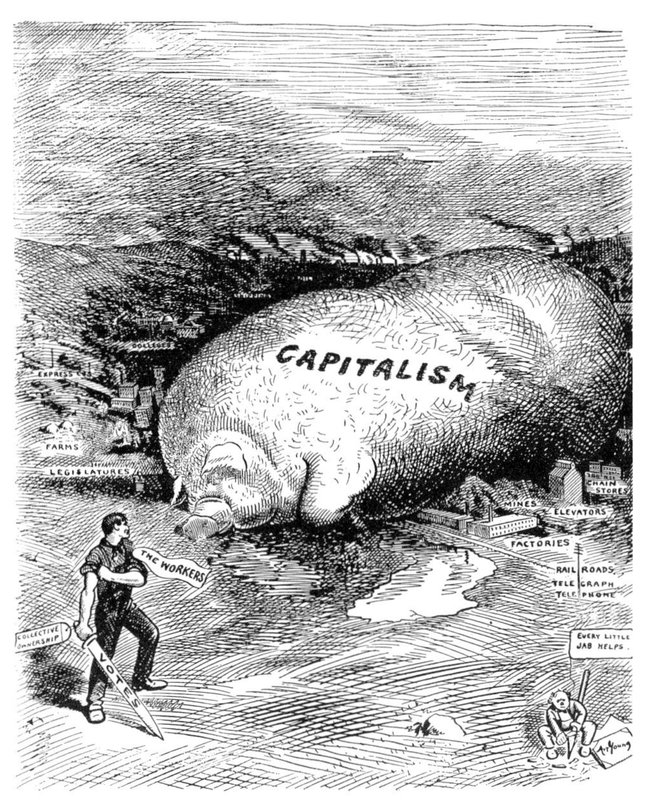

"Time to Butcher," *a radical cartoon which appeared in a Kansas weekly, depicts worker as a modern St. George about to slay the gorged hog,* "Capitalism."

looked to Morgan for guidance. Then seventy-one years old, he was at the time suffering from a terrible cold and scarcely able to speak. A statement made by one of his partners seemed to imply that the Trust Company of America, just east of the House of Morgan, was in serious trouble. The unfortunate statement focused attention on a single trust company, and by the following morning it really *was* in trouble. After a rapid survey of the Trust Company of America's assets, Benjamin Strong, who later became President of Bankers Trust and of the Federal Reserve Bank of New York, was able to tell Morgan that the bank seemed solvent.

With the aid of George F. Baker of the First National and James Stillman of National City, Morgan was able to supply sufficient cash to keep the Trust Company of America from closing. A committee of trust-company presidents was organized and they raised $8,250,000 as an emergency fund to support the weaker banks. Morgan and the national banks put up another $1,750,000. The following day he was greeted in the crowded Street as a popular hero. The heat was off the banks. Now it was turned on at the Stock Exchange, where securities tumbled and loans were called. By the end of the morning the Presi-

In 1911, LIFE, *then a humor weekly, ran a Wall Street issue featuring a cartoon of the Street labeled "When We All Get Wise." Boy* (CENTER) *peddles newspaper extra with headline: "Great Excitement—Two Whole Shares of Stock Sold Yesterday."*

dent of the exchange crossed the street to Morgan's office and told him that the exchange would have to close. Morgan raised another twenty-five million dollars within a few minutes so that new loans could be made.

The next day this was all gone and another fifteen million was desperately needed. At a meeting with the bank presidents at the Clearing House, Morgan was able to raise thirteen.

"Anyone who saw Mr. Morgan going from the Clearing House back to his office that day will never forget the picture," wrote Herbert L. Satterlee, his son-in-law. "With his coat unbuttoned and flying open, a piece of white paper clutched tightly in his right hand, he walked fast down Nassau Street. His flat-topped black derby hat was set firmly down on his head. Between his teeth he held a paper cigar holder in which was one of his long cigars, half smoked. His eyes were fixed straight ahead. He swung his arms as he walked and took no notice of anyone. He did not seem to see the throngs in the street, so intent was his mind on the thing that he was doing. . . . The thing that made his progress different from that of all the other people on the street was that he did not dodge, or walk in and out, or slacken his pace. He simply barged along, as if he had been the only man going down Nassau Street hill past the Sub-Treasury. He was the embodiment of power and purpose. Not more than two minutes after he disappeared into his office, the cheering on the floor of the Stock Exchange could be heard out in Broad Street." The thirteen million dollars Morgan had raised proved to be enough.

The conferences continued and new methods of providing funds were discussed. In the middle of the worst day Morgan signed his name to an agreement to guarantee the marketing of thirty million dollars' worth of New York City bonds to take care of short-term notes which were coming due. A wave of brokerage firm bankruptcies was averted when Morgan accepted a complicated plan by which United States Steel took over control of the Tennessee Coal and Iron Company at bargain rates and rescued Moore and Schley, the brokerage firm which had financed the purchase of a majority of the stock. That night Morgan locked the trust-company presidents in his house until they put up twenty-five million dollars as a fund to meet further emergencies. When, early on Monday, President Roosevelt said he would not

While George F. Baer was making his notorious statement implying that God was on the side of the rich property owners, coal miners, including thousands of children, were starving on low wages and dying at an early age of diseases contracted in the mines.

stand in the way of United States Steel buying the Tennessee company, the news was announced as the exchange opened and the market rallied. The corner was turned, but it was years before Wall Street was back to normal.

However, several benefits emerged out of the Panic of 1907. The Aldrich-Vreeland Act, a forerunner of the Federal Reserve Act of 1913, broadened the base which permitted banks to issue currency in times of financial stringency and trust companies came under more vigilant supervision. When Woodrow Wilson became President in 1913, the Federal Reserve System was created, the Clayton Anti-Trust Act of 1914 was enacted, and the Federal Trade Commission was established to prevent unfair competition in interstate commerce.

The Panic of 1907 also marked J. P. Morgan's withdrawal from active business. He began to spend more time abroad, visiting the ancient ruins of Greece and Egypt. The Drexel building was demolished to be replaced by the House of Morgan, but he did not live to enter his new headquarters. His son, J. P. Morgan, Jr., Henry P. Davison, Thomas W. Lamont, and other young men began to run the business. The elder Morgan was by now a noted collector of antiques and art, both for himself and for

View of lower Manhattan, looking across the East River from Brooklyn Heights in 1912, shows the Wall Street area dominated by the Bankers Trust pyramid and the 612-foot, 47-story Singer building, the world's tallest, until the Woolworth tower, going up at right, topped it with 60 stories and a height of 792 feet.

During the Hudson-Fulton celebration, September 25–October 10, 1909, Wilbur Wright made a spectacular flight up the Hudson River to Grant's Tomb from Governor's Island, shown with Statue of Liberty in the background. The following year, Glenn Curtiss landed here after a pioneer flight from Albany.

the Metropolitan Museum of Art, of which he was a founder. He applied the same sweeping methods to acquiring art that he had used in finance, and soon he was the greatest collector in the world.

In 1912 Pierpont Morgan made the most public appearance of his life, just a year before his death, when he was questioned by the Pujo Committee, an inquiry headed by Congressman Arsène Pujo of Arizona, but directed by Samuel Untermyer as counsel. Morgan dreaded the call to testify, but he made a good witness nevertheless—when it suited his purpose. However, the grip of the House of Morgan on America was brought out, and the "money trust," which the congressional committee was out to expose, stood revealed to most of the nation for the first time. Morgan, his partners, and his associates in the First National and National City banks and the Bankers and Guaranty Trust companies held between them 341 directorships in 112 corporations with a total of twenty-two billion dollars in resources or capitalization. These were in 34 banks and trust companies, 12 public utilities, 24 industrials, 32 rail and transport companies, and 10 insurance companies. By his own standards Morgan justified his conduct in every one of the momentous deals he had been involved in or formulated. He sincerely believed that he was a conservator of American capital and investments. That he favored "his kind" he did not deny. That he insisted on his idea of a profit, no matter what the deal, he admitted as a matter of course. He felt that money was a gentleman's stock in trade, and gentlemen should deal

Thomas Alva Edison, whose association with Wall Street began with his improved ticker for the Stock Exchange in 1869, later had his electric-light system underwritten by Morgan. He continued to create inventions largely financed by Wall Street investors, such as the "Business Phonograph" or dictaphone beside his desk.

Between 1900 and United States entry into World War I, Bernard Baruch was a bold stock-market trader and a shrewd developer of mining properties who frankly termed himself a "speculator."

only with other gentlemen on every possible occasion.

He was a giant—the last of the giants—and his way of dominating the money market faded with him. "The era of untrammeled authority for the men who ran big business was over, because the public at large no longer trusted them," wrote Frederick Lewis Allen—which might well stand as an epitaph to "*The Great Pierpont Morgan.*"

A revealing insight into the character of the man can be seen in a remarkable photograph taken by Edward Steichen in 1902. A South American artist, Carlos Baca-Flor, was painting an oil portrait of Morgan and wanted a photograph so he could work between sittings. He told Morgan that there was a young camera genius who should be called in, according to Carl Sandburg in *Steichen, The Photographer:* "Mr. Morgan was willing. It was okeh with him. He stipulated merely that the young camera genius should work fast. He would sit two minutes."

Young Steichen arrived early and posed the janitor of the building at different spots "assuming that God's good sunlight would work the same way on a great financier's face as that of a jocular janitor."

Morgan strode into the room exactly at the appointed hour. Sitting down in the chair which Steichen indicated, he put his cigar aside and Steichen clicked the shutter of his camera.

"Now," said the photographer, "would you please sit a little differently? Just swing your head around and we'll have it."

Mr. Morgan swung his head around, relaxed, and brought it back to the same place and position it had been originally. The subject was at ease and comfortable, which makes a difference in the look of the eyes—which Steichen said were the most penetrating he had ever seen—and in the set of the shoulders.

Again the camera clicked.

"Thank you, sir," said Steichen.

"Is that all?" inquired Mr. Morgan.

"Yes, sir."

The lighting in the picture perfectly reflects the essence of the man— a Titan of America, a man proud to be known as the Money Master. An electric gleam burns in his eyes which gaze straight ahead, defying the world, his hand grasping the arm of the chair as if he were holding a sword or a dagger.

Leading private citizen of the United States and great art collector, John Pierpont Morgan, Sr., was painted by Carlos Baca-Flor, who arranged for a photograph to be made by a young cameraman named Edward Steichen because Morgan could not spare the time to pose.

Symbol of an era. John Pierpont Morgan, Sr., by Steichen, 1903, has been called the world's finest photographic portrait. Unlike the painting on the preceding page, it captures the overwhelming strength and force of the financier—in the hand which grips the chair, in the hypnotic eyes, the dominating brow and chin. In 1913, at seventy-six, Morgan died of cancer in Rome.

12

The First World War

AFTER LOOKING in from the outside for almost twenty long years, the Democrats regained executive power in Washington when Woodrow Wilson became President in 1913. By spring of the following year the United States was embroiled in a series of disputes with Mexico; the country had a foretaste of war when the Navy bombarded Vera Cruz and landed troops to occupy the port; and the stock market went through a spasm of uncertainty. It was hoped that the opening of the Panama Canal would stabilize the uneasy state of affairs and even bring an era of prosperity. However, only two weeks short of the opening date, Germany declared war on Russia (August 1) and France (August 3). Europe became a huge battlefield.

Fifteen billion dollars' worth of American stocks were owned by Europeans and if a concerted attempt was made to turn the securities into money, the sell-off would be disastrous to the economy of the United States. The Stock Exchange closed to prevent a headlong panic, then reopened in December so orderly liquidation could take place. American investors bought the stocks and lifted the mortgage on American industry. As the war progressed they began to buy European securities and the United States, formerly a debtor country, became a creditor nation.

When the United States finally joined the Allies, tremendous sums were needed to run the war—the Treasury Department borrowed thirty-seven billion dollars between 1917 and 1919—and the country at large became familiar with Liberty Loans, Victory Bonds, Allied war debts, rehabilitation loans, loans to Latin America, and the funding required by expanding American war industries. Wall Street stayed open nights to catch up with the load of work. The new Federal Reserve Board unified the banks and made financing easy—yet could not check the orgy of speculation. One reason for this was that the Board in Washington failed to raise the rediscount rate as the Federal Reserve Bank in New York had strongly advocated.

The Morgan firm became not only the chief American financier of the British and French governments, but also acted as their purchasing agent. This led to savage attacks on the banking house by the pro-German press and in such books as Charles A.

Serene-looking Wall Street actually underwent a 3½-month freeze at the beginning of World War I when the Stock Exchange suspended business to prevent panic selling by European stockholders. Shipping, importing, and exporting suffered a slump and banks refused to finance foreign trade.

Collman's *The War Plotters of Wall Street*, published by The Fatherland Corporation, a name which suggests that the publishers were not without bias. A more serious and personal attack on J. P. Morgan, Jr., who now headed the bank, took place on July 3, 1915, when a "Frank Holt" invaded his Glen Cove home while Morgan was having breakfast with British Ambassador Cecil Spring-Rice. The would-be assassin arrived in a taxi, dismissed the driver, and rang the bell. When the butler opened the door, the man drew two revolvers, leveled them, and demanded to see Morgan. The butler's cries of alarm brought the financier on the run. Instantly, Morgan grappled with the intruder. In addition to the artillery he displayed, "Holt" had three sticks of explosives in his pockets, and when Morgan, ignoring the guns, began beating him with his fists, the man cried: "Be careful of the dynamite!" He was at last subdued and held for the police who found that "Frank Holt," former instructor of German at Cornell, was actually Dr. Erich Meunter, under indictment for murdering his wife in Cambridge, Massachusetts, in 1906. He also confessed to the mysterious dynamiting of the Senate reception room in the Capitol at Washington, not long before his capture, as an act of protest against the sale of arms to the Allies. He was taken to the Mineola, Long Island, jail where he committed suicide by diving head first from the top of his cell door to the stone floor.

During the hectic trading of the war days, fortunes were made by both bears and bulls, sometimes within minutes. When Bernard Baruch, called to testify before a congressional investigating committee as head of the War Industries Board, was asked his

Forerunner of the American Expeditionary Force to France was Pershing's punitive expedition into Northern Mexico against rebel General Francisco (Pancho) Villa (seen here riding with troops) after his raids into United States territory at Santa Isabel and Columbus, New Mexico, in 1916.

Munitions explosion on Black Tom Island, off Jersey City, at 2:00 A.M. on July 30, 1916, resulting in $40 million damage ($1 million of it plate glass shattered in the Wall Street area), was traced to German saboteurs who used pencil flame bombs planted in cargo. This scene shows wreckage the morning after the blast.

Although unprepared, the United States declared war against Germany on April 6, 1917. The Draft Law was signed by President Wilson on May 28 and registration began on June 5. These men, minus uniforms, were soon drilling on Governor's Island. Later, they were sent to camp at Plattsburg, New York.

occupation, he replied: "I am a speculator." After the committee recovered from this burst of frankness, Baruch explained how he operated and gave an example of the celerity and courage it took to make a killing on the market.

On December 18, 1916, the ticker was clicking out a speech the new Prime Minister, David Lloyd George, was making at that moment in London before the British Parliament. He was saying: "The Allies will fight on to victory, but—" At that instant and without waiting for the end of the sentence, Baruch gave an order to sell twenty-five thousand shares of United States Steel. To him the word "but" could only mean that Lloyd George was about to give

Wall Street's chief wartime job was selling Liberty Loan issues and the Street made a fine record. Bond parades featured celebrities and even President Wilson (seen here in silk hat). At his right is Admiral Cary Grayson who was Medical Director of the Navy and also his personal physician.

The most vigorous congressional opposition to United States participation in World War I came from Wall Street-hating Representative Charles Augustus Lindbergh of Minnesota, shown with his son.

some hint of peace which, for the moment, would cast a pall on America's booming munitions prosperity. The split-second decision and the heavy sell-order made Baruch almost a half million dollars that afternoon.

When, at the end of January, 1917, Germany resumed its campaign of unrestricted submarine warfare, stocks declined sharply. A series of earlier provocations—the deliberate sinking of the *Lusitania*, with 124 Americans on board, on May 7, 1915; the Black Tom explosion on July 30, 1916, when saboteurs blew up a score of dynamite-laden barges and a munitions plant at the Jersey City docks, killing two and causing damages of more than forty million dollars; as well as other serious incidents—had led to increasing resentment and indignation on the part of the American people. Finally, on April 6, 1917, Congress acted on President Wilson's request and declared that a state of war now existed between the United States and Germany.

Almost two million American troops were eventually landed in France, three-quarters of them embarking from the port of New York, which was defended not only by forts and warships, but a steel anti-submarine net stretched across the mouth of

J. Pierpont Morgan the younger succeeded his more autocratic, less affable father as head of the banking house and became the British and French purchasing agent when the war started. Here he is buying Liberty Bonds from a society woman whose name became synonymous with rules for proper social behavior—Mrs. Emily Post.

Under a canopy in front of Washington's statue on the Sub-Treasury steps, exhorting the crowd to buy bonds, is a young New York City Congressman who was about to trade his swallowtail coat for the uniform of a major in the Air Force and see active duty over the Italian front—Fiorello LaGuardia, future Mayor of New York.

Reigning idols of the silver screen attracted huge throngs when they appeared in person to plug Liberty Loan drives. The crowd listening to Douglas Fairbanks, who toured with Charlie Chaplin and Mary Pickford, packed Wall Street as far as Hanover and stretched to Broadway in the other direction.

"America's Sweetheart," Mary Pickford, wearing the height of 1918 fashion in hats, made an appeal for the purchase of war bonds at City Hall Park. It was while traveling on this tour that she and Fairbanks fell in love, and were later married.

the harbor. German submarines were sighted off the coast on a number of occasions, and on July 19, 1918, the *U.S.S. San Diego*, an armored cruiser, was sunk just ten miles southeast of Fire Island. Six men were lost and six were injured. At first a torpedo fired from a submarine was thought to be the cause, but later it was determined that a drifting mine had been responsible.

Parades, drives, war-bond rallies, meatless Tuesdays, and corsetless women (the steel was needed for armor plate) were the order of the day in lower Manhattan. The Stock Exchange patriotically put Liberty Bond sales ahead of its usual trading, and almost everyone connected with Wall Street acted with an unselfishness that stood out in bright contrast to the greedy behavior of the Civil War years. The Sub-Treasury steps were, of course, the rallying place for patriotic meetings of every kind, and the celebrities of the period were used as magnets to lure vast crowds which choked the four corners and the streets as far back as the people could see and hear.

Charlie Chaplin, Chauncey Olcott, Lillian Russell (in white topee, blouse, and skirt as an honorary colonel in the Marine Corps), John Philip Sousa and his band, Paul Whiteman leading the Great Lakes Naval Training Station band—these were only a few who gave unstintingly of their time and talent to help sell Liberty Bonds at these rallies. Also present at several of these meetings was the dynamic, fiery Teddy Roosevelt who, denied the chance to fight overseas, brandished his fists, laughed his wonderful laugh, and told the public exactly what the American doughboys were going to do to "Kaiser Bill."

Henry P. Davison of the Morgan bank headed the American Red Cross, while Bernard Baruch organized the War Industries Board and mobilized the raw material it needed. When President Wilson named him to this post, he gave up his seat on the Stock Exchange and sold every security he owned which might benefit from government contracts or purchases. But he took with him from Wall Street a number of experts and capable assistants who con-

*Jubilation on Broad Street during the celebration following the signing of the Armistice, November 11, 1918, brought a paper snowstorm to the canyon as 155 tons swirled down on lower Manhattan, resulting in a bill of $80,000 for sweeping it up. Service flag (*LOWER LEFT*) had a star for each employee in uniform.*

tributed to the great success of this organization, which demonstrated for the first time that the winning of a war depended as much on a steady, boundless flow of supplies as upon any other factor.

On Thursday, November 7, 1918—the day of the False Armistice—a great throng of joyous New Yorkers packed the Wall Street district and other focal areas of the city in an uninhibited, wild celebration. However, toward nightfall, when it was learned that the United Press announcement of peace and victory was premature, the crowds dispersed and went quietly home.

After an anxious weekend, at four o'clock in the morning on Monday, November 11, the sirens began to scream again. People awoke to peer out of their windows, shouting questions at each other across the streets; thousands tried to telephone the *Times* and the *Tribune* for some definite news. An hour or so later, the cries of newsboys were heard as they rushed through the streets with bundles of extras on their shoulders, yelling: "Armistice! Peace! It's true this time!"

No one thought the second wave of jubilation could equal the first spontaneous outburst of delirious happiness. But, as the news was confirmed and the details of the signing of the Armistice in a railroad car in the forest of Compiègne—which brought a cessation to all hostilities at eleven minutes after 11 A.M. on the eleventh day of the eleventh month of the year—were published, the second celebration built up to more turbulent heights than the first.

No one reported for work. People gathered in the downtown area, linked arms, and swept in ranks of ten, twenty, and thirty abreast down Broadway, Wall, and Broad streets. Everyone tried to make as much noise as he could—blowing toy horns, shaking clappers and cowbells, singing, yelling, cheering—all in a sort of universal St. Vitus' dance. The relief and the joy, the tumultuous commotion and revelry, were not restricted to Manhattan alone, but were duplicated in Pittsburgh and Peoria and Petaluma and ten thousand other towns and cities across the country. Never before or since in the United States has there been so universal an outburst of mass ecstasy—or so genuine a sense of thanksgiving. One at a time, hundreds of people slipped out of the lines of celebrants and entered St. Paul's or Trinity, to join the solemn rows of worshipers in prayers of thanks.

Outside, in the narrow canyons of Wall Street, the noise and furor of celebration went on. As if they had been rehearsed, the lines of revelers broke out into song after song: "There's a Long, Long Trail A'winding," "Pack Up Your Troubles in Your Old Kit Bag," "Tipperary," "Smiles," "Oh, How I Hate to Get Up in the Morning," "There's a Rose That Grows in No-Man's Land," "Over There," and dozens of others.

The exultant, happy mobs were caught up in a delirium of sound and movement. No one seemed to care about eating, or even drinking—keep going, keep singing, keep dancing, keep kissing. The uproar and pandemonium did not abate for a moment. Girls embraced and kissed soldiers, sailors, marines, anyone in uniform, including Boy Scouts too young to appreciate it. Wall Street was enveloped in a swirling snowstorm of ticker tape, torn-up telephone books, and long, long streamers of toilet paper. A dozen people were making speeches, all at the same time, from the steps of the Sub-Treasury; scores clung

The colorful Curb brokers brought an end to street trading on June 25, 1921, when the last outdoor session was held on Broad Street. Two days later they went indoors and resumed their buying and selling two blocks west in a fine new building at 86 Trinity Place, across from the church.

to the sides of joy-riding, horn-honking autos and trucks; firecrackers and blank pistols went off in rapid bursts. There was laughter and unashamed tears; church bells clanged and ships in the harbor blasted their whistles; Mayor Hylan tried to make himself heard in front of City Hall and J. Pierpont Morgan, Jr., tossed ticker tape out of a window at 23 Wall. Pianos mounted in the rear of trucks pounded out gay tunes and sad, songs of war and peace, and everyone within hearing distance joined lustily in singing out the choruses of "The Star-Spangled Banner," "The Marseillaise," and "God Save the King."

Armistice Day, 1918—a day of sustained, obsessive joy—when everyone was everyone else's friend, pal, buddy, sweetheart. It was the greatest office party in history.

The Prince of Wales, making a triumphant American tour, was given an even greater New York ovation than his grandfather, Edward VII, six decades before, and received the freedom of the city from Mayor Hylan.

In 1919, some sixty years after his grandfather, Albert Edward, had been feted by New York, another Prince of Wales visited the city as Baron Renfrew. He received a typically tumultuous Broadway welcome, for he was the dashing, handsome Prince Charming of his time. Perhaps what endeared him most of all to Americans was his unroyal habit of falling off his horse at steeplechase meets.

In 1921 the Curb Market went indoors. Having organized before the war and tasted the fruits of respectability, the outdoor brokers built an imposing exchange on Trinity Place, across the churchyard from Broadway. The move came as a great relief to the police traffic division and to the increasing numbers of automobile drivers who wished to pass through Broad Street. With appropriate ceremonies the brokers dedicated the roof over their heads and settled down to trade in a dry, draft-free, well-heated building. Strangely, during the first winter that the brokers were protected against the elements, they were hit by the highest percentage of absenteeism in the history of the organization; never before or after were Curb members so frequently the victims of colds, bronchitis, and pneumonia.

Trading in most securities picked up after the sharp dip of November 12, 1919. Before the Liberty Loan drives, there were tens of millions of people who had never owned a security. Now that the ice was broken they began to buy. Many small businessmen, with capital accumulated during the war boom, also came into the stock market. Soon the country was swept by the greatest wave of stock-promotion

After the Curb Market opened its five-story building, it changed its name to the Curb Exchange in 1929, expanded to fourteen stories in 1931, and became known as the American Stock Exchange in 1953.

and wildcat stock sales ever recorded. New automobile companies were incorporated. Oil discoveries on Signal Hill in California, Burkburnett in the Texas Panhandle, and the gas field at McKeesport, Pennsylvania, sparked hundreds of new share-selling outfits, some based on possibility, some on sheer hope, but most on plain thievery. "Turn in your Liberty Bonds," was the promoter's cry. "Give them to us —make a fortune instead of 3½ per cent." And the gullible among the public rushed in to part with their money in the gaudy, temporary stores set up on the Main Streets of America, where miniature wells spouted oil and weird revolving motors whirled in the windows.

Nowhere did people flock to be mulcted in such great numbers as in Boston, where the most confident confidence man of the day, Charles Ponzi, was paying up to 50 per cent interest a month on money deposited with him. Ponzi was extremely mysterious about revealing how he was able to do this. He hinted that the answer lay in International Postal Certificates, an exchange scrip enabling a person to send a coupon bought in the United States at our postal rate to another country, where it is turned in for stamps of that country so that a reply can be mailed without becoming involved in the complicated realms of foreign exchange. Since there is variance

On June 27, 1921, the Curb brokers shed their hats and raincoats and began a new life as indoor traders. However, they retained their old hand signals which were flashed back and forth with clerks who now sat in booths (FOREGROUND AND REAR).

in the postal rates of most countries, some arbitrage is possible. However, in order to roll up the profits Ponzi claimed, it would have been necessary for him to do a business hundreds of times greater than the entire volume of the International Postal Certificate system. There was nothing new about Ponzi's secret. He was merely paying profits out of the capital he was acquiring, and could do so as long as fresh money kept pouring in. Even some staid heads of the smaller Boston banks became enmeshed in Ponzi's get-rich-quick scheme and came to grief with him when the inevitable collapse occurred.

The intersection at Wall Street, where Broad loses half its width and continues north as Nassau, is set precisely at latitude 40°42′25″ and longitude 74°52″. On Thursday, September 16, 1920, the corners were occupied as follows: southeast, the House of Morgan; southwest, the excavation and surrounding barricade for the annex to the New York Stock Exchange, where the Wilks building, owned by Hetty Green's son-in-law, had recently stood; northwest, the Bankers Trust building with its distinctive pyramidal top, designed after the tomb of Mausolus at Halicarnassus; and northeast, the eighty-year-old Sub-Treasury. Next door to the Sub-Treasury, the new United States Assay Office was nearing completion and employees had been at work all morning transferring some of the nine hundred million dollars in gold and one hundred million dollars in Federal Reserve notes from the basement vaults of the Sub-Treasury to the larger and deeper ones of the Assay Office, trundling the treasure over a wooden runway across the alley separating the two buildings.

As noon approached and the gold-movers stopped for lunch, a man drove a rust-brown lattice-sided wagon, covered with a canvas tarpaulin, up Wall from the east. He pulled at the reins and brought the old dark-bay horse to a halt before the doors of the Assay Office. Then the driver jumped to the pavement, tossed the reins across the horse's back to hold him there . . . and disappeared.

The gilded hands of the clock on the tower of Trinity Church, a block west, came together, pointing straight up, and the church bell began tolling the hour.

One . . . Edward Sweet, the millionaire who had formerly owned the famous seafood restaurant at Fulton and South streets, came down the elevator of the Trust Company of America building after visiting his broker's office.

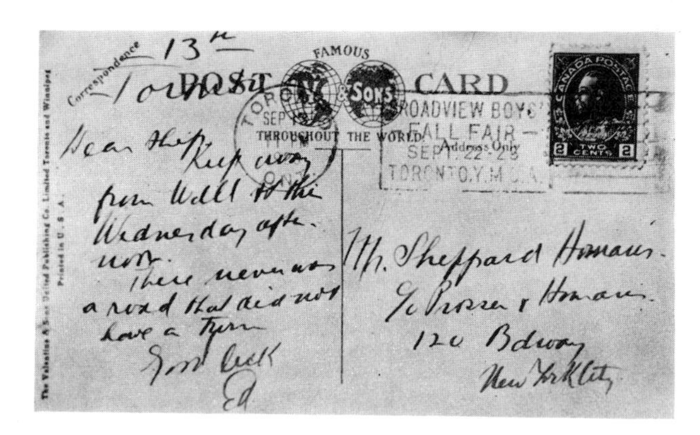

From Toronto, Edward P. Fischer, formerly employed in New York, sent postcards warning of disaster to several Wall Street friends. Since he was known as eccentric, they were ignored. Later investigated, Fischer's cards proved to be only a coincidence.

As the hands of Trinity clock came together at noon on September 16, 1920, a man drove an old wagon up to the Assay Office, jumped to the sidewalk, and vanished.

Two . . . Seward Prosser, President of Bankers Trust, was preparing to leave his fourth-floor office to go out to lunch.

Three . . . Junius Spencer Morgan, grandson of John Pierpont, was at his desk on the Broad Street side of the Morgan building, conferring with John Markle of Jeddo, Pennsylvania, the largest independent coal-mine operator in the country, who had stopped in on his way to his summer home on the north shore of Long Island. With him was his chief engineer and general manager of his mines, A. B. Jessup. Also conferring with them were T. W. Joyce and Walter Dickerson of the Morgan staff.

Four . . . An unidentified man was idly looking into a shop window on John Street, between Nassau and Broadway, more than five blocks away.

Five . . . William H. Remick, President of the New York Stock Exchange, stood chatting with one of the governors near the Reading post, where trading was brisk.

Six . . . Upstairs in the fourth-floor press room of the exchange a financial news editor of the *Times* was playing chess with a reporter and pondering his next move.

Seven . . . Sixteen-year-old Robert Westday, messenger for Curtis and Sanger, brokers at 49 Wall, was striding briskly toward the Broad Street corner.

Eight . . . Arthur M. Anderson, head of the Morgan bond department, sat at his desk on the Wall Street side of the building with his back to the window, conferring with his assistant, William Ewing.

Nine . . . George W. Merchant was visiting his brother, who was President of the Bank of Cuba, in the building next to the Assay Office.

Ten . . . The Schulte cigar store on Wall Street across from Morgan's was crowded with customers.

Eleven . . . John Coleman, a page boy who had come to Wall Street two years before, was scurrying about the floor of the exchange trying to find his boss.

Twelve . . . A young law clerk, Howard Reinheimer, was leaving the Equitable building at 120 Broadway for an early lunch.

As the last bong of the Trinity bell died away, a tremendous explosive roar erupted in all directions from the ball of fire that completely demolished the old wagon parked in front of the Assay Office.

The *New York Times* newsman looked up from the chess board and casually said: "Oh, there goes 23 Wall," and moved one of his pieces.

The white ball of fire gave off acrid yellow fumes that changed color and rose as a great pillar of dense brown smoke, spitting tongues of green flame. Whirling upward, the column of smoke changed form and flattened out into a black cloud that whirled ever faster as it spread above the towering skyscrapers. A hail of iron fragments — great chunks of metal — shot through the street, crushing skulls, smashing arms and legs, ripping living flesh into shreds. Awnings a dozen floors above street level burst into flame and windows within a half-mile radius were immediately shattered under the first powerful impact of the explosion.

The echoing roar of the blast reverberated and bounced from building to building, causing still more windows to vibrate and collapse. The silence that followed the last fading rumble of the explosion was broken by an eerie, incongruous note—a gentle, bell-like tinkling as millions of shards of glass fell from sill to sill and ledge to ledge until striking the pavement below in a rain of deadly splinters.

When a count was finally made on that cruel Thursday in September, 1920, thirty innocent people were known to be dead.

Edward Sweet must have been passing very close to the horse and wagon when they were atomized, for all that was ever found of him was one finger with his ring still upon it.

The interior of the House of Morgan was littered with plaster and glass, and the steel mesh over the windows was twisted as if made of wax. A wild rush of air had swept in at the instant of the explosion, and papers, dust, bits of furniture, and broken glass eddied about until the blast expended its force.

Clerks and secretaries were knocked to the floor. Junius Morgan was covered with slivers of glass, although he suffered only a slight gash on his hand. Dickerson and Joyce were badly cut, and the latter was to learn that his twenty-four-year-old son, William, who had been seated at a window nearest the blast site, had been decapitated—the only fatality to occur in the House of Morgan.

Arthur Anderson struggled to his feet and found a large piece of glass embedded in the back of his chair. Had he not been hurled to the floor it would undoubtedly have been driven into his spine. After recovering from his shock, he administered first aid to William Ewing, who had severe head cuts and a badly bruised hand.

Markle and Jessup, mining men familiar with explosives, picked themselves up and rushed to the

Thirty people were killed and 300 were injured when the wagon, loaded with high explosives and chunks of sashweight "shrapnel," blew up, rocking the whole Wall Street district. This picture, taken from the steps of the Sub-Treasury six minutes after the explosion, shows the remains of the horse and harness (LEFT CENTER), *not alongside the House of Morgan* (RIGHT), *as popularly believed, but near the curb in front of the Assay Office, where $900 million in gold had just been stored.*

nearest blown-in window. After one glance into the center of the street, where a shattered automobile lay on its side, Markle burst out with an explanation: "Bolshevists!"

The front of the Schulte cigar store had been blown in and its stock hopelessly scattered, as if by the fury of a hurricane.

The man who had been window-shopping on John Street was knocked to his knees by an iron object which fell from the sky, striking him at the base of his neck. It was a four-inch length sawed from an old-fashioned sashweight and the missile had been blown over the tops of tall buildings for a quarter of a mile before dropping upon the victim.

Lengths of sashweight, that had the effect of shrapnel, and high explosives made up the giant bomb. Some of the chunks of metal were driven to a depth of two feet into the pavement. Others ripped through the body of young Robert Westday. One victim, identified as a Colonel Neville, was found to have twenty-four wounds in his back.

After the last lethal hail of metal fragments and

An official begins identifying bodies of people who were walking along the north side of Wall Street, near the Assay Office, when the explosion caught them.

Civilians, soldier, marine, and a reporter help policeman hold back the curious from bodies of victims lying on the sidewalk near the Morgan building entrance.

Federal troops summoned from Governor's Island helped clear the blast area and guard the Assay Office and the Sub-Treasury. At rear right, a crowd is beginning to gather on the scaffolding of the excavation where the Wilks building formerly stood and the new Stock Exchange Annex was to be built.

Interior of the Morgan office where William Joyce was killed. At left is twisted grille, placed at window to deflect bombs.

the last tinkling of glass on the pavements, an awesome pocket of silence blanketed the area. Then came the groans and screaming of the maimed, the dazed whimpering and hysterical shouts of those who had been shocked by the detonation. A pool of blood marked the spot where the horse had been left standing. Dead girls huddled against each other in a group and then slowly collapsed like rag dolls. A messenger boy lay a few feet from where his hand—still clutching an envelope full of securities — had been severed from his arm.

The explosion had sent a slug of metal through the window of the Bankers Trust, almost hitting President Prosser. All the glass in the windows of the Stock Exchange had been shattered, and although the silk curtains were riddled to tatters, they served to protect all but a few of the brokers who crowded the room.

As the floor of the exchange began to shudder, John Coleman followed the traders who had fled to the sides of the room, afraid that the roof might cave in. Then, as the screams and groans, the shouts and the pounding of running feet, seeped into the hall,

Anxiety and tears mark the faces of relatives and friends of missing persons as they make inquiries and an official consults a list of casualties after the catastrophe. All the dead victims were later identified, but no one has ever been able to uncover the identity of the assassin who assembled and exploded the bomb.

Remick quietly said: "I think we'd better stop trading for the day." He stepped quickly to the gong, rang it, and brought business to a halt. Everyone hurried outside to be of help. The ticker relayed the news to exchanges throughout the country and they, too, shut down for the day.

Seated in his brother's office when the bomb went off, George W. Merchant exclaimed "What's that!" as the window blew in and the glass cut him about his head. After an ambulance surgeon dressed his wounds, he thanked him and smilingly said: "Guess I'll go out now and see the sights."

Help was quick to arrive at the disaster scene. Fire trucks appeared within six minutes and police platoons followed almost at once. Automobiles were pressed into service to take the injured to hospitals until ambulances could thread their way into the congested area. Orderlies and doctors fought through the swarming crowds. Soldiers from Governor's Island and sailors and marines from the Brooklyn Navy Yard were on hand within a half hour to protect the government gold at the Sub-Treasury and Assay Office as well as help the police keep the ever-increasing throngs of curious onlookers out of the way.

In the next few days the police gathered over five hundred pounds of broken sashweight. One was a section that had been hurled all the way up to the headquarters of the Bankers Club on the thirty-fourth story of the Equitable building. On the day of the explosion, young Reinheimer, who had been standing in front of the block-square structure, joined the people racing toward Broad and Wall, crunching over the glass on the sidewalks, then taking to the middle of the street. Strangers excitedly called to each other: "What happened?" From the vantage of the Sub-Treasury steps, earlier arrivals, guessing from the carnage of the scene, stated that a wagon transporting dynamite had accidentally rammed a passing automobile. In addition to the Stock Exchange annex, five other building excavations in the downtown area gave support to the dynamite-wagon theory. However, an immediate police investigation disclosed no record of any such wagon being in the vicinity of the financial district at the time of the blast. An electric-truck marked DU PONT, which was seen earlier, proved to be carrying two hogsheads of paint.

The evidence of the chunks of old pig iron proved to the authorities that they faced "a piece of organized deviltry executed with a terrible effectiveness that dwarfed such anarchist and other radical crimes of the past as the attempts on the lives of Russell Sage and H. C. Frick, the bombs in Union Square, Saint Patrick's Cathedral and Saint Alphonsus' Church," the *Times* said the next morning.

Before nightfall eight different investigations were in progress. Detectives made little headway in questioning the dazed and injured in the hospitals. After visiting five thousand stables along the Atlantic seaboard, they came up with only one clue to the identity of the man—and none at all for the wagon or the horse. A blacksmith on the lower East Side, who had refastened one of the horse's shoes a day or so before, thought that the driver was a Sicilian. But no more was ever learned. He vanished completely and forever. Dozens of men from Hong Kong to Helsinki confessed to the crime in the hope of being extradited to the United States, but none was able to prove any connection with the atrocious deed. Although rewards totaling a hundred thousand dollars were offered, no claimants ever appeared to provide information.

In addition to the thirty known dead, estimates of the wounded ranged from two to four hundred, most of whom suffered cuts from flying or falling glass. Property damages amounted to almost three million dollars, with the House of Morgan worst hit. But the partners immediately set about to restore normal operations. Within four hours of the explosion, a crew was at work clearing up the litter and debris. Laboring through the night, they repaired the damage sufficiently so that the bank was able to open for business as usual the next morning.

At noon on Friday the greatest mass meeting in the history of the Street was held and the crowd, which stretched as far as Broadway and Beaver and Pearl and Cedar streets, listened with hushed attention as speaker after speaker defied the radicals, the anarchists, and the Bolsheviki who were supposed to be responsible for the outrage. But there has never been a feather of evidence that any organized group was connected with the Wall Street explosion of 1920. As Frederick Lewis Allen wrote in *Only Yesterday:* "The American people were coming to their senses sufficiently [after a prolonged "Red Scare"] to realize that no such insane and frightful plot could ever command the support of more than a handful of fanatics."

Aside from Junius Morgan's cut hand, no injury was inflicted on a ranking member of Wall Street's hierarchy. The House of Morgan never repaired the pitted holes blasted in its wall by the chunks of flying sashweight. When a Morgan official was asked "Why not?" he countered with the proper answer: "How?" To remove and replace the massive blocks of limestone would be a gigantic undertaking. To fill in the holes would only make them more conspicuous. One also senses that the House of Morgan carries the marks proudly, like the scars of wounds attained with bravery and honor.

In the horrible blast of explosion and the deadly barrage of hurtling iron, one figure remained serene and unshaken. Hardly fifty feet from the erupting inferno stood the statue of George Washington — imperturbable and unharmed.

J. Pierpont Morgan, Jr., was generally considered the intended target of the bomb, but he was abroad in England at the time. In any event, his office was at the other end of the building on Broad Street.

13

Boom and Bust

WE ARE INCLINED today to look back on the 1920's before the Crash as a gaudy, golden age, the gayest era within man's memory.

But the carefree times, the great market booms, the bathtub gin, the easy money, the grafting, happy-go-lucky politicians, and the new freedoms of women were reflections in only one side of the glass. Many were out of work (two and a half million in May, 1929); the farmer had little cash; installment buying was a new phenomenon, but defaulting on payments had already begun; no more than half the stocks on the exchanges were zooming on that elevator ride; and the majority of all the people took Prohibition, civic virtue, and womanhood soberly, honestly, and seriously.

Those who could afford it did their drinking in speakeasies or in Europe, Cuba, or Mexico, according to their means. The ladies went from euchre to whist to bridge to mah-jongg to the stock market. The tomb of King Tutankhamen was discovered in Egypt and King Tut styles blossomed on Fifth Avenue. Monkey-gland doctors, flagpole sitters, Floyd Collins trapped in a Kentucky cave, Governor "Ma" Ferguson of Texas, Texas Guinan, Al Capone, marathon dancers, Fall and Sinclair, Fall and Doheny, the Two Black Crows, Amos and Andy, Dempsey and Carpentier, Dempsey and Firpo, Dempsey and Tunney, and Emile Coué (who taught you to help yourself by repeating "day by day in every way I am getting better and better") were only some of the people in the news. Calvin Coolidge's campaign slogan was "Keep Cool with Cal" and the electric refrigerator led to the virtual disappearance of the iceman. In the next campaign, Herbert Hoover pronounced Prohibition "a great social and economic experiment, noble in motive and far-reaching in purpose," but on the following St. Valentine's Day in Chicago Prohibition was responsible for the bloodiest gang massacre in history.

During the 1920's, New York replaced London as the principal money market of the world, and "as if to express appreciation of our new role, we raised our skyscrapers still higher," Christopher Tunnard and Henry Reed wrote in *American Skyline*. "No more interesting or exhilarating change has ever taken place in the city than the new skyline created

The greatest Wall Street construction boom occurred in the 1920's. In this aerial view of lower Manhattan, taken on March 30, 1921, all the tall buildings are to the west of the Bankers Trust pyramid (LEFT CENTER). *Behind it are the Equitable and Municipal buildings.*

by the whim of American business men to reach the clouds."

In Wall Street, as in central Manhattan, many of the tallest buildings were begun just before the stock-market crash and opened their doors to a thin dribble of lessees when they were finished. The new Waldorf-Astoria broke ground the day after the market began to break down. The Chrysler building and the Empire State were so short of tenants that night watchmen were instructed to turn on lights in vacant offices to give the towers an appearance of occupancy.

The biography of one skyscraper is typical. On May 1, 1929, George L. Ohrstrom, an energetic thirty-four-year-old investment banker, and Colonel William A. Starrett, the promoter member of the family of master builders, announced that they were going to put up the tallest building in the world, an 840-foot, seventy-story tower, at 40 Wall Street, to be known as the Bank of Manhattan building. Forty-two per cent of the site was owned by the bank, which had bought the land, including a three-story building upon it, for thirty thousand dollars at the end of the eighteenth century.

The builders first erected a financial skyscraper: twelve and a half millions of 6 per cent first-mortgage gold bonds, a second mortgage of six and a half millions, a three-and-a-quarter-million issue of preferred stock, plus twelve hundred shares of common. Even allowing for a 10 per cent vacancy rate, they expected the building to gross five million dollars a year, with a profit of two million after paying interest. They began a race with time in order to have the building completed within a year and thus start earning rentals. Andrew J. Eken smashed all existing records for construction, finishing the structure in

363 days, half the time any comparable building had previously taken to erect.

But the new skyscraper looked down on a different world from that of a year before. General Electric, which had sold at 244 on May 1, 1929, was going for 86⅝. Adams Express had plunged all the way from 705 to 32¼. And Otis Elevator had dropped from 301 to 72½. Some of the firm commitments for whole floors at eight dollars a square foot had been made by companies no longer in business. Half the floors were empty, but were slowly filled with tenants who paid less than three dollars a square foot. Ohrstrom and Starrett struggled for five years and managed to pay interest on the first and second mortgages, amounting to a million dollars annually, before defaulting. After eighteen months of legal warfare among the holders of various equities, the first-mortgage bondholders took over and issued new securities that could be picked up for less than eleven cents on the dollar. The great tower, which cost over twenty million dollars, could have been bought outright for $1,249,483. "This is less than we paid for the forty-three high-speed elevators," George Ohrstrom said ruefully at the time.

In 1941, however, the situation changed radically. The Navy Department rented several offices and the war brought an influx of more new tenants. By 1945, 40 Wall had an occupancy of almost 100 per cent. Then it was possible to raise space rates. By 1956 the value of the building was placed at $16,250,000. Three years later all of the stock in the company was purchased by Webb and Knapp at an auction on October 27, 1959, for the sum of $18,150,000. Ohrstrom and Starrett had done the right thing in the right place. Unfortunately for them, the right time did not come for a quarter of a century.

Eleven years later the Bankers Trust pyramid is hidden in shadow between the Irving Trust and the 40 Wall tower. Other new skyscrapers are City Bank Farmers Trust, Cities Service, 120 Wall, Downtown Athletic Club, New York Telephone, 19 Rector, and 30 Broad.

Another disappointment to the builders was that 40 Wall did not long remain the tallest structure in the world. For years the Woolworth building, which is 792 feet high, was the giant. At the beginning of 1929 work began on the Chrysler building on Forty-second Street, which was planned to top the Woolworth by seventeen feet. The 840-foot tower at 40 Wall was to overshadow the Chrysler obelisk by thirty-one feet, and almost did until the day the Chrysler building was finished. Then, to everyone's surprise, it actually topped the Wall Street building! Working with extreme secrecy, the builders had smuggled a long, needle-like spire into the peak of the Chrysler tower. At the last moment, the spire was raised from the inside so that the midtown structure loomed taller than its downtown rival. However, the Chrysler's eminence was brief, lasting only until the Empire State building was completed in 1930.

Among the other buildings erected in this era were the tower at 60 Wall—which is actually at 70 Pine Street—and is known as the Cities Service building (now third tallest in the world); the City Bank Farmers Trust building at Exchange Place, William, Hanover, and Beaver; the Irving Trust at 1 Wall; the Continental Bank at 30 Broad; the Bank of New York on the site it has occupied since 1799; the Transportation building on Broadway; the New York Telephone building; the Chase National Bank at Pine and Nassau, and the Maritime Exchange building at Broad and Stone.

One building which was never in the skyscraper race, but influences every other building in the Wall Street district, is the great block-square fortress bounded by Maiden Lane, William, Liberty, and Nassau streets—the Federal Reserve Bank of New York, erected in 1924. It has five basement floors, descending to a depth of eighty feet below street level, housing some of the strongest and most capacious vaults in the world. The building is guarded by a force of 135 ex-marines, more than the number of men at Precinct One, the police station for Wall Street, at Old Slip.

The automobile and the radio came into their own in the twenties, not only as part of the daily lives of the people, but as the basis for securities for speculation and investment. The first broadcasting station, KDKA, near Pittsburgh, opened on November 2, 1920, to air the Harding-Cox election returns. The author recalls his first radio experiments—

Narrowest man-made canyon is fifteen-foot-wide Exchange Place, east from Broadway, one block south of Wall. Upper right is the City Bank Farmers Trust tower.

spending Saturdays in Schenley Park with other members of an evening class in "wireless telephony" from the University of Pittsburgh, trying to pick up experimental signals from the Westinghouse station. This was in the summer of 1920 and Army equipment from the recent World War was used to determine whether antennas stuck into the ground or into the air provided the best reception. The subsequent forests of rooftop aerials that spread across the country failed to indicate that the decision was a close one. In 1922 sixty million dollars were spent on radio equipment; by 1929 annual sales had climbed to $842,000,000—an increase of 1,400 per cent.

There were about eight million automobiles in the country in 1922, but by the end of the decade the figure was over twenty-three million. The aviation industry, which had declined after the World War boom, was struggling to survive when it was dramatically impelled upward and onward by an event that began at Long Island's Roosevelt Field and reached its climax on lower Broadway, all within a period of three weeks in the spring of 1927.

In 1919, to bring about closer rapport between his native France and the United States, Raymond Orteig, who owned the Lafayette and Brevoort hotels, offered a prize of twenty-five thousand dollars for the first New York to Paris nonstop plane flight. No one tried to win the award until the morning of May 20, 1927, when Charles A. Lindbergh, an air-mail pilot, took off alone from Roosevelt Field at 7:52 in a gray monoplane loaded down with gasoline. He had stolen a march on Clarence Chamberlin and Lieutenant-Commander Richard E. Byrd who were waiting for the weather to clear before attempting the flight. Luck was with Lindbergh, for the fog which had blanketed the entire coast all the way to Newfoundland evaporated and he had good weather and favorable winds clear across the Atlantic. Carrying several letters of introduction and a five-hundred-dollar check for expenses, he arrived at Le Bourget airfield in Paris in exactly thirty-three hours, twenty-nine minutes, and thirty seconds.

Of that epic flight Frederick Lewis Allen wrote in *Only Yesterday*:

> *No sooner had the word been flashed along the wires that Lindbergh had started than the whole population of the country became united in the exaltation of a common emotion. Young and old, rich and poor, farmer and stockbroker, Fundamentalist and skeptic, highbrow and lowbrow, all with*

The Federal Reserve building was begun in 1922, and as each floor was finished its staff moved in. The round tower at the northeast corner adds to its fortress-like appearance, although it is only a decorative device.

The Irving Trust, with sun's reflection above Trinity steeple, was finished in 1930. An earlier building was torn down after only fourteen years at 1 Wall. Land here is possibly the most expensive in the world.

Intended as the world's tallest when announced in 1929, the 40 Wall building was cheated of this distinction when the Chrysler building secretly added a spire at the last minute that towered 119 feet higher.

one accord fastened their hopes upon the young man in the Spirit of St. Louis. To give a single instance of the intensity of their mood: at the Yankee Stadium in New York, where the Maloney-Sharkey fight was held on the evening of the 20th, forty thousand hard-boiled boxing fans rose as one man and stood with bared heads in impressive silence when the announcer asked them to pray for Lindbergh. The next day came the successive reports of Lindbergh's success — he had reached the Irish coast, he was crossing over England, he was over the Channel, he had landed at Le Bourget to be enthusiastically mobbed by a vast crowd of Frenchmen—and the American people went almost mad with joy and relief.

When Lindbergh returned to the United States three weeks later, he was one of the most popular idols in the whole history of hero worship. He had been given tumultuous welcomes in London and Washington before his arrival in New York on the morning of June 13. But the Manhattan greeting was incomparable. In an interview that appeared in the *New York Times* the next morning, Lindbergh said:

> I never expected anything like it.
>
> People told me that the New York reception would be the biggest of all but I had no idea it was going to be so much more overwhelming than the

others. I simply cannot find words to describe my feelings. All I can say is that the welcome was wonderful, wonderful. . . .

I had a fine view of the strange armada which greeted me in the Narrows. I never saw anything like it in my life. I didn't know that there were so many different kinds of ships. Everything that could boast of a propeller seemed to be there, probably two hundred in all.

There were ferry boats, tugs, tankers, steamships, excursion boats, all decorated and apparently jammed to the rails . . . the noise broke loose, and from then until we reached the Battery I was treated to more different kinds of noise than I thought existed. It sounded like the whole country had decided to let off steam at the same time. . . .

Three years before Lindbergh's historic flight, Woodrow Wilson had died in Washington—an invalid broken in spirit and body. In his last months as President, before his collapse, he had pitted all his strength against the implacable will of the United States Senate in an effort to obtain ratification of a peace treaty that would allow the United States to join the League of Nations. He had almost personally created the League, but the Senate and the country as a whole refused to join it. Apparently, there were not enough people willing to accept the serious international responsibility such a step entailed. "We won the war, didn't we? What more do you expect of us?" was the majority reaction. Even before Wilson's final term expired, the people of the United States had selected their next President—Warren Gamaliel Harding.

Handsome and charming in manner, Harding impressed many voters as a man of strength, a father image. Actually, he was a "cardboard" senator surrounded by a gang of shrewd operators who guided him, thought for him, and, after he was elected President, fouled the White House with their schemes and frauds.

According to William Allen White, Harding was "almost unbelievably ill-informed." One day, after a conference on taxes, he exclaimed to one of his secretaries: "I can't make a damn thing out of this tax

The Cities Service building, also known as the 60 Wall tower, is actually at 70 Pine. Joined to the Wall Street building by a high bridge, it is 950 feet to the top, making it the world's third tallest building.

On June 13, 1927, three weeks after his solo flight across the Atlantic, Charles A. Lindbergh returned to receive the greatest welcome New York City has ever bestowed on any hero. He was greeted in the harbor by a vast flotilla of 400 ships of every description, seventy of them visible in this picture.

problem. I listen to one side and they seem right, and then — God! — I talk to the other side and they seem just as right, and here I am where I started. I know somewhere there is a book that will give me the truth, but, hell, I couldn't read the book. I know somewhere there is an economist who knows the truth, but I don't know where to find him — and haven't the sense to know him and trust him when I find him. God! What a job!"

Exactly two years and five months after he was inaugurated, Harding died in San Francisco and Calvin Coolidge became President. The scandals that boiled up and came to the surface very soon afterward led to speculation that Harding's death was not due to apoplexy, as officially announced. In Samuel Hopkins Adams' novel, *Revelry*, the fictional President committed suicide. In *The Strange Death of President Harding*, Gaston B. Means implied that Harding was poisoned by his wife. In the 1960

Driving up Broadway to City Hall, Lindbergh, sitting on folded top of the first car in the parade, was deluged by an estimated 750,000 pounds of saved-up ticker tape and torn-up telephone books.

Broadway play, *The Gang's All Here*, Jerome Lawrence and Robert Lee favor the Adams ending. "Yet it is not necessary to accept any such melodramatic version of the tragedy to acknowledge that Harding died a victim of the predicament in which he was caught," wrote Frederick Lewis Allen in *Only Yesterday*. "He knew too much of what had been going on in his administration to be able to face the future."

What had been going on in the way of corruption, bribes, graft, kickbacks, and outright thievery was on a scale unprecedented in American history. Secret leases without competitive bidding were given by Secretary of the Interior Albert B. Fall to drill oil wells on government land reserved for the Navy. Among other transactions, he leased the Teapot Dome Reserve to Harry F. Sinclair's Mammoth Oil Company on April 7, 1922, and the Elk Hills Reserve to Edward L. Doheny's Pan-American Company on December 11. After Harding's death it was revealed that Sinclair had given Fall about $260,000 in Liberty Bonds and Doheny had "loaned" him one hundred thousand dollars in cash, without interest or security.

There were congressional investigations, criminal indictments, law suits by the government, and contempt proceedings which stretched on until 1929. Fall was convicted of accepting a bribe from Doheny and was sentenced to a year in jail—but Doheny was acquitted of bribing Fall! Sinclair was also acquitted on the charge of bribery, but he nevertheless served two jail terms for contempt. The bonds which Sinclair gave to Fall came out of a "kitty" set up by four oil-company heads under the name of the Continental Trading Company, Ltd., of Canada. This corporation was formed to be the depository of the twenty-five-cent a barrel kickback Sinclair and the other three received on the sale of oil to their companies. This amounted to three million dollars and not until the deal was exposed did any of the men report it to their companies.

Other scandals of the administration were also uncovered in rapid sequence. Harding had appointed Charles R. Forbes chief of the Veterans' Bureau, and although he was in office less than two years, waste and graft were responsible for the loss of two hundred million dollars. Forbes, who, it was later discovered, had deserted from the Army, was convicted of fraud and sentenced to serve his time in

"Lucky Lindy" (a nickname the pilot hated) was cheered by 100,000 on the way to City Hall where he received the city's Medal of Valor. More than 300,000 applauded him on the route to Central Park where Governor Al Smith presented him with the state's Medal of Valor.

The flyer was escorted to the grandstand by official greeter Grover Whalen and Mayor Jimmy Walker who said: "New York is yours. I don't give it to you. You won it. And one other thing. Before you go, will you provide us with a new street-cleaning department to clean up the mess?"

Warren G. Harding, genial small-town Senator from Ohio who led the "back to normalcy" wave that swept the Republicans into the White House, campaigned in the summer of 1920 from the porch of his Marion home. After his sudden death in 1923, the nation was shocked by the Teapot Dome and Elk Hills scandals involving members of his administration.

Leavenworth. Other convictions followed. Frederick Lewis Allen concluded his report with "... the Harding Administration was responsible in its short two years and five months for more concentrated robbery and rascality than any other in the whole history of the Federal Government."

Robbery and rascality — and welshing — were the crimes the New York Stock Exchange was accused of by Clarence Saunders, who in 1923 executed the last Corner pulled on the Big Board. Saunders was the Horatio Alger hero of the grocery boys, having founded the fast-growing Piggly Wiggly chain. In the middle of 1922 its stock was admitted to listing on the main exchange where it was a reliable, unspectacular performer until November, when a group of bear raiders tried to drive its price down.

This raid angered Saunders and he hastened to protect his investment by launching a buying campaign to send the price back up. As he bought and the bears continued to sell, rumors out of the Chicago Exchange were that Saunders had cornered the market. This was not yet true, but it may have given the man from Memphis the idea of punishing the New York traders. With ten million dollars borrowed from Southern bankers, Saunders set out to trap the Wall Street speculators, who by now were short of Piggly Wiggly and therefore had to go out and borrow stock to cover their sales.

Meanwhile the price, which had been around fifty until they drove it down to forty and incurred Saunders' ire, climbed to 75½ at the opening of trading on March 20. When Saunders called for the short-sellers to deliver all the stock they owed him by the following afternoon, the price went to 90, 100, 110, and hit its peak at 124. Then word reached the floor that the governors of the exchange were meeting to consider action on the stock and it slid back to eighty-two at closing. Late that afternoon the governors announced that trading in Piggly Wiggly would be suspended and that the deadline for the delivery of stock had been postponed until further notice.

This action can only be compared to the referee in a prize fight stepping in after a knockout and informing the winner, without even an "excuse me," that instead of counting to ten, he was going to count up to a hundred, or perhaps 250. For when the rulers of the exchange next made an announcement it was that Piggly Wiggly was permanently stricken from the trading list and that short-sellers would have five days beyond the deadline to come up with stock. In those five days, instead of buying the shares they needed from Saunders at his price, they were able to beat the bushes for Piggly Wiggly stockholders and buy enough over the counter to get square. Had the governors of the exchange not switched rules on him in his moment of triumph, thus saving the skins of many of the members, Saunders would have beaten Wall Street for about twenty million dollars. As it was, the price he eventually paid for the Corner was the loss of Piggly Wiggly and bankruptcy. Two years later the exchange amended its constitution to make the postponement-of-delivery ruling legal.

If Clarence Saunders heaped curses on the Stock Exchange, his scorn had little effect on the great bull market that was building up.

The stock market started its roller-coaster ride leading up to the Great Crash after August, 1927, when the Federal Reserve Board lowered the rediscount rate to 3½ per cent. In seeking a villain to blame for the Great Panic, many point the finger at the Federal Reserve Board, because it lowered interest rates in order to help Britain, Germany, and France, which were in a very bad financial condition. This also released money for stock purchases.

Other factors and individuals have also been held responsible for the onset of the Depression. Some have accused Calvin Coolidge, whose soothing words in January, 1928, encouraged the bull market when brokers' loans topped four and a half billions and Wall Street itself was scared. "The business of America is business," he said. "This is only a natural expansion of business . . . nothing to worry about."

Another factor was the huge load of securities floated by the investment bankers which remained undigested—unsold to the public.

Margin purchases, calling for as little as 10 per cent of the selling price—a million people held three hundred million shares in that shaky manner—were strongly suspected of bringing on the Great Crash.

Those who favor the big-disaster-prelude theory of panics point to the Fall River fire of 1929 and the subsequent payment of enormous claims, which forced liability-insurance companies to liquidate stock- and bond-holdings much too quickly.

Some theorists place the blame on Winston Churchill. As the new Chancellor of the Exchequer he had insisted on an overpriced $4.86 gold pound, which led to the British General Strike, which led to the appeal to the Federal Reserve Board to lower interest rates, which led to etc., etc.—*ad infinitum.*

Or what about Florida? The disastrous land boom, with its 10 per cent "binders," set the example for margin-trading in Wall Street.

Then there were the supersalesmen, the high-powered customers' men, and the banks selling securities of their own manufacture to their clients.

What about the overpriced investment trusts and the needless mergers? More than twelve hundred mergers, involving over four thousand firms, took place in the period. Some of the utility holding companies were such a maze of complicated interrelationships that they have not been untangled to this day.

The great corporations and industrial concerns must come in for their share of the blame, too. For when the Federal Reserve Board attempted to put a brake on speculation in early 1929 by cutting off brokers' loans and margin financing, the companies dashed into the market with their cash reserves to reap the fat interest payments offered.

Secretary of the Interior Albert B. Fall (LEFT), *had persuaded Harding to transfer Navy oil reserves to his jurisdiction and secretly leased Elk Hills to Edward L. Doheny* (RIGHT) *who had "loaned" him $100,000 in cash.*

Harry F. Sinclair, who gave Fall $260,000, smiled heartily despite two jail terms for contempt. Although Fall was sentenced to one year for accepting the bribe, Doheny and Sinclair were acquitted of paying it.

Some of the biggest Wall Street banks did that, too. For example, Charles E. Mitchell of National City, defied the Federal Reserve Board edict, although he was a member of the board of the New York Reserve Bank. Up to this point, the banks had a wonderful thing going for them, for they borrowed money from the Reserve Bank at 6 per cent and loaned it as call money to brokers for 12 or 15 per cent and even more.

One more factor can be mentioned: the gap between stock earnings and prices had widened from ten to one to as much as twenty-five to one, and Radio Corporation of America, the most active in trading and fluctuation, went up to five hundred without ever paying a single dividend.

But volumes could be, and have been, written about the events leading up to those fatal, final ten days in October, 1929. Perhaps all of the factors and individuals involved contributed in one degree or another to the debacle—or possibly none of them was guilty. Because the fever that seized and possessed everyone in the market was as consuming as the frenzies of earlier eras — the South Sea Bubble, the Tulip Mania in Holland, the Mississippi Bubble —an ever-mounting rage to make money by the pot, the bale, the wagonload, without working for it. It was a disease that was not confined to any one group. People reacted to rumors and responded to tips so swiftly, so heedlessly, that the market never remained stationary and the trading volume kept soaring to incredible figures.

There were Cassandras and prophets of doom, such as the statistician and economist, Roger Babson, but he was always predicting disaster, and his voice went unheard now. The investment banker, Charles E. Merrill, had sold out in 1928, stating: "Now is the time to get out of debt." Bernard Baruch wrote: "Several times in 1928 . . . I sold, feeling that a break was imminent, only to have the market continue upward." Then, returning from a trip to Scotland, he reported: "Soon after I landed in New York, I decided to sell everything I could."

The Blizzard of 1929 began on October 24. Stock prices fell sharply and only a hastily formed bankers' buying pool headed off total disaster—but only temporarily. WORLD *artist Samuel Cahan caught the frenzy of the day in this sketch of the activity near Post 2.*

1
2
SAMUEL
CAHAN
STOCK EXCHANGE
10.29.'29
TO THE N.Y
STOCK
EXCHANGE
FROM THE
ARTIST

"All the News That's Fit to Print."

The New York Times.

THE WEATHER
Partly cloudy and slightly colder today; tomorrow fair.

VOL. LXXIX....No. 26,205. NEW YORK, THURSDAY, OCTOBER 24, 1929. TWO CENTS

PRICES OF STOCKS CRASH IN HEAVY LIQUIDATION, TOTAL DROP OF BILLIONS

PAPER LOSS $4,000,000,000

2,600,000 Shares Sold in the Final Hour in Record Decline.

MANY ACCOUNTS WIPED OUT

But No Brokerage House Is in Difficulties, as Margins Have Been Kept High.

ORGANIZED BACKING ABSENT

Bankers Confer on Steps to Support Market—Highest Break Is 96 Points.

THE WEATHER
Today: Partly cloudy and slightly cooler; fresh southwest and west winds
Tomorrow: Fair
Detailed general and flying reports, Page 21

NEW YORK Herald Tribune

LATE CITY EDITION

Vol. LXXXIX No. 30,293 THURSDAY, OCTOBER 24, 1929

Stocks Off 5 Billio[ns] In Severest Brea[k] Of Wall St. Histor[y]

Found Guilty of Theft Of 10 Quarts of Water

Savage Bear Attacks, ... Forced Selling of Big ... Accounts, Almost P... lyze Market in Last H...

181 New Lows Set ... Average Is Off ...

Adams Express Plu... 96 Points, Day's Rec... Loss; 2,500,000 Sh... Sold in 60-Min. De...

By Ferdinand Lundberg

"All the News That's Fit to Print."

The New York Times.

THE WEATHER
Cloudy and continued cold today; tomorrow fair and warmer.

VOL. LXXIX....No. 26,207. NEW YORK, FRIDAY, OCTOBER 25, 1929. TWO CENTS

WORST STOCK CRASH STEMMED BY BANKS; 12,894,650-SHARE DAY SWAMPS MARKET; LEADERS CONFER, FIND CONDITIONS SOUND

FINANCIERS EASE TENSION

Five Wall Street Bankers Hold Two Meetings at Morgan Office.

CALL BREAK 'TECHNICAL'

Wall Street Optimistic After Stormy Day; Clerical Work May Force Holiday Tomorrow

LOSSES RECOVERED IN PART

Upward Trend Start With 200,000-Share Order for Steel.

TICKERS LAG FOUR HOURS

GRUNDY SAYS LOBBY IS NEEDED TO UPHOLD PARTY TARIFF VOWS

Pennsylvanian at Senate Inquiry Asserts Hoover Platform Demands the Rates in Bill.

TELLS OF CAMPAIGN FUNDS

Veteran Lobbyist Active in Raising $600,000 in 1924 and $1,000,000 Last Year.

HITS AT SENATE COALITION

Plane Lost in Channel Gale; 5 Aboard Fail to Reach Paris

HUMBERT ESCAPES ANTI-FASCISTI'S SHOT AT BRUSSELS TOMB

Student Slips as He Tries to Assassinate the Italian Crown Prince.

HEIR CONTINUES PROGRAM

He Places Wreath on Unknown Soldier's Grave and Reviews Guard of Honor.

CROWD MOBS ASSAILANT

Loud-Speaker Can Be Nuisance, McAdoo Advises Magistrates

THE WORLD: FRIDAY, OCTOBER 25, 1929.

Nation's Financiers Declare Security Panic Has No Economic Basis

STREET HAS WORST PROSPERITY PANIC

Yesterday's Collapse Eleventh Since Black Friday in 1869

LAST EXCITEMENT IN 1921

Present Break Featured Mainly by Fall of Prices

Scene in the Heart of Wall Street When the Market Broke in a Record Panic

Crowds in Front of the Sub-Treasury Building Watching Other Crowds Surging About the Stock Exchange Across the Corner

BUSINESS IS SAFE, FINANCIERS ASSERT

MEN ON EXCHANGE KEEP THEIR NERVE

LONDON REFLECTS MARKET COLLAPSE

Prices of American Shares Drop in Throgmorton Street

HEAR N. Y. EXCHANGE SHUT

Pound Touches $4.86, Highest in Several Years

The World

OFFICIAL WEATHER FORECAST
Cloudy and continued cold to-day; tomorrow fair, with slowly rising temperature, fresh to strong southwest and west winds.

OCTOBER 25, 1929. TWO CENTS

Market in Panic as Stocks Are Dumped in 12,894,600 Share Day; Bankers Halt It

Outside J. P. Morgan & Co.'s

Richard Whitney's Cry of "205 for Steel" Halts Decline in Record Day's Disorder on Stock Exchange

EXPERTS TERM COLLAPSE SPECULATIVE PHENOMENON

Effect Is Felt on the Curb and Throughout Nation—Financial District Goes Wild

By Laurence Stern

BUSINESS IS SAFE, FINANCIERS ASSERT

See No Economic Basis for Securities Panic

MEN ON EXCHANGE KEEP THEIR NERVE

In Face of Disaster, They Joke Amid Violent Scene

By Kenneth Campbell

The World Has a Greater City Circulation Weekdays Than Any Other Standard Size Morning Paper in New York.

The World

OFFICIAL WEATHER FORECAST
Partly cloudy and warmer to-day; tomorrow fair; fresh to strong southwest and west winds.

VOL. LXX. NO. 24,903—DAILY. NEW YORK, SATURDAY, OCTOBER 26, 1929. TWO CENTS

Bankers' Pool Halts Panic, Steadies Market; Hoover Holds U. S. Business Sound

Fundamental Basis Prosperous Says President, After Conference With Mellon, Others of Cabinet, and Bankers

FINDS SPECULATION CUT ACTIVITY IN BUILDING

Reserve Report Less Optimistic; Norbeck Not Ready to Push Senate's Wall St. Inquiry

By Elliott Thurston

Text of President's Statement

From The World's Bureau
Special Dispatch to The World

WASHINGTON, Oct. 25.—President Hoover's statement on business conditions in the country to-day, follows:

The fundamental business of the country, that is, the production and distribution of commodities, is on a sound and prosperous basis. The best evidence is that although production and consumption are at high levels, the average prices of commodities as a whole have not increased and there have been no appreciable increases in the stocks of manufactured goods. Moreover, there has been a tendency of wages to increase and the output per worker in many industries again shows an increase, all of which indicates a healthy condition.

The construction and building industries have been to some extent affected by the high interest rates induced by stock speculation and there have been some seasonal decreases in one or two other industries, but these movements are of secondary character when considered in the whole situation.

A temporary drop in grain prices sympathetically with Stock Exchange prices usually happens, but as the Department of Agriculture points out, the overriding fact in grain is that this year's world wheat harvest is estimated to be 500,000,000 bushels less than that of last year, which will result in a very low carryover at the end of the harvest year.

$100,000,000 Made Available by Morgan and Others—Leading Stocks Close 1 to 3 Points Higher for Day

TURNOVER CUT ONE-HALF; TOTAL 5,910,900 SHARES

Wary Investment Buying Ends Demoralization—10 Billions Bull Market Values Gone

By Laurence Stern

Nation's Business Leaders See Stock Crash Benefits

Survey by The World Finds Executives in All Fields Agree That Conditions Are Sound

FALL IS GUILTY OF TAKING BRIBE; JURY FOR MERCY

Former Secretary of the Interior Faces Sentence of Three Years and Fine of $300,000

DOHENY TO BE TRIED NEXT; DEFENSE PLANS APPEAL

Women Shriek When Verdict Is Announced—Lawyer Is Stricken in Court

Convicted Former Cabinet Member

ALBERT B. FALL, Secretary of the Interior Under Harding, Leaving the Court in Wheel Chair After Bribery Verdict. MRS. FALL Is at the Left, Pushing the Chair

SWEARS WARDER BLED FERRARI OF $73,000 IN CASH

Dell'Osso Declares Banker, on His Knees, Pleaded With the Accused Official to Cease His Demands

ALLEGED BRIBE TOTAL NOW PUT AT $93,000

Palumbo, of the Williamsburg Branch of City Trust, Arrested on $100,000 Theft Charge

WOMAN WINS THAW SUIT; GETS $75,000

Night Club Hostess Had Sued for $100,000, Charging Assault

JURY TAKES 45 MINUTES

Defendant Plans Appeal—Verdict Reached on First Ballot

SCHOOL CRITICISM BARED BY THOMAS

Survey Shelved Since 1924 Cites Building Defects, Waste

SOCIALIST ASSAILS WALKER

Asks if 'Bad Conscience' Caused Holding Up of Report

The New York Times.

"All the News That's Fit to Print."

THE WEATHER
Cloudy, probably rain today and tomorrow; warmer tomorrow.

VOL. LXXIX....No. 26,212. NEW YORK, WEDNESDAY, OCTOBER 30, 1929. TWO CENTS

STOCKS COLLAPSE IN 16,410,030-SHARE DAY, BUT RALLY AT CLOSE CHEERS BROKERS; BANKERS OPTIMISTIC, TO CONTINUE AID

LEADERS SEE FEAR WANING

Point to 'Lifting Spells' in Trading as Sign of Buying Activity.

GROUP MEETS TWICE IN DAY

But Resources Are Unable to Stem Selling Tide—Lamont Reassures Investors.

HOPE SEEN IN MARGIN CUTS

Banks Reduce Requirements to 25 Per Cent—Sentiment in Wall St. More Cheerful.

240 Issues Lose $15,894,818,894 in Month; Slump in Full Exchange List Vastly Larger

Group.	Number of Stocks.	Decline in Value.
Railroads	25	$1,128,686,488
Public utilities	29	5,135,734,327
Motors	15	1,689,840,902
Oils	13	1,832,817,778
Coppers	13	824,403,825
Chemicals	9	1,621,697,897

CLOSING RALLY VIGOROUS

Leading Issues Regain From 4 to 14 Points in 15 Minutes.

INVESTMENT TRUSTS BUY

Large Blocks Thrown on Market at Opening Start Third Break of Week.

BIG TRADERS HARDEST HIT

Bankers Believe Liquidation Now Has Run Its Course and Advise Purchases.

U. S. STEEL TO PAY $1 EXTRA DIVIDEND

American Can Votes the Same and Raises Annual Rate From $3 to $4.

RESERVE BOARD FINDS ACTION UNNECESSARY

Six-Hour Session Brings No Change in the New York Rediscount Rate.

The World

The World Has a Greater City Circulation Weekdays Than Any Other Standard Size Morning Paper in New York.

OFFICIAL WEATHER FORECAST
Rain to-day and probably to-morrow; somewhat colder to-morrow; fresh to strong easterly winds.

VOL. LXX. NO. 24,906—DAILY. NEW YORK, TUESDAY, OCTOBER 29, 1929. TWO CENTS

Gigantic Bank Pool Pledged To Avert Disaster as Second Big Crash Stuns Wall Street

Hoover Asked to Clarify Stand on Amended Tariff

Johnson, Harrison, Voice Request—Bill's Fate Said to Be Up to President

SENATOR HIRAM JOHNSON

FOES OF WALKER FAIL TO MAKE HIM ANSWER CHARGES

Thomas Again Challenges Him to Platform to Discuss City Administration

BUT MAYOR AGAIN TELLS OF THINGS ACCOMPLISHED

Fusion Committee Announced, Names of Root and Hughes Missing

WARDER DEFENSE OPENS; AID CALLED

Bank Examiner Leaves Sick Bed to Testify of City Trust

SIX WITNESSES RULED OUT

State Abruptly Closes Without Calling Di Paola

Administration Is Surprised; Reserve Board Not Worried

Slight Business Recession, Effect on Hoover Prestige, Feared at Capital

CHASE NATIONAL Executive in Pool to Support Market Crash

Largest Financial Powers in the City Meet After Day of Hysterical Liquidation Sinking Prices Below Thursday's

OLD MORGAN POOL FAILS ENTIRELY TO AID MARKET

Average Dive Is 38.33 With Industrial Leaders Lower—9,212,800 Shares Traded

SENATOR BURTON DIES AT CAPITAL

Ohioan Was Serving Second Term in Upper House

IN PUBLIC LIFE 40 YEARS

77 Years Old, Had Been Ill Several Months

REPUBLICAN SPLIT OVER KAHN WIDENS

Borah, Norris Join Moses in War on White House "Machine"

OUT AFTER BURKE'S SCALP

National Committee's Counsel Blamed for "Leak" of Rift

The World

The World Has a Greater City Circulation Weekdays Than Any Other Standard Size Morning Paper in New York.

OFFICIAL WEATHER FORECAST
Cloudy, probably occasional rain, to-day and to-morrow; somewhat warmer to-morrow; moderate to fresh north winds, shifting to southeast.

VOL. LXX. NO. 24,907—DAILY. NEW YORK, WEDNESDAY, OCTOBER 30, 1929. TWO CENTS

Rally Ends New Record Day; 16,388,700 Shares Traded; Administration Sees Relief

Treasury and Reserve Board Believe Worst Is Over—Insist Basic Economic Conditions Are Sound

JULIUS KLEIN, U. S. EXPERT, RADIOS ANALYSIS TO NATION

Refuses to Forecast Market but Expresses "Confidence in Economic Future"

Extra Dividends Declared By U. S. Steel, American Can

Payment Made on Basis of Earnings Higher Than in 1928 Quarter

BROADCASTS Administration's Assurance on Market Crash

DR. JULIUS KLEIN

Rise in Prices Follows Sharpest and Lowest Fall in History as Bargain-Hunting Investors Wade In

LOSSES ARE 15 BILLION; 50 BILLION SINCE PEAK

Market Takes Natural Course—Morgan Pool Used Merely for Stabilization

U. S. STOCKS SOLD WILDLY IN LONDON

INSURANCE FUNDS FOR STOCKS URGED

New York American

2 CENTS IN GREATER NEW YORK — 6 A. M. EDITION

No. 16,905—DAILY. WEDNESDAY, OCTOBER 30, 1929—28 PAGES

Today
By Arthur Brisbane

MARKET RALLIES AS INVESTMENT BUYING CHECKS EARLY DECLINES

'LOBBY KING' DEMANDS GAG ON SENATORS

Tariff Foes Talk Too Much, Says Grundy; Says He Would Silence 2 of His Inquisitors

Daladier Unable To Form Cabinet; May Call Briand

KAHN RESIGNS AS TREASURER IN G.O.P. FIGHT

New York Banker Tells Moses He Cannot Serve in Face of Party Lack of Unanimity

AIR LINER SAFE; AVOIDS STORM

Can and Steel Vote $1 Extras; Conditions Sound, U.S. Reports

Trade Deflation Not Likely, Says Klein.

WAGES HIGH

Reserve Board in Closed Session.

Changes at a Glance

THE following table shows the wide fluctuations in leading stocks in the most active market in history on the Stock Exchange and Curb Exchange yesterday.

Record Sale of 16,410,030 Shares

BANKERS AID

Stocks Drop 5 to 45 Points, Recover.

New York American

2 CENTS IN GREATER NEW YORK — 6 A. M. EDITION

No. 16,906—DAILY. THURSDAY, OCTOBER 31, 1929—32 PAGES

Today
Dividends Are Loud. And Hear John D. R. The Women Resolve. 200 American Dividends.
By Arthur Brisbane

ROCKEFELLERS INVEST MILLIONS AS STOCKS RISE 10 TO 36 POINT

PRESIDENT YIELDS TO COALITION ON TARIFF

Hoover Will Accept Compromise Rather Than Fail Farmer

CALLS WATSON

Readiness to Quit Stand on Duties Is Told to Stalwarts

New $15,000,000 Theatre-Hotel For Broadway

Shubert-Kramer Building to Contain 4,600-Seat Auditorium.

LET LOBBYISTS WRITE TARIFF, GRUNDY URGES

Yes, Even Commas!—Amazed Senators Also Told Eyanson Served Country as Partner

WARDER PUTS BANK BLAME ON SUBORDINATES

Denies Delaying Examination of Ferrari Books; Daughter Admits Getting Gift of Car

THE BIG FELLOW TALKS!

JOHN D. ROCKEFELLER, SR.

John D. Rockefeller, Sr., Says:

"BELIEVING THAT FUNDAMENTAL CONDITIONS OF THE COUNTRY ARE SOUND AND THAT THERE IS NOTHING IN THE BUSINESS SITUATION TO WARRANT THE DESTRUCTION OF VALUES THAT HAS

TWO-DA HOLIDA VOTED EXCHAN

Bankers Report ditions Decid Better in N

LOANS REDU

10,727,320 Share Investing, Large Purc

The World

OFFICIAL WEATHER FORECAST
Cloudy and not quite so cool to-day; probably light rain; to-morrow showers and warmer; fresh southeast winds.

OCTOBER 31, 1929. TWO CENTS

Buying Strong, Stocks Rise; Rockefellers Join in Move; Exchange to Close Two Days

Announcement of Investments From Pocantico Hills Believed First Time Financier Ever Commented on Market

BANK GROUP EXPRESSES THE UTMOST OPTIMISM

Lamont Announces Meetings Will Continue Until Dust of Storm Blows Away

Abetting Speculation Laid to G. O. P. Heads by Robinson

Declares Coolidge and Hoover Encouraged Wild Buying by Statements

MINORITY Leader Who Blames Prosperity Talk

JOSEPH T. ROBINSON

Investors Are Forced to Bid for Bargains — Public Again Rushes In—Foreign Orders Now Soaring

PURCHASES ESTIMATED AT 350 TO 500 MILLION

Opening 2 Hours Late To-Day—Rediscount Rate Cut Now Expected

ACADEMIES REACH FOOTBALL IMPASSE

Army and Navy Heads Deadlocked Over Eligibility

SUPERINTENDENTS CONFER

No Compromise Seen After Talk—Hoover Is Silent

ONTARIO UPHOLDS LIQUOR SALE LAW

Premier Ferguson Re-elected on Policy of Control

CARRIES IN WHOLE CABINET

Progressives, Bone Dry Element, Badly Defeated

TRANSACTIONS ON THE NEW YORK STOCK EXCHANGE

TUESDAY, OCTOBER 29, 1929.

Day's Sales.	Monday.	Saturday.	A Year Ago.	Two Years Ago.
16,410,030	9,212,800	2,087,660	3,483,770	1,676,570

Year to Date.	Same Period 1928.	1927.	1926.	1925.
950,797,190	708,649,607	464,944,575	376,924,360	363,084,123

[illegible]

1929 High.	Low.	Stock and Dividend Rate.	First.	High.	Low.	Last.	Net Ch'ge.	Closing Bid.	Ask.	Sales.
90	25¼	Contl. Baking, A	35	35	25¼	25¾	− 9¼	25½	35	17,200
63¾	45	Contl. Bank N. Y. (1.20)	45	45	45	45	− 4	45	48	1,000
92	40½	Contl. Can (2½)	48	49	40½	44⅛	−14⅛	44	45	56,100
110½	50	Contl. Insurance (2)	61	69½	50	59	−11	58	60	17,500
28⅝	6½	Contl. Motors (80c)	8¼	8⅞	7½	8¼	− ¾	8	8¼	49,500
47⅛	25	Contl. Oil of Del.	25	25¾	25	25¾	− 1¼	..	25½	34,000
126¾	82	Corn Prod. Refin. (†3½)	95⅛	98¾	90	94	− 5⅜	94	94½	35,600
144⅞	138¼	Corn Prod. Ref. pf. (7)*	140½	140½	140½	140½	− ½	139¾	140	760
82¼	20⅛	Coty, Inc. (g2)	21	27	20¼	23	−10	23	24	31,600
125	25	Crosley Radio (†1)	25	29¾	25	28	−11½	28	30	9,100
79	40	Crown Cork & Seal	42	42	40	40	−12	38	52	1,600
121¾	80	Crucible Steel (5)	86¼	80	80	80	− 6	80	83	4,200
116⅝	109	Crucible Steel pf. (7)	109⅞	109⅞	109⅞	109⅞	− ⅛	109¾	112	200
5½	¾	Cuba Cane Sugar	¾	1⅛	¾	1⅛	+ ⅜	..	..	400
17	9	Cuban-Amer. Sugar	10	10	9	9	− 1¼	9	10	3,200
95	60⅛	Cuban-Amer. Sug. pf.*	66	66	65	65	− 2	66	67	170
67⅞	40	Cudahy Packing (4)	40⅛	41⅜	40	40	− 3½	40½	41	5,100
118	112½	Curtis Publish. pf. (7)	113	113	113	113	..	112⅝	113½	100
30⅛	7⅞	Curtiss-Wright	10⅝	11⅛	7⅞	9⅝	− 3¼	9⅝	9½	159,100
37⅞	14	Curtiss-Wright, A	16⅞	18¾	14	18	− 1⅝	18	19	34,000
115½	108½	Cushman's Sons pf. (8)*	110½	110½	110½	110½	..	110½	114	40
121½	58⅛	Cutler-Hammer (3½)	73	76	60⅝	71	−18	71	75	300
126½	63	Cuyamel Fruit	100½	100½	94	94	−11¼	..	95	1,700
69⅛	21¼	Davison Chemical	33¾	33⅞	21¼	25	−10⅛	25	28	15,600
46⅞	27½	Debenhams Sec. (a2.31)	29¼	29¼	28⅜	28⅜	− ½	28¼	30	500
128	116	Deere & Co. pf. (7)*	119	119	117½	117½	− 2	117½	119	270
226	141½	Delaware & Hudson (9)	152	152	141½	144¾	−25¼	144	145	5,800
169¾	120¼	Del., Lack. & W. (†7)	138¼	145½	138¼	145½	+ 8½	145½	150½	10,200
77½	54	Denver & R. Gde. W. pf.	56	56	54	54	− 3	45	54	600
64½	33	Devoe & R., A (†3)	33	33	33	33	− 3¼	32	38	1,500
115½	112	Devoe & R. 1st pf. (7)*	113	113	113	113	..	100	112	40
164	125⅛	Diamond Match (8)*	126	137	125⅛	135⅛	+ 6⅝	135⅛	136	860
11¼	6½	Dome Mines (1)	8	8	6⅝	7	− 1	7	7½	3,800
54¾	12	Dominion Stores (1.20)	22½	23	12	14	−11	16	25	8,200
126¾	71	Drug, Inc. (4)	71	72¼	71	72¼	−19	72	80	[illegible]
4⅞	2⅜	Duluth, S. S. & Atl.	2½	2½	2¼	2½	[illegible]	[illegible]	[illegible]	[illegible]

[illegible]

1929 High.	Low.	Stock and Dividend Rate.	First.	High.	Low.	Last.	Net Ch'ge.	Closing Bid.	Ask.	Sales.
102½	55	Int. Match pf. (3.20)	62½	65	55	55⅛	− 6⅝	55	56	24,200
39⅛	26½	Int. Merc. Marine ctfs.	30¼	30¼	28	28½	− 2	28½	29½	7,800
72¾	26¾	Int. Nickel of Can. (1)	30	36	26¾	31	− 7	31	32	208,700
41¼	23	Int. Pap. & Pw., A (2.40)	23	30	23	30	− 2	28½	30	8,400
33⅛	14¾	Int. Paper & Power, B	20	20	20	20	− 3	20	21	1,300
26⅛	10⅝	Int. Paper & Power, C	14½	14½	11½	12½	− 3¾	12½	13	26,200
108	95	Int. Print. Ink pf. (6)*	98½	98½	98½	98½	− 1	98½	99	40
59	34	Int. Rys. of Cen. Am.	34	34	34	34	− 2	..	33	300
80¼	68	Int. Rys. of C.A. pf. (5)*	68	68	68	68	− 2¼	68	69	80
90	55½	Int. Salt (6)*	63	63	63	63	..	50	70	30
77½	55	Int. Shoe (2½)	60	60	55	55	−10	55	59½	5,800
159½	118	Int. Silver (†8)	129¾	129¾	129¾	129¾	− 7¼	..	..	200
119	103¼	Int. Silver pf. (7)*	113⅞	114	110	110	+22	108	114	60
149¼	61	Int. Tel. & Tel. (2)	71	76	61	71	−17	70	71¾	195,300
93½	25⅛	Interstate Dept. St. (2)	32¼	32⅞	25⅛	31	− 3½	30	32	5,300
97	82	Inter. D. St. pf. (7) x w*	85½	85½	82	82	− 3½	..	82½	250
38⅞	24½	Intertype Corp. (f†1¾)	27	27	24½	24½	− 5½	24	25	800
72½	30	Investors Equity (2)	30	30	30	30	− 5¼	29½	30	3,000
69	39	Island Creek Coal (4)	40	40½	39	39	− 6½	..	41	2,100
84½	40	Jewel Tea (†4)	40	40	40	40	− 9	40	45	5,000
242¾	107	Johns-Manville (3)	128	134	107	115	−17	110	115	41,300
123	119	Johns-Manville pf. (7)*	121	121	120	120	− 1	120	121½	140
126	117	Jones & Laugh. pf. (7)*	120	120⅛	120	120	..	120	121½	270
108⅞	60	Kan. City Sou. (5)	77⅛	77⅛	60	65	−12⅛	64	65	6,400
70½	63⅛	Kan. City Sou. pf. (4)	67	67	67	67	− ½	67	67½	300
37⅞	20¼	K'mann Dep. Strs. (1½)	21½	21½	20¼	21½	− 1½	21	21½	3,000
24	4	Kelly-Spring. Tire	5	5½	4	4¾	− 1¾	4¼	5	27,800
100	30	Kelly-Spring. T. 6% pf.*	35	35	30	30	− 6	..	30	410
94⅞	35	Kelly-Spring. T. 8% pf.*	35	35	35	35	− 6	..	40	100
59¾	21½	Kelsey-Hayes Wh. (2)	29	29	21½	22¾	− 7¼	21½	23	17,400
96	85	Kendall Co. pf. (†6¼)*	86	86	86	86	..	85	86	70
104⅞	65	Kennecott Copper (5)	69⅛	69½	65	65¾	− 4⅞	65¾	66⅛	164,000
57⅞	45¼	Kimberly Clark (2½)	49¾	49¾	47	47	− 3	46½	47	1,200
109¾	80⅛	Kin. (G.R.) Co. pf. (8)*	82	89	80⅛	89	− 3½	80½	90	340
78¾	5⅛	Kolster Radio	8⅛	8⅞	7	7	− 3¼	8	8½	26,100
105⅞	95	Kraft Ph. Ch. pf. (6½)	105	103½	103½	103½	− 2	103½	105	1,500
23	12¾	Kresge Dept. Stores	13⅛	13⅛	13⅛	13⅛	− 1⅞	13	15	500
57½	35⅛	Kresge (S.S.) Co. (1.60)	39½	39½	35⅛	35⅝	− 4⅝	35¼	37	28,900
114	70½	Kress (S. H.) Co. (n1)	70½	70½	70½	70½	− 6¾	70	77½	1,500
46⅝	24½	Kreuger & Toll (1.34)	28½	29⅞	24½	25	− 5⅛	25	25⅝	117,700
122½	41	Kroger Gr. & Bak. (c1)	47¼	56	41	45	−14¾	44½	45	57,800

Daily Worker

WORKERS OF THE WORLD UNITE

Entered as second-class matter at the Post Office at New York, N. Y., under the act of March 3, 1879.

NEW YORK, THURSDAY, OCTOBER 31, 1929

SUBSCRIPTION RATES: In [illegible] Outside New York.

Compradaily Publishing ... New York City, N. Y.

STOCK MARKET CLOSES FRIDAY AND SATURDAY

Raskob Admits to "Temporary" Losses to Business

Morgan Manipulates

Frantic Efforts Made to Save Banks

Despite the combined efforts of Wall St. bankers to save the stock exchange by throwing countless millions of dollars on the market, the extreme seriousness of the situation is shown by the closing of the stock market until noon today and the announcement that the stock exchange will be closed Friday and Saturday. During the remaining half-day that the stock exchange will be open this week, J. P. Morgan, Lamont, Mitchell and other leading gfinanciers hope to be able by the manipulation of huge funds and limitless propaganda in the capitalist press, to prevent a repetition of the tremendous break of Monday and Tuesday.

Realizing the fateful consequences to the "stabilization" of the whole financial and business system that may ensue if the downward fall of the stock market is not retarded in some way, the most desperate means are being used by Wall Street. The propaganda aimed at leading small investors to believe that the crisis is near an end and that instead of selling they should invest even more money continued yesterday. The tactics of Tuesday, in throwing millions on the exchange only a few minutes before closing time were repeated.

The Chicago stock exchange will open today only from 11 a. m. to 2 p. m., and will be closed Friday and Saturday. The St. Louis exchange yesterday continued its fall.

John J. Raskob, one of the nation's leading stock market operators and financiers, admit that general business conditions will suffer, but claimed that it will only be "temporary."

[illegible]

Continued on Page Thirty-four

After Coolidge's reassuring interview in January, 1928, the market began its great spiral. On March 3, General Motors went to 150 on a 1,200,000-share day. Radio was the sensational stock the following week, climbing 18½ points on the 12th, opening 21½ points over the closing on the 13th and, even though the exchange investigated a technical Corner, closing down only sixteen under its high for the day. On March 16, the ticker was thirty-two minutes late. A new trading-volume record was set on the 26th. The next day sharp selling sent General Motors down almost forty-eight points. Then there was a short up-and-down period, and on June 11 the overpriced Bank of America securities dropped an average of one hundred points on the San Francisco Exchange and went from two hundred to 110 on the New York Curb. The next day the New York Stock Exchange felt the impact when a selling spree sent the volume for the first time over the five-million-share mark and the tape fell two hours behind. Radio slid down 23½, but few other stocks sustained more than faint losses. Hoover was the Republican choice against Al Smith for the Presidency and, when he accepted the nomination, he said:

> *One of the oldest and perhaps the noblest of human aspirations has been the abolition of poverty. . . . We in America today are nearer to the final triumph over poverty than ever before in the history of our land. The poorhouse is vanishing from among us. We have not yet reached the goal, but, given a chance to go forward with the policies of the last eight years, we shall soon, with the help of God, be in sight of the day when poverty will be banished from this nation. There is no guaranty against poverty equal to a job for every man. That is the primary purpose of the policies we advocate.*

After that speech trading bounced upward, hitting a 1928 high on November 23, when almost seven million shares were bought and sold. On December 7, it broke again, Radio dipping seventy-two points to 296. If the company's stock was priced at ten times its earnings it would have been selling for around one hundred. "The market is not discounting the future but the hereafter," said Max Winkler. International Harvester dropped from 368½ to 307 and Montgomery Ward lost twenty-nine points. However, after a short spell of teetering, a few dark weeks, the upward climb began once again. The Federal Reserve Board in Washington wanted to halt the gambling which was utilizing more and more of the country's surplus cash, but did not want to raise interest rates, on the theory that no percentage they could set would be high enough to discourage a speculator from borrowing when he was after a profit of 200 or 300 per cent. The Board therefore informed its member banks that it would not lend money to be used on the market. The New York Reserve Bank kept pleading for permission to raise the New York interest rate, but the Board in Washington refused, hoping its ruling against speculative loans would discourage further inflation.

As a result, there was a short drop in the market and a natural increase in the cost of call money. On March 26, it jumped from 12 per cent to 20, stock prices dropped, and trading almost hit 8,250,000 shares. The call for more margin sounded throughout the land, and many investors had their holdings sold out. The end of the upswing seemed to have arrived, but it was then that Charles E. Mitchell and

In the Depression following the Crash, Herbert Hoover, savior of starving Belgium in World War I, stubbornly resisted all efforts to grant direct aid to jobless Americans.

several other powerful bankers put many millions of bank money at the disposal of the brokers. He was the hero of the day for averting a panic, but he had cut the Federal Reserve System's throat. Business on Wall Street improved, money for speculation in the convalescing market became easier to borrow, and in June prices of stocks went up again. It reached the point where one respected broker suggested that the inflated prices for gilt-edged stocks were actually bargains because "these securities will gradually be taken out of the market."

The crest was reached on September 3, 1929, when thirteen leading stocks *cost an average of two and two-thirds times as much as they had eighteen months before.* Then, soon after, the market broke, but, by September 19, it had climbed back to a higher level than on the 3rd. By October 4, it was down again and many solid stocks looked like bargain buys (United States Steel at 204, General Electric fifty below its high, Radio at eighty-two). And a new high in brokers' loans — $6,800,000,000 — had been reached. The "undigested" investment trust and new merger securities accounted for part of this.

Stocks went up again. And they came down. This was not true of the whole market, however. As James Kellogg III and William E. Downie wrote in *The Stock Market Crash of 1929:*

> *It is erroneously thought that in a Bull Market every group of stocks participate in the sustained rise of the market. This is fallacious, and 1929 was no exception in this respect. While the market was climbing upward to its pinnacle, about half of the group listed declined in price, while half went to new highs. The groups that declined were amusements, apparel, automobiles, chain stores, fertilizers, leather, meat packing, motion pictures, rayon, rubber, silk, sugar, textiles, tobacco....*
>
> *The groups of stocks that participated in the rise were the airplanes, agricultural implements, building equipment, business and office equipment, brass, chemicals, department stores, electrical equipment, foods, household products, iron, machinery, mining and smelting, oil, paper, phonographs, radios, railroad equipment, shipbuilding, shoes, steel, telephone and telegraph, U.S. Steel, utilities, operating as well as holding companies.*

Contributing to the seesaw market were: 1) the rise in rediscount rate, from 5 to 6 per cent made tardily by the Federal Reserve Board on August 8; 2) the collapse of Hatry and Company in London that month, causing British holders of American stocks to liquidate their holdings in order to protect their other commitments; 3) raising of the Bank of London's rediscount rate to 6½ in September; and 4) refusal of the Massachusetts Public Service Commission to permit Edison of Boston to split its stock four for one. The last was a wise and cautious refusal by the commission, but coming on October 11, it threw the delicate market into another frenzy.

On Saturday, October 19, the short session was rocked by a selling surge which shrank total values by three billion dollars. Five million shares were traded. Canny investors thought that this was the break they had been waiting for and bought stocks, expecting a rally.

Monday was a six-million-share day, slanting downward; on Tuesday volume went almost three hundred thousand shares over and the market started to recover, but lost again during the last hour. On Wednesday, October 23, there was a serious break and the ticker reports were an hour and forty-four minutes late. The *New York Times* average of fifty leading railroads and industries dropped 18.24 and the margin calls flew out thick and fast.

On Thursday, October 24, the Stock Exchange opened with prices steady but the great volume offered—in blocks of up to twenty thousand shares—and the heavy sell-orders sent the prices plunging down and the ticker limping far behind executions. After the first hour the day looked like the blackest. Who was selling? The brokers were selling — selling out their margin accounts who could not cover. The reaction which this produced in the whole securities field was: Get out of the market! Everything started to toboggan — junk, gilt-edged, conservative, gambler's stocks — as instructions arrived to sell at any price obtainable. But buying orders lagged so far behind that even the leaders dropped up to five points between sales.

"Where were the bargain-hunters who were supposed to come to the rescue at times like this?" asked Frederick Lewis Allen in *Only Yesterday.* "Where were the investment trusts, which were expected to provide a cushion for the market by making new purchases at low prices? Where were the big operators who had declared they were still bullish? Where were the powerful bankers who were supposed to be able at any moment to support prices? There seemed to be no support whatever. Down, down, down. The

The nightmare position of many speculators who had put up no more than 10 per cent of the cost of their stocks was pictured in LIFE'S *"On a Margin."*

roar of voices which rose from the floor of the Exchange had become a roar of panic."

Seward Prosser of Bankers Trust, Albert H. Wiggin of Chase National, William Potter of Guaranty Trust, and Charles E. Mitchell, the erstwhile bull, of National City met at the J. P. Morgan offices with Thomas Lamont, senior Morgan partner. A fund of $240,000,000 was hastily subscribed. The Morgan floor broker and Vice-President of the exchange, Richard Whitney hurried from the meeting to the United States Steel post where the last sale was for 195.

"I bid 205 for ten thousand," he said, loudly. Then he hurried to the posts of a dozen or more other leading securities and offered to buy ten thousand shares of each. This was the brake which forced the juggernaut of panic to a temporary halt. It was a day when almost thirteen million shares were traded.

On Friday and Saturday, trading was steadier, although the market softened toward the end. As they had been doing for days, the brokers and their staffs worked through the night—and all day Sunday—to straighten out their accounts. By Monday morning, October 28, they knew where they stood: they needed more margin. So the sellouts began again. Now the big traders were being wiped out and it looked like the whole country was liquidating everything it owned. This was the day the greatest losses were listed and it looked like the worst the market could sustain. But on the next day, Tuesday, October 29, the market was to plunge deep into the blackest quagmire it has ever known.

The inability of the ticker to keep up with the plummeting prices meant that the market on the floor was operating half-blind. Outside of New York, where brokers were stymied by a late ticker and clogged wires cutting them off from the center of activity, business was conducted in a panic-stricken, hysterical void. In St. Louis, Phil Leslie, now a writer for television, had graduated from board boy to assistant margin clerk at Lorenzo E. Anderson and Company. His experience was typical:

> *For one thing, the ticker couldn't begin to handle such a volume as it was called on to handle that day, and as a result we out in the provinces had no idea at all what any stock was selling for at the moment, because the last quote we had on the ticker might be an hour or two hours late. . . . Part of the panic—much of it—that rough day, was due to the fact that communications simply clogged up and broke down. . . . And things happened too quickly to reach our margin customers and ask what they wanted to do—there just weren't enough phones. . . . After the first few tries at reaching a customer, we had to just give it up and sell him out, for whatever we could get, and as fast as we could . . . And, of course, the tremendous losses the firm took, through the fact that customers simply couldn't get up money enough to cover, resulted in the big wave of bankrupt firms across the country.*

The scene on the Big Board was the worst in its history and the volume of stocks traded was the greatest—16,410,030.

Many members of the exchange wanted to close down for a few days, but others were fearful that once closed the Stock Exchange would not reopen. Providentially, on Wednesday, October 30, a sharp, heartening rally took place and over ten million shares were traded. On Thursday the upturn continued and at noon the governors felt it was safe, in the face of the firmer tone, to declare the exchange closed for the balance of the week.

"The organizations of the Stock Exchange houses have reached a point of complete physical exhaustion," they said.

STAGE BROADWAY SCREEN

VARIETY

PRICE 25¢.

Published Weekly at 154 West 46th St., New York, N. Y., by Variety, Inc. Annual subscription, $10. Single copies, 25 cents.
Entered as second-class matter December 22, 1905, at the Post Office at New York, N. Y., under the act of March 3, 1879.

VOL. XCVII. No. 3 NEW YORK, WEDNESDAY, OCTOBER 30, 1929 88 PAGES

WALL ST. LAYS AN EGG

Going Dumb Is Deadly to Hostess In Her Serious Dance Hall Profesh

A hostess at Roseland has her problems. The paid steppers consider their work a definite profession calling for specialized technique and high-power salesmanship.

"You see, you gotta sell your personality," said one. "Each one of we girls has our own clientele to cater to. It's just like selling dresses in a store—you have to know what to sell each particular customer.

"Some want to dance, some want to kid, some want to get soupy, and others are just 'misunderstood husbands'."

Girls applying for hostess jobs at Roseland must be 21 or older. They must work five nights a week. They are strictly on their own, no salary going with the job and the house collecting 10 cents on every 35 cent ticket. To keep her job, a girl must turn in at least 100 tickets a week during the cold season and 50 in the summer months. In a dull week girls buy their own tickets to keep up the record.

If a partner wishes to sit out a dance, he must pay for the privilege. "Sitting-out time" sells at eight tickets an hour, or $2.80. It's usually a poor sport who will come across with less than $3, many kicking in heavier for a little genial conversation.

The girl who knows her professional dancing trade will keep an alert eye open for potential "sitter-outers," ascertain their hobbies and talk herself into a whole string of tickets. In this way she not only earns money easily, but saves wear and tear on her evening dresses and slippers.

Big money rolls in if she has a good line. One of the most successful girls at Roseland takes this part of her work so seriously that she reads up on current events (sports and stock market included) and has a smattering of current literature and art.

"There are two types of hostesses at Roseland," she said, displaying high brow leanings. "They are the 'mental' and the 'physical.' Surprisingly enough the physical ones are not those who make the most money. One customer will buy three tickets from them at the most. They rely on their sex appeal and go dumb between dances—and that's the surest way to lose a partner, going dumb.

Mental Girls

"The 'mental' girls, being good conversationalists, can wise-crack with the flippant, sympathize with the lonely and know how to salt the fresh boys and make them like it. I have one client who has been coming up every Monday night for two and a half years. Some times he dances all evening, other times we sit out every dance and just talk. He's a good spender, but his wife doesn't understand him."

Usually the hostesses change every two years, although one or two girls have been there for eight years. Some marry, some go into the chorus, others get hat-checking

(Continued on page 63)

Hunk on Winchell

When the Walter Winchells moved into 204 West 55th street, late last week, June, that's Mrs. Winchell, selected a special room as Walter's exclusive sleep den for his late hour nights. She shusshed the Winchell kidlets when her husband dove in at his usual eight o'clock the first morning.

At noon, Walter's midnight, his sound proof room was penetrated by so many high C's he awoke with but four hours of dreams and a grouch. Investigated at once, after having signed the lease of course.

Right next door, on the same floor, is the studio of the noted vocal instructor, Kinney. Among his pupils are Ona Munson, Irene Delroy and Marjorie Peterson. They love Winchell like you love carbolic acid.

And Miss Munson is reported to have requested that an amplifier be started hereafter when she runs up the scale.

Demand for Vaude

Springfield, Ill., Oct. 29.

Petitions requesting Publix theatres to resume vaudeville in Decatur, Ill. are in circulation in that city.

Petitions specify that vaudeville at one or more of the three larger Publix houses would furnish employment to a number of Decatur musicians and stage hands and provide larger variety of local entertainment.

Paul Witte, Publix manager in Decatur, states that he believes vaudeville will find a place in Decatur before the season is over.

Pickpocketing Dying Out

Chicago, Oct. 29.

Some 1,000-odd pickpockets who used to make Chicago what it was are no more. A confidential list in the hands of government revenue men shows them to be operating in bottles.

In the last eight months there has not been a complaint or an arrest for pocket picking.

Flirting Contest

Paris, Oct. 29.

New idea here: "flirting contest" at the Bal Tabarin cabaret.

Gals are permitted to flirt only to a limited degree with a committee of judges regulating their manner of approach.

DROP IN STOCKS ROPES SHOWMEN

Many Weep and Call Off Christmas Orders — Legit Shows Hit

MERGERS HALTED

The most dramatic event in the financial history of America is the collapse of the New York Stock Market. The stage was Wall Street, but the onlookers covered the country. Estimates are that 22,000,000 people were in the market at the time.

Tragedy, despair and ruination spell the story of countless thousands of marginal stock traders. Perhaps Manhattan was worst hit in the number of victims. Many may remain broke for the rest of their lives, because the money that disappeared via the ticker tape was the savings of years.

Many people of Broadway are known to have been wiped out. Reports of some in show business losing as much as $300,000 is not hearsay. One caustic comment to that was that the theatre is enough of a gamble without its people to venture into Wall street.

Prominent showmen, several identified with the picture industry

(Continued on page 64)

FILTHY SHOW OF SHUBERTS GOOD FOR SCREEN

Chicago, Oct. 29.

Shubert's latest musical of their "Night" series, now in Chicago, is so filthy that one of the cast admits embarrassment while in the performance.

The second act of this scramble called "Broadway Nights," is the

(Continued on page 63)

Soft Drink Smuggling

Chicago, Oct. 29.

Bootlegging charged water and ginger ale into the main Loop hotels is recent.

Water, at hotel prices, is 45 cents a bottle. Under the new plan a legger brings in a case at 25 cents a bottle. Ginger ale coming through these channels retails at 15 cents. Hotels get 50 the bottle.

Kidding Kissers in Talkers Burns Up Fans of Screen's Best Lovers

Talker Crashes Olympus

Paris, Oct. 29.

Fox "Follies" and the Fox Movietone newsreel are running this week in Athens, Greece, the first sound pictures heard in the birthplace of world culture, and in all Greece, for that matter.

Several weeks ago, Variety's Cairo correspondent cabled that a cinema had been wired in Alexandria, Cleopatra's home town.

Only Sodom and Gomorrah remain to be heard from.

HOMELY WOMEN SCARCE; CAN'T EARN OVER $25

No homely ones on Broadway!

And now it looks as if Crosby Gaige may have to postpone production of "One Beautiful Evening" because the Main Stem is devoid of the non-beauts necessary for the casting of the show.

Arthur Lubin, caster for the producer, for several weeks has been trying to land the right type of women. A most unusual piece, the drama has an all-women lineup, and, although as many as 23 are needed, all must be homely—and middle age or over, except for two who can be young.

Vera Caspary wrote the play and it centers about conditions at a club for girls where requirements of residence demand that the girls must not earn over $25 per week in order to live under its roof.

That's why they must be homely.

Ads for Execs

Chicago, Oct. 29.

Newspaper ad calling for potential executives for the Publix-B. & K. organization here, drew heavy response, with over 100 applicants.

From all walks of life, with several $20,000-a-year men among the mob, seeking a chance to break into the show business.

Studio in Church

A new Roman Catholic Church, Holy Angels, newly opened on East 47th street near 1st avenue, New York (Italian Parish), has rented out its upper story as a motion picture studio.

Visugraph, industrial producing concern, has established its headquarters there.

Boys who used to whistle and girls who used to giggle when love scenes were flashed on the screen are in action again. A couple of years ago they began to take the love stuff seriously and desisted, but the talkers are reviving the ha ha for film osculators.

Heavy loving lovers of silent picture days accustomed to charming audiences into spasms of silent ecstasy when kissing the leading lady are getting the bird instead of the heartbeat. The sound accompaniment is making it tough.

Such a picture romancer as John Gilbert is getting laughs in place of the sighs of other days, and the flaps who still think he's grand are getting sore. One little flap had to be quieted by an usher when making a commotion during a Gilbert picture at the Capitol, New York. The person sitting next to her, like many others in the house, took Gilbert's passion lightly. The girl jumped to his defense and started to bawl out the Gilbert derider.

Not only has Gilbert received the bird lately, but all of the other male screen players who specialize in romance. Charley Farrell in "Sunny Side Up" draws many a giggle from his mush stuff.

In the silents when a lover would whisper like a ventriloquist, lips apart and unmoved, and roll his eyes passionately, preparatory to the clinch and then kiss, it looked pretty natural and was believable. The build-up to the kissing now makes a gag of the kiss.

When the kiss is with serious intent, the laughs are out of order. It's burning the impressed female fans to see their favorite kissers kidded when kissing.

In Reverse

Seems the only type of love stuff received as intended since advent of the talkers in the comedy love scene. The screen comics are becoming the heavy lovers and the heavy lovers comedians.

The normal kiss, delivered with the usual smack, sounds like an explosion. For that reason clinch scenes in the early talkers had them rolling in the aisles.

Toning down their kissing to make it noiseless has made bum kissers of the screen's best lovers, but, audible or silent, the kisses are getting laughs that don't belong.

Hollywood, Oct. 29.

Soft pedal on dialog in romantic love scenes in the future. Hereafter, the sacchrine stuff will be

(Continued on page 63)

14

The Third Revolution

ONCE THE FIRST shock had subsided, most people were courageous and even ruefully humorous about their plight. Windows of closed stores displayed such signs as "Opened by Mistake" and "Busted and Disgusted." In a sketch of *The Ziegfeld Follies*, Eddie Cantor asked a hotel clerk for a room on the nineteenth floor. The comeback line was: "For sleeping or jumping?" London was rife with rumors that you had to pick your way among the corpses lying on Wall Street. In the French novel *The Wicked Village* (the title did not refer to Manhattan), Gabriel Chevallier wrote: "People are jumping out of skyscraper windows to smash their skulls on the pavement. I'm telling you, you have to watch out or you get a suicide falling on your head. You have to take a good look upwards every step you take."

The suicide legend of 1929 was exactly that—a legend. In Joe Alex Morris' *What a Year!* he demolishes the tale of wholesale self-destruction: "There were only 44 suicides in all Manhattan between mid-October and mid-November 1929 compared to 53 in the same period of 1928. The same was generally true of the rest of the United States. More people killed themselves during the summer months of 1929, when the market was booming, than during the months of the big crash."

People in distress were sustained by the knowledge that almost everyone else was in the same boat—an extremely large boat, for it held fifteen million unemployed and their dependents in the bleak winter of 1932–33, the trough of the Depression. One of the most onerous things people had to endure was the persistent stream of optimistic predictions made by prominent individuals, headed by President Hoover, that "prosperity was just around the corner." A brisk seller in 1931 was a slim book *Oh, Yeah?* quoting all of these premature soothsayers. A runaway best-seller of the period was Eddie Cantor's *Caught Short!* Published in November, 1929, it sold hundreds of thousands of copies, not only in bookstores but at the *Ziegfeld Follies*. "I remember going backstage one evening," said M. Lincoln Schuster recently, "and telling Eddie that twenty-two thousand copies had been sold that day." The royalties helped the comedian recoup some of his losses on the market and the jokes helped the country retain its sense of the ridicu-

Most of the new skyscrapers in lower New York were half empty after the Crash of 1929. Pinched by the Depression which persisted despite the repeated assurances of President Hoover and his Cabinet that "prosperity is just around the corner," the nation as a whole regarded Wall Street with suspicion and distrust.

lous. There was the one about the two fellows who jumped from a bridge together because they had a joint account. And the Morgan partner who was going to give the chauffeur a hundred shares of United States Steel, but decided on something more substantial—ten dollars in cash. The Rockefellers announced that they were buying stocks when the market hit its worst day and Cantor said: "Sure, who else had any money left?"

Since few people were buying apples, the International Apple Shippers Association offered to let the unemployed have boxes of apples on credit. That was the start of the most common symbol of the Depression, the street-corner apple-sellers. In lower Manhattan so many men joined the ranks that they were frequently strung out, a dozen to the block. When they became too numerous, they were banished to the side streets. The Crash not only led to vast numbers of unemployed, but resulted in cutting down the working hours and days of those who still had jobs as well as the wages paid to them. Despite wage cuts that often amounted to as much as 40 per cent, the employed felt themselves fortunate indeed to have any kind of income. The Hoover government was adamantly against a dole, preferring to create the Reconstruction Finance Corporation and pour millions

Many unemployed sold apples obtained on credit in order to survive. They became so dense in the downtown area that they were banned from the major streets.

into aid for distressed banks, railroads, and insurance companies, hoping that the money would somehow trickle down to the jobless, the foodless, and the homeless. Men in increasing numbers began to shuttle about the country by boxcar, and at one time it was estimated that two hundred thousand teenage boys (and girls dressed in boy's clothing) were roaming across the United States, searching for jobs, food —or merely to ease the family's burden at home.

On Wall Street prices at the end of 1929 were, on an average, half of what they had been three months before. From Washington a flood of reassuring statements were ground out and distributed, but although the economy perked up slightly during the first quarter of 1930, a severe reaction set in. If only the trading of securities had been affected, the Depression would not have been the nightmare it was to become. However, a wave of retrenchment swept the country. On every side there was doubt, uncertainty, and fear. A miasma of despair haunted the land. Few brave men were left in business or in industry, almost as if they had expended all their courage in pushing the market when it was on its way up and had none left to help

Shelter as well as food was an urgent problem of the early thirties. The grimy docks and Skid Row at Whitehall and South streets offered poor protection for increasing numbers of homeless men.

The law of supply and demand brought bread down to a nickel a loaf when wheat prices dropped 50 per cent and people could not afford to pay the old price. The Zito Bakery now charges five times as much.

Rich as well as poor had their troubles. J. P. Morgan's $3-million CORSAIR *ran aground off Isleboro, Maine, requiring a Coast Guard cutter and tugs to free it.*

them begin again at the bottom. The bull market had been one sustained, reckless drunken spree and now most businessmen were too hung over to do anything but groan, feel bad, retrench.

By the end of 1930 business was 28 per cent below normal. In addition to the brokerage houses which had been forced to shut down in early November, 1929, others were dying of malnutrition. Overcapitalized investment companies and underfinanced ones were falling by the wayside. More than one thousand banks failed in 1930 as real-estate prices followed stocks in establishing new lows. In spite of official statements of optimism, conditions became even more grave in 1931 as people everywhere began to realize that the country had not yet seen the worst of the Depression.

Herbert Hoover, who had been such a great success as the relief administrator for Belgium, during the First World War, either did not know how to relieve the distress of his own countrymen or else, misguided by his advisers, decided that they must pull themselves up by their own bootstraps. His inaction or wrong action, his torpor and resignation, might more readily have been forgotten had his successor not

The principal effort made by Hoover to alleviate the slump was to create the Reconstruction Finance Corporation, aimed at unfreezing bank assets, in the hope that benefits would trickle down to the public.

"It seems there wasn't any depression at all!" is the caption of this Fitzpatrick cartoon commenting on a speech by former President Hoover in December, 1935, after the country was on the way to recovery.

Most historians agree that the chief factor in the United States' economic comeback was President Franklin D. Roosevelt (shown with son James) whose fight against the Depression began the moment he entered office, at a time when every bank in the nation was closed.

immediately shown that something could be done. As it was, Hoover ended his term making hopeful pronouncements and becoming the target for scathing comment, bitter, hostile cartoons, and the abuse of many of his countrymen who were denied the relief he had so generously handed out to foreigners.

To Franklin Delano Roosevelt he turned over an exhausted, almost bankrupt country in which the unemployed and discontented, and all those who suffered deprivations, might have been lured toward communism had economic conditions not improved swiftly. What Roosevelt gave the country was, first of all, a sense of hope and confidence. Acting vigorously, he launched a daring program of legislation aimed primarily at relief and recovery. Many long-needed economic reforms were introduced and a number of ambitious experiments were undertaken, some serving their purpose and others proving to be failures. Economics, "the dismal science," as one economist defined it, is, with the possible exception of tea-leaf

More than charm or sympathy, Roosevelt gave the people a strong, confident leadership, speaking to them in his radio talks as "my friends." During the days of the New Deal he initiated many long-needed economic reforms.

The Spider Web of Wall Street

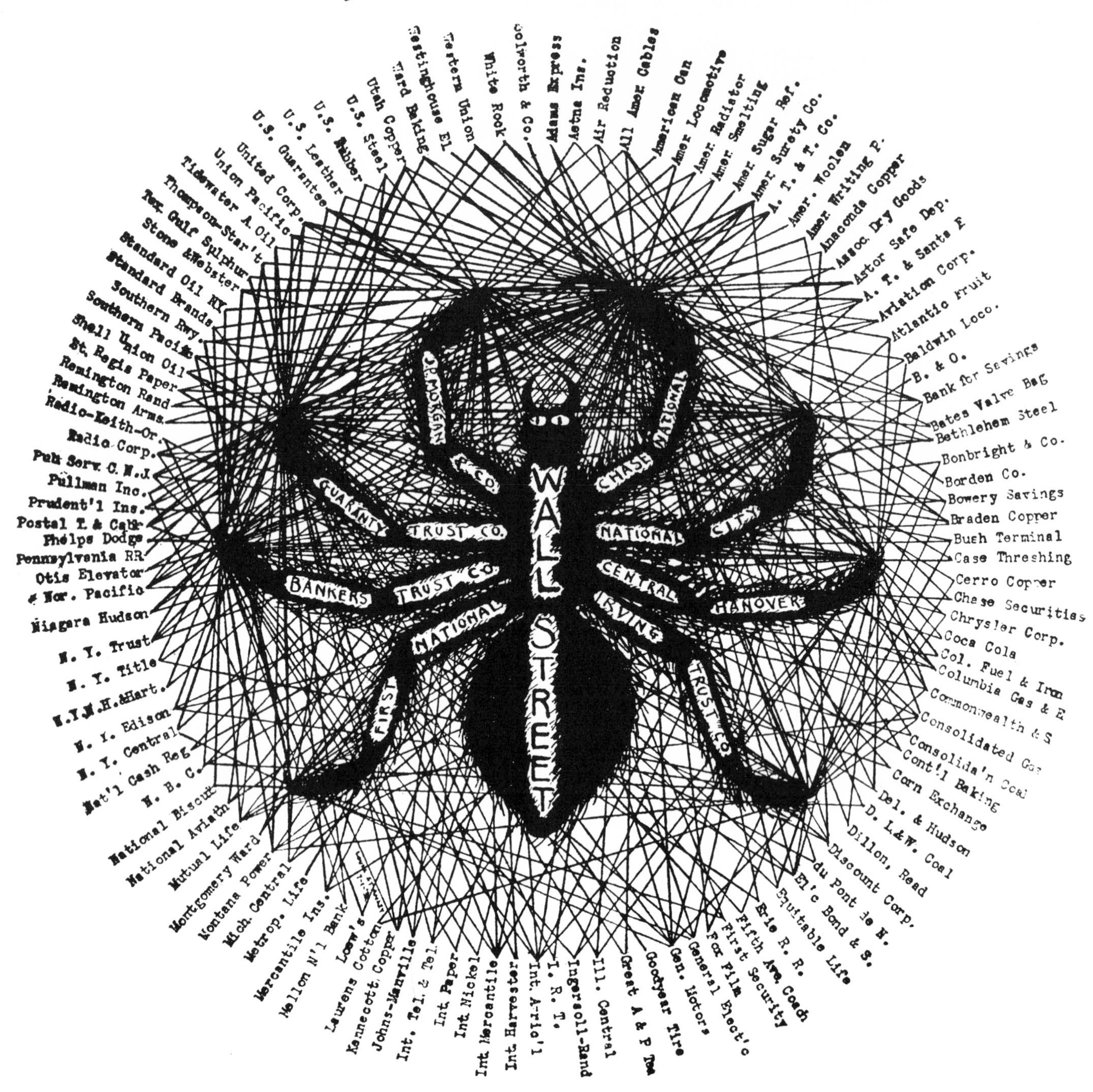

"The Spider Web of Wall Street"—a chart prepared by a Socialist journal in 1932 showing interlocking directorates between eight top New York banks and 120 major corporations—was used as an exhibit in the Senate hearings in Washington. Despite complex look, it was an accurate picture of the situation existing at that time.

reading, the least exacting of sciences. Although errors were made along the way, the New Deal was based on the application of economics to the workings of government and history records that it was the most successful use of economics in government up to that time. As a result of the New Deal, the United States recovered from the worst Depression it had ever known—a Depression that might have made the nation a dismal wasteland and destroyed Wall Street in the process.

"Mr. Roosevelt was at once in both a most advantageous and difficult position," Roger Babson reminds us in *If Inflation Comes*. "He started on top of the heap. The United States was his oyster. He could travel whatever road he chose. It was possible that he could stay on top. It was also possible that he would

Lya Graf, midget with the Ringling-Barnum sideshow, was on her way to try crashing the White House for publicity when she stopped by the Senate committee room at the noon recess. The late Al Nesensohn, a photographer, planted her on the lap of witness J. P. Morgan, who thought she was a child and said: "I've got a granddaughter just your age at home, young lady."

Morgan was impressed with the young Tennessee lawyer, Henry Clay Alexander, who was his assistant counsel during the Senate hearings and later invited him to become a Morgan partner.

Morgan with Senator Duncan U. Fletcher (CENTER), Chairman, and Ferdinand Pecora (LEFT), counsel for the Banking and Currency Committee. The committee found Morgan's business methods highhanded, but uncovered unethical practices in other banking institutions.

find events sweeping upon him which would wrest control from his hands. He could be hurled into a whirlwind of chaos down to a lamentable obscurity —or even worse."

One of the first things F.D.R. and his administration did—in what has been called America's "Third Revolution"—was to get the facts behind the events leading up to the Great Crash so that a disaster such as that one could never occur again. Many an innocent victim had been put through the wringer by certain elements in Wall Street. Now the Senate Banking and Currency Committee, with Ferdinand Pecora as counsel, reversed the process. Such a parade of skeletons came prancing out of so many previously hallowed closets that twelve thousand pages of testimony were printed. Four major New Deal reforms can be directly attributed to the hearings: the Banking Act of 1933, the Truth-in-Securities Act, the Public Utilities Holding Company Bill, and, most important, the Securities Exchange Act, which provided for the establishment of the Securities and Exchange Commission to regulate the operations of exchanges dealing in securities.

Among other things, the committee learned that the House of Morgan was virtually an absolute monarchy run by J. P. Morgan, Jr., who held a power of life and death over the twenty partners, any or all of whom could be shown the door at any time. He alone decided how half the yearly profits were to be

A reluctant witness before Senator John G. Townsend, Jr., was New York Stock Exchange President Richard E. Whitney (LEFT), *described as "arrogant, imperious, a born leader with charming manners . . . a dictator of the old guard intent on maintaining the Exchange as a private club to be run as they damn-well pleased."*

Samuel Insull (LEFT) *built the third largest public-utility empire—consisting of 95 holding and 255 operating companies valued at $2.5 billion. His own investment of $7 million mushroomed to $100 million before the structure collapsed. He fled to Greece, but was extradited to stand trial for embezzlement and fraud. During the trial, which ended in his acquittal, he demonstrated the telegraphic skill he had acquired years earlier when he was Thomas Edison's clerk.*

divided. The firm not only picked and chose its clients for mergers but literally required an introduction before it permitted anyone to become a depositor. Wealth alone was not sufficient. The customer had to be eligible in other ways because the Morgan bank was interested only in the accounts of the steel and auto manufacturers, oil and telephone companies, and utilities. In 1927 it held deposits of half a billion dollars; in its worst year in 1932, it held $340,000,000.

Ivar Kreuger, match-company king and international financial wizard, defrauded United States investors of billions by intricate financial juggling. When he was exposed in 1932, he committed suicide.

Albert H. Wiggin, head of the Chase National Bank, borrowed $8 million from the bank to sell Chase stock short (while serving on committees to stabilize the falling market) and made a $4-million profit.

Joseph W. Harriman, President of Harriman National Bank and Trust Company, juggled depositors' funds and attempted suicide to avoid arrest. After his trial and conviction, he is seen (LEFT) *on his way to prison.*

In order to obtain an introduction, a potential depositor had to see one of a limited number of bank chairmen, such as Charles E. Mitchell, Seward Prosser, William Potter, M. Buckner or Artemus Gates of New York Trust, Harvey D. Gibson of Manufacturers Trust, Charles G. Dawes of Central Trust of Chicago, Myron C. Taylor, Norman H. Davis, and others in the highest echelons of finance. Morgan saw nothing wrong in this, nor would he admit that this

Charles E. Mitchell (RIGHT), *of National City Bank, leaving court after being acquitted of criminal charges of income-tax evasion through the efforts of his attorney, Max D. Steuer (rubbing hands). However, he had to pay the government $1,348,222 in a civil suit.*

The Pecora probe unearthed 12,000 pages of shocking evidence and led to many reforms in the conduct of banks, holding companies, securities underwriters, and stock exchanges. Here legislators watch F.D.R. sign the "Blue Sky" Securities Law, intended to protect the public from the sale of worthless stock issues.

situation put his company in a position to receive favors in return. "They are friends of ours and we know that they are good, sound, straight fellows," he said. He controlled the money, there were no government regulations, no bank examinations, but, he declared, his firm voluntarily furnished the Federal Reserve Board with an informal statement—in strict confidence. "Anyone," Mr. Morgan said, "could obtain this information by asking." No one, even with ten million dollars on deposit, ever asked.

Another result of the investigation was the creation of the Securities and Exchange Commission to regulate stock trading and the exchanges. Joseph P. Kennedy (CENTER) *was the first of the hard-hitting chairmen.*

The last time anyone dared ask in public was twenty years earlier, when J. P. Morgan, Sr., had given testimony before the Pujo Committee. This was the only public statement concerning the operation of the bank that had ever been made—until the Pecora cross-examination. The attitude of gentlemanly dealing and righteousness which cloaked the father fell in graceful folds around the son, whose thinking, as brought out in testimony, paralleled his father's.

The committee learned that new issues of promising stocks were first offered at cost or near cost to a "preferred list" which included Calvin Coolidge; General John J. Pershing; Charles A. Lindbergh; Hoover's Secretary of the Navy, Charles Francis Adams; Wilson's Secretary of War, Newton D. Baker, and his Secretary of the Treasury, William Gibbs McAdoo; Bernard M. Baruch; Kuhn, Loeb and Company; Richard E. Whitney; Charles E. Mitchell; Albert H. Wiggin; George F. Baker, and many other

James M. Landis, second SEC Chairman, left in 1937 to become Dean of the Harvard Law School. He was succeeded by William O. Douglas, who put pressure on the Old Guard of the Stock Exchange in 1938.

SEC scrutiny and regulations (hailed in this New York HERALD TRIBUNE *cartoon) as well as self-policing by the exchanges restored confidence in Wall Street and led to a fair, ethical market.*

On the day of the showdown with the diehards led by Richard Whitney, the announcement came that Whitney was barred from trading on the Stock Exchange for embezzling clients' funds, that his firm was bankrupt, and that he had surrendered to the District Attorney. The Old Guard immediately capitulated to SEC rules.

notables. If you were not on the Morgan preferred list, you were practically a financial nobody.

The fortunate visitors to the ground floor at the House of Morgan included several men who were guilty of much more than simply eating high off the new-issue hog. On the basis of evidence supplied by the Senate committee as well as Wiggin's own testimony, stockholder suits were filed against the Chase National Bank which resulted in Wiggin personally paying two million dollars in damages and other colleagues an additional half million.

Commenting on the bank closings which brought down the curtain on the Hoover administration, the committee reported: "From the very mouths of these trusted leaders, there came forth an amazing recital of practices, to which the catastrophic collapse of the entire banking structure of the country seemed but the natural climax."

From the end of the First World War to the Crash, National City manufactured or helped to manufacture at least twenty billion dollars' worth of new securities. It acted as wholesaler and retailer of these stocks and bonds, and also participated as a speculator in these same stocks on the market. Although this was against the law, the bank created the National City Company, with the same stockholders, so inseparable from the original organization that the certificate of stock ownership in National City Bank

(2) *The* QUEEN MARY *takes on a pilot to guide her through the channel until she is safe at pier for docking.*

(3) *The Coast Guard's* CALUMET *meets th*

START SEQUENCE HERE
PROCEED CLOCKWISE

(1) *The steamer* WASHINGTON *passes the Ambrose Lightship, which sends an immediate report of her arrival.*

To aid the needy and prime the economic pump, the Roosevelt administration created many public works which still stand today. None has weathered the years better than

(7) *Tugboats from five companies, Mor*

(8) *Unloading cargo at the pier. Below the net is a diver getting ready to submerge to inspect the hull.*

ASHINGTON *with inspecting officials.*

e murals in the rotunda of the Custom ouse. Painted by Reginald Marsh and his aff, they show eight stages of a ship's ar-val in the port of New York.

zell, Meseck, Olsen, and Barrett, nudge NORMANDIE *into her dock.*

(4) *Public health, immigration, customs, and steamship line officials are transferred from the* CALUMET.

(5) *Passing the Statue of Liberty, passengers get first close view of buildings in the Wall Street district.*

(6) *The press interviews a celebrity (in this case, Greta Garbo). Marsh painted many friends into the scene.*

John D. Rockefeller, who retired from Standard Oil in 1911, was also a great success in the business of staying alive. On his ninety-first birthday in 1930 he cut this cake. He died at the age of ninety-eight.

and the beneficial interest in the National City Company were printed on reverse sides of the same sheet of paper.

Thousands of trusting investors were high-pressured into buying a glittering assortment of foreign garbage in the guise of Viennese, German, Greek, Peruvian, Chilean, Hungarian, and Irish government bonds. They were not only high-pressured, they were switched to other securities so that the salesmen could collect double commissions and they were sold out when they fell behind on payments. The bank peddled securities door-to-door and simple people were swindled because they had implicit faith in so venerable an organization as the National City Bank.

This is only one example, unearthed by the Senate committee and documented in Ferdinand Pecora's *Wall Street Under Oath*, of the flagrant practices indulged in by some of the largest banking institutions. Albert Wiggin had six personal corporations to keep his various stock-trading interests separate, and his management of the Chase Bank and the Chase Company was every bit as profitable—and shocking—as that of Charles Mitchell at National City.

After the elder Rockefeller's death in Florida, in May, 1937, his body was met at the Tarrytown, New York, station by his son, John D. II (LEFT) *and his five grandsons* (LEFT TO RIGHT), *David (now of the Chase Manhattan Bank), Nelson (later Governor of New York State), Winthrop, Laurance, and John D. III.*

Celebration of the two hundredth birthday of George Washington in 1932 included the construction in Bryant Park, behind the New York Public Library, of this replica of Federal Hall, where he was first inaugurated.

It was because of their own testimony, as well as that of a score of other bankers and security underwriters, that the New Deal government created legislation to split banks away from companies designed to create and float securities, thus removing temptation from the custodians of money to favor themselves when investing funds entrusted to their care. The Morgan bank split into J. P. Morgan and Company and Morgan, Stanley and Company. Most of the other big banks dropped their badly tainted underwriting departments, while those firms engaged predominantly in underwriting securities went out of the banking business entirely. All have survived without hardship, especially to the investing public.

Changes were also made in the conduct of the stock exchanges in spite of the stubborn, unfriendly testimony of Richard E. Whitney, who in 1933 was the President of the New York Stock Exchange. Until the committee hearings, the organization had been untouchable by any government agency. It was operated strictly as a private gentleman's club—and an extremely select one at that. "It is a perfect institution," Whitney said, and then displayed a strange ignorance of such terms as "pool," "syndicate," and "pegging." He went on to add that it was "a God-given market" and Wiggin did not "churn up the market." The committee found, however, that "far from being an impartial forum for the free play of supply and demand . . . the Exchange was in reality neither more nor less than a glorified gambling casino where the odds were heavily weighted against the eager outsiders."

The Securities Exchange Act was passed on June 6, 1934, but Richard E. Whitney and the Old Guard refused to knuckle under. The commission brokers, who dealt with the public, knew that there would be no confidence in the Big Board again until the much-needed regulations of the Securities and Exchange Commission were put into effect, and a bitter battle for control of the exchange was therefore waged for several years. How long the "private club" advocates would have been able to hold out is a matter of conjecture, but they were betrayed from within. Right on the heels of a government ultimatum that the New York Stock Exchange would either alter its operations to comply with the law or close down, there came the almost unbelievable announcement on March 8, 1938, that Richard E. Whitney's company had been suspended from trading on the Stock Exchange, that it was bankrupt, and that Whitney, alone, was the embezzler who was responsible. That same afternoon, the exchange agreed to comply with the Federal regulations.

John Davison Rockefeller, Sr., who had retired

from active participation in his vast business interests at the turn of the century to devote himself to the business of keeping alive, was far more successful than most men. He lived for ninety-eight years in spite of a stomach disorder and various other ailments. He also devoted himself to giving away much of his money — a burden taken up by his son after John D., Sr., died in 1937. Throughout the thirties the Rockefellers had been constructing Rockefeller Center, a complex of structures in midtown Manhattan, because when the Crash came John D., Jr., had found himself stuck with the land. He had obligingly assembled the parcels of property for the directors of the Metropolitan Opera House who had intended to erect a glittering new auditorium on the site. But this dream — like so many others — vanished swiftly in October, 1929, when an entire era came to an abrupt end.

Except for several nervous dips in the market, economic recovery moved slowly ahead in the 1930's and Wall Street struggled out of its black hole. Stocks and trading, however, were painful, even forbidden

Downtown Skyport in 1940 was at the foot of Wall Street. Providing service to and from Long Island, it proved to be far ahead of its time and suspended operations during the war. Behind the pontoon craft is the Cities Service building.

The Cities Service building could also be seen from the Third Avenue El as it curved from Pearl Street into Coenties Slip on its way to South Ferry. Elevated railways were first built in the early 1880's. The Third Avenue line was the last to vanish. It made its final scheduled run in May, 1955, and was demolished in 1956.

words to many people, and the securities market was considered a barren field for young men with ambition. The price of a seat on the New York Stock Exchange declined each year from the high of $625,000 paid by Ferdinand Straus on February 15, 1929, until a low of seventeen thousand dollars was recorded in 1942. Trading became so sluggish, especially on the smaller exchanges, that the ticker would only chatter sporadically, a group of pretty tourists in the galleries would mark the highlight of the day, and, for want of something better to do at lunch time, brokers would take the forty-minute, five-cent ferryboat ride to Staten Island and back.

War in Europe broke out just as the industry and economy of the United States were reviving, and the country began to hum with vibrant activity that was felt everywhere. Now the problem of the Roosevelt administration was the reverse of what it had been at the start. In 1933, the goal had been to prime the pumps, create jobs, and encourage spending. By 1940 the problem was to build up the industrial capacity, find enough people to fill the jobs, and discourage spending and inflation.

"First we fought against breadlines and bankruptcies," Roger Babson wrote in *If Inflation Comes*, "next, against backlogs and bottlenecks. In the thirties, heavy industries were starved; in the forties, they were glutted. From struggling to put depressed prices *up* to the levels of 1926, we turned to face the problem of holding them *down* to these same levels."

The West Side El ran down Greenwich Street to Battery Place. Geographers have concluded that this is the spot where Verrazano came "a-land with our boat" in 1524. The buildings at the left were razed to make way for the Brooklyn-Battery Tunnel. Just before the war, the El was torn down and its steel was shipped to Japan.

15

The Second World War

"YESTERDAY, December 7, 1941—a date which will live in infamy—the United States of America was suddenly and deliberately attacked by naval and air forces of the Empire of Japan." With these words, President Franklin D. Roosevelt, addressing a joint session of Congress, asked for a declaration of war against Japan. The request was a mere formality, for the Japanese attack on Pearl Harbor had already embroiled the United States in a global war.

The war was not only a challenge to the American people, numbed momentarily by Pearl Harbor. It was also a test of Wall Street, a test that the reformed Stock Exchange passed with flying colors. It was not necessary to close down the Big Board, which was prepared for the crisis by more than two years of increased United States involvement in the European conflict before Pearl Harbor. Also the system of controls introduced by the legislation of the thirties eliminated the fissures and canyons of speculation and prevented either desperate panic or wild upswing. As the authors of *New York: World's Capital City* wrote:

> *The supreme test of Wall Street's contribution came during that global war. It was not merely a monetary contribution. . . . A more accurate measure was the degree to which American industry was enabled to outproduce the world as a result of . . . specific genius for mastering multiplicity—giving it order, unity and direction.*

Investors, recalling the "War Babies" of the earlier world conflict, had been buying industrials with growth potential ever since Hitler embarked on his series of fatal invasions. British securities kept declining until the evacuation of Dunkirk and then slowly climbed back. The American stocks which fell continued to go lower until April, 1942, when the rebound began.

In 1938 the New York Stock Exchange had elected its first salaried President, William McChesney Martin, Jr., a former floor member and Chairman of the Board of Governors. When he enlisted in the Army in February, 1941, he was succeeded by Emil Schram, who was Chairman of the Reconstruction Finance Corporation. On May 18, 1942,

On September 25, 1941, Mayor Fiorello LaGuardia opened a three-month celebration of the 150th anniversary of the Bill of Rights with an address to 6,000 on the site of Federal Hall, where the document was ratified by Congress. The fiery Mayor said that Americans would never submit to any "new order" or any dictator.

the exchange celebrated the 150th anniversary of its founding by closing from noon to 1:00 P.M. and staging a huge war-bond rally on the steps of Federal Hall. For the second time in its history (the first had been the Liberty Loan campaign of 1918), the New York Stock Exchange actively and openly recommended a security for purchase—war bonds. By December of that year, the exchange brokers and their firms had sold almost thirteen billion dollars' worth of the government securities, surpassing their quota of nine billion dollars. For this achievement the New York Stock Exchange was awarded a government commendation presented personally by the Secretary of the Treasury, Henry Morgenthau, Jr.

The market climbed steadily throughout 1942, but tapered off in the summer of the following year when action on the war fronts slowed down as the Allies marshaled their forces for the great battles that were to come. When the tide surged in our favor in 1944, with victories in the Pacific and the successful invasion of France, the market again went up and continued strong until it reached its peak during 1946.

In financial terms, the war cost the United States about 350 billion dollars, one-seventh of which went to our Allies in the form of Lend-Lease. The total cost, for all the warring nations, has been estimated at one trillion dollars, with property damage amounting to 231 billion dollars. (These estimates do not include the eight-year war in China.)

At least 40 per cent of the United States cost was paid for by Federal taxes collected during that period. In spite of this, corporation profits after taxes doubled in the years between 1939 and 1944. The rate of climb of personal income was even higher.

In the five years from 1939 to 1944 the average weekly industrial wage, including overtime, almost doubled — from $23.86 to $46.08 — while working hours rose from a weekly average of thirty-eight to forty-five. Many farm workers went into industry, but agricultural mechanization took up the gap and farm productivity doubled over that of the First World War. Because of scarcities in consumer goods and the drive against inflation, personal savings were almost 150 billion dollars by the end of the war. Stiff credit curbs, rent ceilings, price ceilings, and rationing all contributed to the thumping total. These controls, which the administration demanded although Congress was reluctant to act on them and which were at first accepted with some misgivings by the public, were coupled with two other anti-inflation measures — higher taxes and a wage

On the morning of December 7—"a date which will live in infamy"—a sneak attack on Hawaii by the Japanese brought the United States into World War II. This Pearl Harbor scene, one of the most remarkable combat photographs ever made, was snapped at the exact moment the powder magazine of the destroyer SHAW *exploded.*

Among other wartime innovations and precautions were air-raid drills and dim-outs such as this one which shows the East River and the Wall Street area at night from Brooklyn Heights.

Wall Street led brokers across the country in launching the sale of E bonds. Secretary of the Treasury Henry Morgenthau, Jr., at microphone, congratulated members of the Stock Exchange on their accomplishment.

freeze. In spite of these brakes, the amount of savings continued to climb, topping all previous records. Another innovation of the war years—and one that is still in force—was the Federal withholding tax, the "pay-as-you-go plan," suggested by Beardsley Ruml, former Chairman of the Federal Reserve Bank in New York, and adopted by Congress in 1943.

During the war another stage in the managerial revolution was almost completely effected with the ascendancy of the specially trained expert as the leader of industrial and business firms. As *Time* magazine reported:

> *Death and taxes had all but eclipsed the great owner-management dynasties epitomized by Carnegie, Ford and Rockefeller. In their place had come the professional managers, the engineer-trained technicians . . . [who] took over industrial societies so huge that the average owner [stockholder] seldom exercised more than theoretical control. Profits were still the test of efficiency . . . but the tremendous diffusion of ownership enabled the professional manager to give first concern to the economic health of the whole corporate body.*

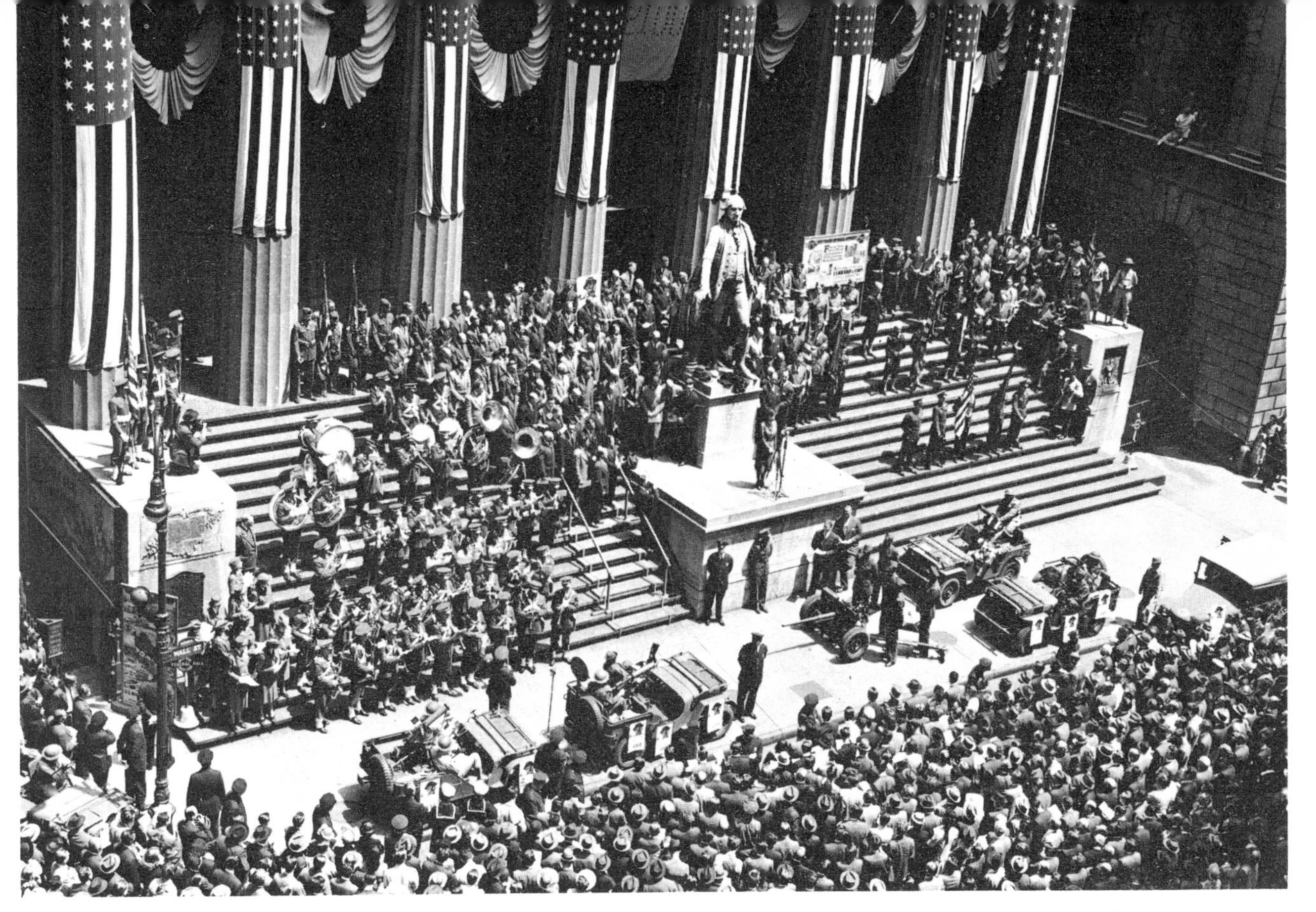

It was a great day for Wall Street when the New York Stock Exchange celebrated its 150th anniversary on May 18, 1942, by closing the Big Board from noon to 1:00 P.M. and staging a mammoth war-bond sale on the steps of Federal Hall supported by a military display of bands, jeeps, peeps, tanks, and light artillery.

Tradition was broken when girl clerks and messengers began to appear on the exchange floors as replacements for young men who were off to war. This young lady served at Post 11 of the Curb (now American) Exchange.

Exchange President William McChesney Martin, Jr., enlisted in the Army in 1941 as a private and later became an officer. He was succeeded by Emil Schram who served as President for ten years.

The lighter side of war financing. Debutante chairman Virginia McCulloch pins War Stamp Victory Buttonaire on Bernard Baruch at the President's Birthday Ball in the Waldorf-Astoria Hotel while Cynthia McAdoo stands by.

Morale in the war-production plants became as important as military morale, and government as well as individual factory departments were set up to nurture it. The Office of War Information tried to solve the problem of chronic absenteeism and frequent job desertions from the thirty-thousand-worker Du Pont plant at Hanford, Washington. Quick turnover and labor shortages were attributed to the fact that no one knew the nature of the product being processed. Patriotic pep talks and personal appearances by movie stars and other celebrities were used to raise morale, but security was so effective that only after the war did the Office of War Information, the movie stars, and the thirty thousand workers learn that the product they were making was uranium for A-bombs.

The sociological approach to better company spirit, often called Human Relations in Industry, was only one indication of the reforms, first begun by the Roosevelt administration in the mid-thirties, which continued to benefit the working man and minority groups during the war. Women invaded every field and made a place for themselves which they did not relinquish after the war ended. The Negro flocked north in greater numbers than ever, and few returned to the South. Labor took a stronger hand in politics, although, unfortunately, some labor groups were responsible for strikes which caused delays in wartime industry.

John Pierpont Morgan, Jr., died in 1943 at the age of seventy-six and Thomas W. Lamont succeeded him as Chairman of the House of Morgan which incorporated as a state bank, offered its stock for sale to the public, and became a member of the

Although signs stating "Hours: 10:00 A.M. to 3:00 P.M." appear on bank windows, leading the public to believe that bankers work a short, easy day, the most important functions begin after the doors close. With increased business during the war, large banks like Chase (LOWER CENTER) *worked around the clock.*

Messengers from various branches of Chase bring the day's work to the head office at Pine and Nassau streets after 5:00 P.M. Men here are bundled up against bitter-cold winter evening.

Checks and papers arrive at Branch Rack by direct messenger and by express shipment. Employees work in two late shifts, from 4:00 P.M. to midnight and from midnight to 8:00 A.M.

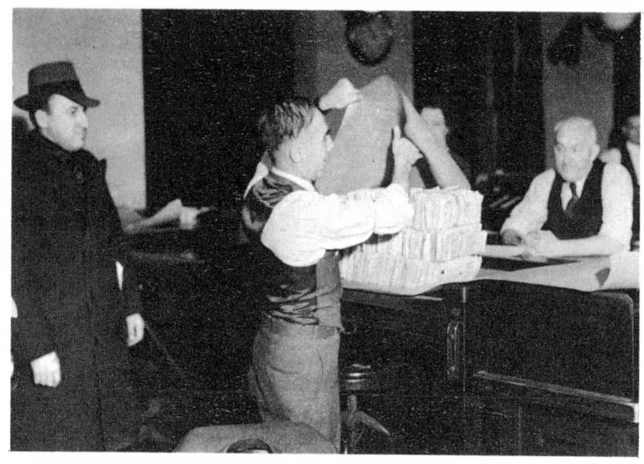

Evening Rack staff bundles the hundred thousand checks representing an average day's business and sends them to the New York Clearing House for distribution to other banks.

After messengers return with another hundred thousand checks from the Clearing House, sorting gets under way. Many bank employees work at day jobs as well and call this "moonlighting."

During a peak period at Night Check, the huge room roars with sound, resembling a mechanical "Anvil Chorus," as all the adding machines clatter out their sums at the same time.

The late night staff eats lunch at 3:00 A.M. in the thirty-third-floor dining room. Students and daytime workers in need of additional income make up a large percentage of moonlighters.

A heavy volume of night mail arrives after midnight. It is sorted, opened, and distributed to IBM operators who put items in proper bins and list them on a separate tape for each bin.

Registered mail arrives under armed guard at 6:30 A.M. and is taken to the Registered Mail Department where it is unpacked, inspected, opened, and routed to the proper destination.

Federal Reserve System. Until that time it was the largest private bank in the world. J.P., Jr., was much more urbane than his father, but he was far less powerful, mainly because the times had changed and even a Morgan was no longer able to do the things which the elder Morgan had accomplished with impunity.

In this world war, as in the first, Bernard Baruch was a guiding light in mobilizing raw materials and production, although this time he served as coach rather than quarterback. He also acted as a talent scout for the administration in placing men who had worked with him in key positions in the departments where production and economic codes were formulated and administered. In addition, since he had experimented with rubber substitutes as early as 1904 and taken part in the formation of Continental Rubber, his experience was most valuable in the search for synthetic rubber when he assumed the chairmanship of the Rubber Committee.

The shortage of manpower on Wall Street during the war was a critical problem which was solved in part by the introduction of womanpower. For the first time, girls replaced young men, who had gone to war, as clerks on the floor of exchanges everywhere. The previous all-male domain was none the worse for the invasion, but the girls did not stay on the floor after the veterans returned and were reinstated in their old jobs.

However, women have remained in the banking world of Wall Street, where they obtained a firm foothold starting in 1940. Many of them run a home

At 8:15 each morning a Chase officer works the combination to open the main vault. After the massive steel door swings out, cash and coin are distributed to tellers and another day begins.

DAILY NEWS

FRANKLIN DELANO ROOSEVELT: JAN. 30, 1882—APRIL 12, 1945

The New York Times.

LATE CITY EDITION

PRESIDENT ROOSEVELT IS DEAD;
TRUMAN TO CONTINUE POLICIES;
9TH CROSSES ELBE, NEARS BERLIN

U.S. AND RED ARMIES DRIVE TO MEET

END COMES SUDDENLY AT WARM SPRINGS

ALL CABINET MEMBERS TO KEEP POSTS

PM Daily

Daily Mirror

F.D.R. DEAD

...d Comes at Warm Sprin...

New York Herald Tribune

LATE CITY EDITION

President Roosevelt Is Dead;
Truman Sworn In as Successor

9th Army Crosses Elbe, 50 Miles From Berlin

New York Post

NIGHT EXTRA

WORLD GRIEVES FOR PRESIDENT ROOSEVELT

TRUMAN'S 1ST ACT:
NO DELAY IN PARI...
Calls Victory Conference

NIGHT EDITION

The Sun

LATE NEWS

ROOSEVELT MOURNED;
TRUMAN TAKES OFFICE

New York World-Telegram

EXTRA

Five Cents

ROOSEVELT DIES SUDDENLY

New York World-Telegram

NIGHT

Five Cents

FUNERAL TRAIN TAKING ROOSEVELT TO CAPITAL

9th Speeds On Leaving Elbe Far Behind

Mourning Nation Waits On Last Journey Home

The death of President Roosevelt came suddenly on April 12, 1945, just short of Allied victory. Typical of the mourning for him was that of a small stationer in the Wall Street area who did not open his store the next day and hung a sign on the door: "Closed because of the death of a close friend."

and look after their children in the daytime while moonlighting during the evening shift or the graveyard (midnight to 8:00 A.M.) shift. Most moonlighters in the Wall Street district, however, hold down a full-time position by day in addition to one at night. Some profess to be bored with too much leisure, others are saving for some special project, but the great majority need the added income to support large families, send someone through college, or pay continuing medical or hospital bills for a dependent. The practice, which began in the war years when there was a scarcity of clerical help and a flood of billings and checks to be processed, has continued ever since. For one thing, office space and expensive office machines can be utilized more economically when the costs involved are spread over two or three shifts. For another, banking firms realize a great saving in interest costs if they can process their paper immediately.

During the fall of 1944, F.D.R. waged his fourth presidential campaign, this time against Thomas E. Dewey, who had been a vigorous prosecutor of crime when he was District Attorney of New York County, achieving such fame that he was later elected Governor of the state. The President came to New York on October 22, partly to let the people see him and judge his physical fitness, which was the subject of campaign innuendo and rumor. The next day, C. P. Trussell reported in the *New York Times:*

> *There was left no doubt that he wanted to be seen by as many New Yorkers as possible. To give the widest opportunity he traveled fifty-one miles in an open automobile [in the rain], at times hatless, through four boroughs . . . letting the elements have their way while he had his. . . . At his news conference on Friday in Washington the President, by word and action, had indicated that the fire-horse urge of activity and personal campaign was upon him. He anticipated, though somewhat face-*

The announcement of Germany's surrender on May 7 sent crowds scurrying to newsstands for details. This photograph was taken at the corner of Wall and Nassau, in front of the Federal Hall National Memorial.

On V-J Day (August 14), marking victory over the Japanese in the Pacific, uptown crowds invaded Wall Street, but the unrestrained delirium of the Armistice Day celebration at the end of World War I was missing.

*V-E Day was a joyous occasion on Broadway at Wall, outside of Trinity Church. Newsreel cameramen (*LEFT AND RIGHT*) photographed crowd scenes from the tops of their automobiles.*

At the war's end, thousands of returning servicemen who disembarked in the port of New York were greeted by this huge red-white-and-blue sign at the outer end of a pier in the lower Hudson River.

tiously, that he would step into a fifty-mile gale here along with the rain. It was not that bad, but he was soaking wet almost from the start of his journey to the end. Once he stopped briefly, discarded a much-soaked suit, donned another and went on.

At Ebbets Field . . . [he was cheered] by a crowd of 10,000 roaring Brooklynites, most of them under cover. . . . Mr. Roosevelt left his automobile, stood hatless before the microphone and, facing a lashing rainfall, made his appeal. . . . The power of his voice as it filled the ball park was reminiscent, fans said, of an announcement of a change of Dodgers' batteries.

Mayor LaGuardia said after the trip that the President had stood it better than he had. On the basis of the reception all along the route, he told the President, he was prepared to predict that the Presidential plurality next month in New York City would be exactly 762,347.

Tossing a suspicious glance at the Mayor, Mr. Roosevelt asked him how he knew such things.

"I counted them," the Mayor said.

The actual figure was 769,849, just 7,502 more than La Guardia's estimate. He was less than 1% off!

In anticipation of the end of the war, the Stock Exchange embarked on an extensive public-relations program and its first advertisement in newspapers in July, 1945, was an extremely wise and unselfish one. It urged all owners of government E Bonds to hold them and not sell or switch to any other securities. After this initial approach to the public the advertising campaign pursued the theme of the soundness of American corporate stocks, pointing out that the need for new capital for expanding industry would continue and increase in the years ahead.

When the Second World War ended with the final capitulation of Japan on August 14, 1945, there was none of the dismaying downward movement in the market or in business in general which had characterized the end of every other war in which the United States had been involved. There was no inflation, either. It appeared that the United States had learned at least one lesson in economics.

16

Prosperity and Progress

THE FIFTEEN YEARS following the end of the Second World War were distinguished by a vital, healthy economic growth, especially if viewed as one ascending curve, and not as a day-to-day series of fluctuations. Values and volume on the Stock Exchange reached almost unheard-of totals, and although common-stock prices logically climb along with wages and cost of living, stocks have actually raced ahead of both. However, the great phenomenon in Wall Street and the investment industry as a whole was, and continues to be, the tremendous broadening of the base of investors as prices and number of shares increased.

Not until 1952 was a census of stockholders attempted, and then the total was estimated as almost six and a half million. This figure included all individuals owning shares in publicly held corporations in the United States. By 1956 the figure had increased more than two million, and early in 1959 it was about twelve and a half million—almost double the number of seven years before. Of the twelve and a half million shareholders, more than two-thirds (8,510,000) held stocks listed on the New York Stock Exchange.

By comparing the state of the market at four distinct points — 1959, 1949, 1932 (when it was at its lowest depth), and 1929—the following table reveals just how great the growth has been:

	12/31/59	12/31/49	12/31/32	12/31/29
Stock Issues . . .	1,507	1,457	1,237	1,293
Bond Issues . . .	1,180	918	1,549	1,543
Total Issues . . .	2,687	2,375	2,786	2,836
Number of Shares (in millions)	5,847	2,151	1,311	1,127
Value of shares (in billions)	$307	$73	$22	$64*
Av. per Share. .	$61	$34	$17‡	$57†
Annual % of Turnover	15	23	32	119
Common Stocks Paying Cash Dividend	953	930	288	554
Median Yield . .	3.8	6.7	*Not Available*	
Preferred Stocks Paying Cash Dividend . . .	403	405	*Not Available*	
Median Yield . .	5.1	4.3	*Not Available*	
Av. Daily Vol. (in millions)	3¼	2	2½	4¼

* Value of shares at high point (9/1/29), $89 billion.
† Average per share at high point, $89.13.
‡ Average per share at low point (7/1/32), $11.89.

The oldest public building on the island, St. Paul's Chapel, first opened on October 30, 1766, received a $200,000 renovation which restored its original appearance and refurbished its blue, white, and gold interior. The St. Paul building across Broadway, the world's tallest at the turn of the century, was razed in 1959 to make way for the Western Electric building.

Lower Manhattan, glowing like a convention of fireflies, hummed industriously after the war ended and wartime controls and restrictions were lifted. The economy boomed as a flood of pent-up money put Wall Street into a fever of activity, optimism, and prosperity.

The decline in prices from the highs at the beginning of 1960 (Dow Jones industrials down from 679 to 608 in midyear) indicates that the low yield reflected the fact that investors were acutely aware of one pitfall into which the 1929 market had plunged — the abyss between price and earning of securities. The possibility of another debacle such as that of 1929 seems remote indeed under the watchful eye of the government and the exchanges. Every experience since the passage of the Securities and

Bache and Company, climbing to second-ranking position among securities houses, staged the first fashion show ever held in a broker's board room in co-operation with Saks Fifth Avenue.

Three of the Saks models posed with Harold L. Bache, head of the firm and nephew of the late Jules S. Bache, who founded the company, which now traded a half million shares of securities a day.

Using a Teleregister stock price board as a backdrop, the Bache-Saks style show attracted 500 women, most of whom had never before entered a brokerage house.

Exchange Act has strengthened the belief of the experts that it cannot happen again.

The New York Stock Exchange—borrowing a leaf from American Telephone and Telegraph (1,736,681 stockholders in 1960), General Motors (760,442) and Standard Oil of New Jersey (569,600)—has been campaigning ever since the end of the war to bring more customers into the market, using the same reasoning as the corporations: the more people financially involved with a corporate destiny, the larger the proportion of the community that is sympathetic to the corporation and its aims. During the progress of this campaign, the number of women stockholders increased to over 52.5 per cent; totaling four million, they now constitute the largest single group of shareowners. However, men still hold about three hundred million more shares than women.

The influence of the New York Stock Exchange on the postwar increase in new investors of limited capital has probably been equaled, if not surpassed, by the missionary work of a single brokerage house. Presently known as Merrill Lynch, Pierce, Fenner and Smith, Inc. — formerly Merrill Lynch, Pierce, Fenner and Beane—it is also known familiarly as the Bureau of Missing Persons, The Thundering Herd, We the People, or simply, WE. These brokers are as different from Jacob Little and Jim Fisk as the Bank of England is from Jesse James or Willie Sutton. The firm, which has grown to be the largest in the world, is the creation of the late Charles E. Merrill, described by Martin Mayer as "the first authentically great man produced by the financial market in 150 years." As Mayer wrote in *Wall Street: Men and Money:*

> *The Drews and Goulds, the Cookes, the Morgans and the Livermores—these men existed in a tight little island of their own making, where the public were sheep to be shorn. They made the alleys of Wall Street dark and dangerous places, and they kept for themselves as much as possible of the benefits that came from the system which produced their fantastic riches. Merrill brought in the public, not as lambs to be fleeced but as partners in the benefits. Today a man who loses his shirt in the market is the victim of his own stupidity or greed, not of the machinations of insiders. The climate of the 1930's helped, the New Deal laws helped, and many individuals helped, but the prime mover was Charlie Merrill.*

An investment banker earlier in the century, Merrill had specialized in founding chains of stores (McCrory, Safeway, Kresge, Western Auto Supply). He got out of the market in 1928 and out of the brokerage business in 1930 with enough cash to lend five million dollars to the firm which took over his customers. When he decided to return in 1940 he drew on his chain-store experience to weld an organization that stripped the mystery from brokerage operations and created a new image of the broker as an approachable human being.

Regular balance sheets and profit statements of the house were made public. The firm's interest in any securities it floated was stated on the first page of each offering. Customers' men were placed on flat salaries so they would have no incentive to load and unload customers, plug stocks, or churn accounts. Nor did they have to bring their own accounts into the office in order to survive. The firm began a series of aggressive, unorthodox, but legitimate advertising campaigns to bring in clients. Every facility was utilized to build business among people who were new to the market or those who appreciated Merrill Lynch service and especially ML research and information. This has perhaps been the keystone of the firm's success, for it provides, without charge, the most detailed, expert data on any investment at the request of any client. The information it furnishes is as thorough and reliable as anything anyone, short of a Bernard Baruch, could obtain.

These methods resulted in a network of 131

The Manhattan entrance of the Brooklyn-Battery Tunnel, which cuts under Battery Park and Upper New York Bay to emerge three miles east in Brooklyn.

offices, an army of more than one hundred vice-presidents, membership in about forty-five exchanges, and over 445,000 customers by 1960. There are 1,850 account executives and 5,450 other employees. In 1959 the research department reviewed forty-five thousand portfolios, ranging in value from a few thousand to many worth millions of dollars. There are girls who do nothing all day, every day, but clip coupons off customers' bonds; men who start work at 1:00 A.M. wiring orders to Europe; and members on the floor of the Fresno Cotton Exchange, the Cocoa Terminal Market in Amsterdam, and the Winnipeg Grain Exchange.

The impact of Merrill's revolution in Wall Street has been enormous. The firm he organized in 1940 quickly assumed a commanding lead. Today it consistently handles well over 10 per cent of the business transacted, not only on the New York and American exchanges, but on the forty-three other markets in which firm members hold seats, on the over-the-counter and commodity markets, as well as in underwriting and municipal bonds.

The counterpart of Charles E. Merrill in the Wall Street real-estate field during these growing years was Charles F. Noyes whose faith in downtown property left him holding a great deal of it from 1930 until the upturn began at the war's end. By then he owned almost a hundred properties on Broadway alone, and when he began disposing of them in the brisker post-

The toe of Manhattan from Governor's Island by day—the world's greatest concentration of improved real estate, with more than a dozen buildings over 500 feet tall.

The same view at night—F. Scott Fitzgerald's "white glacier . . . a miracle of foaming light suspended by the stars," and Le Corbusier's "limitless cluster of jewels."

war years, his personal income went as high as four million dollars a year. But this affluence does not prevent him from being one of the hardest-working men on Wall Street, or from enjoying his work to the hilt, whether it was acting as rental agent for a dismal loft in an old building or acting as the primary broker in the sale of the Empire State building for $51,500,000, collecting a fee of about a million dollars.

Noyes and his firm deal in properties almost anywhere, but his favorite neighborhood has always been the Wall Street district. For sixty years the firm has had its main office there and to Noyes the tip of Manhattan Island, up to City Hall, has always been the loveliest view—and collection of real estate—in the world. In these 120 acres of ground there was property with an assessed value of 750 million dollars even before the erection of the hundred-million-dollar Chase Manhattan building, the total almost equally divided between land and buildings. The thirty-seven parcels on Wall Street itself are valued at more than 150 million dollars.

During the postwar period two venerable institutions of the Wall Street district celebrated anniversaries. In 1947 Trinity Church parish commemorated the 250th anniversary of the signing of its royal charter by Governor Benjamin Fletcher. As the wealthiest parish in the world, because of its real-estate holdings, Trinity has either founded or given substantial aid to more than fourteen hundred churches, schools, hospitals, and other institutions. One of these, St. Paul's Chapel, which was dedicated in 1766 as the uptown branch of Trinity, was restored to its original colonial appearance at a cost of two hundred thousand dollars in time for its 185th anniversary. The oldest public building on Manhattan, St. Paul's originally stood close to the grassy bank of the Hudson before the river was pushed back as land was filled in. By 1960 the turn-of-the-century St. Paul building, across the street, as well as the adjoining bank building, had been torn down to make way for the new thirty-one-story headquarters building of Western Electric.

Going into the 1950's Wall Street became predominantly a market for investors interested in long-term income rather than for speculators seeking short-term quick profits. With margin determined by the Federal Reserve Board, usually requiring from 50 to 90 per cent of the purchase price, the number of people who used this method of stock-dealing

During the television quiz show craze, a top winner was eleven-year-old Leonard Ross, reported to have won $164,000 answering questions on the stock market. He was deluged with appeals for advice. With him is seventy-eight-year-old Alice Morgan, who had taught investment planning and won $32,000 on the "$64,000 Question."

The bicentennial of the birth of Alexander Hamilton, first Secretary of the Treasury, was commemorated at an American Stock Exchange luncheon with a speech by the Reverend Alexander van Cortlandt Hamilton, a descendant, as American Exchange President Edward T. McCormick listened.

dwindled to less than 20 per cent of the total. In 1929 the proportion had been exactly the reverse.

John Brooks, in his book of that title, called the big boom of the fifties "The Seven Fat Years." But after a setback in the middle of 1957, the market recovered, passed its former high in the autumn of 1958, and continued on an upward trend until the end of 1959. During that time Wall Street proved it could stage stirring events and exciting scenes without reducing its customers to beggary or subjecting them to heart failure. There were proxy fights and the launching of big special stock issues, one specialist's courageous, public-spirited stand in the case of Pantepec Oil, a plane crash on Wall Street and an automobile firm's crash on the market, the rise and fall of the quiz-show financial expert, and the brief flutter of stock dives and bond rises when President Eisenhower suffered a heart attack on September 26, 1955, and a digestive upset on June 9 of the following year. The news of the President's attack was responsible for a 7,716,650-share day of trading, while the announcement of his seizure of ileitis resulted in a volume of 3,628,600 for the day, new lows for 153 issues, and a temporary shrinkage in stock values of four billion dollars.

The construction of the Brooklyn-Battery Tunnel wiped out several square blocks of dingy slums at the rim of lower Manhattan and cut forty minutes of driving time to Coney Island. The Cortlandt Street Ferry to Weehawken closed down and Sean Thomas O'Kelly, first President of Ireland to visit the United States, received a tremendous shower of ticker tape from four hundred thousand people who greeted him on his way from the Battery to City Hall. Emil Schram retired as President of the New York Stock Exchange in 1951 and G. Keith Funston moved from the presidency of Trinity College into Schram's position.

In 1954 the Corn Exchange Bank, ranking twentieth on the list of United States banks, merged with the Chemical National to become the seventh biggest, and in 1959 the Chemical Corn Exchange joined with the New York Trust Company to become fourth largest. That same year J. P. Morgan and Company merged with Guaranty Trust Company to form the four-billion-dollar Morgan Guaranty Trust. In 1948 there were twenty-four member banks in the New York Clearing House, which exchanged checks through clearings totaling 373.7 billion dollars that year. A decade later there were only twelve banks in the Clearing House, but the total amount of the checks exchanged was 628 billion for the fiscal year ending September 30, 1958, and 641 billion during the following fiscal year.

Blizzards and floods, strikes and threats of strikes, the stalemate war in Korea and the continuing Cold War between the West and the Soviet Bloc, failed to halt the upsweep of the market and of American prosperity. General Motors, requiring 325 million dollars for additional plants, raised the sum easily by issuing 4,380,683 new shares of its stock early in 1955. Just a year later an even greater stock sale was held.

One of the most publicized stock promotions of the postwar period was to finance the revolutionary rear-engine Tucker Torpedo. A campaign was launched to sell $20 million of stock and to buy the Dodge engine plant in Chicago—but the automobile never went into production and investors were wiped out.

Weather
SHOWERS, CLEARING
Details on Page 2

Daily Mirror

3c In Suburbs
5c Elsewhere

Vol. 22. No. 284. NEW YORK, [illegible]DAY, MAY 21, 1946 C FINAL EDITION ★★

4 KILLED AS PLANE RAMS 40 WALL ST.

3 Army Men, WAC, Victims, Craft Strikes at 58th Floor

CRASHES IN LOW FOG, SETS FIRE TO BUILDING

An Army Air Force C-45 transport, flying blind at 650 feet through low fog, crashed into the fifty-eighth-floor offices of the Atlas Corporation in the seventy-story 40 Wall Street building at 8:10 P.M. on May 20, 1946, killing all on board but none of the 500 evening workers in the building (daytime population: 5,000).

A familiar sight on lower Broad Street for thirty years was the sign of the union hall of the Industrial Workers of the World, a stone's throw from the center of capitalism they sought to abolish.

In a bitter strike of the United Financial Employees against the Stock and Curb exchanges, a worker goes into 11 Wall Street entrance of Big Board despite heckling of picket. A mass sitdown of strikers, across from the original wall, was broken up by police. The union lost when brokerage-firm clerks took over their jobs.

This was the marketing of 10,200,000 shares of Ford Motor Company common—the first public offering of Ford stock in the half-century of the company's existence.

Blyth and Company headed the group of seven investment-banking firms which managed the great syndicate, consisting of 722 security distributors. The Ford Foundation, which had owned the stock but decided not to keep all its eggs in one basket, received $642,600,000 in one check about a month after the registration statement was filed with the Securities and Exchange Commission.

The blizzard of December 26, 1947, was as heavy in snowfall as that of 1888, but not as devastating. At the Battery, commuters from Staten Island walk single-file from the ferry to the subway station.

Another corporate activity that absorbed the attention of Wall Street and stockholders everywhere was the series of proxy battles for control of giant corporations during the mid-fifties. Robert Young of the Chesapeake and Ohio Railroad engaged Harold Vanderbilt, the Commodore's great-grandson, J. P. Morgan and Company, and William White, President of the New York Central, in a titanic struggle for the domination of Central's board of directors. In the newspaper-ad, letter-writing, and personal solicitation war, each side spent a million dollars to present its story. Newspapers throughout the country carried full-page advertisements signed by James A. Farley, former Postmaster-General of the United States, who had been a member of the Central board for 14 years and, naturally, a backer of the status quo. Farley endorsed management and blasted Young. Young and his wife owned huge blocks of stock and he controlled even more. He revealed that Farley was the owner of 100 shares of New York Central. In his position as head of a rival railroad, Young was able to bring into the open many charges of mismanagement, Morgan domination, and what he headlined in full-page ads as "Little

When the CHICAGO TRIBUNE *jumped to the wrong conclusion after the early lead piled up by Thomas E. Dewey in the 1948 election, headlining Republican victory, President Truman jubilantly displayed paper on his return trip to Washington.*

White Lies." On June 14, 1954, Young was declared the victor by more than a million share-votes.

Other celebrated proxy battles of the period included Charles Green's successful take-over of United Cigar-Whelan in 1951; Ben W. Heineman's victory over Lucian C. Sprague and the management of the Minnesota and Saint Louis Railroad; Louis E. Wolfson's failure to gain control of Montgomery Ward in 1955; and Charles Green's unsuccessful attempt to replace Spyros Skouras and Darryl F. Zanuck at Twentieth Century-Fox Pictures.

On January 10, 1955, following a tip on the stock by Walter Winchell in his Sunday night broadcast, there were buy-orders for 357,500 shares of Pantepec Oil awaiting David Jackson, the American Exchange specialist in that issue. Orders to sell amounted to 234,500 shares. Jackson was shy 123,000 shares of filling his buy-orders. In order to maintain a liquid market he had to go short that number of shares—with the prospect of losing $123,000 every time the stock went up a point. That morning the floor of the American Exchange was a bedlam, all centered around Jackson, who had received a respite of one hour to make his decision. The specialist announced that he would open the stock at 8⅞, the price that most of his sell-orders quoted and only 2⅛ over Friday's last price. Jackson could have named a much higher opening price, which would have protected him but cost the eager buyers much more if the stock should slide. Absorbing the 123,000 shares he did not

The largest stock issue in history was the sale of 10,200,000 shares of Ford Motor Company common by the Ford Foundation in 1956. Here reporters at the National Press Club in Washington get the first details.

No. 1

New York, N.Y. January 26, 1956

1 1-8/210

Pay to the order of

• The Ford Foundation • $ 642,600,000.00

Six hundred forty-two million six hundred thousand Dollars

Blyth & Co., Inc.
The First Boston Corporation
Goldman, Sachs & Co.
Kuhn, Loeb & Co.
Lehman Brothers
Merrill Lynch, Pierce, Fenner & Beane
White, Weld & Co.
Representatives of Ford Underwriters

By Blyth & Co., Inc.

PAID JAN 26 1956 THE FIRST NATIONAL CITY BANK OF NEW YORK

CERTIFIED JAN 26 1956 PAYABLE ONLY AS ORIGINALLY DRAWN AND WHEN PROPERLY ENDORSED THE FIRST NATIONAL CITY BANK OF NEW YORK TELLER

To The First National City Bank of New York
Head Office
Fifty-Five Wall Street
New York, N. Y.

By Charles R. Blyth
By Lawrence ...
Authorized Signatures

Proceeds of the Ford stock sale, amounting to $642,600,000, were paid to the Ford Foundation in the largest check of its kind ever issued. The seven leading underwriters were headed by Charles R. Blyth.

Several years before the above meeting, flanked by senior partner Edward A. Pierce (LEFT) *and managing partner Winthrop H. Smith, sentimental Charles E. Merrill was moved to tears at his birthday party. More than any other man, Merrill was responsible for bringing stock-market investment to the average American.*

"We the People." The last partners' meeting of Merrill Lynch, Pierce, Fenner and Smith was held on October 24, 1959, with 113 members of the firm present. Three months later the nation's largest brokerage firm was incorporated and all the partners except Michael W. McCarthy (sixth from right at speakers' table in rear) became vice-presidents. McCarthy became the President of the corporation.

have to balance his buy-orders, he announced the trade of 357,500 shares for the ticker—the largest block of stock ever to change hands on the floor of any exchange. Pantepec did not go higher. John Brooks, in *The Seven Fat Years,* related the end of the story:

> The sudden flare-up of the speculative interest in Pantepec proved to be short-lived—as is often the case in such flurries—and in the week that followed Jackson's big Monday, the stock did not reach 8⅞ again; instead, it slipped off into a decline that was to continue for some time. During that whole week, Jackson kept buying Pantepec to cover his enormous short position, at prices ranging from 8¾ down to 8⅛. By closing time on Friday, he was practically covered and, on totting up the figures, discovered that he had no reason for gloom. His personal profit from his week-long dealings in Pantepec—quite apart, naturally, from the sense of well-being experienced by one who has acted in the public interest—came to just about fifty thousand dollars.

THE STORY OF A STOCK TRADE. *One day in 1957, Ann Pater came to the Cincinnati office of Merrill Lynch after discussing a proposed investment with her husband, Raymond C. Pater, Jr. With George A. Edwards, an ML account executive, she checks statistics on Phillips Petroleum common and decides to buy 200 shares.*

Edwards hands "buy 200 Phillips at the market" order to ML teletype operator, Maria Pacini, who sends instructions to the head office in New York.

In the New York wire room, Olga Macowchick tears the message from incoming teletype machine and routes it on multichannel belt system to the Order Desk.

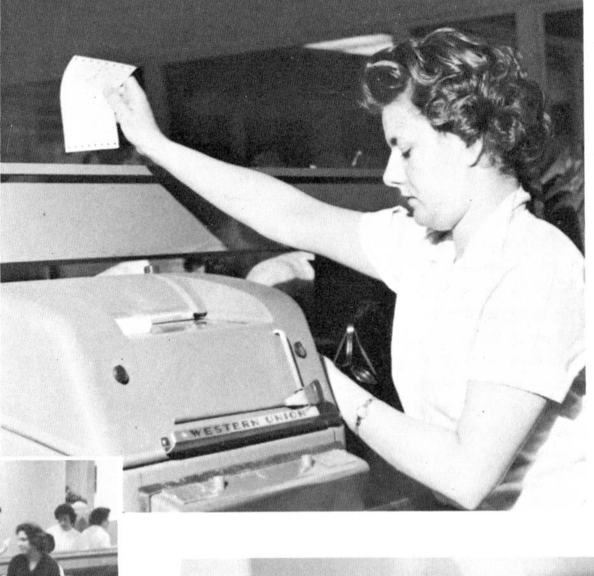

Part of ML's wire room, the largest in the world, which extends through the Cities Service building from Pine to Cedar streets. It is supercharged with noise and excitement during Big Board hours.

At the Order Desk, Frieda Wendell has taken the Cincinnati order off the belt and is telephoning it to a clerk on the Stock Exchange floor.

In the San Antonio office of Bache and Company, almost at the same time that the Cincinnati transaction began, Robert K. Pincus (LEFT) *decides to sell his 200 shares of Phillips, checks quotation, and gives "sell at the market" order to Jay Lewis Rubin, customers' man.*

Teletypist Jerree Nacker gets the order from Rubin and quickly transmits it to Bache's Wall Street headquarters . . .

. . . where Eugene Dugas tears it off receiving machine and puts it on belt conveyor . . .

. . . extending from rear right. The message from San Antonio travels across the big, busy Bache wire room . . .

. . . until it is intercepted by Helen Kascewicz, who is in constant touch by private wire with the Bache booth at the edge of the Stock Exchange floor.

At the ML phone booth on the side of the Stock Exchange trading floor, a phone clerk jots down the order for 200 Phillips. Knowing that member Charles Marsico trades at Post 8, he presses button for him.

The button activates Marsico's number—156—which flops down on the large annunciator boards that cover part of the north and south walls.

Floor broker Charles Marsico, then an ML partner, habitually glances at boards. Seeing his number, he hurries to the booth.

At the phone booth, Arthur Paine hands the order from Mrs. Pater to Marsico, who hurries, but does not run, to Post 8.

The destination of both brokers, Post 8 (TOP LEFT), is the only place at the New York Stock Exchange where Phillips Petroleum is traded.

Bache clerk Roger Fenn jots down phone order from Miss Kascewicz and presses button for Donald M. Lovejoy, one of the firm's partners on the floor, who is assigned to Post 8 and trades in Phillips stock.

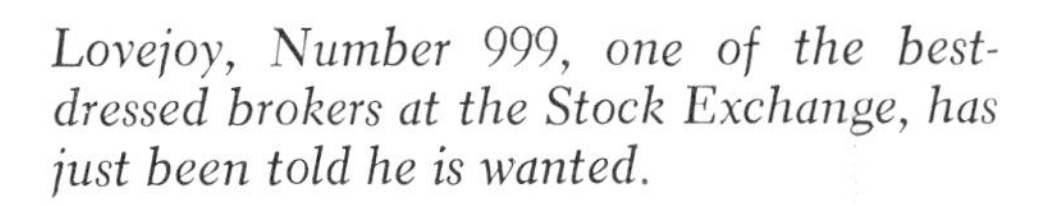

Lovejoy, Number 999, one of the best-dressed brokers at the Stock Exchange, has just been told he is wanted.

Checking for himself, Lovejoy sees his number and heads at a brisk pace for the Bache telephone.

Sell-order in hand, Lovejoy automatically proceeds to Post 8. However, he does not run, for he could be fined up to $50 if he did.

"How's Phillips?" asks Marsico of Kenneth R. Williams, specialist in that security. Lovejoy listens. Neither broker reveals whether he is buying or selling. Williams says: "45 bid, 45½ asked."

Marsico decides to offer a price in between and says: "I'll bid 45¼ for 200." He is immediately taken up by Lovejoy, who says: "Sold!" The deal is made, nothing passing between the brokers but their word. Despite pressure, rush, and noise, deals are always binding.

Marsico who bought (B) and Lovejoy who sold (S) jot down price, number of shares, other firm, broker's number. Williams notes price and amount in his Phillips book.

CHARLES K. MARSICO
No. M
B
200
P
Bache
999
45¼

P
200
2-ML
156
45¼
FEB 18 1957 FEB 15 1957
BACHE & CO.
920 FEB 12 '57 OO-11

Marsico hands the note which he wrote to page Thomas Gutheinz and tells him to deliver it to the ML phone booth. . . . Gutheinz gives the memo, now a confirmation of purchase, to Paine who will phone the information to Miss Wendell at once.

Lovejoy shouts "Squad!" — the traditional cry for a page boy. . . . Barry Lasner responds to Lovejoy's call. Familiar with the Bache floor man, he does not need to be told where to go. . . . At the nearest Bache phone, Lasner hands confirmation of sell-order to Thomas White, who will relay it to head office.

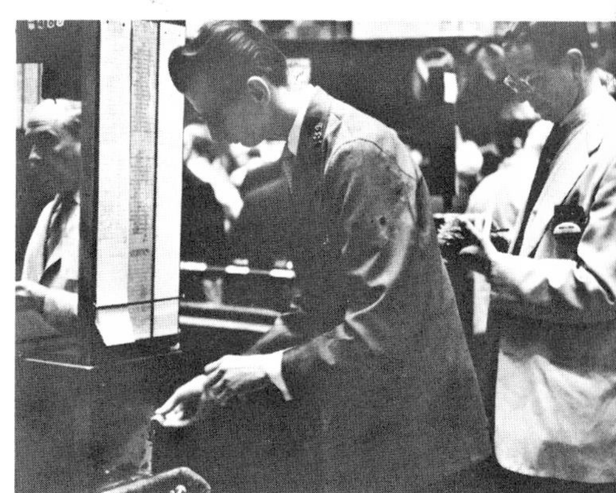

Alexander Sazanovitch, in black coat, is a Stock Exchange reporter who records transactions. He marks down "P . . . 2s . . . 45¼" for "Phillips, 200 shares at $45.25 a share". . . . He tells a page to dispatch the note to the central stock-ticker sending station. . . . Slipping the message into a carrier, the page inserts it into a pneumatic tube which relays it to the ticker department where it is typed on ticker machine.

In less than a minute, depending on market volume, the transaction is flashed on the screen and goes out over wires to 3,100 tickers throughout the country.

In the Merrill Lynch wire room, Alfred Sampron has been handed confirmation of purchase by Miss Wendell and puts it on the direct wire to the Cincinnati office.

Mrs. Pater, who has just seen a sale of 200 Phillips for 45¼ on the Teleregister screen behind her, gets confirmation from Edwards that she has bought the stock at that price.

In the Bache wire room, at the other end of the phone from Thomas White, Tom Hatrick gets news of the stock sale. He makes a notation and sends it to the operator in direct touch with San Antonio.

Client Pincus reads confirmation from the Bache New York office that he has sold his 200 Phillips at 45¼ as Rubin checks the ticker. Brokerage commission was less than 1 per cent on $9,050 sale, which took less than five minutes overall.

To the New York Stock Exchange Clearing House, under the trading floor, Bache messenger comes to deliver, and ML man to pick up, stock certificates for 200 Phillips shares traded.

Old certificates are surrendered at the office of Phillips, which acts as its own transfer agent. Then Beverly Shaw makes out new ones in the name of Mrs. Pater.

17

Wall Street Today

OF ALL THE patients admitted to Wall Street's hospital—the Beekman-Downtown at 170 William Street—over 60 per cent are victims of heart ailments, many undoubtedly precipitated by undue excitement and business pressures. The hospital records almost no cases of collapse induced by mental stress, and the district has practically no psychoanalysts. Apparently, people on Wall Street are too busy worrying about losing their money to have any time left to worry about losing their minds.

Practical and sober in business matters, the people of Wall Street nevertheless do have a sense of humor. When Merrill Lynch, Pierce, Fenner and Beane spent a tidy fortune on new office signs and stationery changing its name to Merrill Lynch, Pierce, Fenner and Smith, a triumphant, attention-catching ad appeared in *The New Yorker* reading: "Who has BEANE? We have BEANE! J. R. Williston & Beane."

But there are still people obtuse enough to be taken in by the most obvious of confidence games. The Annetja Jans case, for example, has been superseded by the Edwards Estate racket, another inheritance fraud in which gullible "heirs" are encouraged to pay legal fees for a supposed assault on the title to all the property between St. Paul's Chapel and the center of Greenwich Village. One of the scheme's promoters for whom a warrant was issued lived in Houston, Texas, on Robin Hood Street.

Otherwise, crime in Wall Street is confined to the high-pressure selling of low-grade stocks, the average number of embezzlements, and an occasional daylight holdup or payroll-snatching.

Many things have changed on Wall Street, but it is still 520 average strides from St. Paul's to Trinity, and the only rent the shoeshine men in front of each must pay for their concessions is the chore of shoveling the snow from the churches' sidewalks. In Trinity Churchyard there are 1,186 gravestones (1,018 still legible), including those of William Bradford, the Revolutionary patriot and official printer to the First Continental Congress; the unfortunately mated Lady Catherine Cornbury; Robert Fulton, with a bas-relief taken from a self-portrait; Francis Lewis, a signer of the Declaration of Independence; Hercules Mulligan, patriot and confidant of Washington; John Watts, last royal Recorder of

New York; Albert Gallatin; Captain Isaac Berryman (of whom it is written: "Boreas' blasts and Neptune's waves/Have tossed him to and fro,/But by the sacred will of God/He's anchored here below."); and Alexander Hamilton. At St. Paul's there are 810 stones (679 with legible inscriptions), including those of Richard Coote, the Earl of Bellomont; Christopher Colles, who first conceived the plan of the Erie Canal; General Richard Montgomery, who died in 1775 during the assault on Quebec; the Sieur de Rochefontaine; George Frederick Cooke, an English actor who, in 1810, refused to perform *Richard III* until the orchestra played "God Save the King"; and Thomas Addis Emmet, a distinguished lawyer and brother of Robert Emmet, the Irish patriot who was hanged for treason in 1803.

This is the town of the quick as well as the dead, where the pedestrians heavily outnumber the drivers. Jaywalking is the rule rather than the exception on Wall Street, where there is not a single traffic signal after you leave Broadway. The city fathers keep toying with the idea of closing off Nassau, the shopping street, to motor traffic from noon to 2:00 P.M., making it a temporary mall. In early Manhattan the Indians bartered two- and three-foot oysters, two-foot Staten Island lobsters, and five-hundred-pound sturgeon caught in the Hudson. Now on Nassau Street tiny Blue Points are two dollars a dozen and smoked sturgeon is six dollars a pound.

Staten Island, no longer famous for lobsters or Commodore Vanderbilt, is still distinguished for its nickel ferry ride and Todt Hill, which rises 409.8 feet, the highest coastal point between Maine and Florida. The bridge to Brooklyn no longer charges one cent for pedestrians or a nickel for cows (now prohibited), and the borough's high spot is the promenade deck on Brooklyn Heights where Colonel Washington Roebling watched the bridge under construction.

A ship enters or leaves the port of New York every twenty-two minutes throughout the year. There are four thousand craft—barges, lighters, carfloats, floating grain elevators, and floating derricks—which are tugged about the harbor by five hundred powerful tugs. If all the land rimming the port of New York

At Old Slip, the day squad of Precinct One marches out of the police station to line up and receive instructions. The Wall Street district has always been the best-policed in the city. Years ago a "Deadline" was in effect — known criminals caught below Fulton Street were hauled off to jail on sight.

In the early morning light, the 813-foot Chase Manhattan building towers over the squat Federal Reserve Bank (in front and to the north) and appears to be taller than the 950-foot Cities Service building (to the left and east). In the background are the docks of Brooklyn (LEFT) and Governor's Island (RIGHT).

"In the shape-up, which is the method by which longshoremen are chosen for jobs . . . [New York] preserves one of the few medieval hiring systems that remain in a progressive world," wrote Brooks Atkinson. At the foot of Wall Street is banana dock.

were straightened out in one line, it would be 579 miles long, 320 miles of it made up by New York City alone. There are 170 steamship lines, 15 railroads, 42 airlines, and 500 truck lines serving the port, and the Department of Sanitation operates a 250-man navy to dispose of garbage.

Commuters from outside the city arrive by train and bus—an army six hundred thousand strong—each working day, mainly through Grand Central and Penn stations and the Port Authority Bus Terminal. But thousands more come by car through the Brooklyn-Battery Tunnel, the Queens Midtown Tunnel, and over the East River bridges from Queens, Brooklyn, and Long Island. Now that all but two of the ferries from Jersey have vanished, a great many commuters from across the Hudson flock into the city through the Holland and Lincoln tunnels and the Hudson and Manhattan Tubes. A small trickle of commuters is beginning to land at the new Port Authority heliport near the foot of Broad Street. However, the main flow of Wall Street workers and visitors is handled by six municipally owned and operated subway lines from every part of the city, bus lines, taxicabs, and the Staten Island ferries which carry sixty thousand passengers daily.

Sixty thousand Staten Island fares mean thirty

As the passenger ferries between New Jersey and Manhattan shuttle back and forth across the Hudson, spilling Wall Street workers onto West Street, the commuters fan out to fill the downtown office buildings.

thousand round-trip passengers, divided equally between shoppers, uptown workers, and downtown workers, leaving an estimated figure of ten thousand Staten Islanders who work in Wall Street. Added to an average of 150,000 who arrive by subway and forty thousand who come by bus, taxi, and automobile, Wall Street has a working population of about two hundred thousand. Almost another hundred thousand people drop in each day on various business matters or merely to wander about the streets and look around.

Few in the bustling crowds pay much attention to the block-square fortress which houses the richest bank in the world, the Federal Reserve of New York, with assets of thirteen billion dollars, and, incidentally, the repository of currency, coin, gold, and securities worth another hundred billion dollars. The building has nine freight elevators to carry money, the 125 guards have a shooting accuracy averaging 85 per cent, and the reference library receives 1,300 different periodicals and financial-information releases regularly Each day two million "mutts" or mutilated bank notes are destroyed and one counterfeit note is discovered.

Some people are under the misapprehension that the Federal Reserve is a private superbank. Others believe that it is owned by the government. Actually it is neither—and both. The Federal Reserve System is a privately owned nonprofit institution serving the public interest. It was set up by Congress to create and maintain credit and monetary conditions most favorable to the country's prosperity, while keeping the purchasing power of the dollar as strong as possible.

The twelve-bank system—New York is the largest and the others are in Boston, Philadelphia, Cleveland, Richmond, Atlanta, Chicago, St. Louis, Minneapolis, Kansas City, Dallas, and San Francisco—was a congressional compromise between centralized power, a serious defect of the first and second Banks of the United States which foundered, and regional participation. As such, it is a unique system of central banking tailor-made to suit the nation's needs.

Only about half of the banks in the United States belong to the Federal Reserve System, but these six thousand member banks, which include all national and qualifying state banks, hold about 85 per cent of all bank deposits. They own stock in the Federal Reserve in amounts equaling 3 per cent of their own capital and surplus and must comply with Reserve requirements and other regulations. In return, they may borrow from the Reserve banks, use the many Federal Reserve services, and receive a 6 per cent annual dividend on their stock.

The Federal Reserve provides a place where banks can obtain extra currency when needed and where they can keep their own reserves, so that money panics and runs on banks can be, and have been,

About 150,000 Wall Streeters pour into the district each weekday by subway via the six lines transporting passengers from Brooklyn, Queens, uptown Manhattan, and the Bronx. A smaller flood flows in by bus and taxi and a few brokers walk to work from the Downtown Athletic Club.

To steeplejack Carl Stengard, Wall Street is a wonderful place to get away from He gets to see it from a bosun's chair at the top of the flagpole on the 60 Wall tower each time the beacon light burns out and he goes up to replace it.

This breath-taking view from the Chase Manhattan building looks straight down on the roof of the Federal Reserve, then north along William Street to Foley Square and government buildings (to the right are the Brooklyn Bridge approach and the Alfred E. Smith Houses), and uptown to the Empire State building at the horizon.

In 1882 two young men from Providence, Charles H. Dow and Edward D. Jones, formed a company to provide an hourly financial news bulletin service. Seven years later they began publishing a daily paper made up of news reprinted from the bulletins — the WALL STREET JOURNAL. *In 1902 Clarence W. Barron bought the company and made it national in scope.*

On January 2, 1897, Dow Jones began publishing daily average closing prices of selected active industrial and railroad stocks, adding a public-utility list in 1929. By adjusting the divisor for stock splits, a comparable average over the years is always available.

While everyone quotes the current Dow Jones Averages, few people know how the figures are determined and, until the stocks were assembled for these pictures, no one had seen them all together. Goodbody and Company supplied 100-share certificates of the 30 industrial (CENTER), *15 utility* (LEFT), *and 20 railroad stocks. On August 22, 1960, the value of these shares was $374,187.50.*

The New York Federal Reserve Bank usually holds fifty billion dollars in cash, bonds and gold. Millions of dollars arrive daily in armored trucks from the city's banks, for deposit to their credit.

Armored-car guards deliver paper money in sealed containers from the banks. Later, the money is sorted to determine its fitness for further circulation or whether it should be "retired" and destroyed.

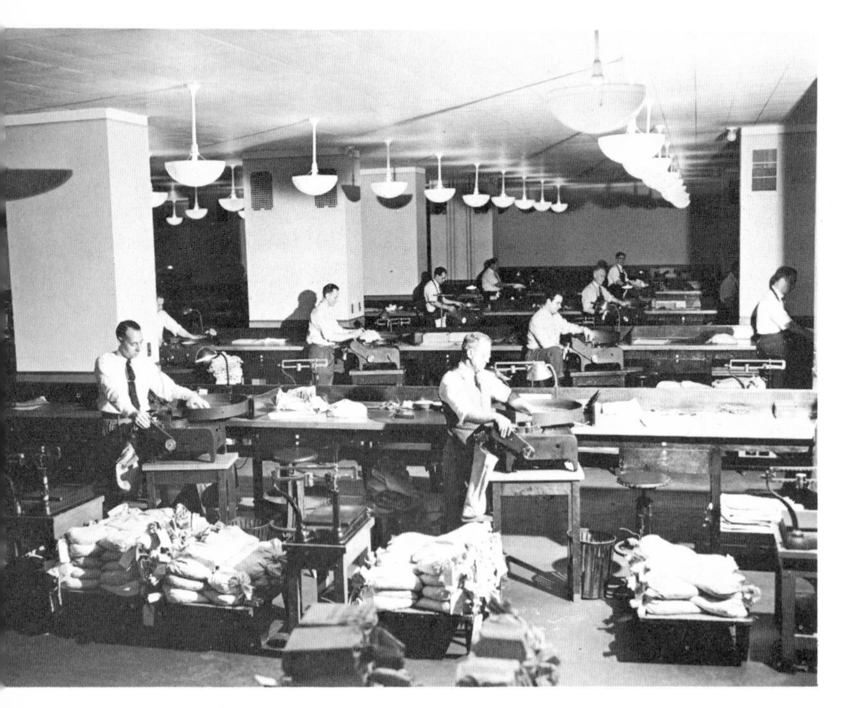

Coin deposits are verified by checkers who operate machines which automatically count the contents of the bags. Tons of pennies, nickels, and silver coins pass through the Federal Reserve each day.

Currency is also counted by machine and sorted in one operation. It is at this point that counterfeits are detected and ragged, worn bills are removed and are replaced.

averted. The system also provides a nation-wide clearing house for checks, a unified organization to hold the funds of the United States government and thus act as the government's banker, and a voice for the banker, the businessman, and the average citizen on questions and decisions of monetary policy.

The most important job of the Federal Reserve is to keep the country in economic balance by increasing or decreasing its holdings of government securities, via the Open Market Committee, which functions in New York; changing the reserve requirements of banks as well as the margin requirements for stock-exchange trading; and fixing the discount, or interest rate, at which it will lend money to member banks. It also makes other loans, administers credit regulations, collects and analyzes economic information, conducts international banking operations, and supervises and examines member banks.

After deducting operating expenses, dividends to member banks, and additions to surplus, all the

New currency from Washington arrives by registered mail and is checked and counted. Packaged in bundles of four thousand bills, there are about 800,000 pieces of money visible in this picture.

Federal Reserve banks act as clearing houses and ship checks to each other by air to save interest, using fire-resistant, crash-proof containers. New York sends out a ton of checks a night.

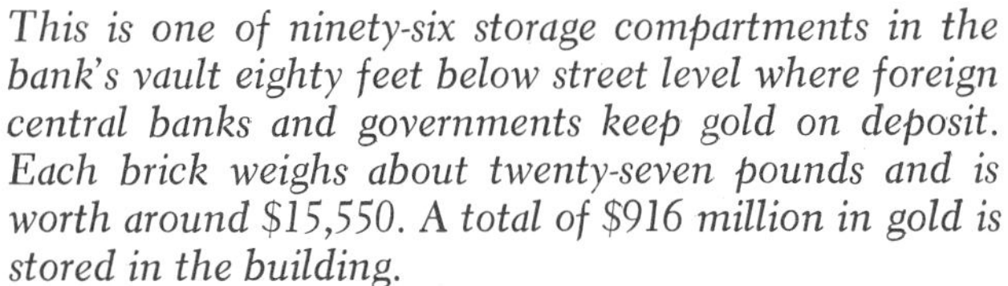
This is one of ninety-six storage compartments in the bank's vault eighty feet below street level where foreign central banks and governments keep gold on deposit. Each brick weighs about twenty-seven pounds and is worth around $15,550. A total of $916 million in gold is stored in the building.

When currency has been mutilated or is found too worn to be continued in circulation, it is destroyed. However, before being sent to Washington, it is canceled and sliced in half horizontally.

Treasury bonds, notes, and certificates of indebtedness which the Federal Reserve redeems or exchanges are sorted, listed, and prepared for shipment to Washington in this department.

At Old Slip, conveniently across the street from the police station, is the United States Assay Office, where gold and silver bricks are made for foreign countries, mining companies, and jewelers.

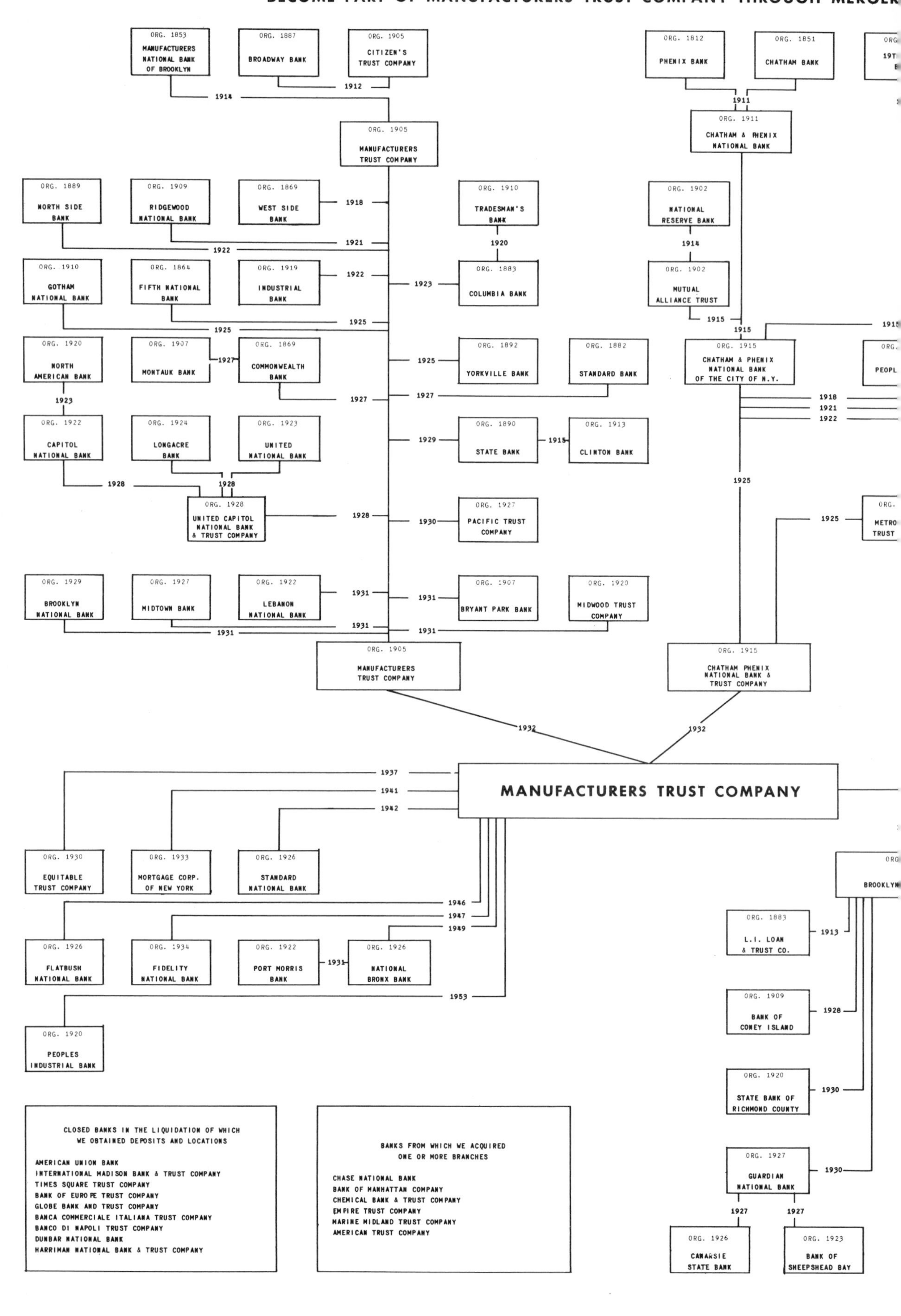

HISTORY CHART—MANUFACTURERS TRUST COMP
SHOWING THE ORIGINS AND AMALGAMATIONS OF THE VARIOUS INSTITUTI
BECOME PART OF MANUFACTURERS TRUST COMPANY THROUGH MERGER
ORG. 1853 MANUFACTURERS NATIONAL BANK OF BROOKLYN
ORG. 1887 BROADWAY BANK
ORG. 1905 CITIZEN'S TRUST COMPANY
1912
1914
ORG. 1905 MANUFACTURERS TRUST COMPANY
ORG. 1812 PHENIX BANK
ORG. 1851 CHATHAM BANK
1911
ORG. 1911 CHATHAM & PHENIX NATIONAL BANK
ORG. 1889 NORTH SIDE BANK
ORG. 1909 RIDGEWOOD NATIONAL BANK
ORG. 1869 WEST SIDE BANK
1918
1921
1922
ORG. 1910 TRADESMAN'S BANK
1920
ORG. 1883 COLUMBIA BANK
1923
ORG. 1902 NATIONAL RESERVE BANK
1914
ORG. 1902 MUTUAL ALLIANCE TRUST
1915
ORG. 1910 GOTHAM NATIONAL BANK
ORG. 1864 FIFTH NATIONAL BANK
ORG. 1919 INDUSTRIAL BANK
1925
ORG. 1920 NORTH AMERICAN BANK
ORG. 1907 MONTAUK BANK
1927
ORG. 1869 COMMONWEALTH BANK
ORG. 1892 YORKVILLE BANK
ORG. 1882 STANDARD BANK
ORG. 1915 CHATHAM & PHENIX NATIONAL BANK OF THE CITY OF N.Y.
1918
1921
1922
1923
ORG. 1922 CAPITOL NATIONAL BANK
ORG. 1924 LONGACRE BANK
ORG. 1923 UNITED NATIONAL BANK
1929
ORG. 1890 STATE BANK
ORG. 1913 CLINTON BANK
1928
ORG. 1928 UNITED CAPITOL NATIONAL BANK & TRUST COMPANY
1930
ORG. 1927 PACIFIC TRUST COMPANY
ORG. 1929 BROOKLYN NATIONAL BANK
ORG. 1927 MIDTOWN BANK
ORG. 1922 LEBANON NATIONAL BANK
1931
ORG. 1907 BRYANT PARK BANK
ORG. 1920 MIDWOOD TRUST COMPANY
ORG. 1905 MANUFACTURERS TRUST COMPANY
ORG. 1915 CHATHAM PHENIX NATIONAL BANK & TRUST COMPANY
1932
MANUFACTURERS TRUST COMPANY
1937
1941
1942
ORG. 1930 EQUITABLE TRUST COMPANY
ORG. 1933 MORTGAGE CORP. OF NEW YORK
ORG. 1926 STANDARD NATIONAL BANK
1946
1947
1949
ORG. 1926 FLATBUSH NATIONAL BANK
ORG. 1934 FIDELITY NATIONAL BANK
ORG. 1922 PORT MORRIS BANK
1931
ORG. 1926 NATIONAL BRONX BANK
1953
ORG. 1920 PEOPLES INDUSTRIAL BANK
ORG. 1883 L.I. LOAN & TRUST CO.
1913
ORG. 1909 BANK OF CONEY ISLAND
1928
ORG. 1920 STATE BANK OF RICHMOND COUNTY
1930
ORG. 1927 GUARDIAN NATIONAL BANK
1927
ORG. 1926 CANARSIE STATE BANK
ORG. 1923 BANK OF SHEEPSHEAD BAY
CLOSED BANKS IN THE LIQUIDATION OF WHICH WE OBTAINED DEPOSITS AND LOCATIONS
AMERICAN UNION BANK
INTERNATIONAL MADISON BANK & TRUST COMPANY
TIMES SQUARE TRUST COMPANY
BANK OF EUROPE TRUST COMPANY
GLOBE BANK AND TRUST COMPANY
BANCA COMMERCIALE ITALIANA TRUST COMPANY
BANCO DI NAPOLI TRUST COMPANY
DUNBAR NATIONAL BANK
HARRIMAN NATIONAL BANK & TRUST COMPANY
BANKS FROM WHICH WE ACQUIRED ONE OR MORE BRANCHES
CHASE NATIONAL BANK
BANK OF MANHATTAN COMPANY
CHEMICAL BANK & TRUST COMPANY
EMPIRE TRUST COMPANY
MARINE MIDLAND TRUST COMPANY
AMERICAN TRUST COMPANY

Family tree of a fast-growing bank. Manufacturers Trust Company today is the result of mergers and purchases which involved eighty-six other banks as well as vigorous expansion of new branches. It has 114 offices, all in New York City, offers seventy different banking services, has over $3 billion in deposits, and is sixth in size in the United States, fifth in the city. The stockholders of the Manufacturers Trust and the Hanover Bank have approved the merger of the two.

Federal Reserve banks turn the balance—profits earned mainly from holdings of government securities—back to the Treasury. The New York bank's yearly contribution runs over seventy million dollars.

The activities of the twelve Federal Reserve banks are co-ordinated and supervised by seven men appointed to fourteen-year terms by the President. These men constitute the Federal Reserve Board, in Washington, which formulates national credit policies and supervises their execution. It is now headed by the former first salaried President of the New York Stock Exchange, William McChesney Martin, Jr.

The appointment of Martin and the image he projects symbolize the new wave that has engulfed and washed away the old order of banking. Within almost every reader's memory is the stereotyped picture of banks and bankers as austere, forbidding, coldly formal. In the old days the average man could obtain a loan—provided he could prove he did not need the money. Those who desperately needed loans some years ago could borrow money at almost usurious rates of interest from local finance companies who frequently were known to stand by to snatch the borrower's car, furniture, or house the moment he fell behind in his payments. Then banks all over the land began to emulate an imaginative, daring California financier, A. P. Giannini, possibly because the Bank of America, which he founded, had become the largest in the world. By conducting banking as a personalized business rather than as an impersonal profession, providing innumerable customer services, competing with the finance companies and offering decent interest rates, opening convenient branches with friendly managers and personnel who never looked down their noses at the small depositor, the Bank of America has been able to roll up deposits of ten and a half billion dollars, held in seven and a half million deposit accounts in 664 branches throughout California, a state where the banking

Looking up Broadway from Bowling Green, over which former Mayor Abraham De Peyster (1692–1695) still presides. The statue was presented by a seventh-generation direct descendant.

The modern Number 2 Broadway building, on the site of the Produce Exchange, is across from Bowling Green, bracketed by Number 1 Broadway (LEFT) *and the Custom House* (RIGHT). *Here it is seen from a spot on Battery Place where the El station once stood and Giovanni da Verrazano once landed.*

ower Broadway to the Battery, seen from he top of the Irving Trust building. On this hort stretch of the longest street in the vorld (it extends 150 miles to Albany) is the ite of Adriaen Block's first rude camp. In he bay, above the liner, are the Statue of iberty and Ellis Island.

Trinity Place at Christmas time. Twelve floors and 111 office worlds were caught in Berenice Abbott's photograph of the Cunard building during the holiday season.

Occupying ten of the skyscraper's sixty stories, a crew of 1,223 men constructing the Chase Manhattan building took a half-hour off to pose for their picture. The photograph cost the bank $10,000 in lost working time. The completed structure houses 15,000 office workers—as well as the Burr-Hamilton dueling pistols.

Few people ever look at the Stock Exchange statuary. The group of eleven figures in white marble typifies American commerce and industry, with "Integrity" (CENTER) *flanked by "Wealth Producing Sources."* RIGHT: *"Agriculture" and "Mining" groups;* LEFT: *"Scientific Appliances," "Motive Power," "Designer and Mechanic." The waves at extreme ends denote ocean-to-ocean influence of the exchange.*

laws are far more sympathetic to branch-banking than New York.

California-style banking has spread eastward and the stereotyped banker of yesterday has been replaced by a friendly official who is still governed by sound banking principles but no longer acts in the aloof, formal manner of prewar days. He cannot afford to. There is too much competition for the dollar about to be deposited or to be borrowed. This competition has been responsible for the wave of bank consolidations during the late 1950's, as bankers merged facilities in order to operate more efficiently and less expensively, and joined talents to broaden their services and influence.

The merger movement, which has been so pronounced among banks and businesses in recent years, has not been noticeable among Wall Street brokerage firms, where the trend has been to build up and expand organizations from within, rather than to combine them. The only distinct structural change has been for firms to incorporate rather than continue unwieldy partnership agreements. The other trend, already noted, was toward bringing more people into the market and providing them with information and service, no matter how small the account might be at the start.

The influx of new investors has been accompanied by a marked increase of interest on the part of the general lay public in stocks and the stock market. In 1959, the number of visitors to the New York Stock Exchange rose to almost four hundred thousand, nearly 20 per cent more than the previous year. What these visitors saw was the activity on the floor of the exchange, an extremely familiar sight, but one which is confusing and difficult to explain.

The floor, two-thirds the size of a football field, frequently looks like one right after a game that has ended in a riot. However, what appears to be confusion and chaos is really the most efficient and orderly method that American finance has worked out for the trading of securities. This is an auction market, where on an average day forty thousand packages of stocks and bonds are bought and sold by some nine hundred brokers, who make up the active two-thirds of the New York Stock Exchange membership. For a substantial sum ($110,000 to $157,000 in 1959) a man may purchase the privilege of trading on the floor with other members—that is, after he has been thoroughly investigated and voted in as a member.

He cannot delegate this privilege to anyone else, not to a partner, an employee, or even his wife—especially not his wife, for women are barred from working on the floor. If he cannot function in person, he turns his business over to another broker who executes transactions for him. There are exchange

"Stage door" of the New York Stock Exchange at 11 Wall is used by brokers, the floor staff, and a thousand other Big Board backstage workers.

The Stock Exchange floor forty-seven minutes before opening is almost deserted. Windows at the Broad and New Street ends are fifty feet high, ninety-six feet wide. With the skylight, they provide abundant light.

Five minutes after trading starts, the floor is jumping with activity as brokers begin executing overnight orders. At lower left is Post 8, where Phillips Petroleum is traded; on the wall at left is annunciator board for paging members. The flag is that of New York State.

On the next two pages is Marvin Newman's "Floor of the Stock Exchange" shot taken from a hole in the ceiling five stories up. The scene brings to mind Russel Crouse's skeptical 1938 comment: "It's still the largest green baize table in the world." But the trend from gambling to investment for income grows stronger each year and the ethics of brokers are high.

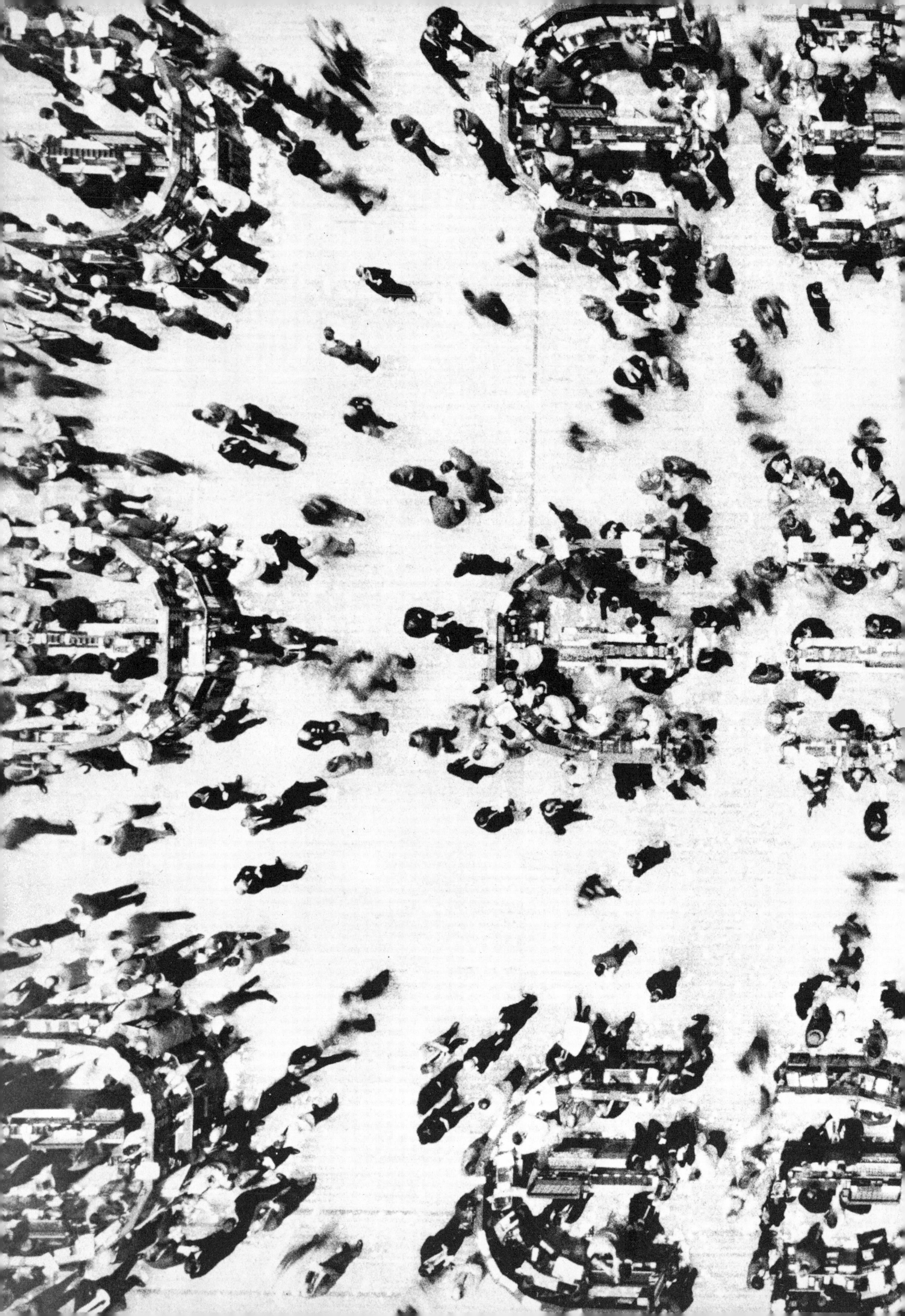

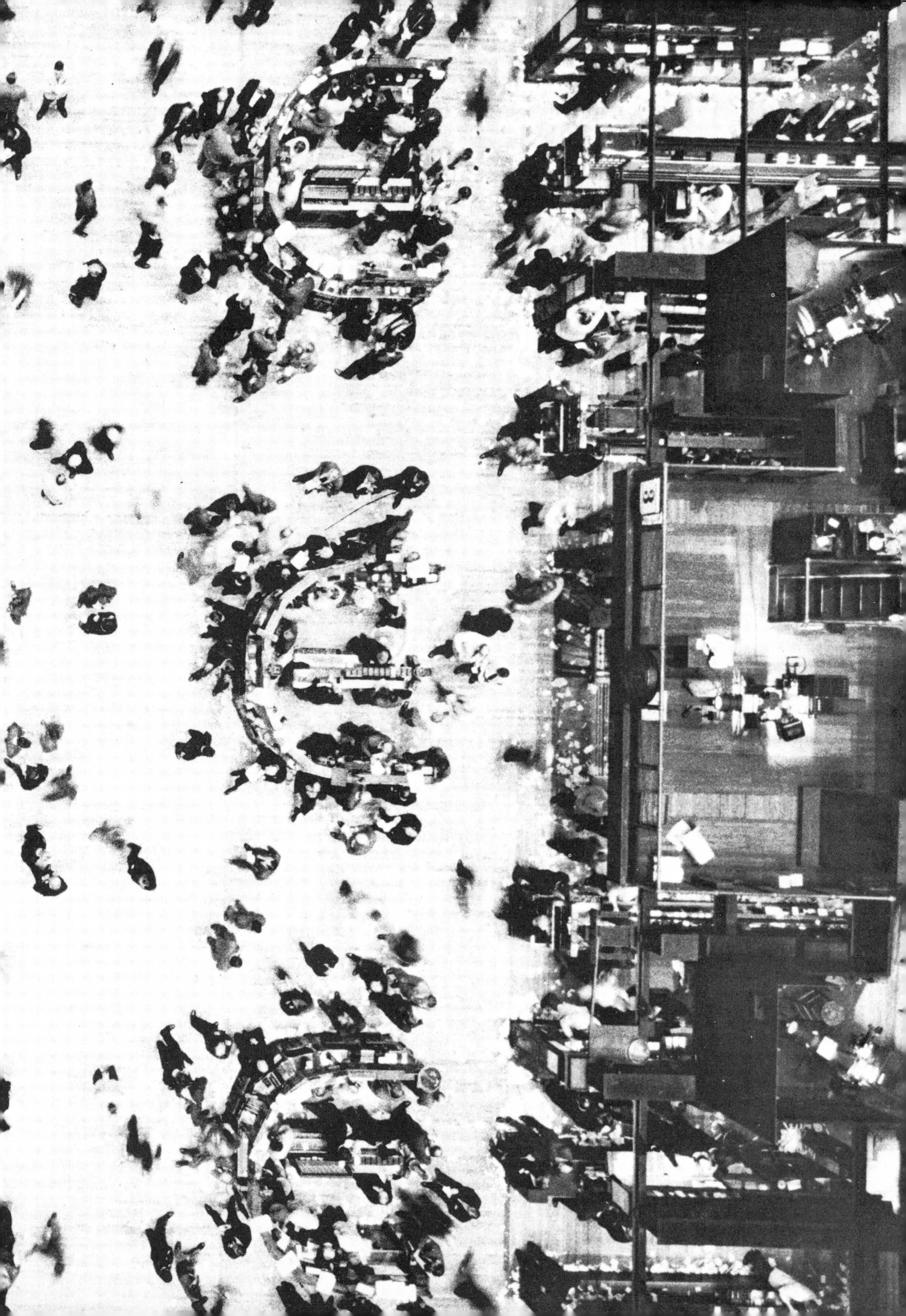

The catch-all for stocks on the floor is Post 30 where about 230 of the least-active issues listed are traded. Post 30 stocks are bought and sold in ten-share lots, instead of the usual units of hundreds.

A family team of specialists dealing in American Tobacco, Curtiss-Wright, Telautograph, and fifty others (RIGHT TO LEFT): *John A. Coleman, his son, Thomas A., and his brother, William A.*

members, known as floor or two-dollar brokers—although their fees range from $1.25 to $4.00, averaging $3.30—who do nothing but represent absent or never-on-the floor members. The latter hold their memberships as investments, or for the trading privileges it gives their brokerage firms. Among these are 165 members who live and have offices out of town.

Of the total membership, 1,051 members are associated with 661 brokerage firms, each of which can refer to itself as "Member of the New York Stock Exchange." These firms are subject to the rules and regulations of the New York Stock Exchange and the Securities and Exchange Commission, as are any partners and employees who are not themselves members of the exchange. At the beginning of 1960 the New York Stock Exchange "community" throughout the country consisted of 6,226 members and either partners or stockholders of firms (including 427 women), 24,898 registered representatives—not all customers' men, since 1,143 were women —42,490 other employees of members, and 1,386 employees of the exchange.

The majority of the firms associated with the New York Stock Exchange are commission houses dealing

The brother team of William M. Meehan (LEFT) *and Joseph A. Meehan are specialists in Ford and RCA, which, as Radio, was a pet roller coaster of their late father, Mike Meehan.*

Pausing at the water cooler are two of the Merrill Lynch team, Arthur L. Kerrigan (LEFT), *floor general, and Allen A. Pierce.*

with the public and over half of the exchange members are commission-house brokers. Another quarter are specialists who act as common denominator between buyer and seller. Then there are over a hundred odd-lot brokers who handle transactions not rounded off in one-hundred-share units, 170 two-dollar brokers, and about thirty-five floor traders, doing business for themselves, operating with their own capital, getting into and out of different stocks all day long, trying to stay ahead of the market. They find it less expensive to maintain a seat than pay brokerage commissions to others.

On January 1, 1960, there were 1,507 issues of stock in 1,116 companies valued at $307,708,000,000 listed on the Big Board and 1,180 bond issues with a market value of $105,422,000,000. The total number of shares of stock was 5,847,000,000. This is a staggering figure that can perhaps best be visualized by thinking of each share as a single certificate. If that were the case, piles of these single shares placed side by side on the floor of the exchange would cover every bit of space and rise to a height of thirty feet, about as high as the railing of the visitors' gallery.

While only about 2 per cent of all domestic public corporations have their common stock listed on the New York Stock Exchange, they are by far the most important segment. These corporations employ one-fifth of all civilian workers; their assets are about 30

Another second-generation broker is Bernard E. Smith, Jr. (LEFT), *the son of "Sell 'Em" Ben Smith, with Harold Hirschberg.*

In the following spread, John Groth, a renowned combat artist who covered the battlefields in World War II and the Korean War, has captured the movement, pace, and conflict of the Stock Exchange in a vigorous, incisive style that no camera can match.

John Groth
New York Stock Exchange

per cent of the total capital invested by private business; and they make 35 per cent of all corporate sales and about 65 per cent of all corporate profits—fourteen billion dollars in 1958.

The total value of all the bits of paper which members of the exchange could trade as 1960 began was over 413 billion dollars. Since the assessed value of all the property on Manhattan is around sixteen billion dollars, this sum would purchase more than twenty-five Manhattan islands.

In addition to the members on the floor of the exchange there are the clerks who work for them at the telephones, relaying orders from and confirmations to the home office, and the clerks who work for the specialists at their posts. Specialists' clerks wear red badges, phone clerks yellow ones, and relief clerks, for either, green. Members wear all-white oval badges, except for the odd-lot brokers—the DeCoppet and Doremus men can be distinguished by their pink-

John Groth's quick, informal sketches of members of the Stock Exchange on the trading floor graphically evoke the shifting moods and tempo of their working day.

and-white insignia from the Carlisle and Jacquelin men who wear green-and-white ones.

Among the employees of the exchange itself, the different jobs are designated by the jackets worn. Quotation clerks and tube men wear black jackets (although at some posts quotation clerks wear gray jackets with a yellow patch number); the pages all wear gray jackets; the exchange supervisors (one at each post) wear black jackets and identifying badges, while the reporters wear black jackets, too.

Although the rules require the selling member to report each transaction, a Stock Exchange reporter eavesdrops for every sale, makes a note of the stock symbol and price, pops the note into a cylinder which is inserted into a pneumatic conveying tube which swiftly delivers it to the central stock-ticker sending station. There a girl types the transaction so that it appears simultaneously on ticker tapes and projection screens throughout the country and in the corners of the exchange trading hall. From the conclusion of the transaction to its appearance on the tape ordinarily takes less than two minutes, unless trading is so heavy that the ticker falls behind.

A quotation clerk reports bids and offers, rather than actual transactions, and his messages go up to the central quotation room, where some seventy girls sit answering the queries of member firms. Traffic in quotations has gone as high as 173,793 queries a day (October 29, 1937) and currently runs over eighty thousand daily. When the ticker is inactive on sales, bids and offers are printed to keep it running. During a three-and-a-half-million-share day about 1,750 feet of tape are used per ticker. At the frenzied peak of the 1929 Crash, October 29, five miles of tape slithered out of each ticker to record the more than sixteen million shares traded. (Richard E. Whitney later said that twenty-one million shares was closer to the actual total, although five million never got on the tape.) In that fatal year, the three thousand ticker machines leased out by the New York Stock Exchange's Quotation Company consumed one million miles of tape.

Except under special circumstances no woman is allowed on the floor of the Stock Exchange, but almost a thousand work upstairs, including these forty who answer phones in the quotation room.

Nimble-fingered girls such as this one operate the complex IBM machines in the Stock Exchange Clearing House, the central point for the transfer of shares members have traded on the floor.

After lunch at the Stock Exchange club on the sixth floor of the building, President G. (for George) Keith Funston (RIGHT) chats with James C. Kellogg III, former Chairman of the Board of Governors. Behind Funston is the bronze statue of a Bull and Bear locked in combat, bought by the club at the Jesse Livermore auction.

In addition to 3,100 stock and 175 bond tickers in operation in the almost three thousand offices of Stock Exchange member firms, there are 621 Teleregister electrical quotation boards in brokerage offices.

Sitting in the three thousand "funeral parlors," as the board rooms of the brokerage houses have been called, keeping a hypnotized eye on the electronic antics of Teleregister panels or the Translux tape projections, are the regulars—their numbers estimated between three hundred thousand and half a million. Among them are people who cannot buy a stock, pat it on the head, put it away, and, more or less, forget about it. These are the amateur professionals who are "in the market." Some are would-be Bernard Baruchs and Jesse Livermores, and occasionally a would-like-to-be Hetty Green. A large percentage of them are retired farmers and merchants who find golf frightening or a bore and a daily routine a necessity. There are the lucky ones who are trying to do even better and the hapless souls who say they only want to get even again. Most of them have done well, but regret they did not buy twice as much or did not wait for a higher price before selling.

There are, of course, the system players—systems based on cycles, sunspots, charts, reports, numerology, astrology, tea leaves—and why not? Didn't the S.E.C. bar a Wall Street financial adviser who admitted his predictions were partially based on portents he read into the comic strips? There are also regulars who are respected by fellow board-room sitters as experts on one stock or one industry. Some are a delight and a source of income for their account executives. Others rarely do anything more than sit. The hero of the board room is the one who passed on a tip that paid off. The villain is not so much the man who offered a sour tip as the one who touted his neighbor off a profitable one.

For some men the board room is a club, a home away from home, an office where he gets his messages, a tower of rumors and a grave of hopes. If the regular lives in California, the time difference may find him in his seat downtown at 7:00 A.M. and, at 12:30, when action in New York closes, he can turn his full attention to the Pacific Coast Exchange, which operates simultaneously in San Francisco and Los Angeles.

Whatever some people may feel about the regular and the board room, they are both an integral part of the Wall Street story. Not only are they both here to stay, but their numbers are growing as more people find themselves with more time—and more money—on their hands.

As more women become shareholders, the "boiler-room" stock-salesmen have developed new techniques to part the ladies from their money, taking advantage of methods of communication never dreamed of by their 1920 counterparts. Instead of limiting themselves to the well-worked field of widows and orphans, the con men have begun to concentrate on the well-to-do housewife who shares a joint checking account with her husband. Before a selling crew invades a town, the stock is given an expensive but subtle build-up on television. For instance, if the promoter has acquired a million shares of a limping gadget manufacturer named the Coogle Carrot Curler Company at a penny a share, he buys time on local television stations and uses it to show commercials demonstrating the product several times a day for several weeks. This is one time when the advertiser does not care if he sells his product or not—he may even lose a nickel on every carrot curler ordered. But when the horde of telephone salesmen ring up the ladies of the town and offer them Coogle Carrot Curler Common, at the ridiculously low price of a dollar a share, they do not have to explain what a carrot curler is or what a sensation they have created recently in the kitchens of the community.

Mrs. Housewife too often proves to be a sitting duck and is given no opportunity to consult her husband about the investment. Still dazed by the fast spiel and the lure of a quick profit on a stock that is climbing fast, she hands over a check to the messenger who arrives at her door, stock in hand, almost as soon as the telephone salesman has finished his pitch. The fat profit, of course, never materializes. And by the time the monthly statement arrives and the husband gets his surprise, it is a sad one.

This has been an extremely effective get-rich-quick scheme—for the operators—because it is a new twist on the gold-brick racket, a more subtle one to fit the times, and one aimed at an almost untapped field, the newly prosperous, financially inexperienced wife who can be persuaded that putting two and two together will result in the sum of twenty-two.

But returning to the legitimate companies and Wall Street, there are several score of stocks now traded on the two Manhattan exchanges as well as

A record-breaking flashlight photograph showing almost the entire Stock Exchange main hall was taken with a battery of Sylvania bulbs which gave a light burst equal to the output of 300,000 watts. The picture was made just before closing time, when 599 men were visible on the floor.

A gong rings every second for the last ten seconds before quitting time at 3:30 P.M. Immediately after the final bong, trading is prohibited. The tension breaks, the members relax and head for the exits.

Robert Bookman, one of the most urbane members, was a floor (or two-dollar) broker. A fastidious dresser, he always rolled up the cuffs of his coat, shirt, and trousers at work, unrolling them at the end of the day.

Charles Marsico rests his weary feet after a day of walking and trading (eight to twelve miles) for Merrill Lynch. Since We the People became a corporation Marsico has been one of the vice-presidents.

over the counter which provide a sense of historical continuity for a span of more than two centuries. Everyone knows that the Street is old, but comparatively few people realize how many big American firms began here and how long ago they were founded.

The most ancient of the firms that have maintained an independent identity is P. Lorillard Company, established by a young French snuff-grinder at 4 Chatham Street (now Park Row) in 1760. Pierre Lorillard, killed by Hessian soldiers during the Revolution, was succeeded by his sons, Peter and George, who began to advertise chewing and smoking tobacco as well as snuff in 1789. In addition to "Segars and Ladies twist," they sold pigtail, hogtail, plug, and prig or carrot tobacco. In 1830 their wholesale house was at 42 Chatham Street. When Peter Lorillard died in 1843, former Mayor Philip Hone recorded in his celebrated diary:

Died this morning at his seat in Westchester County, Mr. Peter Lorillard . . . in the 80th year of his age. . . . He was a tobacconist, and his memory will be preserved in the annals of New York by the celebrity of "Lorillard's Snuff and Tobacco." He led people by the nose for the best part of a century and made his enormous fortune by giving them to chew that which they could not swallow.

Lorillard stock has been on the Big Board since the dissolution of the Tobacco trust in 1911. In 1958 it moved its headquarters uptown to the blue-tinted twenty-nine-story Lorillard building at 200 East Forty-second Street. Nowadays it sells almost a half billion dollars' worth of tobacco, almost all of it in the shape of cigarets, a form the original Pierre would have difficulty recognizing.

Among the other early firms listed on the New York Stock Exchange and the dates of their founding (or the dates of the founding of the original companies out of which they evolved) are:

Devoe and Raynolds Paint Company (now a division of Merritt-Chapman and Scott Corporation,

Although the average transaction occupies two inches of ticker tape, the length of paper going through each ticker on an average day is between one-quarter and one-third of a mile, as shown by the 1,500 feet of tape stretched out on the floor of the Stock Exchange after a typical trading session.

1754; American Bank Note Company, 1795, Revere Copper and Brass, Inc., 1801; Colgate-Palmolive Company, 1806; Consolidated Edison and Delaware and Hudson Company, 1823; Arnold Constablé Corporation, 1825; New York Central Railroad (through an early omnibus company), 1826; Baltimore and Ohio Railroad, 1827; McKesson and Robbins, Inc., 1833; Phelps-Dodge Corporation, 1834; B. T. Babbitt Corporation, which began handing out samples of its scouring powder from wagons at the Cortlandt Street Ferry in 1836; Hat Corporation of America (Knox, Dobbs, Cavanaugh),

Widespread interest in stock fluctuations led J. R. Williston and Beane to install a ticker in the lobby of the Brass Rail Restaurant. Stock tickers in uptown New York restaurants were an innovation, but they were first installed in Wall Street eating places almost a century ago.

Thousands of investment clubs have been organized since 1955. This is the Bridge Investment Club of Westfield, New Jersey, composed of four couples who meet to play cards and pool their funds to buy $100 worth of stocks once a month.

1838; Adams Express Company, 1840; George H. Morrill Company (now a division of Sun Chemical Corporation), 1840; Gimbel Brothers, Inc., 1842; United States Rubber Company, 1843; Allied Chemical Corporation, 1845; Pennsylvania Railroad, 1846; Philip Morris, Inc., 1847; Charles Pfizer Company, 1849; Singer Manufacturing Company (formerly Singer Sewing Machine Company), 1851; Western Union Telegraph Company, Erie Railroad, and Corning Glass Works, 1851; Otis Elevator Company, 1853; W. R. Grace and Company, in 1854, now as then located on Hanover Square; Austin Nichols and Company, Inc., 1855; Manhattan Shirt Company, Joseph E. Seagram and Sons, Inc., and the Borden Company, 1857; Macy's, E. R. Squibb and Sons (now a division of Olin Mathieson Chemical Corporation), and the original firm that later became Johns-Manville Corporation, 1858; Great Atlantic and Pacific Tea Company, 1859.

On the American Stock Exchange, which itself dates (as the old Curb Market) from 1849, one stock is listed representing a firm, the Insurance Company of North America, that was doing business in New York in 1792. Another listing is R. Hoe and Company, Inc., which began manufacturing simple, hand-powered printing presses at 63 Fulton Street in 1805, and now produces high-speed newspaper presses such as those used by the *Wall Street Journal* today. Other firms which began in early Manhattan and are now listed on the American Exchange include: Black, Starr and Gorham, 1810; Sidney Blumenthal and Company, Inc., 1854; Angostura-Wuppermann Corporation, 1825; Chesebrough-Pond's, Inc., 1873.

The over-the-counter market deals in the stocks of many banks and insurance companies which started in old New York: The Bank of New York, 1784; Chase Manhattan and the Providence Washington Insurance Company, 1799; Manufacturers Trust Company and First National City Bank of New York, 1812; Hartford Fire Insurance Company, 1818; Chemical Bank New York Trust Company, 1824; Hanover Bank, 1831; Morgan Guaranty Trust Company, 1839; Dun and Bradstreet, Inc., 1841; United States Life Insurance Company in the City of New York, 1850; Pacific Insurance Company of New York and Irving Trust Company, 1851; Hanover Insurance Company, Aetna Life Insurance Company, Home Insurance Company, and United States Trust Company, 1853.

In addition to these venerable companies, the over-the-counter market deals in as many as fifty thousand other issues of stocks. Despite the fact that it is the largest, it is the least-known stock- and bond-trading market in the United States. First of all, the term "over the counter" is outmoded. It is almost entirely an over-the-telephone market, although cables, telegrams, and the mails are also used to negotiate and close transactions. It differs from the two New York and the regional exchanges in that the members act for themselves in almost every case—buying from one individual and selling to the next customer. Since it is theoretically possible to make whopping profits (or losses), trading over the counter is supervised by the National Association of Securities Dealers, Inc., a voluntary self-policing group set up by Congress in 1939 as an experiment in self-regulation by the dealers with the encouragement and overall supervision of the Securities and Exchange Commission. Almost every reputable dealer in securities selling direct to the public, including Stock Exchange members who also deal in unlisted issues, is a member of the NASD. As of June 30, 1960, there were 4,372 members, many more than the number belonging to all of the exchanges in the United States. Working for these members were 90,180 registered representatives, some on part-time, in comparison with the 26,000 registered representatives of the New York Stock Exchange.

Mammoth stockholder meetings, such as this at the Kingsbridge Armory in the Bronx, play a part in improving owner-corporate relations. Here 1/135th of American Telephone and Telegraph shareholders vote in favor of a three-for-one split.

What "Average Voter" is to politicians and "John Q. Public" to editorial writers, "Aunt Jane" is to securities salesmen. At a United States Steel meeting, President Benjamin Fairless greets a typical stockholder, Miriam Cerf, seated with her sister, Carrie Cerf.

Since dealings are not recorded, it has always been difficult to keep any statistics on the over-the-counter market, and since transactions take place at the two ends of a telephone hookup, at the rate of over a hundred thousand a day, there is no such thing as a central market. The NASD constantly checks its members' trades and books and keeps dealer profits down to 5 per cent, which is still higher than the average exchange commission. Members can be disciplined for taking too high a gain, especially when any irregularities are revealed, but it is also possible for a trader to lose his shirt by purchasing for his own account stocks which go sour.

Bank stocks and securities of insurance companies find their market over the counter as do all new

Lewis Gilbert, the leading force behind the small stockholders' fight against management autocracy and for cumulative voting, proper auditing, and full and frank reports, is seen here on a closed-circuit television screen of a joint New York-Chicago meeting of American Machinery and Foundry. His family owns shares in 600 corporations and he makes the goal of corporate democracy a career.

issues, such as Ford when it first went on sale, before they are admitted for listing and trade on one of the exchanges. Small or local issues are traded between NASD dealers, for themselves or clients, and bond issues of states and municipalities as well as mutual funds are almost exclusively dealt over the counter. It is also the biggest market for government bonds.

This is the most flexible of markets and one where the officials are tough policemen. More than one hundred members have been expelled for practices which were frowned upon, and even highly respected companies have been suspended from trading for the unethical actions of a single employee.

While it is possible for a leading new stock like Ford to "graduate" directly to the New York Stock Exchange from the over-the-counter market soon after it has been issued, by far the greater number of new issues on the Big Board come from its younger associate, the old Curb (officially designated the American Stock Exchange on January 5, 1953), which acts as an aging agent or prep school for many an issue the senior exchange eventually appropriates for itself. This might seem unfair, except that it is almost a case of stealing from yourself. The roster of the American Exchange lists around three-fourths of the firms which are also members of the New York Stock Exchange. The officials of both boards work closely together and Edward C. Werle became Chairman of the New York Stock Exchange after having served in that capacity at the American Stock Exchange. Innovations, such as closing on Saturday and remaining open a half hour later the other five days, are usually first tried out at Trinity Place before Broad Street accepts them.

Another sign of growth has been the plan for the formation of a third stock market in New York, The National Stock Exchange, with headquarters at the New York Mercantile Exchange.

In spite of the business pace which keeps Wall Street hopping, it is possible for almost anyone to

The second-ranking stock exchange in the nation is the former Curb, now American, where each session begins by striking a gong on the Little Board balcony overlooking the trading floor.

Before 1921, when the Curb moved indoors, rugged phone clerks hung out of office windows and perched on ledges to signal the Curb brokers on Broad Street below. Now snugly ensconced in rows of booths they still communicate with the traders by means of their fingers.

Members of the American Stock Exchange wear linen coats, wigwag to banks of phone clerks at both sides of the 152-foot-long trading floor, and buy and sell at twenty-two octagonal posts. The membership is about two-fifths that of the New York Stock Exchange, while the daily volume of shares and the number of issues traded in are approximately 40 per cent of the Big Board's.

BROKER ELY MARGOLIS DEMONSTRATES HAND SIGNALS HE USES FROM THE FLOOR

sily recognizable—the letter "L."

Either "three-eighths" or letter "M."

"Eight."

)ne-eighth bid, one-fourth offered."

"One-eighth bid, three-fourths offered."

"Three-eighths bid, seven-eighths offered."

Like the Big Board, the American Exchange holds open house for visitors during trading hours, shows movies of its history, and displays products of listed companies. A Bronx couple, Mr. and Mrs. John Acampora, are guided on a tour by Harold Hart, descendant of Bernard Hart, first Secretary of the New York Stock Exchange.

Watchdog of Wall Street is the five-man Securities and Exchange Commission — "the cop on the corner of Broad and Wall." Seen in session in Washington, they are (LEFT TO RIGHT): *Byron D. Woodside, William L. Cary (Chairman), Edward N. Gadsby, and J. Allen Frear. Absent: Earl F. Hastings.*

Hole-in-the-Wall-Street side of the Stock Exchange Annex is occupied by Morris Bernstein, who has operated the busiest newsstand in the district for forty years. He now sells a million papers a year.

Not many years ago "weekend" was only a society-page word and Wall Street workers labored six days a week. Today they put in thirty-five to forty hours in five days and enjoy 100 per cent more leisure.

The last man residing on Wall Street is Hugh Harley who has filled Number 108 with family mementos and antiques. The five-story house, which also contains his export business, was built in 1794 on Murray's Wharf by shipwrights who used no nuts, bolts, or screws in the seemingly indestructible beams.

find fun and enjoyment in the area. No matter what the people on the floors of the exchanges are doing—or even if they are doing nothing—something is always happening outside. If it is not a ticker-tape welcome on Broadway for some celebrity, then it is a ceremony on the steps of Federal Hall, or the antics of a peddler with a new mechanical toy who furtively sets up his display box while keeping one eye alert for the cops.

The Street is rarely without an interesting excavation or building in progress for the entertainment of sidewalk superintendents. Putting up a skyscraper in the narrow thoroughfares, one contractor said, is like trying to perform a lobotomy in a telephone booth. At 5:00 P.M. the hawkers of beads and bangles and "genuine Nile crocodile bags" suddenly appear.

Whether it is the Hot Pretzel King and Good Humor Man of today or the Rockaway Oyster crier and Hot Corn girl of Andrew Jackson's time, the curbside vendor has always done a brisk business on dignified Wall Street.

Viewed from the Irving Trust tower, Trinity's twenty-story steeple shrinks to needle size. Even in 1907 Henry James wrote: "the spire of Trinity Church, so cruelly overtopped and so barely distinguishable . . . in its abject helpless humility."

(FACING PAGE) *Rear view of Trinity, agains background of Bankers Trust and Irvin Trust buildings, was photographed on winter's night from below, where the Hud son flowed in the days of the first church*

Like an old English crossroad shrine, the Astor Cross stands in Trinity Churchyard. At the top are Mary and Child; facing Broadway are figures of Judah, Shem, Adam and Eve; to the north, Ruth, Abraham, Seth; west, Jesse, Isaac, Enoch; south, David, Jacob, Noah with model of the Ark.

City for Conquest! Lower Manhattan (from under the Brooklyn Bridge) is still a place where an unknown youth with persistence, quick wits, and a winning personality can quickly climb to a big income with a securities house, brokerage firm, or mutual-fund company.

No words can describe the transformation of the tip of New York—the Wall Street scene—as effectively as a comparison of this photograph with the view made in 1836 (page 93), depicting the island from the same point on Brooklyn Heights.

So do the ladies' hosiery salesmen, the dealer in Mickey Mouse dolls ("Take home a Mickey—a doll for a dollah!"), and the caterer who deals exclusively in hot barbecued pretzels. His name is Baruch, but he hastily adds: "No relation!"

Down at the Battery, where the children are packed aboard the Circle Line or the Statue of Liberty boats, men of all ages stare out to sea, watching the big ships bound for Cristobal, Kuwait, Kobe, Cochin, or Calcutta and the tramp freighters which will touch at Dar es Salaam, Coatzacoalcos, Angra dos Reis, and Khorramshahr. They don't seem to see the tugs pushing the barges and the freight-car ferries around the point, or, high overhead, the jets drifting swiftly across the sky.

The Battery once had a lighthouse and before that a flagpole, called The Churn because of its shape. There was a floating bathhouse here before the turn of the century and Castle Garden was the market where greenhorn servants could be hired. A society to keep young Irish girls from falling into evil hands set up headquarters at Number 7 State Street and provided aid to more than fifty thousand colleens. The building, second only to St. Paul's Chapel in age, has lived many lives. Today it houses Our Lady of the Rosary Church.

Up from the Battery, where the bridge fell as the crowds cheered Andy Jackson, to Peter Stuyvesant's fort, now covered by the Custom House where Reginald Marsh found walls big enough for any muralist to paint, to the statue of Abraham De Peyster with his curled wig sitting in Bowling Green where once the statue of George III and his horse was toppled to the ground, is only a distance of three blocks, but marks a span of three hundred years in time.

Stroll up Broadway, and in four minutes you are at Trinity Church, looking down Wall, the street with ninety-nine lives—the street of George Washington's proudest moment, of a hundred panics and jubilations, disasters and wild celebrations; a street that makes the news the world must know every business day; a street with a working population of fifty thousand, but where only one person actually lives now. I asked the last man on Wall Street why he resides there. It is because he has a theory, he said—a theory that the climate on Wall Street is milder, balmier, cooler in summer, warmer in winter, by ten degrees, than the rest of New York.

At day's end the Wall Street buildings empty swiftly, and then the night people move in. Weegee, photographer of THE NAKED CITY, *saw and photographed an anonymous scrublady (next page) at the end of a hall, going about her long, lonely job—cleaning up for the fresh new day ahead.*

18

Looking Ahead

WHAT WILL Wall Street be like a hundred years from now? Will the gleaming new Chase Manhattan building have become a dull, gray pigmy among the five or six giants comprising the Supercity: half-mile-long buildings towering four or five hundred stories into the sky, each devoted to one industry—world finance, universe transportation, international corporate headquarters, insurance? Will there still be personal insurance, as we know it, or will the vastly expanding pension funds have made it obsolete? Will some kind of electronic brain link all the stock exchanges in the world into a single operational unit? Will Man have transcended war, disease, panics — and a 25-pound Sunday Times to achieve such peace that ArtX (Artificial Excitement) will be the leading form of entertainment? Possibly AuMin (Automation-Miniaturization) will shrink the labor force and equipment bulk needed to run the business of the world to such small units that the Supercity will be composed of one long, low, sprawling building with a rocket-skyport roof.

Impossible? Fantastic? Perhaps. But suppose we could push time back to the 1660's and tried to describe to a resident of New Amsterdam the seventy-story Chase Manhattan building which would some day be standing in the fields just beyond Peter Stuyvesant's twelve-foot wall. What would that man have replied to our picture of ordinary life in New York today? He could not even clap us into the booby hatch, for construction of the first insane asylum in Manhattan was not begun until 1677.

Closer in time than the possible one-hundred-year look, and easier to visualize, are practical plans now under way to change the face and contours of the Wall Street district. As a result, in a little more than a quarter of a century, the tip of the island will bear little resemblance to what it is today. Street-widening and the creation of new parking lots are already wiping out the decaying slums (relics of fine old buildings) and undistinguished lofts left from colonial days. The venerable "skid row" along Whitehall and South streets is making way for the Battery Park project, composed of 1,225 dwelling units, replacing ten flop houses, a dozen saloons and pawnshops, and several sail lofts. Eventually the Battery Park North development is expected to sweep away

Architect's view of the proposed $250 million World Trade Center to be constructed along the East River from the Brooklyn Bridge to the Battery. The project is to replace 131½ acres, mainly commercial slums. The flat building at the right is the World Trade Mart; the tall structure is a combined office building and hotel. To the left of the Assay Office is the proposed Battery Park North apartments and the middle-income Battery Park residential development. The present 120 Wall Street building will remain and behind it is the proposed Central Securities Exchange.

the Seaman's Church Institute as well as three additional blocks to the north and west to provide space for 225 higher-income bracket apartments which will cost much more per unit. Three other contemplated walk-to-work residential projects are Park Row (400 units), Park Row Extension (244), and Brooklyn Bridge South West (2,000). The first two will be located behind the County Court House and the Municipal building and the third is planned to occupy a site south of the bridge, just north of the Fulton Fish Market, which will be relocated to make room for the proposed World Trade Center.

The Downtown-Lower Manhattan Association is the originator of the World Trade Center idea—a group of buildings designed to extend from Old Slip to Fulton Street and from Water Street to South, leaving intact only the United States Assay Office at the southeast corner of the project and the American Sugar Refining building at 120 Wall. Otherwise the area is to be occupied by three imposing structures: a spacious World Trade Mart with exhibit space for trade missions and headquarters for every sort of transportation and shipping enterprise as well as commodity exchanges; a towering World

Trade Center Commerce building of fifty to seventy stories for offices, with a five-hundred- to seven-hundred-room hotel occupying the top ten floors; and a Central Securities Exchange building which, the planners optimistically hope, will house the New York Stock Exchange and related activities. The association took the initiative in sparking the World Trade Center with the intention that the Port of New York Authority would take over sponsorship and see the project through in co-operation with Federal, state, and city agencies. Headed by David Rockefeller, the association is continuing its interest and initiative in making the World Trade Center a reality.

The Port of New York Authority is already involved in the reconstruction and modernization of lower Manhattan by operating a heliport and small-boat marina in the East River to the south and east of the other proposed projects. Across the river, south of the Brooklyn Bridge, the Authority is changing the appearance of two miles of waterfront by replacing twenty-six antiquated piers with ten modern ones at a cost of eighty-five million dollars.

Private enterprise, however, continues to erect medium-sized skyscrapers throughout the Wall Street area, with the electronics corporations leading in 1960–1962 building activities. The twenty-million-dollar Western Electric building across from St. Paul's has been followed by the thirty-eight-story, fifty-million-dollar 60 Broad Street building which supersedes eleven smaller buildings and will house the RCA Communications Center. The next site scheduled to be occupied by a skyscraper is the House of Morgan at 23 Wall. Now that the old firm is part of Morgan Guaranty, executives have been considering several plans to construct a new towering structure to replace the massive, squat edifice that has long symbolized the financial power of Wall Street.

The eventual passing of this landmark is a matter of regret to the Street, and suggestions have been made that not only the Morgan building, but Federal Hall National Memorial, across the street, and Trinity Church, complete with churchyard, be moved to the Battery at the tip of the island where they would share this ancient site with Castle Clinton (or Castle Garden), which the Federal government plans to reconstruct as a national monument. These four great landmarks of Wall Street could then form a new historical center in the one place in the downtown area where they will not be overshadowed by tall buildings.

The 60 Broad Street building envelops the six-story RCA Communications network structure which links ninety countries. RCA operations did not stop functioning for even a single minute while the new thirty-eight-story building was constructed around its Communications Center.

There is no doubt in the minds of those people whose decisions count on Wall Street that the district is assured of retaining its role of world financial center from now into the foreseeable future. Nineteen of the Street's leaders were asked to present their views on the future of Wall Street. Their opinions appear on the succeeding pages.

G. KEITH FUNSTON has been the energetic, public-relations-minded President of the New York Stock Exchange since 1951, coming to Wall Street from the presidency of Trinity College. Here he is seen before a replica of the façade of the Stock Exchange, on display in the Exhibit Hall, which is visited by more than 400,000 people each year.

In looking ahead to the 1970's we can reasonably expect to see even greater changes in America's investing habits.

The recent past, with its sharp growth in the nation's shareowner family, perhaps illustrates one of the most significant changes likely to occur. Between 1952 and 1959 the number of individual shareowners in publicly held companies almost doubled to twelve and a half million. The ratio of adult shareowners in our population changed from one in sixteen to one in eight.

A continuation of this trend could give us a shareowner population of twenty-two million by 1970. If the various business trends evident since 1945 also continue, this could result in a total of over eleven billion shares listed on the New York Stock Exchange by 1970—double the present level. At that time, the Stock Exchange's average volume could reach five and a half to six million shares per day, in striking contrast to the postwar average of 1,700,000. These, however, are bare statistics. They hardly suggest the dramatic changes which our industry, like other major industries, must plan to undergo in the coming decade.

If our vision of economic America in 1970 is accurate, for example, our Stock Exchange community will employ something like one hundred thousand people as against the present level of seventy-five thousand. There will be about thirty-three thousand registered representatives to serve a wider public, a jump of about 35 per cent over the present number. Our Member Firm offices will have reached into more and more communities around the country, growing . . . to an estimated total of 3,400.

Publicly held companies and their transfer agents will be keeping tabs on some sixty-five million stockholders of record, as against thirty-eight million nowadays. The postman will have the added but happy burden of distributing an expected twenty billion dollars in dividend checks annually, against a recent annual level of $12,400,000,000.

These are some of the possibilities for the future. They are by no means guarantees, but they are projections of what we are capable of achieving.

ALFRED HAYES is little-known outside of the banking world, where he is an important figure and a respected voice. Since mid-1956, he has been President of the Federal Reserve Bank of New York. Before that he was with the New York Trust Company as Vice-President in charge of the Foreign Division. As head of the New York Federal Reserve Bank, Mr. Hayes is also Vice-Chairman of the Federal Open Market Committee, one of the Reserve Board's key economic balances. Above Mr. Hayes, who is standing on the steps of the bank, is one of the lanterns which bracket the entrance.

The challenge of the future to New York's financial community lies in the ever-present need for economic growth. New factories, new power plants, new homes, new schools—and space ships, too—will have to be built to bring rising standards of living for an expanding population. The builders of the future will be looking to New York to provide many of the dollars they need to pay for the bricks and mortar and rocket engines. If we are to grow faster as a nation, the supply of those dollars must grow faster.

Encouraging savers, mobilizing their dollars, and directing them efficiently into their most productive economic and human uses is the challenge facing Wall Street. Through its banks, insurance companies, investment firms, and special institutions flow many of our savings dollars to our nation's builders. Some well-meaning people, seeking a short cut, may suggest that we simply manufacture more dollars through the Federal Reserve System. But there are limits on the effective use of created dollars. The great need for saved dollars will continue if we are to secure real growth without inflation.

The opportunities ahead do not stop at the water's edge. Growth is international. Already the leading banker to the world, New York is developing new interests and new skills that foreshadow a still larger role in channeling dollars into world growth.

HENRY C. ALEXANDER, whose association with the House of Morgan began when he was a young lawyer working as counsel for J. P. Morgan, Jr., during the congressional investigations of the 1930's, became President of the banking firm in 1950 and Chairman in 1955. When the Morgan bank merged with the Guaranty Trust Company in 1959 he became chief executive of Morgan Guaranty Trust Company. Son of a Murfreesboro, Tennessee, grain and feed merchant, Mr. Alexander was ten years old when the first head of the House of Morgan, whose portrait hangs behind him, died in Rome.

WALL STREET, New York's "old city," is in the midst of a renascence. Amid the historic landmarks, there is pulsing a redevelopment to which hundreds of millions of dollars already have been committed and which ultimately will involve hundreds of millions more. Some of the projects will be publicly sponsored because of their civic nature, but . . . most of them will be the product of private initiative.

Downtown Manhattan's firm grip on its place as the financial hub is assured by the practical impossibility of creating a substitute. How, and where, could we duplicate the convenient grouping of facilities which make up the financial community—commercial banks, investment bankers, securities and commodity exchanges, the Clearing House, the Federal Reserve Bank, and others?

Wall Street's problem is not the typical one of old urban sections—erosion and abandonment. Its problem rather is growth—how to accommodate the additional thousands of people who will be needed for its important work. Automation already has a good start in Wall Street, and we will see a good deal more of it. But the main force in the financial community will always be people, and we must find ways to make room for a good many more of them in the active, busy years ahead.

SYLVIA F. PORTER, financial editor of the NEW YORK POST, *is the most widely published writer on business, economics, and money today, her daily syndicated column appearing in 350 newspapers. She also edits the weekly newsletter,* REPORTING ON GOVERNMENTS, *devoted to the government bond market and developments in government finance, and has written five books on this subject and economics in the home, the latest being* HOW TO GET YOUR MONEY'S WORTH. *She is standing on Pine Street near William, under the plaque that marks the first site of the* EVENING POST, *which began publication here in 1801.*

AN ANSWER to the question, "What is the future for women in 'Wall Street'?" is, I think, implicit in just a few statistics. Specifically:

Women perceptibly *outnumber* men as stockholders in this opening year of the decade of the 1960's. The proportion of shareholders who are women is 52.5 per cent compared with 47.5 per cent who are men.

The largest single group of stockholders in the stock market consists of the housewife. The total of housewives owning stocks is a towering four million.

The number of women working in banks—a traditional stronghold of men—tops 350,000 as against only thirty-six thousand as recently as 1939. Women now represent almost 60 per cent of all bank employes and 10,500 women are bank officers.

And over twenty-two million women are working in our country today, a whopping one-third of the labor force, 36 per cent of all women of working age.

These few statistics underline the spectacular future for women in the field of finance in the years ahead. For they shout with unmistakable clarity that:

The opportunities for women in brokerage houses will skyrocket. Women can be as good as any man in this field and many women in brokerage houses this very day are absolutely topnotch. Actually, survey after survey emphasizes that women bring an imaginative and yet common-sense approach to stock investing which frequently can make them superior to men.

The opportunities for women in banks will soar. Study after study pounds home the fact that women possess skills peculiarly suited to banking, not duplicated by men. There is no question that, with proper training, women can fill with superb efficiency any position in a bank.

The opportunities for women in my field of reporting and interpreting every development that touches on the bread-and-butter side of life will balloon. The American woman of this decade will be as avid for knowledge about every aspect of finance as any American man. The eagerness of the American woman for information in this sphere is, I believe, one of the truly new developments in the newspaper profession.

There isn't any sphere of finance that women aren't already starting to penetrate and women are just beginning—*just*. The progress just in my short time as an adult has been breathtaking. Nothing can stop it and I see no reason why anyone should try to stop it.

What are the limits to the opportunities for women in Wall Street, then? My answer is that the limits are limited only by our own imaginations, our own ambitions, our own abilities—which means that the limits are limitless.

DAVID ROCKEFELLER, youngest son of John D. Rockefeller, Jr., is President and Chairman of the Executive Committee of the Chase-Manhattan Bank, Chairman of the Board of the Downtown-Lower Manhattan Association, and serves in the same capacity for the Rockefeller Institute for Medical Research. On his desk in the executive offices of the bank is the "nest egg" featured in Chase Manhattan advertising. Behind him is a drawing of the World Trade Center which has been proposed by the Downtown-Lower Manhattan Association.

DOWNTOWN New York is and, in my opinion, will continue to be the financial capital of America. Today foreign trade and investment are becoming increasingly important to the lifeblood of the American economy. It is logical, therefore, that the proposed World Trade Center should be located in close proximity to the headquarters of many leading financial institutions which are instrumental in financing the flow of international trade and investment.

Looking ahead ten or fifteen years I visualize striking changes in the fringe areas surrounding the New York financial district. Numerous fine new buildings will be erected, the streets will be widened, and better transportation provided. It would not be surprising to see twenty million square feet of new business space added to the entire downtown area in that period. The World Trade Center project alone will require probably five or six million square feet on a thirteen-and-a-half-acre tract centering at the foot of Wall Street.

Another fifty to seventy-five thousand people will be working downtown, in addition to the present 350,000 estimated daytime population. And some thousands of them will be living in the new residential developments which are planned.

Downtown New York has a wonderful historic past—yes. But it also can look forward to a thrilling future.

CHARLES F. NOYES, the dean of New York real-estate men, is seen here revisiting his first office at 61 Beekman Street, where he worked at the turn of the century at a salary of $8 a week. From where he is seated, he can see seven of the several score of properties he has acquired in the past sixty years.

For twenty-five dull, dark years I demonstrated my faith in the future of the Wall Street district when many people sold it short. That faith has been most gratifyingly justified in the bright decade which has just ended.

Now the future of our downtown area promises to be even greater than the recent progress and it will only be limited by the amount of good real estate which remains to be developed.

For with the essential financial principals centered here, all the auxiliary functions, such as lawyers, accountants, public-relations and tax advisers, must remain close to the exchanges and banks and other financial institutions they serve. While certain divisions, such as the trust departments of banks, may move uptown, the head and direction will remain in Wall Street.

The trend toward walk-to-work housing down here should be given every encouragement, and so should the World Trade Center which, like the United Nations, is bound to enhance the position of New York as the World's Capital City.

Look around you in Wall Street and engrave today's scene deep in your memory, for it is going to change so much in twenty years that a Rip Van Winkle could return and would not recognize it.

EDWARD C. WERLE, elected three times as Chairman of the Board of Governors of the New York Stock Exchange, is the only man who has also been Chairman of the Board of the American Stock Exchange. He is a partner in Scheffmeyer, Werle and Company, specialists at Post 6 and specialists in the marketing of rights. On the spot where Mr. Werle stands on Wall Street once stood the tree under which, according to legend, the Buttonwood Agreement was signed in 1792.

Now AND in the years ahead we will see substantial changes in the Wall Street community—changes in the number of people working here, in methods of doing business—and in the services offered to investors everywhere.

Yet the changes that excite me the most lie in the improved equipment and facilities that loom ahead. The trading floor of the New York Stock Exchange, of course, will probably look much the same to the casual visitor. Markets are, after all, people—busy people. A broker's services are personal, and nothing presently on the horizon will replace his judgment, discretion, and experience. But the electronic age will supplement his decision-making and broaden his activities.

For one thing, there will be less paper work. Transactions will be handled faster, although to anyone who has observed the floor in action this hardly seems possible. The order entered by voice on one end of a phone wire is apt to appear as a printed message on the other end. Or a printed order may be mechanically transcribed into a spoken message.

And there are other possibilities as well. Today each sale on the trading floor must be recorded on a slip of paper and sent via a pneumatic tube to a ticker operator five stories above.

What of tomorrow? The ticker operator may well be stationed on the trading floor itself. In his hand he may have compact electronic equipment the size of a package of cigarettes or a memo pad. By punching a few keys he'll be able to tell the world of investors the latest prices of the stocks he's responsible for. And high-speed electronic computers will determine whether it's the high or low price for the day, and automatically transmit complete price data to quotation boards across the country. In much the same way, individual bid-and-ask prices may be available instantaneously. In Member Firm offices, the individual investor's records may be kept on magnetic tapes.

Such is the possible shape of the future in the securities industry. That future, to be sure, is strictly a dream; it is scarcely on paper yet. But men are working hard today to give substance to that dream.

S. SLOAN COLT, in addition to being Chairman of the Board of Commissioners of the Port of New York Authority, is Chairman of the Board of the Bankers Trust Company and former President of the New York Clearing House Association and the New York State Bankers Association. He is also a leader in civic and philanthropic affairs.

One out of every four people in the New York Metropolitan Area gains his livelihood directly or indirectly from the movement of waterborne freight through the port. Thus, the task of maintaining the position of the port is of primary interest to all in this region. The magnitude of this task becomes apparent when we consider that this area, which now has some 16,400,000 people, will have nineteen million people in 1975. Modernization of the port's marine terminal facilities thus assumes a paramount place in meeting the challenge of the future.

During the next ten years, construction of Port Authority marine terminal facilities will amount to an investment of four hundred million dollars. Vast projects are currently under way, such as the ninety-million-dollar redevelopment of the Brooklyn-Port Authority Piers to provide two miles of the Brooklyn waterfront with the most up-to-date and modern facilities for handling oceanborne commerce. In addition, the Port Authority is currently undertaking a project for development of the Elizabeth-Port Authority Piers which will provide a dynamic terminal area in a location which is now marsh land. At the same time, development will continue in Port Newark to provide improved and expanded facilities for this increasingly important point of commerce for the New Jersey-New York region. When both of these latter projects are completed, they will represent a total investment of 250 million dollars and will contribute to maintaining the leading position of the Port of New York. . . .

In the field of commercial aviation, Port Authority programs will continue to be carried out in order to increase the capacity of the region's airport system. The completion of the $150,000,000 Terminal City at New York International Airport will provide a modern "aerial gateway to the United States." LaGuardia Airport, currently undergoing a fifty-six-million-dollar redevelopment program, will provide increased and improved service to the region. In addition, the Port Authority will continue to improve and expand the other air terminals—Newark Airport, Teterboro Airport, and the West Thirtieth Street Heliport—to meet the growing demand for air travel. New facilities, such as the Downtown Manhattan Heliport, which will be constructed in the Wall Street area, will help to meet the challenge of tomorrow's air age.

The Port Authority will continue its studies of projects which will contribute vitally to the future of the New York Metropolitan Area. For example, the Port Authority, at the request of the Governors of the states of New York and New Jersey and the Mayor of the City of New York, is studying the possible design and development of a World Trade Center located on a thirteen-and-a-half-acre site along the East River in lower Manhattan. The proposed World Trade Center would provide a centralized, distinctively designed facility for serving the world trade community. It would furnish convenient, efficient facilities and services that would expedite and simplify international trade and provide an appropriate symbol of the port's pre-eminence in handling, processing, and financing United States trade. . . .

All of these projects and plans will be aimed at meeting one of the major challenges of our time—the need to develop efficient facilities to handle the increasing flow of people and goods into, out of, and through this great port region. They will assure the continued growth of this, the world's greatest center of business, industry, and transportation.

MICHAEL W. McCARTHY, who was born in Belle Plaine, Minnesota, population 1,500, is now boss of five times as many people in his capacity as President of Merrill Lynch, Pierce, Fenner and Smith, Inc. In 1940 he was an executive of Safeway Stores in California when he met Charles E. Merrill, who brought him to New York to reorganize and streamline the backstage operations of ML, one of which, the news wire room, is shown here.

The Wall Street of yesterday, as we knew it, has changed drastically. More and more millions of people have become shareowners and in the coming years the ownership of American industry will continue to broaden. This will come about not only through further increases in the number of investors, but also as the result of more privately owned companies becoming publicly owned. Additionally, as the economies of the countries of Europe and other parts of the world expand, our market place will grow in international importance.

If we are to benefit from the greater opportunities we must assume greater responsibilities. We intend to expand our public educational programs in which we pioneered twenty years ago and, although we already have 130 offices in the United States and abroad, we will extend our service facilities to more cities throughout the world. We believe that, just as the nature of the securities market has changed, old concepts and methods must also change. The means for meeting industry's need for capital, securities research, communications systems, and electronic processing of the vast paper workload must be studied constantly in order to provide both the users and suppliers of investment funds with the most efficient service. That is our continuing obligation.

EDWARD T. McCORMICK pauses in Trinity Churchyard on way from work. President of the American Stock Exchange (seen across Trinity Place), he is a former member of the Securities and Exchange Commission, a Certified Public Accountant, economist, and wrote UNDERSTANDING THE SECURITIES ACT AND THE S.E.C.

A PROJECTION into the future a decade away is surrounded by considerable risk. However, when one looks back at the accomplishments under our capitalistic system, we can, with considerable confidence, look to the future for continued and expanding economic growth. The long-term view is bright indeed and, given a period of peace and a lessening of world tensions, the present rate of growth should not only be maintained but should be enhanced.

Every week, almost each day brings to light somewhere in this country some new product, a more efficient method of production, or a fresh line of research. Each new idea stirs intelligent curiosity and opens up before it new horizons. Each improvement in production technique invites and stimulates rivalry for future improvements.

Research expenditures alone have grown from less than one billion dollars in 1941 to considerably more than four billion dollars today. It is believed that this spending will reach nearly sixteen billion dollars a year by 1975. Industrial research will provide an ever growing array of new methods, procedures, and products to enrich our living standards.

Living standards have risen more than 65 per cent in the United States during the past twenty-five years and a greater increase is predicted for the period ahead. During a like period of twenty-five years, the average spendable income which now amounts to $4,400 will have risen to eight thousand dollars per family (in 1955 dollars). The promise is more jobs with higher income and more leisure time in which to enjoy it.

The population growth will have stimulated consumer demand not merely for food and clothing but for new homes, roads, hospitals, schools, and churches. The impact of this demand on our economy will be tremendous.

Our people will become more and more aware that ownership of the tools of production can be secured through stock investment and our stock-owning population should expand to nearly double the present total. The number of companies listed on our stock exchange will have increased substantially and it is not beyond present vision to foresee trading volume on the American Stock Exchange rising to a daily turnover of four million shares.

J. CLARENCE DAVIES, JR., stands at Coenties Slip and South Street, watching the demolition of ancient store buildings to make way for the erection of Battery Park. New York City Commissioner of Real Estate and Chairman of the New York City Housing and Urban Renewal Agency, Mr. Davies is the son of the collector of New York illustrations who left the J. Clarence Davies Collection to the Museum of the City of New York.

THE YEARS ahead for the Wall Street area will almost certainly be enormously influenced by at least two foreseeable programs not now in existence.

The first of these will be the addition of a supply of both high-rent and middle-income housing, within a few yards of the "Morgan Corner" at Broad and Wall. This change envisions an area of landscaped housing, with air, light, good design, and convenience almost beyond belief for workers of the financial district. The project, now known as Battery Park, will remove the antiquated and obsolete buildings from the southerly side of South Street, the westerly side of Whitehall Street, the northerly side of Water Street, the westerly side of Broad Street, the northerly side of Pearl Street, and the easterly side of Coenties Slip, and includes seven blocks of substandard, old, deteriorated structures beyond practicable repair. There will be, in addition to Battery Park, at least two or three other major housing projects utilizing private capital, plus the government's power of condemnation, without which the land could not conceivably be assembled. These will, in all probability, be built prior to 1975.

The second great factor which will change the area will be the International Trade Mart to be constructed north of Wall Street and along the East River frontage. This magnificent conception can, and I believe will, bring a vastly greater number of workers to the perimeter of the section where the light and air, if fresh and unconditioned air is ever used in the future, are available and permanent. Traffic studies and routing can do much to unblock the interior, hard-to-reach area, and enough housing can mean a substantial reduction in transportation snarls. Utilizing this part of the island for residential development is both logical and inevitable.

These two changes will make a real difference in improving the area and taking advantage of the narrowest, most attractive, and geographically best section of Manhattan Island.

ROBERT STOTT, seen in his office at Wagner, Stott and Company, specialists on the floor of the New York Stock Exchange, is a former Chairman of the Board of Governors of that body and one of the leaders of the young reform group which opposed the conservatives who dominated the exchange until the middle of the 1930's.

In pondering the future of share ownership in America, something more than impressive statistical growth comes into focus. By 1970, teenage students throughout the country will be learning what makes the stock market tick, and why—and America will be all the healthier for it.

The exciting prospect of teaching our youngsters the meaning of the investment process is long overdue. In my own school days we learned the basics of history, plane geometry, and all Gaul being divided into three parts. But we learned virtually nothing about economics and our American capitalism.

As recently as 1951 a survey revealed that only 4 per cent of the 9,240,000 students enrolled in the nation's high schools were expected to take a course in economics. Just one state had made economics a requisite for high-school graduation.

Since then, of course, much has happened in the vital realm of the classroom. Schools beyond number have enlarged their curriculum to include economics, capitalism, and stock ownership. They have added new courses, new texts, and teaching techniques.

In Western Springs, Illinois, for example, the eighth-graders at McClure Junior High learn their arithmetic not by traditional formulas but by following the market tables in a daily newspaper and keeping individual books showing the price movements.

In Nyack, New York, the teacher of a senior class decided to let his students explore the risks and rewards of stock ownership by becoming owners themselves. He proposed that each student ante up fifty cents and that the class invest the proceeds. This led to an enthusiastic search for exactly the right company, and an equally enthusiastic discovery of the range and variety of American industry. Finally one corporation was chosen to be the agent for destiny for the class fund of eighteen dollars, which happened to be just enough to buy one share of the company stock.

Activities such as these, I think, illuminate the shape of the future in America. Not only will the number of investors go up and up, but our schools will be teaching youngsters what share ownership really means.

WALLACE H. FULTON, as Executive Director of the National Association of Securities Dealers, Inc., is the administrative head of the world's largest "invisible market place," the over-the-counter market.

THE NATION's economy is financed through the over-the-counter market. Future expansion in this market must, therefore, keep pace with the demands for new capital from corporations now in existence, from corporations still to be formed, and from Federal, state, and local governments for undertakings to be paid for through debt securities. Almost all new money needed by corporations to finance their growth is raised by members of the National Association of Securities Dealers, Inc., through the public sale or private placement of stocks and bonds.

During the 1950's, underwriters and over-the-counter dealers first offered to the public securities of many new companies in the missiles industry, electronics industry, natural gas pipeline industry, the drug industry, companies developing digital computers and means of automation, industries working to conquer space, as well as the continuously expanding chemical industry. In prior years the securities of electric and gas utilities, airlines, appliance manufacturers, and airplane manufacturers were first introduced to the public through the over-the-counter market. 1970 will continue to find the over-the-counter market the launching point for new industries today unknown.

While the distribution of new securities is an important function of the over-the-counter market, it constitutes only a part of the activity taking place over the counter. The securities of thousands of companies are traded here regularly. Today, the shares of almost all bank and trust companies, and insurance companies stocks; all railroad equipment trust certificates; most real-estate bonds; many railroad, industrial, and public-utility securities; and all bonds of the United States government, its territories, and instrumentalities are handled in the over-the-counter market. It also embraces all municipal securities—issues of states, cities, towns and their instrumentalities. A large volume of *professional* trading of listed securities is also done over the counter. Trading in listed issues goes on between dealers and between dealers and customers such as investment trusts, insurance companies, pension funds, and banks. . . .

The shares of open-end investment companies (mutual funds) sold in the over-the-counter market proved their place as an investment medium for all kinds of investors—both individuals and institutions. Almost sixteen billion dollars were invested in open-end investment company shares at the end of 1959, compared to only two and a half billion dollars in 1950. There is every reason to believe that this impressive record of growth will continue.

At present, the infant of the over-the-counter market is the variable annuity contract, ruled to be securities by the United States Supreme Court in April, 1959. The over-the-counter market has proved its ability to exploit new ideas and this alone gives reason to expect that the variable annuity contract will be familiar to millions of investors by 1970.

When the NASD was established in 1939, it had 2,616 members. Today, mid-1960, there are 4,372 members employing 90,180 registered representatives. As the over-the-counter market continues to expand in the years ahead, the NASD will also grow, projecting its services and guiding principles into new fields for the protection of investors and the securities business.

JAMES C. KELLOGG III has been a member of the New York Stock Exchange since 1936, when he bought his seat at the age of twenty-one. He was Chairman of the Board of Governors in 1956 and is a partner in the specialist firm of Spear, Leeds and Kellogg. First appointed by Governor Robert B. Meyner of New Jersey in 1955, he is a Commissioner of the Port of New York Authority.

Wall Street, as far as the brokerage business is concerned, will change drastically over the next two or three decades. The Stock Exchange is considering the possibility of moving from its present location to one nearby. The move is being studied because of what is known as technological change or automation. Certainly there is a desperate need for the detail work to be done by computers, but the decisions will still have to be made by individuals so that the physical setup will probably remain unchanged.

The new companies and expanding issues will swell the listed securities to well above fifteen billion shares. The trading volume will probably average between four and six million per day and at certain periods will probably run at ten million a day for months at a time.

Dow Jones averages, which are weighted for stock splits and stock dividends, could easily go over the one-thousand mark . . . within the next ten years.

If times continue to change at as fast a pace in the next years as they have in the past ten, all of these things will certainly become a reality, since New York has definitely become the financial center of the world and will continue as such with the constant shortening of distances due to the modern techniques of the "Jet Age." These are some of the possibilities of the future and only time will tell whether or not they will become reality.

CARL MARKS stands in his trading room with its quotation board which tells him the current price of a thousand foreign bonds and stocks. From a background of newspaper distributing, taking want ads, and working as a brakeman on the Pennsy, Mr. Marks came to Wall Street where he worked his way up from bookkeeper to head of his own little ($6,500) firm by 1925. Surrounding himself with astute traders, many still with him and earning the fattest stipends on the Street, he quickly came to the fore in the field of trading foreign securities. Now the firm turns over several hundred million dollars in foreign securities a year, provides the nation's dominant market for shares and bonds of every country on the globe, and trades for its own account and frequently represents foreign governments, but not the U.S.S.R., although in the Carl Marks safes are piles of Czarist bonds and Imperial Russian rubles. Said the NEW YORK TIMES: *"If the Soviet regime acknowledged its fiscal obligation to Carl Marks as enthusiastically as it does its ideological debt to Karl Marx, the Wall Street trader and foreign securities specialist could add another $10 million to his already substantial fortune."*

MONEY IS the economic lifeblood of the world and, like blood, it must circulate to be of value. Today money does not circulate freely between most nations, whether for trade or investment. The words "Venture Capital" do not adequately describe the dangers involved in investing funds abroad under current conditions.

Looking over the past history of foreign investments, it is difficult to find an operation which would have exceeded the success of an equivalent investment here at home. Present conditions are no more encouraging now than they have been in the past and this situation will become worse as more restrictions are created in the future. I sincerely believe that the immense sums throughout the world seeking investment will find their best and safest opportunity in the highest-grade securities of the United States. There are very few other countries where an investment of extremely large sums can be placed with the possibility of eventual liquidation.

Increasingly (and in spite of political urging, tax encouragements, and moral considerations) the private investor has learned by sad experiences to refrain from sending his money to any but the most stable foreign nations. To fill this void we now have government-to-government and international institution financing. The risk of foreign investment has become too great for the individual. The only solution seems to be for sovereign power to deal with sovereign power and eventually this condition must come about.

On the other hand a tremendous amount of foreign capital is flowing into United States industrial securities and in the future so much more will come here that there is some concern over the possibility that foreign capital may take control of key United States corporations. Today there is no law (with the exception of some limitations as to the amount of foreign investments in the communications field) to prevent the Soviet Union, with its vast treasury, from acquiring the domination (and the secrets) of corporations in this country working on classified defense contracts. Steps should be taken to make such a situation impossible.

Of course another war would be so drastic that only 100 per cent government control would be effective. The money and securities markets cannot be expected to withstand atomic assault. In that event not even cash would have purchasing power, and rightfully so. To protect everyone, there must be an instantly-ready, workable plan by which food, clothing, and shelter would be distributed equitably, and production and labor mobilized, with effective controls. There could be no question of inflation in such an economy.

It is a painful paradox that an assault on the United States by communist forces would force us into a type of communistic life—not their type of communism but a pure variety, in which all the people would share alike. If this is so, it is possible that the only practical way to retain our free world would be to go through an economic experience similar to what the enemy would claim they were trying to impose on us.

JOSEPHINE BAY PAUL was a partner in the New York Stock Exchange firm of A. M. Kidder and Company from 1952 to 1956 and has since been President and Chairman of the Board. She was Chairman of the Executive Committee and a director of American Export Lines until 1959 when she became Chairman of the Board. She is a director of the Connecticut Railway and Lighting Company and a member of the Corporation of the Columbia Presbyterian Hospital. In 1956 the annual poll of the Associated Press selected Mrs. Paul as Woman of the Year in Business.

In the years ahead Wall Street will change not only its physical appearance, but another—and even more striking—change will be the greater participation by women in top-layer executive positions. The canyons of lower Broadway today are crowded with feminine workers among whom a limited number have reached the upper level. During the past ten years the employment of women in increasing numbers has become essential and has added a new dimension to the nation's total manpower; in the years to come it will add a new potential for executive manpower.

Frankly there are not enough women in top executive positions in today's business world. A top executive position requires many abilities. It requires a combination of good judgment, emotional maturity, stamina, and enterprise. It is a rare man who possesses these abilities and there are just as many rare women in this country as there are rare men. Women have many talents, many abilities, and I believe the reason that women are not holding more executive positions is that too many women underrate themselves.

Up to 70 per cent of some large business firms is owned by women and a recent study reports that holdings of shares of common stock registered in the names of women are 8 per cent more than those registered in the names of men. In other words, most common stockholders . . . are women.

Many women do an expert job in home management. Isn't it only logical that, as women's interest in corporate business, under the American system in which the stockholder is the boss, increases, women will share more and more on a par with men in the ultimate authority over corporate affairs?

It is my prediction that just as the past ten years have seen an enormous increase in the number of women employed in the Street, the next ten years will see women, through their interest in stocks and bonds, finding their niche in top executive positions in the market where such commodities are traded.

LLOYD W. MASON, crossing Broad Street from the New York Stock Exchange, joined Paine, Webber, Jackson and Curtis following World War I, in which he won the Distinguished Flying Cross as a member of the British Royal Flying Corps. He became a partner in 1929 and managing partner of the New York office in 1947. He has been Vice-President of the Association of New York Stock Exchange Firms.

A REVOLUTION has occurred in the investment industry during the past ten years and is continuing at an accelerated pace. The basic aspect of this revolution is the tremendous distribution of common share ownership throughout the entire American middle class.

A generation ago, security ownership was heavily concentrated in a relatively small number of wealthy individuals. Those persons, who did most of the actual trading in securities, were frequently inclined to approach the market as speculators rather than as investors. In the twenties, it was not unusual for a company's entire common stock capitalization to turn over three or four times in a single year. Today a 15 per cent to 20 per cent turnover is typical.

Present-day provisions of our tax laws, as they relate to capital gains and losses, have placed an effective brake on speculation. Inheritance-tax laws have struck at the large concentrations of stock ownership. Rising incomes, increased sophistication and education of the average American have provided a ready market for the securities that the wealthy were forced to convert into cash for tax purposes. Wall Street investment and brokerage firms organized research departments to offer these new investors topflight advice regarding their new stock ownership ventures. The position of a customers' broker has evolved into that of an investment adviser, as well as a securities salesman, and qualifications for entering the securities business have become increasingly rigorous.

In the future, I believe both of these trends will be accelerated and the results will enable every potential investor to receive the finest of professional assistance. Under this stimulus, we expect the ownership of American industry continually to expand and reach that point where common stock ownership will become as extensive as 1960's automobile ownership. In another generation, every prudent American will own his share of American industry and the dream of our forefathers will be fulfilled—the wealth of the United States will be owned by ALL the people.

BURTON CRANE (RIGHT), *financial writer of the* NEW YORK TIMES, *is seated with Fred Schwed, Jr., author of* WHERE ARE THE CUSTOMERS' YACHTS?, *in the Exhibit Hall at the New York Stock Exchange. Behind them is a panel showing previous homes of the exchange (starting top left and going clockwise), the Tontine Coffee House, the second Merchants Exchange, the interior at Lord's Court, the first Merchants Exchange, the buttonwood tree, Broad and Wall streets about 1830, and the first Broad Street building (1865); in the center is a scene of the Panic of 1857. Mr. Crane is the author of* THE SOPHISTICATED INVESTOR.

A FEW thoughts on our future:

Capital is being created in the United States at such a swift rate and is being utilized so efficiently that the return being offered to the investor is steadily decreasing. Up to now wars have always been the great consumers of excess capital. We have rarely had an oversupply for any extended period. Now, we have been without war for fifteen years and prospects for a long span of peace are bright. So, more and more capital will pile up, seeking a favorable investment return. That means more competition for securities, which will therefore increase in price, and that also means lower stock yields. This is a problem we shall probably have to face in this generation. Peace may be as puzzling to our economy as war ever was.

An increasingly large segment of the population faces the problem of living on retirement incomes while living costs continue rising. But those foes of inflation can—and perhaps they will—do something about this, for 40 per cent of the people are over fifty, and fewer than 40 per cent of the people vote regularly. This older group has the power, if it stirs itself, to slaughter any elective officer who tries to cut the buying power of the dollar.

We can expect to see sun power and atomic plants cutting the cost of power; in ten years people will commute daily by three-hundred-mile-per-hour helicopter from Boston and Philadelphia and Washington, landing on flat roofs all over Wall Street; hydrofoil boats will bring thousands of workers down the Hudson, across from Jersey and from Long Island, Westchester, and Connecticut to the marinas around the tip of the island; the commodity exchanges will deal in as yet unheard-of materials; the New York Stock Exchange will not move to California; Wall Street will reluctantly raise salaries to recruit the brighter young people; and some gifted analyst will pioneer in the over-the-counter market and start a much-needed trend.

BERNARD M. BARUCH, who had New York forebears who lived across the street from Captain Kidd's widow—and whose daring operations in the stock market took place in the same vicinity—is seen seated on the steps of City Hall, waiting for the arrival of the Mayor.

WHILE BERNARD BARUCH has been reluctant to offer any advice or rules on how to invest or speculate, he has learned a number of things from his own experiences which he considers worth listing for "those who are able to muster the necessary self-discipline." These are:

1. *Don't speculate unless you can make it a full-time job.*
2. *Beware of barbers, beauticians, waiters—of anyone —bringing gifts of "inside" information or "tips."*
3. *Before you buy a security, find out everything you can about the company, its management and competitors, its earnings and possibilities for growth.*
4. *Don't try to buy at the bottom and sell at the top. This can't be done—except by liars.*
5. *Learn how to take your losses quickly and cleanly. Don't expect to be right all the time. If you have made a mistake, cut your losses as quickly as possible.*
6. *Don't buy too many different securities. Better have only a few investments which can be watched.*
7. *Make a periodic reappraisal of all your investments to see whether changing developments have altered their prospects.*
8. *Study your tax position to know when you can sell to greatest advantage.*
9. *Always keep a good part of your capital in a cash reserve. Never invest all your funds.*
10. *Don't try to be a jack of all investments. Stick to the field you know best.*

"These rules," writes Mr. Baruch in *My Own Story*, "mainly reflect two lessons that experience has taught me—that getting the facts before acting is of crucial importance, and that getting these facts is a continuous job which requires eternal vigilance."

Acknowledgments

A VOLUME OF this scope and size would hardly be possible without the assistance of a number of other persons, and the author is deeply indebted to many skillful, talented, and wise people who have contributed very much to this book.

First, he wishes to acknowledge his debt to the celebrated photographers who were responsible for the several hundred new pictures, made especially for this book, which appear on the preceding pages. Miss Berenice Abbott, whose photographs of the Wall Street district are world famous, devoted several months to the task of recording new scenes of pictorial history and has contributed others which have never been published before. Working with her on this assignment was a particularly rewarding experience for the author. He is also indebted to her for the use of the illustrations from her copy of the rare *New Metropolis* by E. Idell Zeisloft.

Eliot Elisofon's photographs, taken on the floors of the New York and American stock exchanges, are another integral part of the story of contemporary Wall Street and are seen in the last three chapters of this volume.

Andreas Feininger, still another celebrated chronicler of the metropolitan scene, made available his portfolio of unpublished photographs of lower Manhattan, from which have been selected a score of memorable pictures. In like manner the cameraman Arthur Fellig, better known as Weegee, contributed from his collection of Wall Street photos. In the last chapter, the reader will find a number of portraits made for this book by Marcus Blechman, a photographer who usually does not stir from his studio, but who came down to Wall Street to shoot these subjects in their native habitat.

John Groth has drawn notable sketches of the floor of the New York Stock Exchange especially for this book.

People who staff the museums and libraries of New York and Washington were of great help, both in the assembling of historical illustrations and in aiding the author with the research for the text of the book. Arthur Carlson, curator of maps and prints of the New-York Historical Society, with his encyclopedic knowledge of early New York and its illustrations, was most encouraging and co-operative, as were his assistants, Miss Betty Ezequelle and Paul Bride. Miss Carolyn Scoon, assistant curator, and Miss A. Rachel Minnick of the library, were among the other members of the New-York Historical Society staff to whom the author is indebted.

At the Museum of the City of New York the curator of prints and photographs, A. K. Baragwanath, and the nautical curator, William M. Williamson, have both been unstinting in their assistance and the same has been true of Mrs. Henrietta Beall, in charge of photographs, and Philip Rees of the museum's library.

In Washington, D.C., Milton Kaplan, Carl Stange, Virginia Daiker, and Dr. Edward Breitenbach, chief of the prints and photographs division, of the Library of Congress extended their helping hands; the staff of the National Gallery of Art, especially Miss Grace Farrar of the print-room, was most co-operative; Miss Josephine Cobb and other members of the Audio-Visual Records Division of the National Archives delighted the author with the rare Mathew Brady photographs they unearthed; and the United States Coast and Geodetic Survey furnished him with aerial photographs of lower Manhattan.

Other photographs, illustrations, and information were supplied by Fred B. Adams, director of the Pierpont Morgan Library, Henry Grunthal of the American Numismatic Society, Miss Elizabeth Hall, librarian of the New York Botanical Gardens, Miss Ena Yonge of the American Geographical Society, William Stiles of the Museum of the American Indian, Heye Foundation, and Robert E. Logan of the American Museum of Natural History.

Several years ago at the Museum of the City of New York and more recently at the Museum of Modern Art, Miss Grace M. Mayer offered much wise counsel and arranged for the inclusion of the Edward Steichen photographs which appear here. And to A. Hyatt Mayor, curator of prints of the Metropolitan Museum of Art go the author's thanks for his interest and aid.

It is doubtful if a book such as this could have

been produced without the great treasure of research and illustrative material available at the New York Public Library. The Picture Collection, totaling several million items, has been of incalculable assistance and the author's appreciation is matched by his obligation to all the members of the Picture Collection staff, headed by Miss Romana Javitz and her assistant, Miss Franzeska Schacht, for their patience and co-operation.

The other great source of illustrations and information for this book has been the files of Gardner Osborn of the Federal Hall Memorial Associates and the Sons of the American Revolution. Mr. Osborn most unselfishly made available all the material he has personally collected over a period of thirty years and the author is most grateful that he has been permitted to use what appears here.

At the New York Stock Exchange, Robert G. Deindorfer and Richard Callanan have been most co-operative and enlightening. So was Mrs. Rita Marie Braswell, who was in charge of the exchange's extensive library. The American Stock Exchange's John J. Sheehan and George H. Kerrigon matched their Big Board opposite numbers in helpfulness and expertise. James Conway of Chicago, in charge of the public information services of the National Association of Securities Dealers, Inc., the over-the-counter market, came all the way to New York to be of assistance.

Among other officials to whom the author is under obligation are Warren T. Lindquist and Porter Moore of the Downtown-Lower Manhattan Association, Inspector George V. Staker of the New York City Police Department, Mrs. Lee K. Jaffee and Leon Katz of the Port of New York Authority, William E. Boyland, President of the New York City Tax Commission, Mrs. Catherine Supinski of the New York Chamber of Commerce, Robert W. Dill, Collector of Customs, and Orval L. DuBois, Secretary of the Securities and Exchange Commission.

He is also grateful to Paul Meek and Raymond G. Brown of the Federal Reserve Bank of New York, J. C. Boehm of Manufacturers Trust Company, Crawford Wheeler, Christopher Gerould, and Miss Sheliah Murphy of the Chase Manhattan Bank, and James M. Shea of the Bank of New York.

Among the officials of brokerage houses who have helped are William Downie, of Spear, Leeds and Kellogg; Lutrell Maclin, of Paine, Webber, Jackson and Curtis; Francis Prior of Goodbody and Company; LaRue Applegate of Merrill Lynch, Pierce, Fenner and Smith, Inc.; Henry Gellerman of Bache and Company; and the staff of Carl Marks and Company, Inc.

D. Jay Culver, Harry Collins of Brown Brothers, and Erik Monberg were untiring in their efforts to find illustrations of every description relating to Wall Street and its personalities. The author also wishes to thank Harry Grund of Wide World and Associated Press Photos and Philip Miller of that organization. Glenn Neville of the *New York Mirror*, Robert Lasch of the *St. Louis Post-Dispatch*, Null Adams of the *Memphis Press-Scimitar*, and Abel Green of *Variety* are among the editors who have been most gracious in their assistance, and Martin Mayer, Kenneth Dunshee, Roger Butterfield, Alvin M. Josephy, Phil Leslie, and Ted Taylor are writers who have not stinted with time and advice when the author called upon them.

The roster of others who have contributed information and illustrations ranges from Frank Braden, the circus press agent with the definitive story of the midget on J. P. Morgan, Jr.'s lap, to Mrs. Seton Henry, whose mother served frog legs to the creator of the Statue of Liberty. Joseph Galdi of Mutual Shares Corporation made available his collection of *Valentine's Manuals*, Hugh Harley, his old New York prints, Harry T. Peters, Jr., of Orange, Virginia, the Currier and Ives material collected by his father, now at the Museum of the City of New York, and William Deatly, the historical art collection of the Title Guarantee and Trust Company.

Others who must be included in this acknowledgment are Georgie Price, Cass Gilbert, Jr., Captain Anton L. Mare, USN (ret.), Agnes Rogers (Mrs. Frederick Lewis Allen), Clinton B. Axford and Mrs. Gloss Edwards of the *American Banker*, Arthur Rosenberg of the National Studios, Arthur Cardiner, who found many rare books and magazines relating to the subject, Fritz Bamberger of Esquire, Inc., Michael Skinness of Standard Oil Company of New Jersey and Nick Parrino of Cities Service Corporation.

And, in conclusion, a word of thanks to the nineteen Wall Street leaders who have contributed their forecasts and opinions of the future of the Street, which comprise the major part of the last chapter.

L.L.L.

Picture Credits

The following abbreviations have been used in referring to picture sources:

AMNH—American Museum of Natural History
ASE—American Stock Exchange
FHMA—Federal Hall Memorial Associates, Inc.
LLL—Leonard Louis Levinson
MCNY—Museum of the City of New York
ML—Merrill Lynch, Pierce, Fenner and Smith, Inc.
MMA—Metropolitan Museum of Art
NYHS—New-York Historical Society
NYPL—New York Public Library
NYSE—New York Stock Exchange
PNYA—Port of New York Authority

Title page—Andreas Feininger
2—Berenice Abbott
4—same
5—Leonard Stern, courtesy PNYA
6-7—Andreas Feininger
9—Berenice Abbott
10—William Samenko, Jr., courtesy PNYA
11—Charles E. Rotkin, courtesy Cities Service Co.
12—Edward Steichen, print from the Museum of Modern Art
13—Peter Eckel, courtesy PNYA
14—Berenice Abbott
16—upper; same; lower: *The Story of the City of New York* by Charles Burr Todd
17—sketch by Albert Operti, courtesy AMNH
18-19—all: murals by Reginald Marsh in Custom House, photos from National Archives
20-21—all: murals by Ezra Winter in Cunard Line Great Hall, photos by W. A. Probst, courtesy Cunard Steam-Ship Co., Ltd.
22—upper: map by Jacomo di Gastaldi, from *Navigatione et Viaggi* by G. B. Ramusio, courtesy NYPL; lower: painting by Walter Bollendonk, courtesy MCNY
23—courtesy FHMA, from MCNY
24—painting by Alfred Fredericks, courtesy Title Guarantee & Trust Co.
25—upper: courtesy FHMA, from MCNY; lower: Hartgers view, drawn by Kryn Fredericks, from *Views of Early New York*
26—Montanus view, probably engraved by Jacob van Meurs, from *Views of Early New York*
26-27—Hugo Allard map, probably engraved by Romeyn de Hooge, from *Views of Early New York*
28—redraft of Castello plan, from survey by Jacques Cortelyou, 1660, rectified and enlarged by John Wolcott Adams and I. N. Phelps Stokes, 1916, from *American Historical Prints*, NYPL
29—upper: *Wall Street in History* by Martha J. Lamb; lower: courtesy FHMA, from NYHS
30—top row: oil on wood panel, artist unknown, courtesy NYHS; NYPL; supposed portrait found in Dongan's mansion, later in Caleb Lyon Collection, courtesy NYHS—middle row: *History of New-York*, NYPL; oil painting, artist unknown, courtesy NYHS; Sarony & Co. lithograph, NYPL —bottom row: enamel miniature by Christian F. Zincke, courtesy NYHS; *New York: Past and Present* by Evert A. Duykinck in *Frank Leslie's Popular Monthly;* engraving from painting by Sir Joshua Reynolds, NYPL
32—upper: *New York: Past and Present;* lower: painting by E. L. Henry, courtesy Title Guarantee & Trust Co.
33—*History of the City of New York* by Martha J. Lamb
34—Maerschalckm map, from *The Story of the City of New York*
35—*History of the City of New York* (Lamb)
36—upper: lithograph from *Valentine's Manual*, courtesy Joseph Galdi; lower: *A Tour Around New York* by John Flavel Mines
38—painting by C. E. Mills in the Franklin Union, Boston, Bettmann Archive
39—*Frank Leslie's Popular Monthly*
40—*The Story of a Street*
41—upper: *Atlantic Neptune*, NYPL; lower: engraving by John C. McRae, Library of Congress
42—upper: *History of the City of New York* (Lamb); lower: fictitious view or "peep-show" print by François X. Habermann, MMA
44—George Washington Bicentennial leaflet, NYPL
45—illustration by E. A. Abbey, NYPL
46—illustration by Joseph Ropes, from *Life of Captain Nathan Hale*, NYPL
47—same
48—upper: *History of the City of New York* (Lamb); lower: NYPL
50—upper: NYPL; lower: *Pictorial Field-Book of the Revolution* by Benson J. Lossing
51—upper: *Pictorial Field-Book of the Revolution;* lower: Library of Congress
52—*History of the City of New York* (Lamb)
53—illustration by Henry Wolf, *Harper's Monthly*
54—*"Manna-hatin," The Story of New York*
55—NYPL
56—illustration by H. A. Ogden, courtesy NYHS
57—NYPL
58-59—top row: painting by John Vanderlyn, courtesy NYHS; B. McN. Stauffer Collection, NYPL; *Critical Period* by John Fiske, NYPL; same; painting by Robert Field, courtesy NYHS; author's collection—middle row: author's collection; NYPL; same; same; same; author's collection — bottom row: engraving by W. Sharp after painting by George Romney, *Century Magazine*, NYPL; *Pictorial Field-Book of the Revolution;* same; same; same; same
62—upper: illustration by Harry Fenn, from *The Story of a Street;* lower: *History of the City of New York* (Lamb)
63—*Critical Period*, NYPL
64—upper: *Columbia Magazine*, NYPL; lower left: illustration by A. Bobbett, *Harper's Monthly*, NYPL; lower right: mural by Peixotto, courtesy the Seamen's Bank for Savings
65—upper: *The New Metropolis* by E. Idell Zeisloft; lower left: engraving by Peter Lacour and A. Doolittle, from *American Historical Prints;* lower right: *Frank Leslie's Illustrated Newspaper*, courtesy NYHS
66—upper; painting by Daniel P. Huntington in the Brooklyn Museum, photo courtesy NYHS; lower: *History of the City of New York* (Lamb)
67—*The New Metropolis*
68—courtesy FHMA, from NYHS
69—upper: drawing by W. J. Condit, photo by Andreas Feininger, courtesy MCNY; lower: painting by Francis Guy, photo from NYHS
70—*History of the City of New York* (Lamb)
72—upper: Phelps Stokes Collection, NYPL; lower: *History of the City of New York* by Mary L. Booth
73—Phelps Stokes Collection, NYPL
74—painting by John Trumbull, courtesy NYHS
74-75—*History of the City of New York* (Lamb)
75—NYPL
76—upper: engraving from painting by Benjamin West, from *History of the City of New York* (Lamb); lower: Phelps Stokes Collection, NYPL
77—upper: *American Historical Prints;* lower left: Rogers Fund, courtesy MMA; lower right: painting by William P. Chappel, courtesy NYHS
78—author's collection
78-79—*American Historical Prints*
79—NYPL
80—*History of the City of New York* (Lamb)
81—Bennett view, from *Megarey's Street Views in the City of New-York*, courtesy National Studios
82—courtesy NYHS
83—upper: NYPL; lower: engraving from painting by Alonzo Chappel, NYPL
84—Eliot Elisofon
86—both: courtesy FHMA
87—upper: courtesy NYHS; lower: courtesy FHMA
88—upper: drawing and engraving by H. Fossette, photo by Andreas Feininger, courtesy MCNY; lower: *History of the City of New York* (Lamb)
89—painting by Anthony Imbert in the Museum of the City of New York, photo courtesy NYHS
90—both: *History of the City of New York* (Lamb)
92—upper: engraving by Samuel Maverick from painting by Anthony Imbert, courtesy NYHS; lower left: NYPL; lower right: engraving from painting by Alonzo Chappel, author's collection
93—engraving by W. I. Bennett from painting by J. W. Hill, from *American Historical Prints*
94—upper: courtesy FHMA, from NYHS; lower: water color by J. W. Hill, Phelps Stokes Collection, NYPL
95—mural by E. C. Henry, courtesy New York Central Railroad
96—courtesy MMA
97—courtesy NYHS
98—same
99—courtesy MCNY
100—upper: engraving by W. I. Bennett from painting by Calyo, Eno Collection, NYPL; lower: Edward W. C. Arnold Collection, lent by MMA, photo courtesy MCNY
101—upper: painting by J. Ackerman, J. Clarence Davies Collection, courtesy MCNY; lower: courtesy MCNY
102—engraving from painting by Oliver I. Lay, *Harper's Monthly*, NYPL
104—lithograph by N. Currier, Eno Collection, NYPL
105—*New York Illustrated News*, courtesy NYSE
106—upper and middle: *Harper's Weekly;* lower: *History of the City of New York* (Lamb)
107—*Illustrated London News*, photo by Andreas Feininger
108—both: engraving from lithograph by N. Currier, NYPL
110—upper: J. Clarence Davies Collection, courtesy MCNY; lower; courtesy MCNY
111—*"Manna-hatin," The Story of New York*
112—upper: courtesy New York Central Railroad; lower left: courtesy ML; lower right: *Scientific American*, Erik Monberg Collection
113—left: National Archives; right: Library of Congress
114—*New York Illustrated News*, NYPL
115—engraving by Henry Papprill from drawing by J. W. Hill, from *American Historical Prints*
116—upper left and right: courtesy MCNY; lower: Harry T. Peters Collection, courtesy Harry T. Peters, Jr., photo from MCNY
117—both: lithographs by N. Currier, NYPL
118—upper: National Archives; lower: photo by Andreas Feininger, courtesy MCNY
119—upper: photo reproduced by Andreas Feininger, courtesy MCNY; lower: courtesy the Seamen's Bank for Savings
120—upper: Local History Department, NYPL; lower: *Illustrated London News*, courtesy the Bank of New York
121—upper: Mathew Brady Collection, Library of Congress; lower: Edward W. C. Arnold Collection, lent by MMA, photo courtesy MCNY
122—upper: stereopticon view by E. and H. T. Anthony & Co., courtesy NYHS; lower: courtesy FHMA, from NYHS
123—engraving by W. B. Closson from daguerreotype by Brady, NYPL
124—courtesy MCNY
125—drawing by "our artist, Mr. Thwaites," *Harper's Weekly*
126—Mathew Brady Collection, Library of Congress
127—upper: *Illustrated London News;* lower: lithograph by Currier & Ives, photo by Andreas Feininger, courtesy MCNY
128—*Harper's Weekly*
130—*Harper's Weekly*, Erik Monberg Collection
131—*Frank Leslie's Illustrated Newspaper*, Erik Monberg Collection
132—same
133—*Harper's Weekly*, Erik Monberg Collection
134—same
135—both: same
136—upper: illustration by Arthur Lumley, from *Ten Years in Wall Street;* lower: photo by A. Tennyson Beals, from MCNY, NYPL
137—upper: *Harper's Weekly*, Erik Monberg Collection; lower: *Illustrated London News*
138—upper: artist unidentified, Erik Monberg Collection; lower: *Harper's Weekly*, Erik Monberg Collection
139—*Harper's Weekly*, Erik Monberg Collection
140—left: *Illustrated London News*, NYPL; right: stereopticon view by E. and H. T. Anthony & Co., NYPL
141—*Harper's Weekly*, Erik Monberg Collection
142—same
143—colored lithograph by Schumacher & Ettlinger, Edward W. C. Arnold Collection, lent by MMA, photo courtesy MCNY
144—National Archives
146—contemporary print, courtesy FHMA
147—upper: author's collection; lower: tintype, courtesy NYHS
148—upper: *Frank Leslie's Illustrated Newspaper*, Erik Monberg Collection; lower: *London Graphic*
149—upper: Phelps Stokes Collection, courtesy NYSE; lower: illustration by Arthur Lumley, from *Ten Years in Wall Street*
150—upper: illustration by Arthur Lumley, from *Ten Years in Wall Street;* lower: *Harper's Weekly*, Erik Monberg Collection
151—*Frank Leslie's Illustrated Newspaper*, courtesy NYHS
152—upper left and right: Mathew Brady, National Archives; lower: *Harper's Weekly*, Erik Monberg Collection
153—*Frank Leslie's Illustrated Newspaper*, courtesy New York Central Railroad
154—lithograph by Currier & Ives, NYPL
155—upper: drawing by Matt Morgan, *Frank Leslie's Illustrated Newspaper*, courtesy NYSE; lower: *Frank Leslie's Illustrated Newspaper*, Erik Monberg Collection
156—both: *Frank Leslie's Illustrated Newspaper*, Erik Monberg Collection
157—*Harper's Weekly*, Erik Monberg Collection
158—*Frank Leslie's Illustrated Newspaper*, Erik Monberg Collection
159—all: *The Days' Doings*, Erik Monberg Collection
160—courtesy NYHS

162—Currier & Ives print by Parsons and Atwater, photo by Andreas Feininger, J. Clarence Davies Collection, courtesy MCNY
163—drawing by I. Pranishnikoff, *Harper's Weekly,* photo by Andreas Feininger, courtesy MCNY
164—courtesy NYHS
165—left: *Esquemeling's Buccaneers of America,* NYPL; right: photo by Ernst Hanfstaegl, courtesy AMNH
166—courtesy NYHS
167—upper: courtesy MCNY; lower: courtesy NYHS
168—both: courtesy Consolidated Edison Co. of New York, Inc.
169—courtesy Mrs. Seton Henry, photo from Frick Art Reference Library
170—courtesy MCNY
171—drawing by Schell and Hogan, *Harper's Weekly,* Erik Monberg Collection
172—upper; *Harper's Weekly;* lower: cartoon by F. Graetz, *Puck*
173—upper left: courtesy New York Central Railroad; upper right: Brown Brothers; lower: NYPL
174—sketch by Stanley Fox, *Harper's Weekly,* Erik Monberg Collection
175—colored lithograph, J. Clarence Davies Collection, courtesy MCNY
176—rephotographed by Andreas Feininger, courtesy MCNY
177—upper: photo by John Francis Strauss, *Camera Work No. 3;* lower: drawing by C. Graham and W. A. Rogers, *Harper's Weekly,* Erik Monberg Collection
178—upper left: courtesy Remington Rand Corp.; upper right: courtesy Burroughs Corp.; lower: courtesy Otis Elevator Co.
179—both: courtesy New York Telephone Co.
180—woodcut from *One Hundred Years of New York and Environs,* Whittelsey Fund, courtesy MMA
181—drawing by Hrohjon Hawley, courtesy Consolidated Edison Co. of New York, Inc.
182—courtesy MCNY
183—Brown Brothers
185—*Harper's Weekly*
186—drawing by De Thulstrup and Bodfish, *Harper's Weekly*
187—courtesy NYSE
188—upper: courtesy MCNY; lower: J. Clarence Davies Collection, courtesy MCNY
189—upper: photo by Byron, courtesy MCNY; lower: copyright Pach Brothers, Inc.
190—drawing by Charles Broughton, probably *Harper's Weekly,* courtesy NYSE
192—drawing by T. V. Chominski, from photo by Rockwood, *Harper's Weekly*
193—cartoon by W. A. Rogers, *Harper's Weekly*
194—upper: Clark Collection, courtesy National Gallery of Art, Washington, D. C.; lower: drawing by E. J. Meeker, *Harper's Weekly*
195—upper: Berenice Abbott; lower: Charles Latere, courtesy FHMA
196—courtesy NYSE
197—upper: Berenice Abbott; lower: courtesy NYSE
198—all: courtesy ASE
199—same
200—upper: drawing by T. Dart Walker, *Leslie's Weekly,* Erik Monberg Collection; lower: *Munsey's,* NYPL
201—upper left: caricature by Homer C. Davenport, from *Wall Street by the Back Door;* upper right: copyright Pach Brothers, Inc.; lower: Brown Brothers
202—Brown Brothers
203—both: same
204—cartoon by Homer C. Davenport, photo by LLL, Library of Congress
205—upper: cartoon by Art Young, NYPL; lower: cartoon by Harry Grant Dart, *Life,* NYPL
206—copyright Pach Brothers, Inc.
207—upper: drawing by Monk, photo by Andreas Feininger, courtesy MCNY; lower: Brown Brothers
208—copyright Pach Brothers, Inc.
209—upper: Brown Brothers; lower: courtesy the Pierpont Morgan Library
210—courtesy the Museum of Modern Art
212—courtesy NYHS
213—upper: Acme; lower: Wide World
214—upper: United Press International; lower: Brown Brothers
215—upper: Brown Brothers; lower: Culver Service
216—upper: Culver Service; lower: Brown Brothers
217—Culver Service
218—United Press International
219—courtesy ASE
220—Brown Brothers
221—both: courtesy ASE
222—upper: courtesy George Cavaniss; lower: LLL
224-25—courtesy George Cavaniss
225—both: same
226—upper: same; lower: courtesy Morgan Guaranty Trust Co. of New York
227—courtesy George Cavaniss
228—courtesy Morgan Guaranty Trust Co. of New York
230—courtesy Fairchild Aerial Surveys, Inc.
231—same
232—left: Berenice Abbott; right: copyright Ezra Stoller, courtesy Federal Reserve Bank of New York
234—left: Andreas Feininger; right: H. Craig Severance, Inc., architects, courtesy National Studios
235—Weegee
236—upper: United Press International; lower: Culver Service
237—upper: Culver Service; lower: United Press International
238—Brown Brothers
239—upper: Wide World; lower: United Press International
240-41—photo by LLL, courtesy MCNY
242-43—courtesy *New York Times* and NYPL
244—same
245—Culver Service
247—NYPL
248—courtesy Abel Green, *Variety*
250—Andreas Feininger
251—upper: United Press International; lower left: Weegee; lower right: Berenice Abbott
252—upper: Wide World; lower left: cartoon by Cesare, *Outlook,* NYPL; lower right: cartoon by Daniel R. Fitzpatrick, courtesy *St. Louis Post-Dispatch*
253—upper: Wide World; lower: Culver Service
254—Louis Stanley, *New Leader,* NYPL
255—upper left: photo by Al Nessansen of Acme, Wide World; upper right: Brown Brothers; lower: Wide World
256—upper: Brown Brothers; lower: Wide World
257—upper left: copyright Pach Brothers, Inc.; upper right and lower left: Wide World; lower right: *New York Mirror* staff photo
258—upper: Brown Brothers; lower: Wide World
259—upper left: Brown Brothers; upper right: cartoon by Brown, *New York Herald Tribune;* lower: Wide World
260-61—all: murals by Reginald Marsh, photos from National Archives
262—both: Wide World
263—Brown Brothers
264—Andreas Feininger
265—Weegee, courtesy Cities Service Co.
266—Berenice Abbott
268—Wide World
269—Brown Brothers
270—upper: Andreas Feininger; lower: courtesy NYSE
271—upper: courtesy NYSE; lower left: Wide World; lower right: courtesy ASE
272—Brown Brothers
273—courtesy Chase Manhattan Bank
274—all: same
275—all: same
276—Culver Service
277—upper left: Andreas Feininger; upper right: Wide World; lower: Brown Brothers
278—courtesy Standard Oil Co. (N. J.)
280—Andreas Feininger
281—Berenice Abbott
282—all: Eddy Van Der Veen, Black Star
283—Berenice Abbott
284-85—both: same
286—upper: Associated Press; lower: Tommy Weber, courtesy ASE
287—courtesy ML
288—courtesy Glenn Neville, *New York Mirror*
289—upper: Berenice Abbott; lower: Wide World
290—upper: Ray Platnick, Culver Service; lower: Fran Cancellare, United Press International
291—upper: Wide World; lower: courtesy Blyth & Co., Inc.
292—Ted Burrows, courtesy ML
292-93—Standard Flashlight Co., Inc., courtesy ML
294—upper and middle left: Camera Center, Cincinnati, courtesy ML; middle right: Marcus Blechman; lower left and right: LLL
295—upper and middle right: Zintgraff, San Antonio, courtesy Bache & Co.; middle left, lower right and left: LLL
296—all: Eliot Elisofon
296-97—Jerry Cooke
297—all: Eliot Elisofon
298—all (except transaction notes): Eliot Elisofon; extreme lower left: courtesy ML; extreme lower right: courtesy Bache & Co.
299—all: Eliot Elisofon; ticker-tape fragment courtesy NYSE
300—upper left, middle left, and lower right: LLL; upper right: Camera Center, Cincinnati, courtesy ML; middle right: Zintgraff, San Antonio, courtesy Bache & Co.; lower left: Jerry Cooke, courtesy NYSE
302—Elwood P. Johns, courtesy Chase Manhattan Bank
303—Berenice Abbott
304—courtesy Standard Oil Co. (N.J.)
305—Berenice Abbott
306—courtesy PNYA
307—Speed Hanzlick, *New York Mirror,* courtesy Cities Service Co.
308—Erich Locker, courtesy Chase Manhattan Bank
309—upper: all LLL
310—all: courtesy Federal Reserve Bank of New York
311—all (except lower right): courtesy Federal Reserve Bank of New York; lower right: Berenice Abbott
312-13—courtesy Manufacturers Trust Co.
314—Berenice Abbott
315—both: LLL
316—Robert M. Mottar, courtesy Chase Manhattan Bank
317—Berenice Abbott
318—same
319—upper left: Eliot Elisofon; upper right and lower: Berenice Abbott
320-321—Marvin Newman
322—both: Eliot Elisofon
323—all: same
324-325—John Groth, courtesy NYSE
326-27—same
328—upper left and right: Jerry Cooke, courtesy NYSE; lower: Eliot Elisofon
330—upper: George, Jim, and John Burns of Schenectady, New York, courtesy Sylvania Electric Products, Inc.; lower: Eliot Elisofon
331—both: Eliot Elisofon
332—Berenice Abbott
333—both: Wide World
334—both: same
335—Archie Lieberman, Black Star, courtesy Lewis Gilbert
336—upper left and right: Eliot Elisofon; lower. Tommy Weber, courtesy ASE
337—all: Eliot Elisofon
338—upper: same; lower: courtesy Securities and Exchange Commission
339—upper left: Eliot Elisofon; upper right: Berenice Abbott; middle left and lower: LLL
340—both: Berenice Abbott
341—Andreas Feininger
342—Berenice Abbott
343—courtesy PNYA
344—Weegee
346—courtesy Downtown-Lower Manhattan Association
347—Adolph Studly, courtesy Emery Roth & Sons
348—Eliot Elisofon
349—Marcus Blechman
350—Elliott Erwitt
351—Marcus Blechman
352—same
353—LLL
354—Marcus Blechman
355—Karsh of Ottawa
356—Marcus Blechman
357—Tommy Weber
358—Marcus Blechman
359—Berenice Abbott
360—courtesy National Association of Securities Dealers, Inc.
361—Eliot Elisofon
362—LLL
363—courtesy American Export Lines, Inc.
364—Berenice Abbott
365—Eliot Elisofon
366—Irving Haberman, Culver Service

Index